Sun Signs
for the
New Millennium

Sun Signs
for the
New Millennium

The Definitive Astrological Guide for a New Era

GERALDINE ROSE AND CASSANDRA WILCOX

AVON BOOKS  NEW YORK

Lyrics from "Forever Young" by Bob Dylan copyright © 1973, 1974 by RAM'S HORN MUSIC. All rights reserved. International copyright secured. Reprinted by permission.

Poetry extract from Charles Bukowski, which appeared in *Three Days Run Away Like Wild Horses Over the Hills,* appears herein courtesy of Black Sparrow Press.

Extract from "Resume" copyright © 1926, 1928, renewed 1954, copyright 1956 by Dorothy Parker is from *The Portable Dorothy Parker* by Dorothy Parker. Introduction by Brendan Gill. Used by permission of Viking Penguin, a division of Penguin Putnam Inc.

Lyrics from "As Time Goes By" by Herman Hupfield © 1931 (renewed) by Warner Bros. Inc. All rights reserved. Used by permission. Warner Bros. Publications U.S. Inc. Miami, FL 33014.

Lyrics from "Aquarius/Let the Sunshine In," words and mysic by MacDermot/Ragni/Rando. Reproduced by permission of Warner/Chappell music Australia Pty. Ltd. Unauthorized reproduction is illegal.

AVON BOOKS, INC.
1350 Avenue of the Americas
New York, New York 10019

Copyright © 1998 by Geraldine Rose and Cassandra Wilcox
Front cover illustration by Ruth Pettis
Visit our website at **http://www.AvonBooks.com**
ISBN: 0-380-78942-6

Library of Congress Cataloging in Publication Data:
Geraldine Rose.
    Sun signs for the new millennium : the definitive astrological
guide for a new era / Geraldine Rose and Cassandra Wilcox.
        p.   cm.
    1. Astrology. I. Wilcox, Cassandra. II. Title.
BF1708.1.G47   1998   98-24816
133.5—dc21   CIP

First Avon Books Trade Paperback Printing: November 1998

AVON TRADEMARK REG. U.S. PAT. OFF. AND IN OTHER COUNTRIES, MARCA REGISTRADA, HECHO EN U.S.A.

Printed in the U.S.A.

QPM   10   9   8   7   6   5   4   3   2

CONTENTS

Sun Signs
for the
New Millennium

INTRODUCTION

As the new millennium dawns, astrology is coming back in from the cold. Condemned by church and establishment for nearly four hundred years, it is now used by more and more people from all walks of life who are prepared to approach the subject with an open mind, and test its practical value in their lives.

Those who would pride themselves on being thoroughly rational and scientific and are quick to say, "How can you believe in all that superstitious nonsense?" might be reminded that to dismiss anything out of hand without investigation is thoroughly unscientific. In any case, it's not a matter of whether you "believe" in astrology. Astrology is not a religion. Nor does it require psychic or clairvoyant skills. It is a body of knowledge, albeit with esoteric and occult connections, that, from its beginnings thousands of years ago in the cradle of civilization of Mesopotamia, has developed into a sophisticated science. A science that is used—as it always has been—by royalty, world leaders, and people in positions of power, even if there are still few who would be willing to admit it.

The debunkers of astrology might also like to ponder on the impressive list of great names who either practiced or investigated it and came to the conclusion that it works. Pythagorus, Plato, Ptolemy, Dante, Kepler, Galileo, Shakespeare, Isaac Newton, Goethe, Ralph Waldo Emerson, Theodore Roosevelt, and C. G. Jung, to name

1

a few. In fact, what Newton is supposed to have said to Edmond Halley (of comet fame) when the latter was berating him for his interest in astrology is often cited as the perfect retort for those faced with the scorn of the skeptics: "I, sir, have studied the matter. You have not."

That there exists a cause-and-effect relationship between events in the heavens and events on earth is what astrology is all about. "As above, so below" is how astrologers have traditionally summed it up. Perhaps one reason why the spirit of our times is so willing to embrace astrology is that the idea of our planet as one vast living organism in which everything is affected by everything else is now commonly accepted. Astrology supports this concept of the unity of everything; it puts our connection with the cosmos into symbolic form.

As for "scientific proof" that astrology works, whether or not physicists eventually discover proof of why the movements of the planets affect us the way they do is beside the point. Astrology, like psychology, is not an exact science, and many say that the kind of proof that would satisfy a rigid rationalist is not possible. Personal astrology is all about discovering the *meaning* that celestial influences bring to our lives. And how do you measure meaning? You can't. No two people are going to experience a particular stellar influence in exactly the same way. In this sense, astrology is an art as well as a science. The art is in the interpretation of the scientific data. Your personal horoscope is a circular map of the heavens calculated for the hour and place of your birth. If you happen to have been born when the Sun was in the sign of Gemini, the Moon was in Leo, and Virgo was ascending, then those are the indisputable facts. How this combination manifests itself in your personality and in your life is where interpretation—the art of astrology—comes in.

The revival of astrology began in England in the second half of the nineteenth century. But it wasn't until the 1930s when newspapers introduced Sun sign columns that "pop" astrology took off. In the 1960s, the interest in everything mystical and esoteric, including the idea of the coming Age of Aquarius, gathered force and followers. It flowed on through the seventies and into the eighties when the term *New Age* was coined to cover a huge choice in which the "me generation" could search for answers to questions about themselves. The personal-growth industry took these New Age subjects, including astrology, as its own.

The current boom in astrology is as much due to computerization as anything else. In ages past, astrologers had to be mathematicians as well as astronomers, and personalized horoscopes were strictly for the important and the wealthy. Now the math is done in a few minutes and everyone has access to accurate personal horoscopes. Computerization has created a huge new market for astrology and has turned it into a growth profession.

Contemporary consumers of astrology know there is a great deal more to it all than "the stars" in the daily paper. It is not uncommon to hear people swapping Moon signs and Ascendants, or bemoaning their current troublesome transit. The classic party line of "I'm a Sagittarius, what sign are you?" has moved on to "I thought you might be a Libra. I've got Libra rising. I meet them everywhere." It seems there is no one under the age of fifty who does not have at least one Sun sign book on their shelves.

People who know nothing about astrology at least know what their Sun sign is because it is determined by their birthday. Your Sun sign is the sign of the zodiac that was occupied by the Sun at the time of your birth. The zodiac is an imaginary circle drawn in the heavens by the Earth's annual journey around the Sun. By dividing each of the four seasons of our solar year into three equal subdivisions, we have twelve signs starting at the spring equinox on March 21.

The twelve signs cover the full spectrum of human nature and human experience. They represent twelve eternal basic personality types. Since antiquity, people born under the sign of Leo, The Lion, have shown leadership qualities and have enjoyed a good banquet. People born under the sign of The Scorpion have always been attracted to the dark and the mysterious side of life. Two millennia ago there were astute Capricorns who denied themselves a new toga in order to invest their money in olive groves that would pay handsomely in five years. Today they plan their investment portfolios with the same foresight and good judgment.

Although the essence of the signs of the zodiac is unchanging, the stage on which they are played out is forever changing. And as we hurtle into the new millennium, these changes are occurring faster than ever before. Nobody, including astrologers, is able to predict exactly where these changes will lead us. History has taken quantum leaps in the past, but never before has change occurred at such a rate or on such a broad scale.

The new millennium has spawned mass expectations that the new century will correspond with the beginning of a new, positive direction for humankind. On top of that, many have jumped onto the popular New Age bandwagon of the Age of Aquarius with all its promises of instant peace, harmony, and understanding. Yet few understand what this Age of Aquarius really means.

There is a tradition in astrology that each sign of the zodiac governs in turn a long cycle in history that is a little more than two thousand years in duration. These cycles are called The Great Ages.

They move backwards through the zodiac, so according to the theory, since the beginning of the Great Age of Pisces roughly coincided with the birth of Christ, we are now preparing to enter the Age of Aquarius. Curiously, astrologers themselves can't actually agree on whether the Age of Aquarius has in fact already dawned, or when it will. In fact, there are some who believe that the significance of these Ages has been exaggerated and that they represent a far too simplistic view of the astrology of our history. In any case, we should not expect to wake on January 1, 2000, to a new "Aquarian" way of life.

But what we *can* expect, and indeed what we are already witnessing, is a growing Aquarian influence with mass computerization, rapid technological innovation (it seems your "new" computer is obsolete even before you get through the instruction manual), and a culture dominated by the electronic communications industry.

We may not know exactly when the great Age of Aquarius begins, but we do know that at the start of the new millennium we will be in a fourteen-year period heavily colored by Aquarian principles. That's because the planet Neptune, which rules the zeitgeist, the flavor of the times, moved out of Capricorn in 1998 and into Aquarius, where it will remain until 2011. This episode could be likened to a sort of kick start into the Age of Aquarius.

Certainly we can expect new Utopian movements that tap into the Aquarian ideal of the brotherhood of man to emerge. Aquarius is the sign that rules groups of people. And under the influence of Aquarius, the impetus will most definitely be to belong to some kind of group. New ways of living collectively are sure to appear. And as for technology, as they say, you ain't seen nothing yet.

But what is also certain is that the growing Aquarian influence is not going to bring a universal fix for humanity's problems. Those of us who are still naively holding out for some sixties-style Aquarian light and love will probably be disappointed. We already have warnings that the pace of technological advance doesn't come without a price. All around us, the social implications are being felt, and there's much talk about the depersonalization of human existence, and the "politics of group identity." On the one hand we see a positive collective push towards global unity to save the planet for us all, and yet on the other, we see tribal and national affiliations becoming stronger as people define themselves by what race, religion, corporation, or group they belong to and cling to the security that a sense of belonging brings. And if you don't feel you really belong to a specific group, then where do you belong? The danger of the Aquarian influence is that those people who do not identify themselves by which group they belong to, but rather see themselves as individuals, will suffer increasing isolation and alienation.

When an astrological trend moves too far in any one direction, balance always comes in the form of the opposite sign. So sometime during this fourteen-year Aquarian episode, the influence of Leo will be felt. Leo stands for the rights and the power of the individual, and people will begin to appreciate that everything innovative was originally conceived in an individual human mind. The Aquarian need for group cohesion versus the Leonine value of individual creative thinking and independent action is sure to be an issue in the early years of the new millennium.

During this time, each of us will be challenged in our own way. And astrologically speaking, that means in our own Sun sign way.

Your personal horoscope is, of course, complex, just like you. Perhaps you have read that your Moon sign and the sign that was rising at the time of your birth are major influences on your personality. And it's true, they are. Your Moon sign is the picture of your emotional conditioning. It describes your instincts and is your protective emotional mechanism. In times of stress, you often become more like your Moon sign and less like your Sun sign. Your Ascendant (or Rising sign) is your persona, the face you put on to interact with people and operate comfortably at work and in the outside world. Often people mistake your Ascendant for your Sun sign because it describes how you come across.

It does not diminish the importance of the Moon, the Ascendant, and all the other planets when we say, however, that the first and most important step that you will take on your own unique astrological journey is understanding your Sun sign. No matter what other revelations your horoscope has in store, it is your Sun sign that is the bottom line.

It would seem that if a rose is a rose is a rose, then astrologically speaking, an Aries is an Aries is an Aries. A Taurus is a Taurus is a Taurus. And a Gemini is a Gemini is a Gemini.

Having said that, it's important to understand that a Sun sign is an archetype, not a stereotype. Each of us must tread the path of our Sun sign, whether that is Aries, Taurus, or Gemini—but in our own individual way, and within the context of our culture and our own time in history.

Take Michelangelo, Albert Einstein, and George Washington, for instance. Add Mikhail Gorbachev, Elizabeth Taylor, and Glenn Miller. Different eras, different lives, different destinies. But Pisces, all. Each traveling his or her own path to follow the Pisces star.

It's also important to realize that no one sign is an entity unto itself. It does not exist in isolation. Nor does any sign have a monopoly on any one human trait, talent, virtue, or foible. It is not only Virgos who are prudent, meticulous, and cautious. Or Pisces who can be gentle, compassionate, and imaginative. Geminis are not the only quick-witted, bright, and multitalented people. Nor are Scorpios the only ones who are passionate, deep, and ambitious.

The more you get to know about Sun signs, the more you appreciate that every sign has a positive and a negative side to its basic archetypal nature. The truth is that most of us display a mix of the two, and if we come out on the positive side most of the time, we are doing well. Certainly there is no such thing as a good or a bad sign.

Which is why Virgos can also be critical, narrow-minded, and stingy. Why Pisceans are notorious for being lazy, irresponsible escapists. Why Geminis can be nerve-racking, unreliable, and inconsistent. And why Scorpios have earned a reputation for being secretive and Machiavellian.

Nevertheless, when you start to put together your own Sun sign database from your observations of family, friends, and colleagues, you will be intrigued to discover how uncanny it is that the sweet-toothed Taurean is inevitably the one who has his eye on the last slice of cake. How feet-conscious Pisceans can never bring themselves to throw away their comfortable old shoes that are falling apart. How Geminis talk at a hundred miles an hour, changing subject in midsentence. And how bargain-hunting Cancerians can't see the absurdity of spending ten dollars on gas to drive to a distant store where they can save five dollars on groceries.

The reason why no sign has exclusive ownership of a particular personality trait is that the twelve signs of the zodiac are all interconnected and related to each other.

Some are related, for example, by *element*. There are four elements; Fire, Earth, Air, and Water. The elements represent the way you deal with other people and your environment.

The three fire signs are Aries, Leo, and Sagittarius. All of them, each in its own way, respond with passion, ardor, and vigor. Fire-sign people are dynamic types, born enthusiasts. They are self-motivated, and like fire itself, they are quick to ignite. Their reactions are fast and sometimes furious.

The earth signs—Taurus, Virgo, and Capricorn—have a practical and prudent approach to life. Realistic and cautious, Earth signs pride themselves on keeping both feet on the ground. They value common sense and reliability, always aiming to preserve and build upon their resources.

All three air signs—Gemini, Libra, and Aquarius—react to situations in a rational way. Air is the realm of thought, ideas, and the intellect. Cool and analytical, airy people are skillful communicators and are distrustful of overly emotional or fiery reactions, in the belief that the right decision can always be reached by good reasoning.

The water signs—Cancer, Scorpio, and Pisces—are the signs that govern the emotions. Watery people are at home swimming in the deep pools of feelings and sensitivity. Their response to life is the most subtle and instinctive. Sooner or later they learn to trust their intuition, which is strong, often making their best decisions on the grounds that it "feels right."

We can also divide the signs of the zodiac according to the three qualities—cardinal, fixed, and mutable. The qualities describe our general approach to life, our attitudes, our modus operandi.

The four cardinal signs are Aries, Cancer, Libra, and Capricorn. These signs are linked by their drive and sense of purpose. They have no shortage of energy to pour into achieving what they want out of life. Goal-oriented and enterprising, they are the initiators of the zodiac. Cardinal people are born with a "go for it" attitude.

The fixed signs of Taurus, Leo, Scorpio, and Aquarius are, as the term suggests, fixed in their approach to life. And often in their attitudes, too. Persistent, tenacious, determined, and steadfast, they are the rocks of the zodiac and are blessed with strength and willpower. When they are confident of the path they are treading, they can be relied upon to stay with it to the end.

The four mutable signs of Gemini, Virgo, Sagittarius, and Pisces are linked by their ability to adapt to changing circumstances. They have an inborn restlessness and are the most flexible types of the zodiac. Not only can they easily adjust to varied situations and environments, they have a good instinct for when to bail out and move on if something is clearly not working out.

Another important connection exists between signs that oppose each other on the wheel of the zodiac. To find your opposite sign, start at your own and count forward six. If you're an Aries, your opposite sign is Libra. If you're a Scorpio, it's Taurus, and so on.

Our opposite sign is the one that we love to hate because it's like looking in the mirror of our own shortcomings. It's the sign with the characteristics that frequently annoy us the most, but that, truth be known, are precisely the ones we would do well to cultivate. You could say that the best of what the opposite sign has to offer is what we need to counteract the worst side of our own sign. Yet it is precisely because they are at opposite ends of the same pole that they also have a lot in common.

When it comes to understanding our true nature and finding our best path in life, there are few tools that come close to the revelations of an astrological birth-chart. If knowledge is power, then surely self-knowledge is the most important power we can acquire in order to gain greater control over our own lives. Here lies the value of astrology.

The commonest questions that people ask astrologers concern the age-old issue of fate and free will. They ask, "Is this destiny?" "How much free will do I have?" The truth is that nobody has the answer. All reputable astrologers are likely to position themselves somewhere in the middle between the extreme camps of total determinism and arbitrary use of free will. The fact that we are born with our own unique horoscope, which is rather like a blueprint for our life, is in itself an indication that we are all subject to the hand of destiny. Yet, through experience, astrologers invariably come to the opinion that the more aware of your nature you are, the more you are able to seize the measure of control that we all have. In response to the eternal debate of destiny versus free will, astrologers are fond of quoting the ancient adage *Astra inclinant, non necessitant*—"The stars impel us, they do not compel us."

Voltaire (who, oddly, had little time for astrology) struck on the perfect metaphor when he remarked, "Each player must accept the cards life deals him or her. But once they are in hand, he or she alone must decide how to play the cards in order to win the game." Students of astrology would say the "cards" that life has dealt you are revealed in your horoscope, but they would also agree that *how* you play those cards is where the free will comes in.

Clearly, those who would aim to maximize their free will would be wise to gain some knowledge of astrology.

FOR THOSE BORN ON THE CUSP . . .

A lot of nonsense has been spoken on the vexed question of cusps. People like to think that if they were born "on the cusp," that is, around the time when the Sun moves from one sign into the next, it somehow makes them more interesting. That they are, for instance, neither a Taurus nor a Gemini, but a fascinating blend of the two. That's the first popular misconception about cusps we'd like to dispel.

The second misconception is that the cusp extends two or three days either side of the switch in signs. And that if you were born anywhere in this period, you were born on the cusp.

There is actually a precise moment in time when that switch occurs. If you were born within an hour or so of that moment, you may have a bona fide reason for saying that you were indeed born on the cusp between two signs. Though we feel urged to say, experience tells us that no matter how close a Taurus may come to being born at the beginning of Gemini, for example, he or she is still a Taurus. Likewise, Geminis born very early in that sign are definitely Geminis and not Taureans.

Every astrologer has had the experience of breaking the news to a client born on the day when the Sun moves from one sign into the next that they are not born, after all, under the sign they have been reading in the newspapers for years. So if you were born on the day when the Sun changes sign, you need to give your exact time of birth as well as the date and place to an astrologer, or one of the astro-computing services that exist in all major cities, and have the matter settled once and for all.

Then you can study your Sun sign with confidence.

ARIES

March 21–April 20

Ruling planet

MARS

The goal is to live with godlike composure on the full rush of energy like
Dionysus riding the leopard without
being torn to pieces.

Joseph Campbell—born March 26

THE ARIES NATURE

Numero Uno. Number One. The First. However you translate it, there can only ever be one "first." Born under the first sign of the zodiac, an Aries knows there has to be something special just in that.

So why *is* Aries, the sign beginning March 21—not January 1—the first of the twelve signs of the zodiac?

March 21 is the day of the spring equinox in the northern hemisphere. The first day of spring. It's the time of the year when life is being born anew after the symbolic death of winter. The time when the sap is rising, the birds are nesting, fertility is returning to the earth, and the very life force is palpable all round. The astrological correspondence with this new beginning is Aries, the sign of The Ram. Aries is the sign of primal energy. People born under the sign of The Ram are vital, dynamic, and creative. All that it means to be alive.

Being the first sign of the zodiac is only one of the firsts that Aries can lay claim to. It's the first of the fire signs. All fire signs (and that

includes Leo and Sagittarius) are energetic, exuberant, and extroverted. Aries is also the first of the cardinal signs. The others are
Cancer, Libra, and Capricorn. Being cardinal gives Aries people a
strong sense of purpose, and the urge to create structure and be
productive.

All these firsts add up to the Aries surefire formula for success
and achievement. The kind of success born of the special Aries gift
for making things happen.

Aries are not comfortable with the concept of leaving their lives
in the hands of destiny. They are firm subscribers to the force of free
will. When they feel Dame Fortune isn't smiling down on them, they
don't wait for her to turn her wheel in their direction. They'll shake
her by the shoulders and get on with making their own luck.

Aries simply *must* act on their ideas, their dreams, on the destiny
they believe is theirs. Their well-earned reputation as self-starting go-
getters is born out of their compulsion to make their mark. As
strongly self-directed, driven types, Aries generally require less external motivation than other signs. They're the last to be in need of
weekend motivation workshops or a personal coach. These are the
leaders, pioneers, and prime movers of astrological lore. Simply the
best people to get the show on the road, and to get themselves and
everyone else fired up. Aptly enough, getting "fired up" is a popular
phrase in the Aries vocabulary. The Aries flames really soar whenever definitive action and quick decision making are called for. When
an opportunity or a crisis must be handled *now*, others are invariably
impressed by the innate Aries talent to get stuck into the problem at
hand and resolve it.

An Aries friend can be worth his or her weight in gold in life's
emergency moments. When Pisces is temporarily overwhelmed by a
mountain of practical problems, when Libra is in the midst of a mega
vacillation, or even when Scorpio is immobilized by an obsession
with Mr. or Ms. Totally Unavailable, your Aries friend is the one
you need. The one who can fix your car, find you somewhere to live,
and balance your budget. The one who will force you gently to make
up your mind, and convince you that there are plenty of equally
desirable fish in the sea. In short, Aries can be relied on to get you
up, out, and moving.

This is the sign that doesn't hang around debating the pros and
the cons of a problem. They take the fastest, most confident action
to arrive at a solution. *Action* is a key Aries word. *Fast* is also high
on the list. Not all Aries behave like human dynamos. There are
plenty of quiet, more subdued and reflective Aries around. (They're
sure to have their Ascendant or more than one planet in water and

earth signs.) But these types of Rams are still Rams even if the drive and desire for achievement is less on display for all to see.

Being big on action, it follows logically that Aries are usually short on patience. In fact, they quietly despise dawdlers, dabblers, ditherers, prevaricators, and procrastinators. But there are times in life when a little tossing around of the pros and cons is a virtue. Aries can sometimes be too radical in their belief that he who hesitates is lost. The truth is that they have a problem with the wisdom of waiting because biding your time is a concept that is foreign to the Aries ethos. Every astrologer has had the experience of advising an Aries client that, due to temporary difficult influences, the stars decree that it would be in Aries' interests to lie low and wait for the cosmic winds to change. Every astrologer also knows that it's one thing to offer advice to an Aries, but whether he or she accepts it is another matter.

When one high-flying Aries business agent was advised that during his upcoming Saturn transit he would have to knuckle down, put his social life on hold, concentrate on business, and wait for the rewards to come later, his response was, "But it's not in my nature." He quickly discovered, though, that his usual impatient hard-hitting approach was getting him nowhere fast and that being an Aries didn't automatically exempt him from learning the lessons of a Saturn transit.

The Ram positively thrives on challenge and competition. Much of Aries' worldly success can be attributed to their courage and their willingness to take risks, give it a go, and move fast. You can't keep a good Aries down for long. A battle or two may be lost, but they always believe the war can still be won.

Aries are the warriors of the zodiac, born with the fighting instinct. And in the battleground of life, they're the first to be out there on the field wielding their sword, their business card, or their checkbook. Sometimes, their famous confidence is all the ammunition they need. That's if they haven't already disarmed you with their charm.

In ancient mythology Aries was the Greek god of war. In Rome he was called Mars. We know Mars as the planet that was named after the god of war because it shines red—the color of blood, lust, and aggression. And most Mars-ruled people love the color red.

You don't need to have an overactive imagination to see that the symbol of the planet Mars is an erect penis. Ariens are reputed to be as hot and enthusiastic in the bedroom as they are in the boardroom. On the physical level, Mars represents the spark of energy essential for the creation of life itself. Metaphysically speaking, it is the spark of initiative and creative action.

If their intimate relationship with the god of war is what makes

Aries people so competitive and dynamic, it also accounts for the times when they are unbearably pushy, aggressive, and selfish. This is the flip side of Mars. For all of us, no matter what Sun sign we're born under, Mars is the planet that symbolizes our ego; our sense of self. And we all need a healthy sense of self to give us self-worth. Without these, there can be no self-realization.

The connection between our sense of self, self-worth, and self-realization is fundamental to understanding what the sign of Aries means, and to understanding what makes an Aries tick. All human endeavor starts with this consciousness of self. And it's why Aries is the first sign.

French philosopher René Descartes (born March 31, 1596, under the sign of The Ram) lived at a time when the certainties of our place in the universe were being overturned. In the face of the growing evidence, it finally had to be accepted that the Earth was no longer at the center of the universe, and that we were in perpetual motion around the Sun, and not vice versa. This great discovery challenged previous ideas about who we were and what we knew. Descartes wanted to know if there was indeed anything at all that was absolutely certain and forever beyond doubt. So he put himself to the intellectual task of pushing doubt as far as he could. His conclusion was the one philosophical maxim that everyone can quote: "I think, therefore I am."

Descartes had deduced that there was only one thing that he could *not* doubt. And that was his own existence. For to doubt, you must think. And to think, you must exist. In other words, consciousness of self is the *only* thing that cannot be doubted.

Aries is the sign of self-awareness. Traditionally, astrologers have called Aries the "infant of the zodiac." After all, the infant exists at the center of its own little universe, relating first and foremost to its own needs. The infant's world expands as it grows and develops. The title of the infant of the zodiac has left Aries open to superficial misinterpretation. It most certainly does not mean that people born under Aries are more childish or immature than any other sign.

Far from it. The Ram is frequently a very urbane and sophisticated beast, even polished and soigné. He or she is acutely aware of the importance of appearance and presentation, and in this sense Aries is a very self-conscious individual. But when they're fired up, high on the rush of their own adrenaline, even the most worldly of them can't help exuding a magic, childlike quality that is fresh, invigorating, and contagious.

Indeed, when Aries are "on the rush of energy, like Dionysus riding the leopard," as popular mythologist Joseph Campbell has put it, it's extraordinary how they manage to do it with "godlike composure." Aries can be in the thick of it all, thriving on the cut and thrust, and still keep their cool.

When we think of Campbell, most of us think of his popular phrase "Follow your bliss." As he explains in his book *The Hero with a Thousand Faces*, it takes courage to renounce the safe and predictable path and do what we feel compelled to do. It takes courage to live the life of a hero and follow our bliss.

It also takes self-awareness, self-esteem, and a strong sense of purpose. All Mars qualities. Which is why following their sense of destiny and their bliss seems to be a burning issue for Aries people in particular. Likewise, anyone who is born with the Sun in the first house of his or her horoscope (which is the house of Aries) will relate to the Aries-style urge to impress themselves and their achievements upon the world.

Aries accepts that to get somewhere in life, a Ram's gotta do what a Ram's gotta do. And if that means trampling over a few sheep on the way, then too bad. Lesser mortals should just make sure they're not one of those sheep.

People frequently admire or even envy the achievements of Aries, but are reluctant to acknowledge that it takes guts to go all out for what you want. There are plenty of risks along the way, but Aries embraces risk. Truth be known, Aries gets a buzz out of risk. The bigger the risk, the bigger the buzz. If success means venturing out into the unknown, then Aries, the pioneer of the zodiac, can call on the self-confidence and courage required. Certainly they don't need to seek permission from others to do it. The only approval they need comes from themselves.

The story of Isak Dinesen (aka Karen Blixen) as she told it in *Out of Africa* has all the ingredients of a classic Aries saga. Risk, enterprise, and the sheer force of will to do what she wanted to do.

Blixen escaped the claustrophobia of European society at the turn of the century by marrying a Danish aristocrat headed for Africa. But when her dissolute husband disappeared for months on end, the hard work of running their coffee plantation was left entirely in her hands. Her energy was endless, her lust for life insatiable, and through it all she wrote prolifically. Blixen was a true Aries fighter. When serious illness threatened her life, and when fate knocked her down—as it often did—she got straight up and started again. Absence, it should be noted, does not make the Aries heart grow fonder. It wasn't long before a dashing new lover, alias Robert Redford in the movie version, was flying in over the Serengeti and landing on her front lawn, delivering the romance and passion Aries simply has to have.

Times have changed. We have progressed—in some ways at

least—and a lot of the Blixen adventure is now politically incorrect. Shooting lions and exploiting native labor is no longer brave and tough. It's certainly no longer heroic. But you have to agree that, as an Aries and a woman of her day, Karen Blixen followed her bliss.

One curious aspect of the Blixen story that wasn't brought out in the movie, but one that is also pure Aries, was the pride she derived from her title by marriage: Baroness Blixen. In fact, losing the title, the status it carried, and the doors that it opened was her major concern when her husband divorced her.

For a person born under the sign renowned for a healthy self-confidence, it may seem odd that this should have upset her. But to understand this paradox, you need to know that most Aries, whether they admit it or not, are into status and image. In the 1980s when greed was good, most made no secret of it. During the purging of the nineties and the trend against excess, however, it became an Aries truth that many sense was best kept closer to their chest.

Even today, Aries remains slightly in awe of titles. They privately relish being called Professor, President, or Chairperson. Many an Aries has blushed when caught fondling their first pack of business cards, or giving their brass nameplate a quick polish. Bold Aries get quite embarrassed when others notice the telltale signs of their little vanities.

Where more self-effacing types might be content with a decent paycheck and a satisfying life of relative anonymity, Aries yearns for acknowledgment and kudos as tangible evidence of success. Sometimes they just can't help glowing in their own glory, and don't seem to notice that others are not so much green with envy, but wilting under the harsh glare of the Aries ego. Modesty is not high on the list of Aries virtues.

You see, Rams *need* recognition. The sense of inner satisfaction is, frankly, not enough. Most crave the hard evidence of their success as proof that they are valued by our society and the material world. And so long as money is connected with status and achievement, Aries will strive to be rich. Many strive hard to be very rich.

But let's not be petty, let's be generous—as they usually are. Who could deny them a little relishing of their rewards? At least they're honest enough to know what they want.

In fact, in all matters, Aries are generally pretty direct, up-front types. On the whole, what you see is what you get. The firm handshake, friendly manner, and direct eye contact may be the first clue that you've just met a Ram. Your immediate impression is that you're dealing with someone to be reckoned with. You might also have picked up on the aura of restrained but unmistakable sexual power.

The Ram has a strong physical presence. Charming? Certainly. Charismatic? Quite possibly. Aries can be undeniably sexy.

For an extra lesson in Aries spotting, take a quarter out of your pocket and look at the image of Thomas Jefferson. The typical Aries face is lean and angular with a sharp, well-chiseled nose. Often the nostrils are slightly flared. Another giveaway is the eyebrows that meet in the middle, shaped like the curved horns of a Ram or like the glyph that is the astrologer's shorthand symbol for Aries. When the eyebrows knit in intense conversation—like they frequently do—look for the roll of flesh that protrudes over them. A bit primordial perhaps. A touch of the caveman, some would say.

The head is the part of the body ruled by Aries. Curiously, a high proportion of them have a scar somewhere on their face or under the hairline that is the legacy of a childhood accident. Makeup seems to hold a fascination for Aries women. They use it cleverly to maximize and dramatize their looks. Even devotees of the natural look are loath to renounce that perfect red lipstick.

Allowing for genetic or racial characteristics, of course, red hair and a ruddy complexion often go with Aries. The sign on the Ascendant modifies the physical profile of every Sun sign. But unless Aries are born with one of the heavier or rounder Ascendants, such as Taurus, Cancer, or Pisces, they are usually lean and muscular, even to the point of being sinewy, with body weight evenly distributed. You can often pick Aries by the way they move. Faster than most, in a staccato, almost jerky motion. It's as if there is a high tensile energy stored up in the Aries body, ready to be unleashed any moment.

All that energy must go somewhere. No one born under the sign of The Ram can feel happy and fulfilled without an outlet for it. Which brings us back to following your bliss, and what it really means. Following your bliss most definitely does not mean living a totally self-centered life. It's not carte blanche for selfishness or self-gratification.

Lazy is not a word that you read on the list of Aries characteristics. But there are plenty of Rams who are so intent on "following their bliss" and doing their own thing that they're quite prepared for others to work hard and support them while they're on their personal quest, whatever that may be. One forty-something Aries artist we know has never had a regular job. Nor does he make any money from his pictures. But painting pictures is what he calls his work, and he's perfectly comfortable with the idea of living off public assistance and generous gifts from his mother until he makes it. He's one of those Aries who think they're somehow superior to everyone else, and this gives them the right not to have to do just anything to make a living. Don't they know that other people also dream of following their bliss? What if everyone on the planet stopped doing the menial, boring jobs, laid down their tools, and went off to follow their bliss? It's not that Aries are allergic to hard work; they can be the hardest workers of all, but only when it's something they want to work at.

There's another sign that can also be content to allow others (usually a partner) to support them while they follow their bliss, and that's Libra. Libra is the opposite sign to Aries, and opposite signs have a lot in common.

Try hinting to such an Aries that his or her lifestyle might be just a teensy bit selfish and you're likely to encounter aggressive Mars at its worst. Attack is the best form of defense, according to Aries, and a Ram on the defensive is capable of hurling cruel, scathing remarks. If you've been burnt by the fire of the Aries fury, we wouldn't dream of asking you to accept excuses. But could it be that the deep, dark cause of the Aries anger, belligerence, and sometimes even violence is the outer manifestation of a thwarted ego, temporarily out of control? A sign that thrives on action and immediacy is not programmed to handle frustration philosophically.

Take the case of Vincent Van Gogh (born March 30). Volumes have been written about Van Gogh, and how and why he shot himself, and whether he really went mad, or whether he really intended to kill himself.

One thing we do know, Van Gogh wasn't starving and down and out. He was paid a monthly stipend by his art-dealer brother who bought all his paintings. A century after his death, his pictures fetch the highest prices in the world. Yet only one sold in his lifetime. His premature death has become one of the great tragic heroic myths of art history. Could one of the causes be that Van Gogh suffered from "Aries thwarted success syndrome"? It's not easy for the ambitious Aries personality to cope with continual lack of recognition and success.

The personal story aside, Van Gogh's pictures are bursting with the heightened energy of the Aries life force. People liken the sky in *Starry Night* to vortices of swirling energy, and enthuse about the ecstatic color in *Sunflowers*. In his self-portraits we see, again, the typical Aries face; lean features, fleshy knitted brows, intense gaze, and red hair.

Frustration, thwarted ambition, and a surfeit of anger can be evidence of a Mars gone wrong and an Aries out of balance. Just as opposite signs have things in common, so, too, do they have valuable lessons to learn from each other. Libra is the sign that rules getting along with others. Its prime virtues are give and take and a willingness to compromise and accommodate other people. These are precisely the attributes that Aries need to cultivate in order to offset their tendency to rush in with little or no regard to the consequences, and to always put self first. There goes that four-letter word again. Self.

Libra is ruled by Venus, the goddess of love, harmony, and beauty. According to myth, Venus and Mars had a long ongoing relationship. When things were not going well between them, Mars forced himself upon Venus, and the children born from this rape were called Phobos (alarm), Metus (fear), and Demos (dread). But when the love was mutual, they created Harmonia and Eros, the god of erotic love.

This is a poetic way of explaining that unless Martian Aries integrate some essence of the gentle Venusian Libran qualities, they'll find people backing off for fear of getting their fingers—and their feelings—burnt. Conflict is likely to spoil their personal relationships and their professional environment. These are the aggressive Aries who create enemies by being too combative and too blatantly competitive.

The Aries who takes on board some of what Libra has to offer is the noble Aries who is simply superb at eliciting cooperation. This is the charismatic, inspiring Aries whom others respect and admire, the Aries who is the natural leader who creates harmony and still gets things done. As for Eros, when Mars meets Venus on equal ground, it's love and passion as the gods intended.

Normally the Aries drive is inspiring. But when the Ram is riding high, there is always the danger he or she will begin to feel invincible. It's all too easy for the Ram to push too far, too hard, and to feel too "godlike" and lose that composure. The Ram who crosses that line between healthy drive and addiction to achievement can go into overkill. Many Aries risk becoming workaholics, and sometimes victims of self-induced high blood pressure, headaches, and migraines. Aries can be far too naive in not wanting to admit that they are not indomitable and that they, too, have a body that can let them down from time to time.

There is a story from Hans Christian Andersen (born April 2) about the archetypal Aries addiction to action and excitement. It's about the high you get when you're on a roll and you don't want to get off. The story is called "The Red Shoes." Do you remember how the little girl tricked her blind grandmother into buying her a pair of shiny red shoes, instead of the plain black ones that a proper young lady should wear to church on Sunday? Those red shoes turned out to be magic shoes. Whenever she put them on, she spun into an ecstatic dance. In the beginning, she was thrilled.

But one day, tired of dancing, she discovered that she couldn't stop. When she tried to remove the shoes they wouldn't come off.

On and on she danced, beyond the point of exhaustion, crying out for the shoes to stop, but of course, they wouldn't. Finally she begged a woodcutter to chop off her feet so that she could rest.

"The Red Shoes" is a fairy-tale horror story, but the point will hit home for many Aries who've been dancing in their own red shoes for too long. There comes a point when chasing a high becomes a self-destructive habit that takes over their lives. At least until some of that Libran sense of perspective and judgment clicks in and saves them.

Putting 110 percent into everything means that you're overdrawing on your energy reserves. The Aries drive to succeed and conquer often comes at a high price. It's interesting that the late-twentieth-century disease of workaholism (so common that it has even been labeled a "normal neurosis") is now being rethought as a dangerous and foolish way to live. To live life in the fast lane was, only a few years ago, seen as glamorous and enviable. Not anymore. This issue is food for thought for Aries.

"The Red Shoes," though, does not have to be an Aries story with an unhappy ending.

For one contemporary Aries heroine, Gloria Steinem, the pioneering women's magazine she created in the early 1970s turned into her red shoes.

Aries excel at first. Steinem's *Ms.* magazine was one of the first publications to challenge and change our perception of women. But somewhere along the line, *Ms.* magazine took control over Steinem's life. Working tirelessly to keep the magazine on the newsstands, she became more and more exhausted. By her own admission, she had lost perspective on the situation, and had to reach burnout before the turning point came.

Many Aries need to learn when to stop the fast-forward button and press pause in order to review the situation. It's actually an essential factor in progress.

Steinem has that Aries charisma, leadership, and dynamism. Yes, she used it for self-promotion but also to promote the cause of millions of other women. The Aries with a true sense of purpose places great store on honor and being honorable—particularly when he or she is in a position of leadership and responsibility. Aries at their best will move mountains to keep their word and to stand by their commitments, especially if the welfare of others depends on them.

The highest expression of Aries is there for all to see and admire when they pour their courage and drive into the common good. This is when those who live or work with Aries are energized themselves, and reap the rewards of the Aries talent for making things happen.

Aries at their finest embrace challenge. They know that the purpose of life is diminished, and that challenge is scarcely any challenge at all, if we do not have goals that move beyond pure self-interest.

Viktor Frankl, philosopher, psychiatrist, and Auschwitz survivor, was an Aries who explained the true meaning of life for the sign that rules the self. In his book *Man's Search for Meaning*, he wrote, "If the meaning that is waiting to be fulfilled by man were really nothing but a mere expression of self . . . it would immediately lose its demanding and *challenging* character."

Aries the warrior wants to fight a war that's worth winning. This is the challenge. And this, more than anything else, is the meaning of living life as a hero.

THE ARIES CAREER AND DIRECTION

In the small hours of the morning, young ambitious Aries is jolted into consciousness by a brainstorm, a brilliant idea for a new type of business that is guaranteed to succeed. Other Sun signs may have a similar idea, but Aries is almost certainly the one who will have talked to the bank, rented the office, hired the staff, and installed the phone and fax . . . all before noon.

An equally keen Gemini will have spent all morning on the phone running it past friends. A Pisces might have decided before getting out of bed that yes, it was a stroke of genius, but not worth all the trouble. Virgo would be worrying about how the details could be sorted out. And by breakfast, Taurus would have come to the conclusion that it was all too risky, and it's better to play it safe and stick to a steady job. But not Aries. For enterprise, initiative, and sheer speed of action, Aries scores top marks.

In the concrete and chrome towers of corporate culture there are plenty of openings for Aries to do what they do best: compete. In fact, there's almost nothing that a Ram likes better than locking horns with the competition. Except, of course, emerging as the winner.

What makes Aries so famously successful in the world of big business and high finance is their ability to marry passion with the pragmatic. Their will to succeed lights a fire under their "just do it" attitude. If any sign has attitude, it's Aries.

J. P. Morgan and John D. Rockefeller were both Rams. Incidentally, Morgan, who was one of the most powerful men in America one hundred years ago, made his own niche in astrological history by remarking, "Millionaires don't use astrology. Billionaires do."

As brilliant as they are at grasping the big picture, Rams prefer to leave the tedium of filing, sorting, and checking to someone else. Their boredom threshold is low, and time-consuming jobs in which there's no way to cut through tedium annoy them. Aries have limited patience with detail. Dealing with masses of data and minutiae is not an impossibility for Rams, but it's definitely on the far outer edge of their talents. Anyway, why would they want to? From youth, Aries realize the good sense of doing work in which their assets are maximized. One Aries man we know, when questioned by his boss on his late reports and accounts, said: "Either I can get the paperwork done and not do the job, or I can get the job done and leave the paperwork. Which do you want?"

Follow-through also tends to be a problem. As good as they are at getting things going, it must be said that Aries are better starters than they are finishers. They make excellent project workers. When something excites them and captures their imagination, they'll be there—mind, body, and soul. But as soon as the job is up and running, The Ram will already be looking around for a fresh challenge. Challenge is the staple diet of the ambitious Aries. And risk is the spice that keeps bringing them back for more.

No responsible astrologer would advise Aries not to run with a new challenge or not to take a well-calculated risk. There are, though, some Aries who are hooked on risk and challenge to the point of foolhardiness. For all of us, the sign to come is believed to offer qualities that we need to consciously develop to offset any of our own excesses. For Aries, that means taking an appreciative look at the Taurean virtues of patience, caution, thinking before you act, and looking before you leap. Some Aries will scoff at this suggestion. But the older and wiser ones who've learned the lesson of Taurus the hard way are sure to concur.

If Aries rush in where angels fear to tread, it's because they cannot bear the thought of missing out. In fact, you could say that for Rams, not taking risks can actually be riskier. Pent-up frustration is far more damaging to the Aries physical and mental health than a job that doesn't work out.

That's why so many Aries are self-employed, work on commission, or freelance. They're ideally suited to jobs in which the rewards are in direct proportion to their talent and the effort they put in—and jobs in which they don't have to answer to anyone. They could be working as a journalist, builder, promoter, entertainer, agent, or mechanic. Whatever job it is, what they should be looking for is maximum autonomy.

Rams like to run their own show as much as possible. New communication technology has created a situation in which not everyone needs to be working together in one place, in a conventional office. And this suits Aries just fine. But the Ram needs to be out in the field interacting with others, at least some of the time. Politicking and wheeling and dealing are what they do best. Aries prefer to talk business face-to-face. Their ability to engage someone with their presence and to get them enthused and inspired is nowhere near as effective down a phone line. They also like to be able to pick up on the body language and vibes coming their way.

Their nose for business, their sharp brain, and their boldness keep Aries moving confidently forward, and their natural appetite for the new places them in a prime position to embrace progress. Undaunted by technology or any other challenge along the way, Aries is ready and willing to learn whatever it takes to gain the upper hand. And win.

This is the sign of the pioneer. And while there may be no undiscovered lands left on earth to conquer, there are plenty of new industries, new services, and new technologies in which Aries can lead the way. They are essentially modernists who pride themselves on being in the forefront of where the trends are going. David Suzuki is an Aries eco-warrior whose personal commitment to draw awareness to the environment continues to inspire millions around the world.

The ultimate Aries career fantasy is to "boldly go where no man has gone before." And to make a fortune in the process. Is it a coincidence that there are two Ariens in charge of the bridge of the starship *Enterprise*—Captain Kirk and Mr. Spock (William Shatner and Leonard Nimoy)? "Star Trek" has become a metaphor for the Aries pioneering spirit of new-millennium mythology.

Of course, in more down-to-earth locations, not every Aries is destined to carve out a brand-new empire. But even those working for others need to realize that the bottom rung of the ladder is not a healthy place for them to linger too long. On day one on the job, Aries is already impressing the boss with their bright personality, their enthusiasm, and their capacity to get things done. By the end of day two, the boss is suggesting to this bright new employee that he or she is a candidate for promotion. It doesn't take long. Nothing ever does with an Aries. One year later, Aries is likely to be comfortably installed in the boss's chair.

But raw ambition alone is not enough to explain why Aries want to be leaders, not followers. Rams have a strong competitive instinct that makes them want to pit themselves against their co-workers and themselves. Reflect for a moment on the fact that Aries is a Ram, not a sheep. All Aries, both male and female, are symbolized by the male of the species. The Aries woman is usually well in touch with her animus, the masculine part of her psyche, and is every bit as competitive as the Aries man.

Aries may not realize it, but they've been set up to strive to be

high achievers by their childhood conditioning. Father was the dominant parent who in many ways, spoken and unspoken, impressed
upon them that accomplishment was what life was all about. Little
Aries quickly learned that the only way to win Father's approval
was by doing something praiseworthy, be it scoring top marks at
school or becoming captain of the hockey team. It is Aries' father
who has played the biggest part in making Aries a success seeker.

Rams of both sexes love the kudos that accompany success. They
relish all the recognition and admiration that is part of the leadership
package. Most Aries, fortunately, are also acutely aware of the responsibility that goes with leadership. When Aries make a commitment to their employees, or associates, or even themselves, they will
do their level best to keep it. Even if it means pushing themselves
to work longer or harder. An Aries in business, and in life in general,
strives to do the honorable thing.

You can trust that if the Ram goes to bat for you, he or she will
almost certainly do a better job than you could yourself. Many an
aspiring artist's career has taken off after the convincing sales talk of
their Aries agent or dealer.

Having said that, self-interest is never entirely off the Aries agenda.
There's got to be something in it for them. Most Aries who've made
it have made it by being tough, dare we say, even ruthless at times.
Which means there's no place in the Aries-run business for those
who can't deliver the goods or cut the mustard. It won't come as a
surprise to those who work with an Aries to learn that The Ram's
compassion threshold is not high. Your Aries boss really doesn't
want to know if you've had a bad morning, if you're suffering from
PMS, or that your boyfriend has just walked out on you. You might
get a nominal sympathetic squeak, but it doesn't come naturally.
How can they identify when their own stamina and get up and go
are legendary, and when they can still soldier on and put in a full
day's work on a broken heart or a dose of the flu? Basically, they
just want you to get on with the job. Though it must also be said
that they can be wonderfully magnanimous, and are not slow in
giving credit where it's due.

Colleagues will forgive Aries for much on the grounds that they
are genuinely exciting to be with and work with, even the ones who
are far more demanding than they should be able to get away with.

No one is as good at rallying the troops as a Ram. The story of
Jason and his quest for the golden fleece is the great Aries myth
about the extent Aries will go to when they've set their heart on
accomplishing a mission, even if it looks like mission impossible.
Jason didn't set off alone to bring back the fleece that was hanging
in the field of Mars in a far distant, unknown land. He rallied his

troops first. Such was the power of Jason's ability to enthuse and inspire that all the heavyweight heroes of ancient mythology rushed to enlist in the expedition. Jason commissioned the biggest ship that had ever been built, the *Argo*. His heroes, who are called Argonauts, manned the oars, and off they rowed in pursuit of Jason's treasure. Jason and his quest for the Golden Fleece is still told to children as an inspiring story about the glory of pursuing your goal.

It's only reasonable to suspect, though, that at some stage on the treacherous journey, one of the heroes, having nearly lost his life on a dozen occasions, might have turned to another and said, "What on earth are we doing here?" Good question. Especially when you consider that the treasure that Jason risked his life (and everyone else's) for is not recorded in mythology as having any special value except as something that was his birthright, and therefore his to claim. The great myths do not record that the Golden Fleece bestowed wisdom on its owner, or that it brought happiness, or love, or a guarantee of virility. No, the Golden Fleece was simply something marvelous that Jason had set his heart on procuring because it was there and he figured he had a chance of getting it. And as for the fate of the argonauts (a lot of them never came back), well, they were all volunteers and were apparently as keen as he.

Even your everyday Aries on a mission to achieve is brilliant at eliciting the manpower and backup needed. If you work for or with an Aries, and you're not born under a fire sign yourself, you might be wise to take a leaf or two out of the Aries book. There will be moments when you will seriously consider the advantages of an assertiveness training course because there will come a time when you simply have to stand up for yourself. Our advice is, learn to say "No." They do . . . all the time. For people who pride themselves on positive action and are quick to say yes . . . "Yes, I can do it," "Yes, we can deliver," "Yes, it's a deal" . . . Aries are equally adept at saying no. No to anything or anyone that would detour them from their path or sidetrack them from the dollars or the deal in question. They are very good at saying no to time wasters and distractions. And they'll flatly turn down jobs or projects that they think have no future or simply don't interest them.

The world of business and high finance is a familiar battleground for mentally active and aggressive Aries. It's a Sun sign that is well represented among stockbrokers, venture capitalists, and futures traders.

By astrological tradition, any career in which sharp thinking combines with physical courage is also an Aries career. You'll find many Rams in the ranks of the armed forces and law enforcement services. General MacArthur was an Aries. So is Colin Powell, who was the

U.S. chief of staff during the Gulf War. An Aries Ascendant is every bit as useful in the horoscope of a fighter. Oliver Cromwell, who organized a revolution (and a very bloody one at that) to overthrow the British monarchy made good use of his Aries Ascendant to do it. If you happen to know someone with an Aries Ascendant, no matter what the Sun sign, they're dynamic and usually drawn to work that won't keep them stuck behind a desk.

Aries William Booth, founder of the Salvation Army, struck on a uniquely Aries way to relieve the misery of the poor. Booth set up an organization along military lines, believing that the most efficient way to get a large, difficult job done was to create an army to do it. What a classic example of the Aries genius for combining passion and pragmatism. In that unique Aries hands-on, can-do manner, Booth accepted that people must be fed and housed before they can become receptive to religion and morality. Only saints can find God on an empty stomach. And most people aren't saints. How honest. How practical. More than one Aries activist has been justifiably labeled a firebrand. For those Aries with a special calling to rally the masses, the charismatic power of their personality is their single most formidable weapon. Think of Maya Angelou and Dennis Banks.

Astrologers say that the Sun is exalted in Aries. It means that the Sun, the source of all energy in our solar system, shines particularly brightly on Aries. The Sun is the planetary ruler of theatrical, glamorous Leo. This Sun link between Aries and Leo has a great deal to do with the vital, magnetic quality that we call the Aries charisma. It's the kind of charisma that makes movie stars. Marlon Brando's got it. So has Omar Sharif. Both Aries. The brightness of the Aries star quality is unmistakable. It blends the raw physical presence of Mars with the brilliance of the Sun.

Male Aries stars of movie history seem to fall into two distinct camps. The first is the exciting, smoldering type who, without doing or saying a thing, simply oozes sex. His excitement hangs on the edge of the dangerous, even taboo, and the antihero emerges—complete with motorbike or fast car, both of which are archetypal Aries power and sex symbols. Then there's the other type: the noble leader with the initiative and the courage to get the important and difficult jobs done. It's Aries-born Spencer Tracy and Gregory Peck whom you can trust to save the day.

You could say that any job that requires your average Ram to draw on a drop or two of his or her own personal star quality could be defined as an Aries job. It could be sales, advertising, or public relations, where the powers of persuasion and force of personality are everything. Aries make great presenters and spokespersons. The Ram's friendly, direct manner instantly charms and disarms. So if the plan is to wine and dine the client with a view to getting the deal signed in record time, send in Aries.

You'll have gathered by now that Aries like to move fast. For a few, speed itself becomes a profession. Their native desire to win, plus their craving for excitement, makes Aries sportsmen and women dangerous competitors. Few will become Roger Bannisters, but there are many out there dreaming about it. And many who actually do make a living in sports and fitness. You'll find them in gyms and on race tracks, working as coaches, motivators, and promotors.

Mars is the planet that rules sharp metallic objects. So in medicine, it's natural that a lot of Aries are attracted to surgery and dentistry. Opticians are also ruled by Aries. The Mars energy is essential, too, in building, engineering, and mechanics. Aries people are usually gifted with their hands. And there is a whole collection of vocations involving mechanical skills and manual dexterity that are populated by Aries. They delight in the elegance of fine machinery. Henry Royce, of Rolls-Royce fame, was an Aries.

Astrologers believe that countries, just like people, come under the influence of certain signs of the zodiac. They believe that the reason England is the nation in which the industrial revolution began is that England is a country with a strong Aries input in its national character. England has always been a nation of inventors. Now, in the postindustrial revolution, new kinds of machines are necessary for our survival—machines that provide a whole new challenge to the Aries inventor.

Rams have an undeniable need to make their mark in the world, to stand out from the crowd. They yearn for recognition. The Aries with a strong creative urge is frequently led into the more esoteric and contemplative domains of the solitary studio.

Here, in the realm of original ideas, the lone Ram can channel his or her passion and apply him or herself to creating work that is truly inspirational. It's an often-overlooked fact that much of what Aries create, be it mechanical, intellectual, or artistic, brings enormous benefit or pleasure to others, as well as themselves.

The Aries artist can be like the Magician of occult lore who draws on a higher power to manifest his passions into the world of form. This is why the planet of the creative impulse is the planet named after the god of war.

Johann Sebastian Bach, born on the day when the Sun enters Aries, March 21, poured his genius into music that is remembered, above all, for its passion. Ultimately it is the Aries passion, in whatever medium it is expressed, that identifies their work. You see, you can't hold passion down. Passion is what puts Aries in the history books. J. S. Bach, Vincent Van Gogh, William Wordsworth, Saint Theresa of

Avila. Aries, all. It proves, Aries, that if you know what it is that you want to do or create in your life, you don't need any urging from anyone to do it. Nor do you need any advice from anyone telling you how to go about it.

Aries know that their passion will drive them, their intuition will steer them, and their sense of honor will keep them on the right road.

The Aries road to fulfillment.

LOVE AND FRIENDSHIP

Casanova was a Ram. Many Aries find it secretly gratifying that the famous seducer was one of their own. For those of you with an eye on an Aries, you can rest assured that even if his memoirs contain a few exaggerations, Casanova had something going for him.

Perhaps the fainthearted should look elsewhere. But if you are ready for the promise of primordial sex, and figure you can match the Ram's high libido, and if you are excited by the prospect of what a lover with a total lack of inhibition can bring out in you, then go for it. With Aries, the chemistry is palpable right from the start. Aries have got it. They know that they've got it. And they know that you know that they've got it. And you want it.

Only contemplate a relationship with an Aries if you're willing and able to engage in a bit of psychic warfare. Your best strategy is to be interesting rather than interested. Don't hold back from making it clear that you've got a life that's going somewhere. Even over the first cup of coffee, Aries will be testing you. Are you a challenge? Will you pass the excitement test? Will you be able to stand the pace?

Friends have to pass Aries tests, too. You won't be phoned if you've been designated boring, frumpy, unadventurous, tame, or just plain. Ariens want companions who can match their own joie de vivre. If they've organized a night out (and no one, except maybe a Leo, can organize a night out like an Aries), they'll barely be able to disguise their frustration if you cancel. Mind you, there is always that question of Aries self-interest. If something or someone better should happen to come along on the day of your long-planned reunion, you might easily find yourself canceled. But it will be handled with such charm that you'll be quite understanding. Guilt won't give an Aries away on the phone. Guilt is a neurosis that Aries rarely suffers from.

Speaking of big nights out and good times, Aries are up there with the other fire signs as the great entertainers and the most magnanimous of hosts. They give fantastic dinner parties, and can't bear the thought of a guest leaving unimpressed. You can even rely on your far-flung Aries friends to entertain your other friends who may be passing through town. Especially if they're single and desirable.

Aries will readily accept you as a kindred spirit if you suggest an Indian or Mexican restaurant for your first rendezvous. There are sound astrological reasons for this. The chili plant is ruled by Aries. Over the beef vindaloo, you can show your newfound Aries friend that you're one of the initiated by suggesting you catch the latest show after dinner. It's impossible to be too spontaneous or too adventurous with an Aries.

With Aries, you'll have a faithful friend you can rely on in a crisis. Can't pay the rent? Aries will organize the cash. Your car's broken down and you don't know where to go? They'll get it towed to their trusted mechanic. Aries would have to be first choice for best man at your wedding. He'll get the groom to the church, sane and sober, because his reputation for efficiency and organization is on the line.

The Ram will do much to quickly restore your faith in the power of positive thinking. On the other hand, they will expect you to quickly recover from whatever temporary bind you're in. The "poor me" syndrome won't wash with Aries. They'll be looking for the evidence that you're in control of your own life, just as they're in control of theirs.

If you're contemplating romance with a Ram, there are some specific pointers that you'd be best to heed if you want to officially become an item.

First, go all out to look better than your best. If an Aries views you as a serious candidate, he or she will have spent a great deal more time than will be admitted, posing and preening in front of the mirror. The Ram is a vain animal. And he or she will be assessing you from the start as a visual asset. If you're having a bad hair day or your skin has erupted, cancel. Okay, you know Aries hate to be stood up or let down. But presentation is critical. If absolutely necessary, invent a relapse of your malaria, or pretend you've been in contact with the dreaded Ebola virus. The tough Ram, ruled by the god of war, can be one of the most squeamish of signs when it comes to bodily ills and ailments. So Aries is unlikely to turn up on your doorstep with a medicine chest and homemade soup.

How you look can make or break a first date. Aries wants a slick, fashionable package. Don't turn up in anything too outrageous, too outdated, or too radical. The Ram won't mind being seen in public with an arty bohemian type so long as you can do it with such style that it looks like funky chic.

One Aries businesswoman we know was recently set up on a blind date by well-meaning friends. Aries, it must be said, can be remarkably blunt. First, she had the nerve to give the subject a preliminary interrogation on the condition of his body. Over the phone she asked him, "How tall are you? What do you weigh?" She even asked him, "Are you toned?" Aries, remember, hates to waste time. In the end, they scheduled to meet at a sidewalk café. Ms. Aries drove up to the café fifteen minutes after the appointed time, to be sure he would be ready and waiting. Then she drove past slowly, giving herself enough time to see that yes, the subject was sitting there decked out in beige acrylic trousers and a vinyl bomber jacket. What could she do? The only thing an elegant, attractive, and successful Aries could do. "Beam me up, Scottie," Ms. Aries said, and kept driving. The moral of this story is, never look like a nerd.

Never sound like a nerd, either. Aries won't spend long on superficial niceties. They go straight into foretalk. It's all part of the testing procedure. Be prepared to pit yourself against them in intellectual argument. Your mind as well as your looks must be a source of stimulation. Your ideas must be fresh and exciting. And you must be confident of your opinions. If you don't agree with what they say, don't echo their convictions thinking they'll like you more. They'll only take it as a sign of weakness.

In keeping with the Casanova tradition, very little time may elapse between sipping cappuccinos and slipping between the sheets. The lightning seduction is, indeed, a tried-and-true Aries technique. However (and it's an *important* however, given the size of their libido), it's nothing short of amazing how long Aries can take in the seduction process if they view you as more than just another conquest. If you represent a long-term relationship, maybe even The One, Aries can rival Scorpio in the power game of love. These are the Sun signs that will devote however long it takes, months if necessary, to be absolutely certain their prey is so primed that there is no possibility that they won't yield. The Ram has inbuilt expectations of being a winner. Losing face is very hard for an Aries. If there's any doubt in their mind that the object of their desire may say no, Aries will wait.

The young Aries has a reputation for carving notches on the headboard—though they like to pride themselves that they would never sacrifice quality for quantity, with a guarantee of success and satisfaction every time.

The first time with an Aries could be like the first time ever. It's sex rediscovered. Like Adam and Eve all over again. Aries understand wickedness. They don't have much truck with all that nonsense about good clean fun. They know that really delicious sex has an element of the wild and the wicked. And they know that doesn't happen when you're being nice, coy, gentlemanly or ladylike.

Instantaneous arousal, animal abandon, and unbridled lust are traditional Aries specialties. Aries lovers are fondly remembered for the trail of clothing from the front door to the bedroom . . . Some trails don't even get that far. A classic Aries fantasy is playing the cavalier crashing through the French windows and taking his mistress on the dining table, with his boots on.

Having ravished her, he's likely to roll over on his back and demand that she has her way with him. The swing from active to passive is an interesting item on the Aries menu, for both sexes. Aries men have a luxuriating passive side. And Aries women have a natural understanding of the male psyche.

Initiation is another Aries fantasy. They'll try just about anything once. Aries can't resist confiding to their lovers, "This is the first time I've ever done this" if it's a landmark in their sexual education. Thankfully, Rams are unlikely to ruin the event by asking, "Was it good for you?" Probably that's because they know it was. It's also because they're not into too much analytical postcoital conversation. If you're a diehard sentimentalist, you could find their pillow talk a little disappointing.

Nevertheless, if you don't pressure them, and let it happen naturally, the tender moments après are probably the only times when tough, proud Aries will reveal that they have their share of vulnerabilities and weaknesses, just like the rest of us.

If the sexual reputation of Aries is frequently discussed, then less well known is the fact that Aries is an arch romantic.

In matters of love, Aries is idealistic, often to the point of positively unrealistic. There are middle-aged Rams who have never married because they're still optimistically hunting for their Romeo or Juliet. If there is any truth to the idea that love is fated, nobody—not even an Aries—can arrange for Mr. or Miss Perfect to appear on command. For a sign that's famous for it's "can do" philosophy, it can be deeply disturbing to The Ram that this is something he or she still cannot do.

Still, they keep hoping. What an intolerable predicament it would be for Aries to find themselves married to a "suitable" boy or girl, and hooked into a mortgage and PTA meetings, only to feel the fires of romance have burnt down to embers. What would happen should a more desirable proposition then arrive on the scene? Aries are not the types to stay and suffer and die of boredom. Eventually they will seek an escape hatch. It's an important truth that Rams who are contemplating marriage should ponder on.

Lovers of Aries can take heart that the happily married Ram is not uncommon. But it takes a strong partner with an equally strong sense of identity to make marriage to an Aries work. Someone who knows when to give way and when to stand firm. Someone with purpose and direction of his or her own. Aries is highly allergic to codependent relationships. The quickest way to the divorce courts is to live your life through them rather than with them.

Life with Aries can be fast and furious. But forearmed is fore-warned, as astrologers are fond of saying. Be prepared for Aries, who, you'll recall, naturally assume executive control of all opera-tions, to try to run the home along their lines. In all fairness, they probably do it unconsciously. It's not that they necessarily intend to take over and rule the roost, it's just their nature to lead and to make sure that what needs to be done gets done. All fire signs have the tendency to dominate their domain. Before you know it, you're obey-ing the new lord or lady of the manor. Woe to the partner of Aries who can't summon enough self-assertion to restore some essence of democracy.

Actually, democracy is something that the Aries who wants a har-monious, stable relationship needs to think about. Remember, one of the keys to getting on with others is cultivating the virtues of your opposite sign. So, Aries, exercise a little of that Libran-style give and take. Resolve to talk things through rather than fight things through. If there is anything that Aries needs to take on board from Libra, it's learning to compromise and accepting the principle of equal rights. Warning to lovers of Aries: There are a few Rams out there who are incredibly hard to live with, because they still believe that all Sun signs are equal—but some Sun signs are more equal than others.

When Aries is being blatantly selfish, you can't be too slow or too subtle in pointing it out. Partners of Aries are probably aware that the Aries *s* word—*self*—may be at the root of quite a lot of their domestic troubles. Stand up for your rights. Be ready to hold on to your own rhythms of life, refuse to get caught up and dragged along by their breakneck speed. Refuse to be made to feel deficient or incompetent if you don't want to live life at their pace. If Aries can't understand the restorative qualities of a good veg-out, that's their problem. Don't let them make it yours. Tell them some people do their best thinking lying down.

Inextricably linked to the *s* word is the *a* word. *Anger*.

Raw, savage, intimidating anger. When the Aries ego suffers a major deflation, they go in for the kill and can verbally annihilate their partner, hitting below the belt and destroying a relationship beyond the point of repair. This is Mars, the god of war, at his personal worst. The Ram's deepest frustrations and anger demand a physical outlet. In private—and it generally is, because Aries would be far too embarrassed for others to see them losing their cool—rage can provoke Aries to smashing a glass table top, or putting their fist through a wall. It hurts. But you won't see them cry. With Aries, it's anger before tears.

But if you're prepared to put up with an occasional clash of egos, and can pit the force of your will against theirs when the occasion warrants it, then their forthrightness will be a breath of fresh air.

Their passion for life will inspire you. Their courage will make you brave. Aries may be a demanding partner. But you know that if your Aries promises to take you to the stars, he or she will try hard to deliver. Pack your bag. The spaceship leaves in five minutes.

THE ARIES PARENT

There is nothing that Aries cannot organize. No little problems that cannot be solved in order to achieve their goals. And if that goal happens to be parenthood, then Aries will quickly and efficiently have nursery, home, and career all humming and running like clockwork. They're very good at factoring new responsibilities into their lives.

Before other signs develop an inferiority complex, it must be said that the Ram's bottomless reservoir of energy helps. Aries parents won't allow themselves to flounder in the sea of extra domestic duties that babies create. Ever resourceful, Aries will streamline their schedule and take it all in their stride.

The original model for the superwoman of the eighties must have been an Aries. While many other women have long since given up the insanity of trying to do it all and have it all, many Aries women are still doing it all, and doing it well. The Aries mother is one woman who is most likely to want to maintain her own career and interests.

For active and busy Aries, however, the desire to reproduce is not usually the be all and end all of their existence. But when baby does arrive, be it sooner or later, proud Aries parents are renowned for moving heaven and earth, if necessary, to see that their child lacks nothing and has every opportunity in life. They won't think twice about working longer hours or taking on an extra job to cover the mounting expenses. In this way, Aries can be truly dedicated parents.

Aries parents will willingly drive ten miles across town to pick up their son from Boy Scouts after dropping off their daughter at ballet lessons. They'll do whatever has to be done so that their children can have the experience and opportunities that will give them a good start in life. Aries know that an early sense of achievement is the best training ground for success in adult life.

The Ram's parental expectations are high. Aries want to see results from their efforts and returns on their investments. This presents no problem if the child has inherited the Aries parent's traits. If your family tree contains one Aries, for example, you can be certain even if you can't unearth another Ram, there will be plenty of family members with an Aries Ascendant, or Moon in Aries.

But every family produces "the odd one out" who is not so much a black sheep as just different. Maybe they are a throwback to their great grandmother's Pisces Sun or Virgo Moon. Maybe they have no planets in Aries at all. Cracks in the Ram's parenting ability can appear when Aries produces a child who doesn't share their drive, who isn't as tough as the Aries parent.

This is the time for Aries to take a quantum leap into the too-often-unfamiliar territory of sensitivity and sympathy. After all, is sleeping in on the weekend a sign that one's teenager is destined to be a lazy nonachiever? Not everyone is born with Aries' tireless energy. And not everyone can be, or wants to be, as competitive as Aries. They should try not to pounce too quickly on their children as they come through the door, nervously clutching their report card. And when they see that they scored 80 percent in mathematics, they should restrain their natural desire to ask what the top mark was, and who got it. They should think about the long-term effects of telling children too often to get their act together. Aries parents can actually be counterproductive by reprimanding their children for being lazy or unmotivated. Tell people often enough that they're lazy, and that's what they'll be.

Aries parents want efficiency and achievement. And discipline, they believe, is the way to get it. At 6:00 A.M., many an Aries parent bears a very close resemblance to a regimental sergeant major. This is not the hang-loose, go-with-the-flow Californian hippy style of parent. A lot of Aries homes are run with businesslike precision, with the house rules stuck to the fridge. Sometimes children of Aries find themselves working overtime to meet the expectations of their Aries parents, and to fit in with their lifestyle. At the very worst end of the spectrum, there are the notorious Hollywood Aries mothers from hell, Joan Crawford and Bette Davis, whose daughters finally got their revenge by telling the world about a childhood at the mercy of their egotistical, tyrannical parent.

Fortunately, far more common are the children of Aries who hold on to positive memories of their energetic, tireless, and wonderfully encouraging mother or father. They'll remember their Aries parent glowing with pride at awards assemblies. They'll be grateful for their words of encouragement. "You can do it" or "Just do your best" will come back when they find themselves struggling with grown-up problems.

Above all, the children of Aries will remember how they rarely went without the things they needed to give them a head start in life. A parent who is a strong, confident role model is infinitely better than all the self-help books on positive thinking and how to make it in a harsh, competitive world.

THE ARIES CHILD

If the new person in your life is an Aries, and if you've been boning up the latest manuals on parenting that advocate demand feeding and self-expression, it might not be long before you're handing the books back half read to the well-meaning friends who lent them to you. Raising an Aries infant may give serious food for thought about the old biblical notion of original sin. Because an Aries child, untamed and untrained, could be a frightening prospect.

From the very beginning, parents of Aries need no persuading that their bundle of joy is already a Ram, not a lamb.

The Mars urge to action starts as soon as your Aries baby climbs over the top of the crib. By the time they reach the floor, they're up and walking. Or running. Just imagine all that raw Mars energy loose in the house without discipline and direction. It wouldn't make for a quiet life. The home with Aries children needs rules. You don't want to crush their adventurous spirit, but early lessons in self-control and respecting the rights of others are going to give you all a happier life.

The Ram's natural instinct to lead, especially if he or she is the firstborn, could be the breeding ground for sibling rivalry. It's curious how many Aries are born into families in which they are either the first or only child. Or in which there is a large age gap between the children. In this sense, destiny seems to place them in circumstances where the doors to personal freedom and self-realization are wide-open.

All infants exhaust their parents at times. But parents of Aries may have cause to feel exhausted more often than most. This is not the child who is going to leave the playground without protest when he or she still has the energy to swing from the monkey bars, and can't understand why you haven't. The famous high level of energy is there from the start. Are all children so tireless? Can they all be so demanding?

You'll find yourself asking these same questions if you have a child with Moon in Aries. For all of us, our Moon sign glows particularly strongly during our childhood years. Indeed, through all our life, it's the dominant force over our instincts and emotions. Moon in Aries children are generally just as energetic and demanding as children with Sun in Aries. Even when they grow up, Moon in Aries people are impatient. When they decide they want to do something, they want to do it *now*.

Both Sun in Aries and Moon in Aries children should be encouraged to share and to learn patience. At birthday parties, teach your little Ram to pass around the cake before taking a slice. On the sports field, Aries will always play to win, but learning to compete for the fun of it, or at least practicing not being too unashamedly keen to murder the competition, will stand them in good stead in the future.

Already, at a young age, the stage is being set for a life of action. While they are still small, your main task will be to provide outlets for all their energy. Channel their natural competitive and combative spirit. Enroll Bruce Lee Jr. in the local kung fu club, and be prepared to applaud a few demonstrations on the living room floor. Dancing is a fabulous medium of expression for Aries children. But guide them along the tightrope between being the star of the show and the star show-off.

Allow Aries boys—and girls—to help with any repairs or building around the home. Hammer in hand, they'll be content nailing blocks of wood together for hours. It may turn out to be more than just a way of keeping them amused. You'll be surprised at just how useful your little handyram can be around the house.

Aries children grow up fast. It won't be long before they are organizing their own games and activities, and happily leading an independent little life of their own. Their precocious sense of purpose, knowing what they want to do from an early age, is, in one way, a relief to most parents.

But relief could turn to despair should their sense of purpose conflict with yours. A battle of wills with a headstrong Aries child could turn into a small war if you let it.

Above all, they need to learn to accept responsibility for their actions. And that can't happen too soon. Because one day, and it's not too far away, your Aries offspring is going to do what they want anyway—with or without your approval. Then your good work will pay off, especially when puberty strikes. Most Aries have early sexual adventures. Guilt and fear have little chance of dampening their libido. "Curiosity killed the cat" is a cautionary cliché that has never washed with a young Aries. You can probably forget the birds and the bees, too. They learned that one long ago. What's needed now is frank talk and practical advice.

The "I am invincible" attitude is the source of many Aries youthful misadventures and dramas. Many older and wiser Rams carry around permanent reminders of their wild, reckless years in the form of war wounds from the sports field, school-yard battles, or falling off the garage roof. They would be the first to admit that their courage, at times, exceeded their capability.

Don't fall into the mistake of thinking that bravery and bravado are only for the boys. Your Aries daughter will covet the shining red sports car in the showroom as much as your Aries son. As a child, she's likely to be a tomboy, but when the hormones kick in, brace yourself for the transformation into a glamorous, sophisticated predator. It will seem like no time at all between climbing trees and climbing onto the back of a motorbike.

Both young Mr. and Miss Aries are extremely fashion-conscious. Looking cool, for the young Ram, is a matter of social life and death. They think the whole world will notice if, heaven forbid, they're caught in last year's sneakers, or jeans with the wrong cut.

If money is short, young Aries will have no hesitation in fronting up to the local supermarket or diner in search of after-school work. You've got to admire their nerve. It's their first foray into the world of enterprise. And it won't be their last. This is the blessing of having an Aries in the family. Aries is not the teenager you will need to boot off the couch and out of the nest. They won't need any motivating to find a job, an apartment, and a life of their own. Since they're born with plenty of get-up-and-go, you won't need to be responsible for their future. It's more likely you'll find your old age more comfortable thanks to their help and generosity.

Your Aries will not live life through you or anyone else. Nor will they want your life to revolve around them. But you can trust that they will be there with help and practical advice, whenever you need it. Above all, your Aries child wants you to be proud of him or her. And given all that young Aries is capable of achieving, what parent wouldn't be?

BORN UNDER ARIES

Quentin Tarantino   Warren Beatty
Peter Ustinov   Tennessee Williams
Marcel Marceau   Eric Clapton
Chico Marx   Jessica Lange
Andrew Lloyd Webber   David Frost
Severiano Ballesteros   Jeffrey Archer
Charlie Chaplin   Émile Zola
Diana Ross   W. P. Chrysler
Alec Bloomingdale   Penelope Keith
Frank Woolworth   Booker T. Washington
Butch Cassidy   Eric Idle
Aretha Franklin   Hugh Hefner
Spain   Daniel Day-Lewis
Arthur Murray   Elle MacPherson
Emma Thompson   Eddie Murphy
Dudley Moore   Superman
Elton John

TAURUS

April 21–May 21

♉

Ruling Planet

VENUS

Have more than thou showest
Speak less than thou knowest
Lend less than thou owest
Ride more than thou goest
Learn more than thou trowest
Set less than thou throwest.

William Shakespeare–born April 23

THE TAURUS NATURE

Sound Taurean advice straight from the heart of the immortal Bard.
Today, Shakespeare's Taurus code of conduct might read:

> *Don't flash your wealth around*
> *Keep the important things to yourself*
> *Never lend money*
> *Don't walk when you can drive*
> *Don't believe all that you hear*
> *Never risk all on one throw of the dice.*

The language has changed, but the meaning is the same. If you're
a Taurus, it's simply stating the obvious. You may have expressed it
less poetically than Shakespeare, but you've been saying these things
for years. Anybody with a Taurus parent, grandparent, or friend is
sure to have been on the receiving end of every classic commonsense

cliché in the book: Don't bite the hand that feeds you . . . Better the devil you know . . . Look before you leap . . . or, even better, "Look twice before you leap," as Charlotte Brontë advised. And yes, needless to say, she was a Taurus.

Why this unswerving devotion to the safe, sure, and sensible?

Taurus is the first sign of the zodiac in the element of earth. All earth signs (Virgo and Capricorn are the others) are concerned with the practical necessities of life. The first sign of each element deals with the issues of that element at its most basic level. So as the first of the earth signs, Taureans are particularly focused on the issues of security, stability, and material possessions. You could say it's the earthiest earth sign of all.

The primary drive for Taurus is to secure those tangible things— home, good job, and money in the bank—that make for a stable life. If their security package of home, family, and steady job is even slightly threatened, Taurus becomes deeply disturbed. The bigger the threat, the harder it rocks them. This is why they extol the virtues of playing safe and sensible. And why they subscribe so completely to the tried and true.

Since Taurus is the sign that rules money and possessions, money is a commodity that Taureans are not the least bit coy about. As honest materialists, they appreciate that money is not only our means of survival, but it is also what buys the time to enjoy the good things of life they also love so much.

As the second sign of the zodiac, Taurus follows Aries. In Aries, the cosmic spark of primal energy and self-awareness is ignited. Then comes Taurus, following logically as the sign that will harness that energy and use it to create something that is solid, tangible, and useful. In Taurus, ideas and energy become manifest.

The symbol for Taurus is The Bull. A stolid beast surveying his meadow of cows, all plump and in milk. Placid and content, so long as nothing and no one invades his patch of sweet, juicy grass or lets his cows loose. This is an uncomplicated creature who seeks the peaceful life and simple pleasures. The Bull wants to know that his cows will still be there in the meadow tomorrow, and that the farmer can be counted on to bring him his bundle of hay on time.

Standing solid on terra firma, Bulls aim to stay grounded. After all, this physical world is where we are, they figure. Transcendental futuristic speculations are all very interesting, but that's all they are— speculations. As for maya, the world of illusion and delusion, karma, the other side, and the rewards—or otherwise—of the afterlife, well, that's something to be handled later. What exists for Taurus is the here and now. They don't want to transcend reality, they want to enjoy reality.

It was the English philosopher Herbert Spencer who coined the phrase "Survival of the Fittest." Spencer was a Taurus, and his famous words are actually a clue to the meaning of Taurus. Human Bulls are physically tough beasts, and with their stamina and ox-strong constitution, their chances of survival in the wild would be good. But in the modern human jungle, the fittest are not only the physically tough, but also the best providers. And let's face it (because that's what Taurus does), money is what provides.

If practical Taurus has a keen appreciation of the value of money and how it obtains for them the security they want, they've got an equally sound grasp of the value of people, too. They live by the principle that the group is stronger than the individual. And the way to prosper is by being part of a mutually supportive unit. So long as the family is still our primary social unit, the combination of family, home, and money—or money, family, and home—will be cross-referenced, mixed up, and sometimes confused in the Taurus psyche.

Taurus is tribal by nature. Blood ties, roots, and heritage are terribly important to them. They're not loners and find it harder than most to live without a firm sense of belonging. In the face of the social changes that now challenge our notion about what a family is, Taurus remains a committed advocate of traditional family values. Only Cancer rivals Taurus in devotion to the family ideal and the desire to belong. A life, a family, and a society at large based on firm ethical principles creates stability and offers the best possibilities for success and happiness, thinks Taurus. This is the sign that also rules ethics and values. And that's why Taureans have such definite opinions on right and wrong, good and bad, what is acceptable and what is not.

From a young age, Taureans set their sights on establishing a good living and acquiring home comforts. Whatever their circumstances, whether they hail from Seattle or Sydney, whether they are born in a tenement or the house on the hill, they are determined to get their rightful share, their slice of the cake . . . as soon as possible.

Indeed, it is uncanny how often destiny sets many Taureans up at a comparatively young age. A lot inherit and plow the money into a home or a business. Many more are helped by their parents, who buy them their first car or give them the deposit on their first apartment. Their parents may never admit it nor even consciously realize it, nevertheless it's often true that the Taurus child is the favorite. Parents are usually only too keen to express their approval of this sensible, reliable child, the one they are confident will use the money wisely, won't go off the rails, and can be counted on to be there every Christmas and in difficult times. Mother looms large in the life of young Taureans. It was Mother who ran the home and dominated the family scene. She was often an emotional tour de force and you wouldn't want to get on her bad side. Taurean women themselves happily assume the matriarchal role, and adult Taureans of both sexes maintain this respect for the matriarchal figure.

If parental approval is as important to our development as psychologists say, is it any wonder that the quietly confident, self-assured Bull is so content to be who they are? Generally speaking, Taurus has less interest in self-examination than any other sign.

If parents can't afford the young Bull a financial kick start in life, then he or she is often lucky enough to marry into money. Taurean orphans do exist, of course, but even they often find a family through marriage, and a clan of supportive in-laws. Another variation on this theme is the young Taurean who has the good fortune to fall easily into a well-paid job in which he or she is favored as a trustworthy supporter of the establishment. Taurus is a person who instinctively fits in.

The first Taurean goal in life is to own their own home. They almost consider it their birthright. If at all possible, twenty-year-old Taureans will be busy negotiating their first mortgage, while their peers are enjoying today too much to think about tomorrow. In middle age, it is The Bulls who will be kicking up their hooves while the others are bogged down by mortgage payments. It would be a smart move for a lot of us if we took this leaf out of the Taurus book.

Is this no-nonsense, money-conscious Bull the same animal with the reputation for regularly wallowing in luxury? Sure it is. Taurus will casually stroll through the door with an armful of Bloomingdale's shopping bags and an air of mission accomplished, and half an hour later be preaching the importance of having money in the bank and cutting back on the household budget. There's no contradiction really. Good money management pays for their pleasures and gratifications. They regard regular indulgence as practically a necessity. Whatever The Bull chooses to spend money on, whether it's a suit or a stereo, it will be the best, and designed to last a lifetime. You see, Venus, the goddess of beauty, love, and pleasure is their ruling planet.

Some planets, including Venus, rule two signs. Taureans share Venus with Librans. But Venus reveals different aspects of herself in each sign. Libra is an air sign in which Venus is more concerned with the purely aesthetic, with style and chic for its own sake. Taurus relates to the physical, earthy side of Venus—the things that are warm, sensuous, comforting, and enjoyable.

Beautiful, self-indulgent Venus urges Taureans to fill their homes with comfortable old-fashioned armchairs, fresh flowers from the garden, precious heirlooms, and their special loves, beautiful pictures and beautiful music. Gardens fall under the rulership of nature-loving Taurus. And nothing is as therapeutic to Taureans, stressed out by the madness and mayhem of a changing world, as the return to their own private Garden of Eden, where they can get their hands in some good clean dirt. The Bull has an innate sense of continuity and is finely tuned to the comings and goings of the seasons. Many an elderly Taurean has strolled around the garden with a grandchild, proudly pointing out the great oak planted as a seedling fifty years before, or the roses that were transplanted from old Uncle George's garden.

Thanks to Botticelli's *Birth of Venus*, we all know that Venus came from the sea, rising up from the waves, voluptuous and fully grown. Beautiful, serene, and gracious, she may have been. But don't be fooled. Venus was no vestal virgin. You don't get the title of Love Goddess by being pure and demure. Venus knew how to strut her stuff. Her self-assuredness and the impact of her beauty on the social circle of Mount Olympus put the noses of the other goddesses somewhat out of joint. They contrived to marry her off to Vulcan, the roughneck of the gods. But marriage didn't stop Venus from indulging in a long-term affair with Mars, god of lust and passion. Nor did it interfere with her infatuation with Adonis, the most beautiful mortal man who ever existed. Ever since Venus fell for Adonis, their names have been synonyms for the perfection of physical beauty. In light of Venus' resume, it's not hard to see why Taureans of both sexes are such suckers for pulchritude. Warm and uncomplicated in their sexual nature, earthy Taureans are more appreciative of the well-covered Titian nude type than the anorexic supermodel waif.

This healthy Venusian appetite for the pleasures of the flesh carries over quite naturally to the pleasures of the table. Good food is a Taurean delight, but too much of it is a common Taurean undoing. Their love of sweets is well known. Many Taureans spend their lives waging sporadic warfare against chocolate éclairs and mounting pounds. Too much food and too little exercise often causes the Bull's waistline to expand with the years. A sedentary life can be a health disaster for Taureans. Without regular exercise, they can develop a variety of health problems associated with too much rich living, including heart disease and diabetes. When Shakespeare said, "Ride more than thou goest," he meant don't waste your energy in a futile flap. He didn't mean it's okay to spend all weekend on the couch without moving a muscle.

Which is not to say that all Taureans are plump. There is one type of Taurus that is tall, lean, and lanky. Think of Fred Astaire, Audrey Hepburn, Shirley MacLaine, Uma Thurman, and Michael Palin. There is also a large group of Taureans who are on the stocky side. For all of us, the sign on the Ascendant modifies our appearance. But even allowing for that, you can spot many Bulls by their barrel chest, short neck, and strong, muscular legs. Similarly, a Taurus Ascendant makes any Sun sign shorter and more thickset. Watch Taureans walking, and you'll notice they saunter rather than stride. Anything faster than an amble is their definition of power walking.

The throat is the part of the body ruled by Taurus. As winter approaches, you can usually spot The Bulls standing at the bus stop. They're the ones with a cashmere scarf wrapped twice around their neck. When a flu virus invades a Taurus, it heads straight for the throat. As children, they're particularly prone to infected tonsils. Thyroid conditions are also associated with Taurus.

But if the throat is the Taurean Achilles' heel, it can also be their greatest asset. People with a Taurus Sun or Taurus Ascendant are often blessed with a beautiful voice, one with a seductive, pleasing quality and a rich timbre. The sign of Taurus or the planet Venus is always strong in the birth charts of singers. Bing Crosby, Barbra Streisand, and Ella Fitzgerald were all born with Sun in Taurus. At home, Taurus is an uninhibited bathroom baritone with a repertoire of favorite arias from the big operas.

Yet rulership by beautiful, artistic Venus doesn't quite account for that down-to-earth, money-oriented side of Taurus. She somehow seems too romantic, too devoted to beauty and art, to be caught up in the vulgar material world. Many renowned astrologers have suggested that the Earth gods and goddesses fill this gap. Their idea is that the planet Earth itself may also be a ruler of Taurus. Certainly Gaia, Mother Earth herself, seems to correlate perfectly with the Taurus nature.

If that's the case, the great god Pan, who is nature and earth incarnate, is an important character in the Taurus mythology. Pan means "All." In other words, Pan is the all-encompassing universal nature god. Nature creates its own laws and can never be tamed. Pan is both kind and cruel, good and bad. For all his or her love of comfort and security, the aware Taurus senses something soulless and incomplete in the overly refined civilized world.

Today, not many people would know who or what Pan was. But almost everybody has heard of Peter Pan. Is it purely coincidental that James Barrie, the creator of Peter Pan, was a Taurus? When he gave Peter Pan his name, was he giving life to a distant descendant of the great god Pan himself? The magical, ageless Peter Pan was lured by his namesake out of the safe, cocooned world of nannies and nurseries into the dangerous but irresistible world of nature— the world Barrie called Never-Never Land. *Peter Pan* is a perennial favorite because, even at face value, it's a charming story. But when we scratch the surface, we get a glimpse of how Taurus, the first earth sign, is linked to the raw forces of nature, and how Bulls need the experience of both worlds; the tame and the wild.

Taurus is a fixed sign. (The others are Leo, Scorpio, and Aquarius). Fixed signs are precisely that. Fixed. They are persevering, determined, tenacious, and constant. All good stuff. Taureans justifiably pride themselves on their staying power, on being the types you can rely on to see a task through to the end.

Just imagine, then, what the practical common sense of the earth element can produce when united with the dogged perseverance of the fixed quality. Great things indeed. Great people, too. Tough, practical people who know what needs to be done and possess the determination to stick it out until it is done. Taurean Ulysses S. Grant helped save the union during the Civil War with this unbeatable combination. The Iron Duke, the Duke of Wellington, who was also a Taurus, used it to defeat Napoleon at Waterloo. The combination of fixity and earth makes for the famous Taurean fortitude, and their ability to wear down the opposition.

We respect and admire Taureans for their true grit and their dependability. People look to The Bull as a Rock of Gibraltar in times of uncertainty and upheaval. They are a life raft that friends and family can swim towards when things get rough. Taurus always has a rabbit to pull out of the hat, or a bank roll out of the cookie jar. Their competence at solving life's practical problems in an efficient, unflustered manner wraps a security blanket around their loved ones. This is the life-affirming Taurus, the gentle, noble, and supportive Taurus at his or her best.

Ah, but "where's the rub?" as Shakespeare might say. In all signs, it is only a short step across the dividing line between their virtues and their vices.

Look at the glyph for Taurus—an imposing set of horns that commands respect. Anyone who's ever locked horns with a Bull, and who's had firsthand experience of the equally famous Taurean intransigence and stubbornness, will not easily forget his or her encounter with the unlovely side of Taurus.

That respect for money can turn into an obsession to the point greed, possessiveness, and meanness take over. The Bull will probably recoil in outrage at this thought. "But I *do* give . . . I'm always called upon to help. People only have to ask." But people won't ask. Or if they have once, they won't ask again. Because if they haven't been called an incompetent fool, they'll be made to feel like one anyway. If the Taurean criticism is not blatantly expressed (which it often is), then it's implied . . . but it still comes across loud and clear.

When Taurus behaves in a stingy and patronizing manner, he or she is abusing the natural power of their birth sign—the power of being blessed with the money and the assets that put them in the position where they can call the shots. From this vantage point, Taurus can fall into arrogant lecturing to the less fortunate on where they went wrong and what they ought to do. The Bull *will* help, and The Bull *will* give, but often reluctantly and at the eleventh hour. And then with so many strings attached that others feel like a marionette dancing to their tune, and forever beholden.

The truth is, Taurus can be alarmingly insensitive to the needs of those following a different life path. It's a failing popular astrology plays down because the causes run deep. Taurus may never make the connection, but deep down, are they resentful? Do they think, "I behaved sensibly and sacrificed a chunk of my personal liberty to get my security. Why can't they do it, too?" It would explain a paradox in the Taurus nature. Otherwise, how could it be that people born under a sign that places so much value on family cohesiveness so often have at least one relative they have alienated? Taureans may secretly envy people with a more free and unfettered lifestyle, but give them the chance to turn back the clock, and you can bet your bottom dollar they'd make the same safe choices all over again.

Once Taurus has formed an opinion on something or someone, that opinion is unlikely to be reviewed. This is the negative face of fixity. It puts blinkers on The Bull, and convinces him or her that changing one's mind is tantamount to a loss of strength, and giving in is a loss of face.

Change, and the fear of it, is a major Taurus issue. Stability-oriented Taureans don't cope very well with change. Yet we all know that the only real certainty in life *is* change. Taureans know it too; that's why they construct as many fortifications against the winds of change as they can.

One way Taureans psychologically bolster themselves against uncertainty is by accepting things the way they are regardless of the right or wrong, or the good or bad, of the situation. Generally speaking, Taureans are unquestioning supporters of tradition. That's the way it has always been, so that's the way it should continue, believes Taurus.

It should come as no surprise that the world's most famous figurehead of tradition and continuity is a Taurus. Queen Elizabeth II pledged her allegiance to her people when she became queen at twenty-three. Destiny frequently places Taureans from all walks of life in a role of responsibility at a younger age than most. From the beginning, the queen saw her role as a continuation of that of her father, and settled into a routine and an image that has remained unchanged in fifty years. Deeply conservative (as a Taurus with a

Capricorn Ascendant could not fail to be), she has won the respect of her subjects through maintaining an image of dignity, hard work, and duty. It's well known that the queen refers to the royal family as "The Firm." And like the Taurus she is the concept of change is something the queen is slow to embrace.

Taurus is a creature of habit. The comfortable, well-trodden path can, in time, become a deep rut that is hard to climb out of. "New" doesn't imply something exciting to Taureans. It takes them a long time to psyche themselves into accepting the new. Even changes that are so minor they seem totally inconsequential to others can for Taureans assume the magnitude of a crisis.

Take the story of the queen's shoes, for example. For years she wore only black or white shoes. They were a safe choice. After all, black or white goes with everything. It took real perseverance on the part of her shoemaker (he must have planets in Taurus) to persuade her to wear taupe. After that breakthrough, beige was added.

If the queen could resist changing the color of her shoes for decades, imagine how difficult the massive events of 1992 were for her. That was her *annus horribilis* when her favorite home, Windsor Castle, caught fire. Devastating enough for a Taurean. But far worse was being forced to deal with radical changes that threatened the existence of the royal family itself. First there was the very public and very unroyal breakdown of Charles and Diana's marriage. On top of that, questions were even asked about the queen's personal fortune, and whether the world's richest woman should continue to be exempt from paying tax.

Without these upheavals, the queen, like all Taureans, would doubtless have been perfectly happy for things to go on as they were, to let sleeping corgis lie, so to speak. Taureans has an inbuilt reluctance to face anything that threatens to rock their steady boat.

There is another British Taurean who, in recent years, has risen to prominence: Tony Blair, the youngest British prime minister since William Pitt the Younger. Blair's image is that of a solid, serious, responsible Taurean member of the establishment. Yet he was swept to power with the expectation that he would be a leader who would make necessary changes. Change is something that *this* Taurean is only too keen to embrace, and he has an astrological factor in his horoscope that allows him to make changes with ease. Blair has a Gemini Ascendant. And Gemini is a sign renowned for its ability to flex, to adapt, and to move with the times.

It's astrological lore that every sign gains from looking towards the sign to come. Gemini follows Taurus. When Taurus appreciates what Gemini has to offer, namely that making changes can be advantageous and that it's often in your best interests to be adaptable, he or she becomes a formidable player. Taurus and Gemini is an excellent combination for someone who needs to make judicious changes without throwing the baby out with the bathwater.

Almost two thousand years ago, the Roman philosopher-emperor Marcus Aurelius said, "What is good for the swarm is good for the bee." This is the classic Taurean tribal group ethic. Taurus believes that the needs of the family, the firm, or the tribe must take precedence over individual whims. Many centuries later at the height of the Italian Renaissance, another Taurean, Niccolò Machiavelli, wrote a famous book on this theme. It's called *The Prince* and it serves as an instruction manual on how to gain political control and how to keep it . . . by whatever means necessary. *The Prince* is still widely read, and is still controversial.

When we describe someone as Machiavellian, it is a clear message that they are not to be trusted and will stab you in the back if they have to. Yet Machiavelli was a thinker who influenced great minds, including Marx, Spinosa, and Shakespeare. Margaret Thatcher, too, is said to be a fan.

Could popular myth have got it wrong? Has Machiavelli been given bad press for being honest enough to advocate what smart rulers and politicians have been doing since time immemorial? Machiavelli's methods were nothing new. He lived in violent times when, for the preservation of the ruler and the state, it was only sound common sense to ensure that dangerous rivals were eliminated. Rightly or wrongly, politicians and people in positions of power are still doing "what's necessary" on the grounds that that the end justifies the means. Even your everyday Taureans are capable of committing their own little Machiavellian acts when it comes to protecting their interests. Beyond practical and tough lies ruthless. Taureans are very skilled at ensuring that they won't lose out, whether it's asking Grandma directly to leave her antiques to them, or having a quiet word with the boss about the upcoming promotion and the fact that they want it. Ever the realist is Taurus.

There's nothing wrong in being a realist per se. But isn't it curious that the sign that prides itself on having a good grasp on reality has a problem acknowledging that the way things look are not always the way things are? So dedicated are Taureans to preserving outer stability that they are often prepared to relinquish inner truth. In problematical situations they frequently adopt denial as a solution, which, of course, is no solution at all.

Astrology teaches us that the remedy for our most negative traits lies in our opposite sign. And for Taurus, that means Scorpio. Scorpio is a fixed, determined sign like Taurus. But Scorpio is in the watery element of feelings and is unafraid to confront major emotional issues. *Transformation* is a Scorpio word. It's something much bigger than change. Transformation demands digging deep into cause and effect and being honest enough to admit where things have gone wrong and what can be done to set them right. It means being willing to probe and, if necessary, to purge.

Scorpio has no trouble with the fact that a personal revolution can sometimes be a good thing, and some attitudes need to radically shift for growth to occur. Taurus, however, needs a lot of convincing. It can be a very painful process for Taurus, whose instinct always is to preserve rather than destroy.

Sex is another Scorpio issue. So is death. And while it's true that Taureans are sensual, eager, uninhibited lovers, as for the deep dark mysteries of lust and passion, well, this isn't really their territory. But it is for the Scorpion. Fate dictates that sometime, somewhere, a sexual attraction will overpower the Scorpio individual, and that sex—or death—may transform the entire course of his or her life.

Interesting, is it not, that the son and heir of Queen Elizabeth is a Scorpio. Charles has already indicated that when he is king, changes will be made, though whether he will ever become king is a question that astrologers were discussing long before the public was. Whatever the future holds for Charles, his Scorpio Sun compels him towards personal transformation. You see, Scorpio seeks to become rich through personal power. And Taurus seeks power through personal riches. That's the difference.

Every Taurus projects a strong identification with "their own." People see in the Taurus leader a figure they can identify with who can guide them to a better life, someone who understands their interests, someone they can place their faith in. "Your path is my path" is the message Taurus puts across. Insiders feel safe and looked after. Unfortunately, outsiders are at best neglected. At worst, despised and persecuted.

Exclusion and inclusion can take Taureans into questionable moral ground. Bigotry is only a short step away. The list of Taurean tyrants is pretty impressive. Adolph Hitler, Pol Pot, Ayatollah Khomeini, Saddam Hussein, Jim Jones. What do they all share? Rigidity. Ruthlessness. Paternalism. All suppressing those who do not conform or belong.

We hasten to say that bigotry is at the extreme dark edge of the Taurus nature. However, many people who've had to wage their own small war against the Taurean intransigence and self-righteousness know that The Bull can be a bully. Taurus the bully emerges when son or daughter questions a Taurus parent's decision and is labeled a delinquent or an ingrate. Or when a colleague dares to point out a better way of doing something and is called a troublemaker. Or when the artist brother has been given a few handouts and becomes the black sheep of the family. People get the clear idea that only when they "come to their senses," will they be readmitted to the herd. Do Taureans genuinely believe that by insisting that people do things their way, they're bringing everyone closer together? Only through sad experience do so many of them later realize that they've driven people away.

If opposite signs have much they can learn from each other, it's also true that they have many traits in common. What Taurus and Scorpio share is the desire for control. When a person in a Taurean's life refuses to conform, it makes The Bull anxious, insecure, and quietly afraid that he or she has lost control.

There is a serious emotional trap waiting for controlling Taureans who haven't managed to get their materialism in perspective. This trap snaps shut Bulls when their attempt to create total security through money overrides all reasonableness.

The myth of King Midas touches the bedrock of how the Taurus pursuit of wealth can go horribly wrong. Everyone has heard of the Midas touch; the magical ability to turn everything you touch into gold. King Midas lived a comfortable life in a comfortable palace. Yet Midas was not comfortable with his lot. He thought that if he were even wealthier, he would be even happier. Now, Bacchus, the god of wine and festivities, owed Midas a favor. Midas asked that everything he touched might be turned to gold. Bacchus consented, but not without warning him that he had chosen unwisely.

At first, Midas's joy knew no bounds. He picked up a stone; it turned to gold. He plucked a flower; it became a priceless jewel. But when he touched his beloved daughter, she turned into a gold statue. The King could not eat or drink. Every crumb of bread turned to a nugget in his mouth. Faced with more gold than he could ever use, and the prospect of starvation, it wasn't long before Midas was begging Bacchus to relieve him of what had become a terrible affliction. Bacchus told Midas that if he went to the river, he could wash away the sin of his greed, and its fatal consequence. From that day on, Midas turned his back on wealth and retired to the country to worship the great nature god, Pan. He went back to Taurus basics. Midas' fall was typically Taurean. But so was his enlightenment. Midas learned that yes, money is very useful. But ultimately, it doesn't buy happiness.

A lot of what makes Taurus happy is being secure enough to enjoy and share the simple good things of life. How can a home or a society be safe and secure without the threat of civil war if there are any who are unincluded and left to fend for themselves? The aware and positive Taurus knows this can only be achieved when people are contented and have all they need.

There is a fairy-tale land where everyone has all they need, and happiness reigns. The magic land of Oz.

In the story, a cyclone carries a little girl called Dorothy away from the drab farmhouse on the Kansas prairie where she lives with her uncle and aunt, and deposits her and her little dog in Oz.

Dorothy is told that only the great Wizard of Oz himself can cast the spell to take her home. And for that, she must travel to the Emerald City. On the way, she is joined by three fellow travelers, each on his own personal quest, each seeking a magic solution to his troubles from the Wizard.

The four travelers in *The Wizard of Oz* are an allegory of the four elements of the zodiac. The Straw Man has no brains. He is the symbol of the thinking, intellectual element of air. The Tin Man lacks a heart. He represents the feelings and emotions of the water signs. And the Lion is a coward because he has no courage. He is fire, of course. As for Dorothy herself, she, like her creator, L. Frank Baum, is a Taurus. Such a surefooted, sensible, down-to-earth little girl mature beyond her years. Dorothy and her three companions form an indomitable team. Fire, earth, air, and water. Complete and strong.

Dorothy, being true to her own earthy nature, is not bewitched by the wonders of Oz. Fantasy will never win out over reality with Taurus. Dorothy is determined to return to Kansas, where it may be less exciting and less colorful, but it's real. It's hers. And the people she loves are there. "Take me home to Auntie Em," says Dorothy as she clicks the heels of her magic shoes.

Taureans who accommodate all facets of human nature and respect different points of view don't need a cyclone to uproot their fixed beliefs. By being open and receptive to people's differences, and by being prepared to change when change is called for, Taureans won't become hardened and fossilized. But they'll still be rock-steady.

The well-balanced Taurus is strong, grounded, calm, and secure. This is the Taurus people are drawn to, the Taurus who has created a rich life of his or her own, and who enriches the lives of others.

THE TAURUS CAREER AND DIRECTION

When Taurean Harry S Truman was president of the United States, he put a sign on his desk that read "The buck stops here." It means if you take on a job, then you take on the responsibility that goes with it.

If a sense of responsibility is your top priority, then Taurus is your

man. Or your woman. Even at the first meeting they present themselves as the one who will have no trouble fitting into the system.
Employers sense they won't turn out to be a wild card. On the contrary, Taurus is punctual, reliable, loyal, and willing to do things the
way you want. But make no mistake. Taurus is no yes man. These
people have a very clear idea of what's in their interests and how
much they're worth.

What Taurus wants from work first and foremost is security. As
much as possible. Second on the list is dollars. As many as possible.
That's why many Taureans choose to work in old, well-established
corporations or government service, joining at age twenty and staying until retirement, which they look forward to, knowing that
they're going to be well provided for with a fat retirement plan.

Having joined the firm, it seems that by lunchtime, The Bull's
superiors have already recognized this employee as a valuable asset
and earmarked him or her as a prime candidate for fast promotion.
Taurus is perfectly placed astrologically for what, in Victorian times,
used to be called "preferment." And Taurus does often seem to be
preferred over others who might be equally able. This is part of the
Taurus luck with money. Being readily accepted can take The Bull
far. Taurus is the employee whom the chairman keeps a fond eye
on. And if the chairman doesn't have a son or daughter to take over
the family business, then Taurus could have it made.

A manner of dignified self-assuredness comes naturally to the Bull.
To others, it sometimes borders on aloofness with a suggestion of
smugness, especially as Taureans know when to keep themselves to
themselves, maybe heeding Shakespeare's advice to "speak less than
thou knowest."

Many Taureans are perfectly happy to work for the same organization for forty years, so allergic are they to change. *Times* change,
though, and the revolving door leading in and out of the workplace
is spinning faster than ever before, with many jobs disappearing as
fast as new methods arrive. The traditional climb up the ladder, à la
Taurus, to middle and senior management can no longer be taken
for granted by anyone. But Taurus need not panic. It is precisely
because they *are* establishment people that many natives of this sign
are likely to be retained in the diminishing ranks of the salaried
world. While no Sun sign can be guaranteed a job for life, there are
plenty of ways in which Taurus can avoid becoming the victim of
downsizing, streamlining, and all those other fancy words for getting
the sack.

The first rule of vocational astrology is that each sign must follow
a direction that is in keeping with its essence. Taurus is the practical
realist. And there are plenty of Taureans who are already coming to

grips with the growing trend to hire people for specific projects as needed, with more and more people becoming self-employed or contracting out their skills. Fortunately for Taurus, good old-fashioned dependability and conscientiousness will never be outmoded. These desirable qualities often bring the self-employed Taurus the regular jobs and the steady income.

Conscious that a reputation for reliability brings more work and more dollars, Bulls will put in the effort needed to deliver exactly what is wanted, and on time. Often they manage to ensure some form of regular income by negotiating a retainer.

The home office is said to be the workplace of the future. And this is one aspect of work in the new millennium that will suit Bulls perfectly. They love being on their own turf. And what could be more satisfying than having one's own creature comforts at arm's reach—especially if they're tax-deductible.

Taurus performs best in a calm, predictable environment. A frenetic workplace, office soap operas, impossible deadlines, and constant comings and goings may be a buzz to an Aries or a Gemini, but such disturbances are anathema to Taureans, who don't think quickly on their feet and who can't give of their best in chaotic situations. As the sign that rules money and possessions, it only stands to reason that people who manage their own resources so well are in an ideal position to manage other people's. Banking, insurance, accountancy, and investment advice are all classic Taurean occupations. Taurus errs on the side of caution, and can be trusted to spread your investments safely over blue-chip shares and property trusts. Property is a major Taurus interest, and many work in real estate. Restoring old houses and selling them off at a grand profit has launched many a Taurus fortune.

Any business that involves the direct exchange of cash and the providing of essential everyday commodities is a Taurus business. That's anything and everything from making and selling produce at a market stall to running their own store or gardening service. Whatever work they do, gaining self-worth and social approval is paramount to Taureans.

Taurus does not go looking for challenge like an Aries, Leo, or Scorpio does. Challenge entails risk. And risk can be a frightening concept to Taurus, and is usually something to be avoided at all costs. Yet an element of risk is often a major factor in success. The fact is, more often than not, Taurus is prepared to trade off the possibility of a bigger and better future for the sake of immediate security. Taurus believes it's only common sense to put regular money before all other considerations, including, sometimes, personal fulfillment. Some would argue that this is just a cop-out. Taurus would say regular money pays the bills.

The Bull is conservative. But if we think beyond the usual meaning of conservative as upholding the status quo, then we enter another dimension of the Taurus nature that opens up an exciting range of possibilities. To be conservative is to conserve things. And Taurus has an important role to play as the conserver and preserver of the zodiac. Some belong to Greenpeace, Friends of the Opera, or world heritage organizations. Others get involved in setting up community gardens, raising funds to restore historic buildings, or joining societies that preserve cultural traditions. Taureans are the backbone of the local square-dancing troupe or the steam train preservation society. At the top of the list is anything to do with nature.

For the more committed Taureans, their love of nature and their desire to preserve can become a calling. Many discover rewarding work in environmental protection. Protecting what is valuable against the threat of destruction is a Taurean gift that everyone benefits from. It's hardly surprising that the world's best known naturalist, Sir David Attenborough, was born under the sign of The Bull. Attenborough's popular television documentaries have inspired millions with his passion for nature.

From all corners of the planet, and generally from a horizontal position somewhere in long grass, comes Attenborough's trademark hushed whispers, making us intimate observers of the wild and the miraculous. We feel privileged to be watching the family of hippopotami taking their mud bath just a few feet away, or the hummingbirds performing their mating ritual. Attenborough brings to every living room around the world the absolute imperative of preserving our natural heritage. It seems all the more important because he does it with rock-solid Taurean credibility. Beauty and conservation aside, Attenborough's programs always lead to the conclusion that the survival of humans cannot be separated from the survival of other species.

Attenborough's final message at the end of his series "The Private Life of Plants is": "We destroy plants at our peril. Neither we nor any other animal can survive without them. The time has come for us to cherish our green inheritance, not to pillage it. For without it, we will surely perish." Wise Taurean words for the new millennium.

Venus, as a ruler of Taurus, leads her subjects into a host of careers, all associated in some way with nature, beauty, and the arts. All Taureans love music, and many forge a career in the music industry, either behind the scenes as agents, producers, and sound engineers, or as performers. Taurus is a sign with the physical stamina that performance demands. Taurean Margot Fonteyn, one of the great prima ballerinas, danced until she was sixty.

But the particular love of Taurus is pictures. Professional artists may be few—not many are going to make it up there with Leonardo da Vinci or Salvador Dali—but Sunday painting is a popular hobby among Taureans. And many more are collectors to the point where, in some Taurean homes, there is hardly a square inch of wall to be seen. Running a small gallery or dealing in art supplies is something that a lot of Taureans do. For professional artists, one thing is certain; the Taurean dedication to their art does not extend to starving in the garret.

The depiction of nature in all her beauty and terror is an obvious Taurean subject. Artistic legend has it that the great English landscape painter Joseph Turner, born April 23, tied himself to a ship's mast during a gale so that he could experience the full terror of the elements. Whether or not this is is true, his paintings are unique in the way they capture the forces of nature.

Many creative Taureans make careers as art directors, layout artists, and graphic designers. Work that is beautiful but also commercial is work that suits Taurus well.

Craft, because it is functional art, also attracts Taureans. They have a natural feeling for the sensual and the tactile, especially pottery. All earth signs love working with wood. The resurgence in popularity of well-crafted furniture, traditional cabinetmaking, and beautiful timbers holds new creative opportunities for Taurus. From there it's a short extension into interior design and decoration. Their style is not at the cutting edge. Taureans are more comfortable and more successful with conventional quality. You won't find them trading in resurrected 1960s plastic beanbags or lava lamps. Selling leather Chesterfield couches and Persian carpets is more their thing.

The pleasures of the senses are part of Venus' territory, and one where there are many options for Taurus. New Age natural therapies that are, of course, ancient arts revisited and revamped require the Venus touch. As practitioners, Taureans have a grounded, centered quality that people warm to. Now that massage, aromatherapy, and herbalism are mainstream, a little Taurus business acumen can turn any of these into a lucrative profession.

Then, of course, there is food. No sign, with the possible exception of Cancer, appreciates so well the inner glow created by a good meal. In fact, food is one subject that is never far from the Taurus consciousness. Both Taurus and Cancer are strongly represented in the food industries. Providing necessity and indulgence in the one package is ideal work for Taureans. Taurus cooks and foodies of all sorts revel in the joy of good simple home cooking. From plowman's lunch to pot-au-feu, their taste is more towards the rustic, whole-some, and generous. A teaspoon of parsnip puree with three steamed snow peas and a decorative radish is barely even their idea of an hors d'oeuvre, and is definitely not to be taken seriously.

No matter what fields Taureans are drawn to, people admire them for their persistence and for being a pillar of strength in difficult times.

The particular virtues (and vices, of course) of every sign are more visible in people who take on leadership roles. Because of their strong identification with their society and their respect for office, many Taureans are elected as president of the local civic organization or the PTA. The Taurus leader is respected for his or her strength, determination, and steadfastness.

In Ireland, one woman has emerged as a symbol of strength in a country fiercely divided by political and religious strife. Mary Robinson, the new human rights commissioner for the United Nations and former president of the Irish Republic, has both her Sun and Moon in Taurus. Excellent stars for any leader who is looked to to bring reasonableness into a conflict-ridden situation. Called a "woman of the people," Robinson has a warm, down-to-earth approach that won her almost 100 percent approval rating in her own country. Robinson hit her message home to the Irish when she said, "The hand that rocks the cradle can rock the system." What a perfect understanding of the Taurus principle that the family unit is a source of great power.

Ordinary Taureans living more ordinary lives also strive to live up to their obligations. They talk duty and application to the job, and they practice it. They believe that hanging in there, seeing tasks through to the end, and keeping your feet on the ground is the surest way to achieve the security and stability that they value so much.

When other Sun signs find their interest in waning and their energy is flagging, Taurus will stay calm, determined, and focused on the job. Under stress, other Sun signs may show less responsibility and give up and walk away.

But not Taurus. Remember, with The Bull, the buck stops here.

LOVE AND FRIENDSHIP

They say that opposites attract. But with Taurus, this is not the case. What Taurus seeks in a friendship, and even more in an intimate relationship, is someone of like mind. In other words, someone like them. Someone loyal, constant, and dependable. Someone who won't ever stand them up or let them down. Someone who won't embarrass them in public or throw them any rude surprises. Someone warm and affectionate, too. Someone who, like Taurus, will display that affection, and be there when needed.

Taurus is not interested in hail-fellow-well-met sorts of friendships. They're not into café society, the social whirl, or street life. And they certainly don't want to waste time with people who haven't got it all together or, worse still, show no sign of getting it together. Conservative Taurus does tend to judge a book by its cover. Let's be honest; some Taureans are frightful snobs, and even the best of them tend to categorize people too quickly.

Taurus figures that if you look well dressed, well heeled, and well behaved, it's a pretty good indicator that you *are* well dressed, well heeled, and well behaved. Any self-destructive behavior, including burning the candle at both ends, is seen as unconducive to a good relationship, and is a real turn-off.

If you get even an occasional urge to don your leather jacket and motorcycle boots, you're likely to be branded a punk. Don't think that your Ph.D. in French Lit or the volume of Tolstoy hanging out of your back pocket is going to save your credibility. Contradictions don't sit well with Taurus. They don't find them interesting, just plain weird. They want to be certain that there are no dubious aspects to your personality.

It's simply impossible to have too much in common with Taurus. They feel most comfortable with friends who share their tastes and their attitudes. Other signs might find this very limiting. But isn't it true that when like meets like, there is a greater chance of mutual understanding and long-term stability?

Generally speaking, flirting and one-night stands are not the Taurean style. At a younger age than most, they set their sights on long-term commitment. They're not especially happy living the single life.

If it's romance you're seeking, casual suggestions of the "let's meet for coffee" or "let's grab a pizza" variety are not going to earn you the initial Taurus stamp of approval. Invite Taurus properly to a restaurant where you know that the quality of food and service is unquestionable. All the better if that eatery is in a scenic location, in a park, or beside the harbor. All the better still if dinner is followed by an evening at the opera or ballet.

If your budget can't stretch to this scenario, there is another option that is equally appealing to The Bull. Pack the trunk of your car with a gourmet picnic and head for the hills. Lolling around in a meadow on a cozy blanket and a pile of cushions, tucking into an Arcadian feast, is likely to lead to all kinds of delicious possibilities.

If you really want to make solid headway in turning a friendship into something deeper, then you'll need to prove yourself on home ground. This is where you will be truly evaluated. Taurus will want to check you out in situ, you can be sure.

Sunday lunch is perfect. You can take all afternoon to go through four courses. A roast is a good idea. Taureans are serious eaters. The seductive scent of lamb and rosemary wafting up the garden path should greet your guest before you do. Stock up on some good wines, and plenty of them. Dessert is the course that should receive your closest attention. Crème brûlée, apple pie, or chocolate mousse with a pile of whipped cream *and* custard are all Taurus favorites. As for the cheese platter, Taurus will be looking forward to it. They love cheese. If you don't know their favorite, get in a selection. And don't forget the other great Taurus weakness, chocolate. All this set against a background of freshly cut roses (a Taurus favorite) and calm-inducing, digestion-enhancing Monteverdi on the stereo (yes, he was a Taurus), and there's really little else to be done except to let nature take its course.

Should you receive the invitation to dine chez Taurus, give extra thought to the gift you will take. Taurus places great store on social gestures. So don't grab any old bunch of carnations. One terribly aesthetic single red rose will be met with quiet contempt, and may cause an instant drop in the temperature. We suggest two dozen minimum, if you're serious.

Ruled by Venus, they may be, but Taureans are no romantic fools. They're not the types to hold out for elusive ideal love. If a prospective partner is available and willing, and his or her background and attitude have been assessed and approved, then Taurus won't waste time looking any further. Practical Taurus is unabashed about summing up a prospect's potential as a good breeder and a good provider. Having been astutely evaluated, you could be a little surprised at the pace of events from here on. The first response from a partner is often "But this is all so quick!" Well, it's not to Taurus. The Bull doesn't like to play games, and will find it impossible not to get physical. To touch and cuddle comes naturally to Taurus.

All that you've ever read about Taurean being slow in their speech and movements (and they are when they're relaxed) does not apply once they've decided that you're the one for them. Once Taurus has seen what Taurus wants, Taurus moves in fast. Eva Perón did it, and very successfully, too. Having set her Taurean sights on the president, she made her way into his bed, his home, and his life in record time. It all started at a dinner when someone had vacated the seat next to him. Eva seized the moment and moved into it immediately. Three days later, she moved into his apartment. That's fast work by any Sun sign standard.

The penchant that the Sun sign columns have for plugging Taurus as a physically passionate sign perhaps requires a little clarification. Yes, Taureans are passionate in a lusty, animal sort of way. You could say they are the sexual fundamentalists of the zodiac. Uncomplicated and down to earth is Taurus in life. And in bed. This is definitely one sign that has the sheer staying power for the legendary weekend love-in.

Taurean women have a quiet but eminently seductive attraction. Michelle Pfeiffer and Bianca Jagger are two such Taureans who emit this gentle and sensuous Venusian charm. It conjures up in the male mind visions of the goddess of love in all her splendor.

There is a type of sexy Taurus man who exudes an almost wicked sensuality. Think of Taureans Jack Nicholson and Harvey Keitel, and you get the picture. On-screen they're cast in roles in which they play a modern Pan. Devilish characters who charm you as they send a shiver up your spine. You know you're dealing with the forces of nature. You know you will succumb.

They're good, they're bad, but they're never really ugly. The magnetism of Taurus is not like the blatant "come and get it" of an Aries, nor the mysterious allure of a Scorpio. It's a magnetism that is earthy and enduring. After all, Taurus is an earthy sign. It's not in their nature to live in a fantasy world, sex included. They want the real thing. Nudity is a big turn-on for both male and female Bulls. The sight of naked flesh is an essential ingredient in their sexual menu. Their idea of lovemaking is not a quickie in a dark corridor. It's more like the languorous experience on a featherbed. Taurus is no prude. They're not averse to the bawdy or the raunchy. Ask popular Taurean novelist Harold Robbins. He's made an excellent living out of it.

A word of warning to the confirmed footloose and fancy-free. Once Taurus has spent the first night with you, and enjoyed it, they'll probably come around the next night, and the next, and every night forevermore. Lovers of Taurus therefore need to think carefully (and quickly) about where they want the relationship to go. You see, with Taurus, possession is nine tenths of the law. And because the Taurus male is a traditionalist at heart, a proposal of marriage is likely to occur sooner rather than later. This is one man who cannot be accused of being afraid to commit.

Having slipped a diamond on your finger, Taurus sees nothing unromantic about suggesting that you spend the afternoon investigating the best deals on washing machines and refrigerators. Ah, don't you love that Taurean pragmatism? Who said romance was dead?

Before you rush out and book the church, here's some advice that may prove invaluable later on. New Age unconditional love is not a Taurus concept.

Conditions apply.

Read the fine print. You'll be expected to hold up your end of the bargain. You'll be expected to be good with money and know how to budget well. You'll also be expected to visit their family, get on with their mother, and be a devoted partner and parent. So far, so good.

If there's anything at all on which you don't totally concur, you should discuss it and resolve it early, well before you get hitched. Don't ever forget, Taureans are habit addicts. If things are trundling along in a certain way, they'll be quite happy to let things keep trundling along.

So if you're the sort of person who likes to remain open to new possibilities, or prefers to play some things by ear, you might want to talk through a whole lot of issues, no matter how small, before they become bigger issues. Are you prepared to spend every Christmas with their parents just because the precedent has been set the past two years? How would your Taurus partner react if you suggested taking off together on a working holiday to Europe? Would Taurus be happy with the idea of having their favorite old couch recovered every few years?

Most important of all is the question of money. If the time should come when, for whatever reason, you become financially dependent on your Taurus partner, will this give him or her the right to call the shots? Taurus is still a little hung up on the notion that the one who brings home the bacon is the boss.

Being taken for granted is a common problem for anyone living with Taurus. At the first sign of any behavior or attitudes that really grate on you, let them know. We know one young Taurean husband whose wife was reluctant to ask him outright not to keep dropping his underwear and towels on the bathroom floor. She thought that if she kept picking them up, he'd get the message. But three years later he was still dropping, and she was still picking up. Three years after that, and talk of divorce, it all came out. "But why didn't you tell me?" lamented Taurus. You see, for a Taurus, if an issue is not raised, it's not an issue. Bulls frequently do not respond to subtle messages of someone else's irritation. How can they when they've got a tough, cast-iron aura that conveniently blocks out any unwanted atmospheric vibes?

The moral of the story for sensitives and for those who value their independence is to get potential problems sorted out straightaway, or move on.

Communication is a two-way street. It's a good idea for partners to encourage Taurus to talk through any difficulties *they* might have about their relationship with you. Taureans so much want domestic peace and harmony that they will try to avoid outright confrontation at all costs, preferring to sweep all the little antagonisms and irritations under the emotional rug. Taureans think that they're handling the situation well by maintaining an appearance of calm, when what is actually happening is that they're slowly eroding their inner peace. And their partner's, too, of course.

This is a very common Taurus dilemma. And so are the consequences. Repression and anger cannot be buried indefinitely. They have to surface somewhere, sometime. Release will inevitably come in an explosion of rage. When they do finally snap, it usually happens without warning. In an instant their famous calm evaporates, and you're face-to-face with Raging Bull. The Taurus display of temper is generally unpremeditated, but it can be truly terrifying. The face turns red, the veins stand out, the eyes literally pop. At such times the otherwise peace-loving Bull will let fly with such viciousness that the verbal shrapnel of their words will cut deep wounds in personal relationships that may never entirely heal.

When the Taurus fury is in full flight, it's futile to try and defuse the situation with words of reason or conciliation. After the dust has settled, quietly but firmly point out that it would be in the best interests of your relationship if it didn't happen again. This is the dark side of the kind, gentle, benevolent Bull. True, it doesn't surface very often, but when it does, it's unforgettable.

Other sorts of problems might arise from the fact that Taurus is very possessive. There is a tendency with Taureans to slip into a very outmoded concept of "ownership" of family members. For those who don't want to be owned, and figure that the role of a partner doesn't include stage-managing their lives, this is an obvious stumbling block.

Taureans are terribly attached to their possessions, too. Do they realize how offensive they can be when they point out that their bottle of vintage port has gone down one inch? Is it really such a big deal if a colleague, desperate for a snack midafternoon, has dipped into their stash of chocolate cookies that they thought was safely tucked away in their bottom drawer? Does any of it really matter in the grand scheme of things?

Should Taureans make such an issue if their partner wants to go out for the evening once in a while with their old school friends without including them? What's the problem if their partner enrolls in an evening class in calligraphy or numerology, even if Taurus can't imagine why they would want to, or what use it could be? Some Taureans have a problem coming to terms with the fact that what is no good for the goose could be just perfect for the gander, and vice versa. The big lesson for a Taurus who wants to hold on to a relationship is to learn that sometimes you can only "have" by letting go.

On the other side of the coin is that partners of Taureans know that they're wanted. And they're valued. Every birthday and every anniversary is remembered. When Taureans phone to say they're on their way home, you can be sure they'll be there soon. The Bull is a domesticated beast. Home, family, and keeping their financial base together comes first for Taurus. They won't run away at the first sign of difficulties. Taurus has the patience and the sense of commitment to stick with it until problems blow over because they subscribe so totally to keeping home and family together; a relationship has to be seriously on the rocks before Taurus walks.

You know where you stand with this person. And you know you can depend on his or her support. If you've had a hard day at work, Taurus will cook dinner, and wash up as well. If you've come down with the flu, Taurus will rush out to the pharmacy, and return loaded with remedies.

Taurus believes love goes with ongoing commitment. They take moral obligations seriously. So when Taurus says, "for better or for worse," they genuinely mean it. And they still mean it ten years later. Marriage to a Taurus can be a marriage in which the fiftieth anniversary is golden . . . in the true sense of the word.

THE TAURUS PARENT

Rare is the Taurus who doesn't look forward to becoming a mother or a father. The normally restrained Taurean pride bursts out for all to see when Taurus' first child is born. Having a child brings to the surface everything that Taurus holds so dear on the importance of roots and family cohesion. They can't wait to write the name of their offspring on the little green shoot that has just sprouted on the family tree.

A child with a Taurus mother or father is blessed with a parent who wants stability for him or herself and for the children. Taurean parents believe in the old-fashioned virtues of regular meals, regular bedtimes, and regular family holidays, in fact, a well-regulated life all round.

Taurus parents give their children a solid sense of home and roots, and will do their utmost to keep the family together. This is the mother or father who's likely to turn down a good career move to a far-flung location because of the upheaval it would cause. All things weighed up, Taurus would probably decide that uprooting the family, taking the children out of school, and putting the dog into a kennel is not worth it. Besides, they've probably put so much effort into planting the garden, building the tree house, and getting their home just the way they love it.

Taurus doesn't move house often. Some never move at all. There are plenty of Taurean homes where you don't even need to switch on the light to know where you're going, or to find something you're looking for. That's because nothing, not even the vase on top of the piano, has been moved for thirty years.

Children of Taurus parents are never going to be deprived of hugs and cuddles, that's for sure. Taureans are physically demonstrative, and bonding with their children is rarely a problem.

Their children will be taught the value of common sense and to stay well away from anything "risky" or "stupid." Parental expectations are picked up early. Children of Taurus know they are expected to stick to their studies, not run around with the wrong crowd, be home on time for meals, and not waste anything, especially their pocket money. Indeed, training in financial management can't start too young, according to Taurus. As soon as they can sign their names, children will be taught to manage their own bank account. Negotiating increments in a son or daughter's allowance will be handled in a very businesslike way.

As Taureans are there for their children, so, too, do they expect their children to be there for them. The Bull is a herd animal, happiest when surrounded by his or her own. The Taurus parent looks forward to family gatherings where the whole tribe can get together. So the first time a teenager announces, for example, that he or she wants to vacation with friends at Christmas, and not go to Grandma's with all the cousins and aunts in accordance with the family tradition, it may be interpreted as a sign of anarchy and perverse individualism.

Taurus parents need to prepare themselves for that inevitable time when son or daughter will break the unwritten rules. Perhaps she'll drop her law degree and announce she's enrolled in acting classes. Or he'll break up with that lovely girl next door whom mother and father already think of as a daughter. Taurus is stubborn, and if there's an impasse, it may come down to the question of "Whose life is it, anyway?"

Taureans may never admit it, but deep down they do cling to the idea that their children and their children's lives are somehow forever under their aegis. There are plenty of Taureans who still view the family as a hierarchical institution. Be honest, Taurus. Have you ever answered your child's "*Why* do I have to do it?" with "Because

I'm your mother/father. That's *why*"? This black-or-white, right-or-wrong approach commonly has two repercussions. The child either becomes the rebel under the roof, or flies the coop at the first opportunity. If it should come to that, it would be sad because Taurus' heart is firmly in the right place; he or she just wants to keep the family together.

The strong Taurean protective instinct never switches off. If anything or anyone is seen as a threat to their children, they'll move in fast. When one Taurus father we know took his young daughter horse-riding for the first time, he was so concerned for her safety that he ran alongside the horse for miles. Hardly advisable for a man who had had heart surgery only six weeks before. Risky? Unnecessary? Foolhardy? Not when Papa Bull was protecting his little girl.

There is perhaps only one thing that will bring deeper satisfaction to Taureans than having children of their own. That comes when they are presented with their first grandchild. You can imagine their pleasure when they take out the family tree and draw in a new branch for the first name . . . of the next generation.

THE TAURUS CHILD

If a calm and loving baby is your idea of a dream baby, then you might want to start counting the months so that baby will arrive between April 21 and May 21.

Taurus is the child you can direct and trust to do as you say from the youngest age. They're happy to settle into the family routine and you won't have to run yourself ragged chasing after your little Bull pulling him or her out of trouble, or working overtime to keep them amused.

Little Bulls love to snuggle and cuddle, but they're also quite happy not to be fussed over and oversupervised. Taureans are generally contented children. And so long as they have the security of knowing you're around, they'll be quite satisfied to organize their own games and manage their own activities.

They love music. You can't start music lessons too young for Taurus. And they'll love to make their own pictures. Their first box of crayons will be sheer magic for these children of Venus.

There's another magic world out in the garden where they can create their own fantasy around every tree and stone. Give them a packet of seeds and show them how to plant them, and you will have set them on a path that will give them much happiness for the rest of their life. Nature beckons early. Young Taureans are content to while away the hours smelling the flowers, and observing the activities of the snails and butterflies. In fact, all children with Sun or Moon in earth signs have fond memories of these early experiences. A Taurus childhood would be lacking something important to his or her development without nature hikes and camping trips into the great outdoors.

Little Taureans are generally robust and sturdy, though they're unlikely to get through childhood without a bout of tonsillitis. Taurus, you recall, rules the throat.

The Bull's enthusiasm for food is legendary. They're sure to have definite likes and dislikes. But little Taureans are not picky eaters who drive their parents to despair by toying with their food. On the contrary, you may have to control their tendency to wolf their food. You might also like to keep a watchful eye on their sweet tooth, which, incidentally, they'll never grow out of. Rationing the Hershey bars and monitoring the contents of the cookie jar is a must.

It's an unusual Taurus child who is described as a handful. They have no need to be attention-seekers. That's because they're usually given all the attention they need. Simply being born under the sign of Taurus means that the child is a welcome addition to the family, and parental approval follows naturally. Perhaps this is why Taurus children seem so self-assured and mature beyond their years. This applies to children born with Moon in Taurus, too. Our Moon sign determines our emotional reactions throughout life, but in childhood it's particularly strong. Both Sun and Moon in Taurus children show signs of that Taurean determination (as well as that bullheaded stubbornness) almost before they're out of the cradle. In no time at all, the normal peace and calm is going to be periodically shattered by sudden outbursts of "No, I won't!"

Taureans of all ages have a very clear idea of what they like and what they don't like. What they want to do and what they most definitely, positively do *not* want to do. Young or old, Taureans are expert at standing their ground. There is bound to be, sometime, a battle of wills that will go down in family history.

Pleading and cajoling won't work and will be taken as a sign of weakness. But if you, too, stand your ground, firmly and resolutely without wavering, you may never need to go through it again. Taurus always responds to an appeal to practical common sense. If your little Bull is stomping and snorting at the gate, refusing to get in the car, lay it on the line simply and directly: "If we don't leave now, we'll be late at Aunt Anne's, and lunch will be ruined." Watch how quickly Taurus jumps in the car.

Taurean possessiveness develops early. Parents may have to nip in the bud the first signs of their unwillingness to share. Books become "my books," the playhouse becomes "my house," as Taurus cultivate an early sense of ownership and constructs their radar system against trespassers.

Young Taurus won't need much encouragement to learn first steps in money management. Only Cancer and Capricorn are as likely to draw up a budget as soon as they get their first allowance. Little Geminis might allocate two thirds of their allowance, for example, towards comic books and after-school snacks. But little Taurus will have figured out that there's always a plentiful supply of banana cake in the fridge, and founded a comic-swapping club so they can deposit 90 percent of their allowance into their brand-new bank account. It's amazing what 90 percent of your allowance will add up to over ten years. Plus interest, of course.

Habits start young. So train them young. And train them well. Because of all twelve signs, Taurus is the one least likely to question what was learned at mother's knee. The way you teach them to fold their clothes, tidy up, and care for themselves—and others—will be etched onto their adult behavior patterns. Get it right and you'll not only be doing yourself a huge favor, but your future son or daughter-in-law, as well.

Parents will find it easy to encourage their young Taureans' emerging sense of responsibility by giving them specific tasks to do at regular times. Bringing in the newspaper every morning, feeding the pets, watering the garden, are real responsibilities that they will take seriously. They won't forget to do it. Reliability is a Taurus trait.

Reliability is something little Taurus needs from you, in return. If you say that you'll do something or take them somewhere, try to be as good as your word. Regular routine is also very important. If meals aren't on time, if bedtime is a different time every night, and people are forever dropping in unexpectedly—in short, if there are too many unpredictable factors in their life—Taurus will feel disturbed. And if their routine gets too out of sync, there could be some angry scenes.

The three R's in raising a Taurus child are: Regularity, Reliability, and Routine.

Taurus children need time to prepare themselves for new situations and new environments. Visits to the dentist should not be sprung on them at the last minute. The first day at school and moving to a new home need to be discussed well ahead. Avoid shock tactics at all costs.

Speaking of school, this is where their powers of concentration will stand them in good stead. Taurus is a sign whose specific talents and skills show up at an early age. From day one they are praised by their teachers for being methodical, attentive, focused, and well behaved. Later on, your Taurus student will impress you with the capacity for in-depth, prolonged study.

You will have every reason to be proud of your Taurus son or daughter. The Taurus child will want to be cherished as an important member of the family. And in no time at all you will find Taurus has taken his or her rightful place in your home . . . and in your heart.

BORN UNDER TAURUS

Malcom X	Jerry Seinfeld
Karl Marx	Edward de Bono
Janet Jackson	David Helfgott
Oskar Schindler	The Red Baron
Pope John Paul II	Florence Nightingale
Anthony Trollope	Eric Bristow
Ho Chi Minh	Liberace
Pierce Brosnan	Glenda Jackson
Vladimir Lenin	Yehudi Menuhin
Billy Joel	Christian Lacroix
Shirley Temple Black	Johannes Brahms
Golda Meir	Rudolph Valentino
Israel	Cher
Peter Tchaikovsky	Robert Browning
Stevie Wonder	Krishnamurti
William Randolph Hearst	Csar Nicholas II
Orson Welles	Emperor Hirohito
Andre Agassi	Immanuel Kant
Sigmund Freud	Elmer Fudd

GEMINI

May 22–June 21

♊

Ruling planet
MERCURY

May your hands always be busy
May your feet always be swift
May you have a strong foundation
When the winds of change shift
May your heart always be joyful
May your song always be sung
May you stay forever young

Bob Dylan—born May 24

THE GEMINI NATURE

Some people pick up shells on the beach. Some have a knack for picking up bargains in shops off the beaten track. Others seem to be able to pick up a new job whenever they feel like a change.

Gemini does all this. But what Gemini excels at is picking up ideas. They pick up people, too. They toss around ideas with those people, and in the process, they'll pick up another idea. Then they'll meet someone else who has a friend who's already working on the same idea.

Confused? You're not the only one. Not when Gemini is around. Sit back and fasten your seat belt because Gemini is just taking off.

Now, as it turned out, that last person knew somebody who, he was sure, would be interested in Gemini's idea (for a sitcom, as it happened). He suggested that Gemini look him up when he was in town. Three months later, Gemini was passing through, and after a quick call from the airport, was lunching with his latest contact, who was very impressed with Gemini and Gemini's idea.

Did you assume that idea was the one for the sitcom?

Think again. That's what Geminis do. The sitcom had been put on hold, while Gemini moved on to something new that felt right for the times. A documentary on eco-entrepreneurs, and how we can save the forests and make a bundle at the same time. A year later, Gemini caught up with his original contact who asked how the project was going. "Which one?" asked Gemini. By then Gemini had put them *both* on hold while he and a friend set up a cyber-fashion café.

If all this sounds a little crazy, we assure you that it doesn't to a Gemini. Throughout this whole convoluted scenario, Gemini is not the least bit vexed or perplexed. The pace, the perpetual movement, and the changes of direction that would unsettle other signs are perfectly normal to Gemini. They cannot tolerate stasis, standing still doing one thing, in one place, for too long.

Change is the only constant. And change is the lifeblood that Gemini thrives on. First this, then that. First yes, then no. One day everything is light and going well. The next day, nothing's working out and changes must be made. No sign can match Gemini for mental gymnastics. That's because it's an air sign. (The others are Libra and Aquarius). Air is the element that rules the realm of the mind and ideas. As the first of the air signs, Gemini is concerned with thought and communication on the most direct level.

Esoterically speaking, the circle of the zodiac is a symbol of human experience and evolution. The circle, like life, is a process, so that no one sign is a complete world unto itself. In the previous sign, Taurus, which is an earth sign, we learned, symbolically, to deal with our physical needs. Only after food, shelter, and security have been met can we begin to relate to others, gather information, and accumulate knowledge. How do we achieve this? By communication. And how do we communicate? With words.

Words are Gemini's world. Words are their passion, their weapons, and often their tools of trade. Gemini knows that to communicate, you have to get out and about, meet people, and talk. Air is light, and when it flows, it becomes a breeze, refreshing and revitalizing.

Never heavy, always light. That's how Gemini appears. They live by the credo "Easy come, easy go." Such a free-flowing formula would leave many rattled and insecure. But Gemini *must* have variety and stimulation. They feel safer when they've got more than one iron in the fire at all times. Freedom and flexibility are their most precious possessions, and if they could take out an insurance policy against their loss, they would. Flexibility is actually one of the great Gemini strengths. If something isn't working out, or if it's becoming too boring or too "heavy," they won't hesitate to move on. And if that doesn't work out, they'll move on again. Of course, the downside to flexibility is that it can leave a trail of unfinished business. The notorious Gemini vanishing act often catches people by surprise—until they understand what Gemini is all about, that is.

A life in which you cannot change course when the winds shift, and in which you cannot sample from a smorgasbord of people, places, and experiences, is no life at all for freedom-and fun-loving Gemini.

Constantly sniffing the air for new opportunities, Gemini is not one to be caught napping. When it comes to trends, fads, and everything that is au courant, Gemini has the nose of a bloodhound. They are experts at getting the most out of something, someone, or some situation for as long as it holds their interest—or until something better comes along. This is why a lot of people born under this sign have earned themselves a reputation as job hoppers (unless, of course, their horoscope contains indications to the contrary such as a Taurus Ascendant or a stack of planets in fixed signs). It's not that Geminis aren't prepared to work hard. In fact, it's not uncommon for them to work twelve hours a day, seven days a week, for months on end, willingly and without complaint. But their heart must be in it. Even so, the day the job is finished, it will be strictly passé. By evening, Geminis could be on the plane to Bali where they can devote themselves twelve hours a day, seven days a week, to unwinding and just having fun. But the active Gemini mind never switches off entirely. As they swing in a hammock, mentally processing candidates for the holiday fling, another part of their brain will already be ticking over on their job options waiting back home.

Home or away, Gemini alternates naturally between being frantically involved and totally uncontactable. One day they're the life of the party, tucking into rich, exotic curries and expounding on the culinary versatility of coconut milk. The next, they're in self-imposed solitary redressing the excesses of yesterday, balancing their yin and yang with mineral water, yoga, and spirulina. For restless spirits who live on high nervous voltage a lot of the time, it's essential to their health that they regularly step back from the action and recharge their batteries.

It's this ebb and flow that makes it hard to pin Geminis down, to get a handle on who they are and what they're all about. They want stimulation, yet they can't tolerate extreme pressure. They're highly social beings, yet they suffer without regular time alone. They have a gift for satire, but are sensitive to criticism. They want romance, but are turned off by schmaltz and sentimentality. It's hardly surprising that Gemini can be so unfathomable to others. They're often accused of "being in two minds." And indeed, they often are.

You see, it is in the Gemini nature to be in two minds. The Twins is a dual sign, two beings, separate but together. In illustrations they're usually depicted holding hands or with their arms around each other. Sometimes they're male, sometimes female. But always they are young adults, the perpetual adolescents of the zodiac. Forever young, as the song goes.

The duality of Gemini is explained in the myth of the celestial Twins, Castor and Pollux. Their father was mighty Jupiter, king of the gods, who descended from Olympus in the form of a swan to seduce the beautiful mortal, Leda. Leda gave birth to a single egg from which emerged The Twins. Like Jupiter, Pollux was an immortal. But Castor was mortal like their mother.

Trouble came when they were attempting to abduct a couple of maidens, and the maidens' betrothed turned up. In the ensuing fight, Castor was killed. Pollux was inconsolable, such was the tightness of the bond between the brothers. So inconsolable that Jupiter took pity on him and declared that The Twins would henceforth share life and death, just as they had always shared everything. One day, one would live in the land of the living, the other in the land of the dead. And vice versa every second day. This, of course, didn't solve the problem at all, as it meant The Twins were still apart, and still unhappy.

So in the end Jupiter placed them together in the stars in the constellation known as Gemini. And since then, Gemini has been recognized as the sign of brothers and sisters, and fraternal relationships. Because of their love of movement, adventure, and experience, The Twins were also appointed to be the heavenly guardians of travelers.

Real-life twins are not so much one person in two halves, but rather two people (or maybe three or four or five) in one, born to be different people at different times, as it were. There is not one of them who is not the real Gemini; they're all genuine. "I am multitudes," said Walt Whitman, the American poet who understood precisely what it meant to be born a Gemini. Certainly they cannot be accused of being boring, limited, or predictable.

Others frequently wring their hands in frustration, accusing Gemini of being inconsistent and unreliable. "But you've changed your mind—that's not what you said yesterday!" Another much-loved Gemini, Ralph Waldo Emerson, hit the right note in defense of The Twins when he said, "A foolish consistency is the hobgoblin of little minds." What a perfect debunking of tedious ungeminian attitudes.

A lot of Gemini's changes of gears and shifts in interests can be accounted for by being born under a dual sign. But it goes deeper than that. Gemini is also the first of the mutable signs. All mutable signs (and that includes Virgo, Sagittarius, and Pisces) are adaptable, and have the capacity to change and move on whenever circumstances demand. Geminis always know when to quit. When it's time to exit, their feet are swift.

Part of being mutable is being receptive and open to "vibes" from people and places. It's interesting to consider how the dual signs (and that's Pisces—two fish linked by one cord—and some say Sagittarius, too, because it's man and beast in one being) are also mutable signs. Duality and mutability are naturally compatible. All people born under dual signs profit from their natural gift of being able to go with the flow.

Being so adaptable is undoubtedly a top Gemini asset. But Geminis do have a tendency to take on too many things and to stretch themselves in too many directions, and turn that asset into a liability. It's a short step from being adaptable to being unreliable, and from being flexible to being inconsistent. Geminis in this negative mode can be downright infuriating. People become justifiably annoyed by their fly-by-night ways, their restlessness, and their talent for changing the ground rules and moving the goalposts as they go.

It's a talent that can be terribly abused in order to satisfy their own interests. Last-minute changes to their plans—and yours—may be caused by something as simple as the fact that it's a beautiful day, the surf's up, and they don't want to miss it. These are the selfish, irresponsible Geminis who expect everybody to fit in around them, and who can't see what your problem is when they phone three times to reschedule a date. Please note, the problem is yours, not theirs. One way or another, Geminis will talk their way around it. The combination of their friendly manner and what *sounds* like logical reasoning catches hold of you before you have a chance to protest. At the time you're sold on their story, you begin to believe that yes, you are too rigid and should learn to "hang loose." Only after you've hung up do you realize that Gemini has pulled a fast one.

Fast thinking and fast talking are how Gemini fends off potentially sticky situations and defuses conflict. Their quick and clever way with words often gives them the upper hand in many situations, especially at work. The communicator is born to excel in any field where a sharp brain and skill in the written or spoken word is called for. That's why so many Geminis are writers, journalists, and teachers. They're great salespeople, and advertising attracts Gemini like a magnet.

Gemini has an unmatchable ability to step into up-front, friendly interaction with people of all sorts. Never short of party invitations, they can always be relied on to lift the mood and, if necessary, entertain the guests single-handedly. The party is a true Geminian milieu where their bright extroverted nature can shine. It's where they can do what they do best: circulate and fascinate others with their ideas, jumping from topic to topic. Where else can they have fun and work the room at the same time? In fact, you only need to invite a Gemini plus one other person, and you've got an instant party. No matter what the conversation turns to, Gemini is sure to have something to contribute. Geminis specialize in knowing a little about a lot of things, and they're not shy about airing their opinions. One minute they're knowledgeably discussing life on Mars. The next, they're explaining the psychology behind the marketing strategies of McDonald's. Watch how they use their hands when they're making a point. It's as if words are not enough.

They like to play the agent provocateur to get an intellectual argument going. And they're refreshingly adept at stealing the wind out of a pompous bore with a well-timed drop-dead line. So what if their opinions offend. Some people interpret their uppity behavior as arrogance, and maybe it is. But from Geminis' point of view, they're just being direct. Broad-minded and unshockable, Gemini delights in telling, or listening to a risqué story. And they're unequaled in the art of innuendo. Yet somehow they never come across as vulgar or gross. Sociable Geminis know exactly how to charm and how to make a good impression . . . when it suits them.

Mind you, there is one uniquely Geminian type of antisocial behavior. They often offend slower conversationalists, especially those given to long-winded monologues, by interrupting and demanding they get to the point. Yet *they* themselves frequently never quite get to the point. Gemini is renowned for changing subject midsentence and expecting you to complete the thought process yourself. And because they find it almost impossible to disguise boredom and impatience, they are capable of abruptly terminating a discussion should they sight someone they consider more interesting or useful. Especially if that someone is an attractive member of the opposite sex.

The party flirtation is a Gemini specialty. Such a social butterfly can be terribly irksome to more earnest or perceptive types who can see straight through their sparkle and social acumen to catch a glimpse of the notorious Gemini superficiality. To accompany the latest buzz words and the buzz notions, Gemini will be sporting the latest gear. They like to be in touch with the flavor of the month. Like their Aries brothers and sisters, they'd hate to be thought of as out-of-date, unkempt, or a nerd. Geminis rarely create a signature style, but they are brilliant exponents of the current trend.

The sign of the teenage twins takes pride in their slim, youthful figure, and generally looks considerably younger than they are. Many middle-aged Geminis can confidently knock ten years off their age and get away with it. Don't ask them for the name of their antiaging cream because it's really not the secret. It's all in the mind, as Gemini would say. Their youthful attitude is the secret.

A lot of Geminis have an elfin face, bright eyes, and a cute, turned-up nose. Kylie Minogue has the classic Gemini face, and figure, too. Judy Garland, Paul McCartney, Michael J. Fox, Joan Collins, and Isabella Rossellini all have "the Gemini look."

The planet that rules youthful Gemini is named after Mercury, the handsome young god with wings on his sandals and helmet. He was the messenger of the gods and often acted as troubleshooter for Jupiter, setting up his rendezvous and helping him to get out of his many amorous entanglements.

Mercury has given his name to the only metal that is liquid at room temperature and, therefore, takes the shape of whatever vessel it's poured into. *Quicksilver* is its common name. Gemini people are often described as being "like quicksilver." They're also called "mercurial," quick-thinking, changeable, and elusive because, like Mercury, they're fleet of mind and foot.

Mercury gives Geminis an upper hand in business. Interestingly, he is not only the planet of trade and commerce, he is also the ruler of thieves, liars, and con men. There's an episode in the Mercurial myths that explains the connection neatly.

Mercury once came across some cattle that belonged to his half brother, Apollo. In a rebellious, mischievous moment (and Geminis have lots of those), he formulated a plan to steal them. First, he attached little shoes shaped like back-to-front hooves on the cattle. Then he herded the beasts into an empty cave. When Apollo came looking for his cattle, he found the footprints—but they were coming out of the cave, not going in. A clever trick, but not clever enough. The scheme fooled no one. Apollo was furious and insisted that Jupiter punish his delinquent brother. But Jupiter and the other gods found the story so entertaining, and were so impressed with Mercury's ingenuity, that he was let off scot-free.

This is the story of how Mercury earned his title; the Trickster of the zodiac. There's a crafty little corner at the back of Gemini minds that sorely tempts them to play clever tricks and do devious deals to get what they want as easily as possible, with minimum work and no waiting. The story of Mercury and the cattle is an insight into how some Geminis seem to get away with things that come uncomfortably close to the borderline zone between right and wrong. People are intrigued by a clever con, and how Geminis can capitalize on dubious schemes, and pull out just in time before awkward questions are asked.

There are many Gemini tricks you never hear about, because they manage to get away with them, but one infamous Gemini trickster who did make the headlines was newspaper magnate Robert Maxwell. Maxwell was stealing millions from a pension fund in order to prop up his ailing newspaper. When his crime was exposed, he disappeared. Maxwell never had to account for himself because when he was found, he was dead. Drowned. To this day, the question remains, did he jump or was he pushed?

Even your average thoroughly honest Gemini knows the value of a white lie or a half-truth—and won't hesitate to bend a few rules for the sake of expediency. Rules are there to be bended a little, as some Gemini somewhere once said.

The Gemini mind can be superbly cool, cunning, and calculating. Exactly the type of mind that successful criminals need to be able to devise their clever schemes and cover their tracks. It's been said that there is little difference between the criminal mind and the mind of the detective. Some of the most famous writers of detective stories are Geminis, including the father of the genre, Arthur Conan Doyle, creator of the detective's detective, Sherlock Holmes.

Holmes stunned the admiring Watson with his almost supernatural powers of deduction his faculty for pure reason, and his flashes of perception. All coolly explained away by his famous quip "Elementary, my dear Watson." Now we say it when we mean that something is so clear and so apparent—at least to those with brains enough to see it—that it shouldn't need to be explained.

Curiously, Conan Doyle and his Gemini alter ego, Holmes, both had an interest in the occult and psychic phenomena. This is a side of The Twins that sometimes takes people by surprise, since Gemini is so keen to be seen as objective and rational. But in his role as the planet of perception, Mercury is very strong in the horoscopes of psychics. In this sense, Mercury operates like the antennae of an insect, sensing and probing for information.

Another Gemini writer who created a classic Gemini hero is Ian Fleming. His character, James Bond, is just about everything that the Gemini man aspires to. It's widely believed that Bond has a Scorpio Ascendant. Scorpio is the sign of spies and undercover operations. Scorpio is also the sign of sex, and the Gemini/Scorpio combination is a wicked and irresistible one.

Slick, urbane, and immaculate in a Savile Row suit, and equally attractive with a towel around his hips, Bond is fluent in several languages, well informed on everything, master of the understatement, and, above all, unbelievably cool. No matter how many times secret agent 007 jumps from the jaws of death a split second before the bomb blows or the chopper smashes, he walks from the devastation stirred but not shaken. Like a real-life Gemini, Bond has no problem switching from one mode to another. Cast adrift in a lifeboat with a beautiful woman, he doesn't waste one second of the ten minutes they've got before the marines pick them up. Geminis are noted for their speed of operation, their technical prowess, and their manual dexterity—all at once, and in more ways than one. A great deal of action and satisfaction can be packed into ten minutes of attention from a sexy Gemini.

Speaking of matters technical, Bond is invariably rigged out with a battery of whizbang weapons and gadgetry. When missiles are speeding towards him, his car headlights convert into torpedoes to save him in the nick of time. Later, the pen in his shirt pocket turns into a detonator and yet again saves the day. Like Bond, Geminis are the best people to have beside you in an emergency. Hands, eyes, and brain operate at lightning speed with perfect coordination. They step in and assume control of the situation, doing what needs to be done quickly and efficiently.

Also like Bond, Geminis tend to accumulate an array of gadgets purchased on the grounds that they're time-savers, and facilitators of their busy lives. Gemini's love affair with the telephone is well known. Mobile phones must have been invented for mobile Geminis. They simply love clever machines that do clever things. What other reason could there *really* be for buying a two-hundred-dollar space-age orange juicer (even if it does deliver your juice five minutes sooner than the others) or a state-of-the-art wok? We know a Gemini who recently bought both these items in one quick swoop on the stores, proclaiming them to be "must-have" modern survival tools.

By being constantly on the go, Geminis get the mental stimulation they need. But it goes without saying that stimulation can easily turn to hyperstimulation. When they're in fast-forward mode, Geminis operate on a high tension level that's similar to Aries. The difference is that Gemini has less stamina than Aries. Some Geminis periodically throw themselves into harsh exercise regimens. Staying tight, taut, and terrific and trying to stay forever young can be an addiction of sorts. In any case, it has turned many a highly strung Gemini into a gym junkie. Yet boredom and sloth, in their own way, can be every bit as stressful for Geminis. This is a sign that needs to be vigilant about pacing themselves and balancing episodes of high and low activity, because a Gemini who swings too high too fast for too long is prone to nervous collapse.

Biologically speaking, Gemini rules the lungs and the oxygenation of the blood. And since they're inclined to be shallow breathers, yoga, tai chi, walking, and swimming are more beneficial to the health of The Twins.

Good health depends on many forces working in harmony. The medical profession itself uses a symbol associated with Mercury. It's the caduceus, Mercury's magic wand, around which are entwined two serpents: one black and one white, representing dark and light, good and evil, health and disease. For the sign that has so many sides to itself, getting everything in good balance and correct proportion is a core issue.

What better example of the many faces of Gemini than the changing identities of Bob Dylan, the minstrel of the sixties. A Woodstock friend of Dylan's once said of him: "There are so many sides to Dylan, he's round."

The mercurial Dylan baffled people with his shifts in style and persona, to the point of telling different stories to different people about how he got his name, and even being evasive about his background. Alternating between crazed activity and retreat, Dylan made himself an enigma. Like a chameleon, he changed his colors, picking up on new ideas and a new image when he sensed it was time to move on. Even the themes of his songs are Geminian: "Like a Rolling Stone," "Blowin' in the Wind," "No Direction Home," and the anthem of the protest era—"The Time They Are A-changing."

Like many Geminis attuned to their Sun sign, Dylan had a sixth sense of what ideas were ripe for expression and exploitation. His timing was spot on when it came to tapping into the mood of the times.

As communicators extraordinaire, more than a few Gemini names have become identified as the voices of a generation or a movement. They seem to be stamped with the freshness and vitality of youth, no matter how old are in years. Though, as it happens, they're often still quite young when they make their first big impact. While young people in the sixties were singing along with Dylan under the obligatory poster of Che Guevara (also a Gemini), there was a universal mass cry for change. This was the time when America and the world were inspired by the ideas and the ideals of John F. Kennedy, the youngest U.S. president. JFK (born May 29) gave official sanction to the mass feeling that things did not have to stay the way they were, and that change was something that ought to be embraced.

In the nineties, another Gemini spokesperson emerged with a message that was, again, right for the time. Burmese prodemocracy leader Aung Sung Suu Kyi appeared on the world stage with the message that the first step to radical change is talk. During her years of house arrest, thousands flocked to her garden gate to hear her deliver the weekly speech that kept their spirits up, and the collective hope for freedom alive.

The power of Gemini comes from the ability to connect with people and communicate. Many, like JFK and Aung Sung Suu Kyi, are charismatic public speakers. Many more express this power through the written word.

One Gemini who touched the lives of millions was Anne Frank, the young Dutch Jewish girl who went into hiding from the Nazis in Amsterdam during World War II. Through all those difficult years, Anne kept a diary. Tragically, only months before the end of the war, the family was discovered and transported to a concentration camp where Anne died. Her father was the only survivor, and when he returned to Holland, it was he who discovered Anne's diary.

Every page of *The Diary of Anne Frank* is pure Gemini, and for Geminis searching for an understanding of their Sun sign, we recommend it as prescribed reading. The diary is all the more remarkable because it was written by someone so young. (Anne had only just turned fifteen when she wrote her last entry.) The style is open, witty, and unaffected. Anne had Mercury's sharp eye and good powers of reasoning that give objectivity. She even called herself "quicksilver Anne."

From her diary, we see that Anne was already grappling with the contradictions that others were quick to point out and that she saw in herself. Even at such a tender age, she was sensitively and intelligently coming to grips with her own multitudes. Her parents called her their "little bundle of contradictions." And she admitted that she had acquired this name for good reason. In her very last entry, Anne made a penetrating analysis of the fundamental Gemini dilemma—namely, how to acknowledge, live with, and use the different sides of their nature. She wrote to her diary:

I've already told you before that I have, as it were, a dual personality. One half embodies my exuberant cheerfulness, making fun of everything, my high-spiritness, and above all, the way I take everything lightly . . . This side is usually lying in wait and pushes away the other, which is much better, deeper and purer . . . My lighter superficial side will always be too quick for the deeper side of me and that's why it will always win. You can't imagine how often I've already tried to push this Anne away, to cripple her, to hide her, because after all, she's only half of what's called Anne: but it doesn't work and I know too why it doesn't work . . . I'm awfully scared that everyone who knows me as I always am will discover that I have another side, a finer and better side. I'm afraid they'll laugh at me, think I'm ridiculous and sentimental, not take me seriously.

For all Geminis, trouble will loom sometime if they are reluctant to explore their "deeper side." Anne understood very well the duality in her nature, and recognized that, as well as playing the clown, she had great capacity for introspection and deep thinking. Her insecurity and fear of revealing her deeper side only served to magnify her lighter, more superficial side. It is, after all, easier to present yourself as light and cool, rather than deep and thoughtful. Far more fun to be the jester than the sage. Far safer, too.

But you cannot repress a part of yourself forever without paying the price. It's ultimately upsetting, even destructive to the Gemini soul, to exist in only one dimension; the light and bubbly. The truth is, many Geminis struggle to express their deeper side. Their capacity for passion and serious deep thought is often glossed over in the popular profiles of their Sun sign.

What if Gemini Marilyn Monroe had been given the serious roles she wanted so much? What if she had been allowed to throw off her dumb-blonde image and sink her teeth into something more thought-provoking and substantial? Marilyn was never allowed to express her duality on the screen. Yet in private, she was very attracted to intellectual men. Apparently Albert Einstein was high on her list of desirable males.

The message for Geminis is, don't deny any one part of yourself. Rejoice in the fact that your multisided nature does not have to make you a "bundle of contradictions." Getting it all together is literally at the heart of the Gemini issue. Geminis must consciously strive to give all the different players in their personality a stage on which to perform.

As always in astrology, help comes from looking to our opposite sign. It provides a counterbalance to our shortcomings, and for Gemini, that means looking to Sagittarius. Like Gemini, Sagittarius is an extrovert, a mover, a mixer, and quick to seize opportunities. Both signs have rulership over travel, education, and learning. But it is the depth and breadth of thinking Sagittarius that wise Geminis naturally assimilate into their nature.

Sagittarius is the sign of truth and philosophy. A Gemini who is able to visualize the big picture, rather than the immediate situation, will acquire a greater sense of purpose and achieve a lot more. When Gemini realizes that thinking is not the same as philosophizing, and that being articulate is not the same as knowing, he or she finds that their energy is less scattered and their life becomes more focused. Until they take the time to look beneath the surface of everything and beyond the immediate advantages of every situation, they will continue to receive all the labels that people pin on them: fly-by-night, restless, unreliable, annoying, and superficial.

When Geminis cease to be driven only by external chatter and stimuli, they enter a whole new dimension. One that is far richer and more empowering.

Geminis need to create for themselves a solid, immovable base—physically and psychologically. For all his enigmatic and changeable ways, Dylan grasped this critical Gemini issue. "May you have a strong foundation . . ." he sang. With a strong foundation, Gemini can take off in any direction and safely return home.

The centered Gemini is truly a force to be reckoned with. When the winds of change shift, others may be tossed and turned this way and that. But not Geminis. They're up in a flash. And just like the winged god Mercury, Gemini will fly on the wind . . . towards the next great adventure.

THE GEMINI CAREER AND DIRECTION

There is an expression we have adopted from Native Americans. Who knows? It might have been a Gemini who first heard it and repeated it, and before you knew it, it became part of our language. The expression is: "Walk the talk. Don't talk the talk."

It means fine words and fine intentions are only fine so long as you act on them. Otherwise they're just empty words.

Bright, quick-witted Gemini never has any shortage of ideas (or words, for that matter). In fact, they often come up with the concepts that others wish they'd thought of. There's no one better to have around when a good idea or a quick solution needs to be found. But Geminis themselves are only too aware that half their ideas end up floating around in the ether, and never become anything more than hot air. They know that it takes time and effort to pull ideas down to earth and turn them into something real.

Geminis are often accused of lack of follow-through, and it's true that it is one of their shortcomings. The long haul and seeing a project through to completion is not a Gemini strength. This is a mentally restless sign. But it doesn't mean that Geminis can't conquer their impatience and their constant urge to be off and doing something different.

We all need a direction in life that fits the essence of our Sun sign. For Gemini, that means seeking work with enough mental stimulation and flexibility, and preferably with the potential for new experiences. Rigid routine is poison to the Gemini soul. Freedom of movement—mind and body—should be a top priority.

If at all possible, Geminis should look for work that won't trap them in a strict nine-to-five timetable. Geminis work best when given enough autonomy to make their own schedules and work at their own pace, albeit superfast one day, and idle chat over endless cups of coffee the next, while they refuel their mental tanks. Their rate of production is rarely constant. That's okay for boring, predictable individuals, thinks Gemini, who equates falling into a routine with falling into a rut. But never fear, when a deadline approaches, Geminis come into their own. They can produce more quality work and solve more problems in the final two hours than the rest of the team has in the last two weeks. Geminis are very impressive under last-minute pressure. When others are getting flustered, are bordering on hysteria, or have given up, Geminis stay cool, keep their wits, and come up with the goods.

But not even Gemini can perform last-minute miracles all the time. They may be sharp and quick, but they're not good under protracted pressure. Every individual Gemini eventually learns where being happily busy stops and overload starts.

Multitalented Gemini has acquired the title of "jack of all trades, master of none." it's hard for them to specialize when their range of talents pulls them in different directions. They often envy people who knew what they wanted from the start, who focused their career in one direction and set out to make it, permitting no distractions. They sometimes wish they didn't find those sidetracks off the main path so beckoning.

Yet it is precisely by making their multiple interests work for them that they often accomplish great things. Then they can really cash in on the special Gemini gift. Versatility. By using it and exploiting it, they can turn it into their major career advantage.

Work that involves doing some of this and some of that is ideal. Writing proposals, reprogramming the computers, entertaining the clients, and training new staff (if necessary, all in one day) suits Gemini down to the ground. All-rounders are becoming much-sought-after employees. Having more than one core skill and being able to perform a variety of functions is now seen as a real plus. It's called *multiskilling*. And Geminis are made for it.

The Gemini versatility and their ability to move in and out of those many sides of themselves is a blessing of their Sun sign. It can be put to good use in almost any field. Quick as a flash, they can change their career direction and, if they feel it's called for, the image that goes with it. It's fascinating how a disproportionately high number of people who change their name, use a pen name or adopt an alias are born under the sign of The Twins. When Gemini's life takes a different course (as it frequently does), they like to give themselves a new name to match the new dimension of their personality. We know a bright and multitalented young Gemini who operates under three different names. When he's selling Persian carpets he calls himself George. In his part-time job running seminars on personal motivation, he's known as Mike. But socially he introduces himself to the girls as Marcus.

Some Geminis go halfway and opt for a change in spelling: Simon starts to sign himself Siimon. Some abbreviate their name: Madeleine becomes Maddy. Others expand: Archie, at the age of twenty-eight, with his Saturn return approaching and realizing that he's not a kid anymore and needs a more serious persona, declares he is now to be called Archibald.

There is one Gemini who has gone way beyond anyone else and abandoned language—or at least letters—altogether, and replaced his name with a symbol: ♀ It certainly makes an impact, but how do you pronounce it? The Artist Formerly Known as Prince has attempted to sever the mental connection between language and sound. No one can deny it's creative. But what has he achieved if people have to resort to calling him T.A.F.K.A.P.? Isn't that still a name?

Gemini is not the least bit resistant to, or fearful of, change. Quite the opposite. Far from feeling derailed, Gemini actually seems to thrive on uncertainty. Uncertainty implies the promise of something new. And there's nothing Gemini likes better than the thrill of the new.

The Gemini personality is better equipped than most to cope with a high level of uncertainty in work. Jobs in which the circumstances change at the drop of a hat, and where correct decisions depend on a lightning assessment of the situation, are perfect for Gemini. That's why you'll find the sign of Gemini or the planet Mercury strong in the horoscopes of financial traders and stockbrokers.

Geminis like to keep their options open. Frequently they cultivate a new career option long before they leave their current job. You often hear of Geminis who moonlight in a completely disparate field to earn a few extra dollars for years, before moving into it full-time. It's such a typical Gemini story.

Another common Gemini pattern is to replace a full-time job with part-time work that pays the rent and allows them to pick and choose and come and go as they want. That way they can keep up their yoga classes on Fridays and be open to whatever else may come up. For many Geminis this is the ideal way to work and live. Success though, depends on having a string of contacts who can open doors and put in a good word. Fortunately, that's often exactly what Gemini, the networker of the zodiac, has.

The key word for Gemini is *communication*. It underpins all their career choices. Any work that fulfils the fundamental function of their sign, namely to connect and interact with others, to pick up and use information, is Gemini work.

Words, words, and more words are often the bread and butter of Gemini. Media is one direction Gemini is drawn to. The mercurial world of radio, for example, is made for the masters of chat. In fact, a strong input from Gemini is an astrological prerequisite for talk-show hosts and gossip columnists. Joan Rivers, whose show is called "Can We Talk?" and Hedda Hopper, the doyenne of Hollywood gossip columnists, were both born under the sign of The Twins.

Sales is an obvious outlet for the Gemini skills. Blessed with the gift of the gab, there's nothing that Gemini can't sell, including steam heaters in the Mekong and umbrellas in the Sahara. They instinctively know how to grab your interest before your antisales defense system locks into place. So beware the bright young sales assistant who uses friendly patter to get you to buy the ten-inch skirt that you know is not you. Very likely, she's a Gemini.

Working as a tour guide (which also satisfies their desire to get out from behind the desk), a market researcher, or a product presenter also uses their talent for talk.

The advertising industry is positively teeming with Twins. This is true Gemini territory because it's a field in which they can blend all their talents. It's where their talent for commerce can be married with their mercurial gift for coming up with new concepts and getting their message across. In a field where speed and hitting on just the right phrase or image is everything, Gemini can go far. The catchy slogan or the jingle that people hum all day is sure to have been created by someone born under Gemini, or with the planet Mercury strong in his or her horoscope. Those who have the added advantage of a well-placed Neptune can reach the very top of their field because these are the people who know exactly what's in and what's out, and can quickly capitalize on a trend before anybody else has the chance to run with it.

It goes without saying that the sign that is "forever young" has an innate ability to sense where youth culture is moving. Geminis of all ages can commercially span the generation gap.

Nations, like people, have horoscopes. Indeed, a horoscope can be drawn for anyone or anything that commences at a certain time, in a certain place. The United States was "born" on the fourth of July. It has the Sun in Cancer, and you can read more about this in the next chapter. Most astrologers believe that Gemini is the sign ascending in the American birth chart, which goes a long way to explaining why America, the land of teen idols and the queen of the proms, is so preoccupied with youth and looking young. A sense of freedom is essential to the Gemini nature. The First Amendment to the Constitution of the "land of the free" is the one that guarantees its citizens freedom of speech.

And just like Gemini people, America has a passion for variety and for everything fast. Fast food, fast service, drive-through everything (from marriages to funerals), 85 television channels, and fried eggs that can be ordered nineteen different ways. So much choice. So little time. So Gemini.

Astrologers have also long associated the city of London with Gemini. London has always been an important center for education, with schools, colleges, and institutions teaching everything you could possibly want to learn. It even boasts the first accredited school in the world for professional astrologers. On a very mercurial level, London is the home of the tabloid press, where newspapers vie with each other to come up with the most provocative headlines, and be the first with the latest juiciest scandal.

Travel is another popular career choice for Geminis. You'll find them working everywhere in the travel industry, as booking clerks, flight attendants, entertainment managers, and travel consultants. Gemini is a mobile sign. Their love of getting around and going places is something they share with their opposite sign, Sagittarius. Any job that enables Geminis to take off with the wind at their heels is a Gemini job. It could be an express courier, taxi driver, airline pilot, or sales representative. Work in which they're not staring at the same faces, day after day, has a lot of appeal for Geminis.

The data and computer industries have created an obvious opening for the Geminian mental acuity. Many Geminis have an exceptional gift for logical analysis. That's why you'll find a high proportion of Twins designing software and finding and fixing bugs in systems. Gemini is an "experiencing" sign that often learns best on the job. They're clever at picking up bits and pieces of information, a lesson here and a pointer there, which is why they succeed in any field that is new or still developing. Gemini often says, "Just show me what to do." Anything to avoid two days reading the manual, or being glued to a chair in a soporific seminar.

Teaching has always attracted a lot of Geminis, as well as people with a Gemini Ascendant. They're in their element before a room full of receptive young minds. The combination of face-to-face interaction and passing on knowledge is ideal. If a student fails to catch on, it won't escape the Gemini teacher. Language teaching is a special

Gemini skill, and it's uncanny how many Geminis choose to study French in school.

At first glance, it might appear that Gemini isn't looking for the status that Capricorn strives for, and is willing to forgo the security that Cancer always puts first. Superficially they may not seem as interested in power and amassing a fortune as a Scorpio. But make no bones about it, Gemini is every bit as career-minded and ambitious as any other sign.

It's just that deep down, Geminis know that success will come if they remain true to their Sun sign. Happiness in their working life comes from freedom, flexibility, and room to move. When they achieve that, then all the rest follows—status, security, wealth, and, most important of all, personal satisfaction.

LOVE AND FRIENDSHIP

Everyone has arrived. All except one, that is. The chair is noticeably vacant, and the conversation is a bit slow. But then halfway through the first course, the doorbell rings.

Gemini certainly knows how to make an entrance.

While Gemini is delivering his or her excuse for being so characteristically late, the atmosphere starts to lift and the dinner really begins to get going. Who is this interesting addition? you may ask yourself. So smart, so presentable, so appealing. Be aware that you've been noticed, too. And it's quite possible you've already received Gemini's instant personality assessment, and been rated either worthy or unworthy of further attention.

The wrong shirt with the right jeans (or vice versa), or a spare tire and limp hair, means you've failed the test. No one of this description could be regarded as the least bit delicious. If you've passed, then you've successfully projected yourself as a bright mind with the right body. And it won't be long before Gemini moves into a more thorough investigation of your interest quotient. It could be that your interest value constitutes no more than your becoming a new friend. Geminis have lots of friends of both sexes, and if they add your number to their phone book, you can look forward to some happy times and good fun. Their network of friends connects them with many interesting people over the years.

New friends of Gemini will have acquired a companion who is wonderful to have around . . . most of the time. The truth is, many friends of Geminis find them alternately stimulating and great fun to be with, and far too restless and highly strung. But since Gemini is always on the go anyway, breezing in and out of people's lives, that point of aggravation is usually averted in time.

Gemini people can pick up old friendships just where they left off, no matter how many years have gone by. And it's not unheard-for Gemini to hint at "once more for old times' sake" when they meet up again with an ex-lover. They hate to let any tempting opportunity pass them by.

If Gemini has marked you out for a closer encounter, then you will be aware of their intentions almost as soon as they are. They are direct, but smooth operators—so smooth that it's difficult to be offended. On the contrary, you'll be made to feel like a million dollars as the Gemini chemistry works its magic. Gemini is brilliant at disarming a prospective lover at that first vital moment when the air's electric and there's the promise that anything could happen.

There's another kind of Gemini romance scenario that may keep you oscillating back and forth between he loves me, he loves me not/she loves me, she loves me not. In the evening they're all yours, attentive and engrossed in everything you have to say. The next morning they phone to cancel lunch. Something unexpected has come up. Where do you stand? Is Gemini subconsciously—or maybe consciously—seeking to keep you dangling while they blow hot and cold, and figure out where *they* want the relationship to go?

If perceptive Gemini has successfully stirred in you that first sexual frisson, he or she will know it. But keep your cool. It will turn Gemini on even more. On the other hand, it would be a mistake to play *too* hard to get. That won't make you any more desirable. Gemini is far too impatient to plan a long-haul conquest. They strike while the iron—and the hormones—are hot. By the same token, if you're not turned on by Gemini's advances, just say so with a smile. They know how to take no for an answer, and don't waste time in pursuing the unobtainable. On the whole, Gemini has little respect for those who choose to live a tragedy of unrequited love when there are plenty more options out there.

If you're keen, it might be best to abandon the standard rules of courtship and surrender to the moment. That's what Gemini does. They'll want to see if you can live up to their capacity for the impromptu and the outrageous. Many a Gemini has pulled off a seduction with a simple but effective line like "How about it?" Even a wink and a nudge could be defined as a bona fide Gemini invitation to an evening of lust and passion. They've got a refreshing sense of mischief, and offer the thrill of the illicit, something naughty—but nice. It's like being sixteen all over again.

Appearances are important to Gemini, but it can't be stressed enough that Gemini won't be really turned on unless there's a meeting of minds. Sex for all the air signs (but especially Gemini and Aquarius) is 98 percent in the brain. Their brain is, arguably, their primary erogenous zone. They will have read the latest best-seller (or at least the back cover), so if *you* haven't read it, just make sure you know what it's about. A partner of Gemini must not be behind the times, an incurable stay-at-home, or scruffy—unless it's in vogue. And even then you would have to be an exponent of shabby chic.

In the bedroom you're going to discover that Gemini's excellent coordination and motor skills are not overrated. What they can do with their hands is nothing short of startling. And they like to talk. Pre-, trans-, and postcoital conversation is an important part of the Gemini sexual experience. Certainly you won't be left nervously holding back, unsure of what to do next. Thwarted lovers of Gemini may remark that it was like going to bed with an instruction manual. But talk can be very humanizing. At least they're not likely to grunt, groan, and roll over. And then there's the Gemini wit. A sense of humor is always a plus in the bedroom.

This is the sign of the lightning strike. Gemini's turn-on, turn-off buttons are quickly activated. You could describe their sexual response as more urgent than languorous. Did Geminis invent the "quickie"? If they didn't, they elevated it to an art form.

And what about the Gemini notorious reputation for fast turnover? Ah, yes, when they're unattached, available, and looking, there's some truth in that. Although most of the time it's a case of more smoke than fire, as they prove to themselves that they've got what it takes.

Because they don't necessarily need the promise of a deep emotional bond in order to respond sexually, their attitude toward romance can be somewhat detached at times. Sex with a perfect stranger may be Gemini's perfect fantasy. Geminis actually do offer clichés such as "Variety is the spice of life" or "There are plenty more fish in the sea" as a quick and easy justification for an abrupt parting of the ways. They find it especially helpful when they want to avoid heavy explanations of the "where it all went wrong" sort.

The flip side is that possessiveness is not a Gemini problem. Nor does Gemini want to be possessed. Gemini wants a partner who is there for them. But they don't want to be joined at the hip in a state of perpetual 100 percent togetherness. You don't find many Geminis who last long in a symbiotic clinging relationship.

All of which brings us to the question of a certain type of Gemini that is, fortunately, not common but definitely does exist. Beware immature Geminis you can't seem to make adult human contact with because they're really in an adolescent narcissistic relationship with themselves. You have the feeling you've met this sort of person somewhere before. They remind you of someone. Then it hits you. You're attempting, in vain, to form a real relationship with a living Barbie doll. Or a Ken. Were Barbie and Ken—so pert, so pouting, so perfect, so plastic—born under the sign of The Twins? Probably.

Getting the right balance between personal space and intimate time together is something that must be worked out in a relationship with a Gemini. The French existentialist Jean-Paul Sartre and his lover, Simone de Beauvoir, came up with their own solution to this dilemma. He was a Gemini, and she the devoted Capricorn. During all their years as a couple, they alternately spent two years together and two years apart. That's a pretty extreme arrangement, just to guarantee some personal space and to prevent a relationship getting jaded. But it's an issue that must be handled if one of you is a Gemini because constant togetherness will become too claustrophobic without time out from each other.

It's important for partners to create their own agenda, and not to slip into the mistake of allowing their schedule to revolve around Gemini's schedule. Equally, problems could arise if Gemini feels locked into a strict timetable. When Gemini shows those notorious signs of restlessness, don't try to confine them. This can be hard for earth-sign people to resist. And the Gemini restlessness can be far too worrying for some water-sign people. If total stability and a comfortable routine are what you're after, think twice before settling down with a Gemini. Mind you, does Gemini really have the problem? Or are they the ones who wisely accept that a thoroughly cozy, predictable life is an impossibility?

Something else you can do to keep your relationship with Gemini harmonious is to develop a policy on how and where you meet. Never agree to meet on a street corner or anywhere where you can be left stranded, cold, thirsty, and seething. The sign that would hate to be called habit-bound actually has the bad habit of running late most of the time. It's a very annoying illogicality in the Gemini nature. Partners are advised to nip this Gemini tendency in the bud. Fast. The first time you are kept waiting, leave. It could be worth your while confirming your date an hour before by phone. That's if you can get through to the aficionado of the telephone. There's every good reason for the major telephone companies to give prototypes of their new mobiles to supermodel Naomi Campbell to test-run. It's sound astrology; she's a Gemini.

They can't be too far away from their sources of stimulation for too long or they would go crazy. Even Geminis who live in the country need a regular city fix and they're never short of spare rooms they can crash in—their network ensures that. Gemini needs to be part of what's in and to be where it's at. They like to lunch at the

trendy cafés, visit the bookshops, and get in a shot of serious shopping. Geminis spend when they've got it. It's not that they find saving money difficult, but they can't defer pleasure long term, like a
Capricorn or a Virgo can if they have to. As in everything, the perpetual swing between opposites comes out in Gemini's handling of
money. Lavish spending usually alternates with periods of penny-
pinching and ruthless budgeting.

If the relationship doesn't work out, don't necessarily expect to be
let down gently with a deep and meaningful heart-to-heart about
where and why it went wrong, what a wonderful person you are,
and how much they respect you. Gemini's famous disappearing act
has taken many a distraught ex-lover by surprise. Even in a long-
term relationship, the cool side of Gemini can leave a partner feeling
emotionally stranded at times. They can be distant, unreachable, and
unsympathetic if cracks start to appear in a relationship. Anyone
close to a Gemini will probably be hurt at some stage by what seems
like—and probably is—terrible insensitivity. Their wit can be sharp-
ened into a sword of sarcasm should they feel someone is starting
to nag or control them.

Compassion and chicken soup is not their strongest point. Geminis
don't like wading into emotional swamps. But if they're honest with
themselves, they'll know that they don't mind being served a little
compassion and chicken soup themselves. Astrologers believe that at
some level we all yearn for some of the things that seem to come so
easily to the following sign. Cancer follows Gemini, and while Gemi-
nians would never want to be as strongly dominated by their emotions as Cancerians are, they do, in some way, long for the emotional
bonds and security that Cancerians build up around them. The Gemini wit, their smooth talking, and their avoidance tactics are often a
cover-up for the fact that they feel awkward expressing their deepest
emotions. Cancerians are deeply sensitive. When Gemini makes a
conscious effort to understand what people are *feeling* as well as what
they're thinking, when they openly display a little more sensitivity,
then their life—and their love life—run a lot more smoothly.

One reason Geminis have a problem with sensitivity and expressing their feelings lies in their childhood. Geminis are born into families in which they learn to stand back from the emotional dynamics
between their parents. Father is usually seen as the more distant or
difficult parent, while mother is regarded as the one who puts in all
the emotional effort at cementing the family bonds. As they grow
up, Geminis deduce that too much giving and caring without much
in return can make for a thankless, unrewarding existence, and they
learn to cultivate a certain detachedness.

Yet for all that, there's something about the Gemini lover that's not often talked about. Gemini is a romantic idealist. The seeds of this idealism may have been sown in a youthful formative love affair that, in their hearts, they've never forgotten. Older and wiser, Geminis may find they're unwilling to settle for a "suitable" partner. No matter how suitable they are, if Geminis are not smitten, they know it would be unwise to commit. But when Geminis *are* smitten, they can be fools for love, and nothing is too romantic or too sentimental for Mr. or Ms. Right. Like a lovesick teenager, they'll send roses by the dozen and chocolates every week.

You know it's for real when Gemini starts to show patience, starts to compromise, and make allowances and excuses for any shortcomings in their partner. Nothing is too much trouble. They become dedicated to making the relationship work.

When Geminis meet their soul mate, they can be as loyal and committed as any other sign. If you are that soul mate, they'll reveal to you those Geminian depths that previous passing infatuations didn't last long enough to uncover.

If you've won the heart of a Gemini, it's because, like Gemini, you value your independence but want intimacy, too. You'll be pursuing your own interests but always look forward to coming home. You'll love getting together with mutual friends but still enjoy your own company.

Could it be that you've found the best of both worlds? With Gemini, it could be just that.

THE GEMINI PARENT

Quite a lot of Geminis get plenty of practice at playing mother or father before they become a parent themselves. That's because they're often the favorite aunt or uncle.

No matter how old they are, there's a part of Gemini that never really grows old. A youthful attitude makes for an easy connection with young minds. They don't seem to forget as quickly as others what it feels like to be four or six years old. Gemini can manage children without being the least bit patronizing or overcontrolling, and without being laissez-faire. Children relate easily to Geminis, and they love them for it.

For many Geminis, plunging into parenthood is not necessarily their most burning ambition. They know that taking on more responsibility has to be carefully weighed against having less time for themselves. But when they do have children of their own, Geminis will discover that it can be more fascinating than they ever thought possible.

Information-hungry Gemini will have accumulated a library of baby manuals and will be eagerly absorbing the dos and don'ts. Even before they're home from the hospital, Geminis will have analyzed the logistics of the situation and made a mental note of exactly what has to be done to ensure that baby will be the newest, most interesting chapter of their life.

At this stage, everything you've read about cool, detached Gemini goes right out the window. Friends who knew Gemini long before baby arrived are often dumbstruck by the degree of Gemini's coo-cooing. There are, though, some new Gemini parents who are inclined to get terribly engrossed in the wonder of it all, even to the point of developing a classic case of New Parent Syndrome. Overnight they become an expert on child rearing and development, determined to share every new observation with their friends. Don't they know that not everyone is riveted by theories of language acquisition in one- to two-year-olds, or the ongoing debate on early toilet training?

No matter how adoring the Gemini mother or father may be, there are bound to be occasions when the timetable imposed by baby (Gemini, remember, is a bit allergic to timetables) will cramp his or her freedom and lifestyle. Gemini rankles against routine. But routine is exactly what baby needs. This is one of the signs that is likely, at some stage, to have to wrestle with the psychological conflict between the needs of baby and their own need for personal liberty.

The Gemini mother who tries to attain Superwoman status, juggling baby, job, and social life, could find she's paying too high a price since, energetic as Geminis are, and as much as they love variety in their life, they're not actually blessed with enormous reserves of stamina. If they spread themselves too thin (which tends to be a Gemini problem), stress overload is bound to hit. When a child comes into your life, something has got to give. And when Gemini parents accept they cannot continue to do it all, the happier and more relaxed they'll be.

Thank heavens Gemini is so deft. You've got to marvel at the Gemini mother or father who can change a diaper with one hand and throw bottles into the sterilizer with the other, all the while with the phone tucked under chin, booking the baby-sitter.

Gemini is unlikely to be sold on the popular ideal that large families are the happiest. They might talk about the importance of zero population growth. Anyway, that's the theory. But it's for their own personal reasons that they're generally quite happy to stop at one or two. Famous last words. Many born under the sign of The Twins who planned a second child have ended up with a third or a fourth, as well. Multiple births run in Gemini families.

Gemini parents are keen that their children get a good education from the start. A parrot mobile, alphabet picture cards, zip-up button-up teddy bear, and every other toy designed to mentally and physically stimulate their child and raise his or her IQ will be suspended over the cot.

They'll be hanging on the day when baby utters his or her first word. That's when the fun really starts. Geminis will love introducing their little one to their first letters and will be terribly proud that their child could read long before going to school. It's debatable who will have more fun playing Junior Scrabble—parent or junior.

As interested as they are in how their children are progressing at school, their own memory of how much they liked their own sense of autonomy when they were young will restrain them from interfering in their children's lives unnecessarily. Gemini is not the type of mother or father who grills children on the details of what they did at school today. But they can be fantastic when guidance is needed with projects and homework, knowing where to find exactly the right book, the latest maps, and up-to-date information.

Gemini is not the smothering, authoritarian, possessive parent that children will want to flee from at the first opportunity. Quite the opposite. Children of Gemini are encouraged to spread their wings, be confident, discover their talents, and develop their own identity. And that's a fantastic start in life for anyone.

THE GEMINI CHILD

Questions, questions, questions. Does every child ask so many questions? Surely not.

The communicator of the zodiac starts young. Is it really that your Gemini child is more curious and inquisitive than others? Quite possibly, yes. Expect them to be early talkers. And walkers. Geminis have excellent motor skills. They'll be quick to learn to tie their own shoes, use a knife and fork, and make their own bed. So get ready for the kindergarten teacher to take you aside at the end of the first week to impress upon you how bright your five-year-old Gemini is. As if you didn't know. You're already aware how keen and alert he or she is, you've been trying to keep up with the pace for years. Now it's her turn.

Even on the first day, Gemini is one of those confident little scholars striding purposefully through the school gates, who wouldn't want to be seen as a crybaby clinging to mother. After all, school opens up a whole new world of exciting things to do and interesting new friends to play with. This is the beginning of Gemini's valuable network of friends and contacts.

Parents will no doubt count their blessings that they've produced such a clever, independent child. Yet it won't take them long to figure out that boredom is the Gemini demon. Or to learn that things happen when little Gemini is not gainfully occupied.

The Gemini child who is at loose ends too often can show signs of turning into a junior rebel—long before he or she understands what a cause is. On an intellectual level, you may be horrified by the Victorian dictum that children should be seen and not heard. But you may be forced to reassess its merits if you don't step in quickly and train your Gemini not to dominate the conversation and interrupt you when you're talking. Otherwise you may have one of those little chatterbox buzzing mosquitoes on your hands who never gives you any peace.

The solution is simple. Provide them with plenty of books, games, and puzzles. Show them how to make things and how to amuse themselves alone. Teach them games they can teach their friends. The growing Gemini child needs the widest variety of educational options, including languages. They're natural linguists and are sure to enjoy traveling.

Teaching them how to conquer their native impatience is important. Geminis' inclination is to lose interest in things before they're finished, or rather to already be developing an interest in something else and wanting to leave what they're doing. There's always something else to grab a Gemini's attention. So you'll need to encourage follow-through, and insist that not too many things are left half done.

By the same token, it helps to know that you're preparing a versatile nonspecialist for their future. Geminis' destiny, you recall, is to have many interests and use their many talents. So if they're full of enthusiasm for ballet classes one month, and the next want to do kick-boxing, or if they inform you after six months of expensive piano lessons that they've decided that the piano is not their instrument and they ask you to buy them a flute . . . well, you might just have to go out and buy a flute. You can always trade it in next year when they inform you they want to learn the guitar.

Gemini is not a sign that responds to emotion as a tool in disputes. Manipulation and emotional blackmail simply won't work. They're crafty enough themselves to see straight through it. Children of this sign respond best to logical, objective reasons for why something can or cannot be done. The Gemini child, like the Gemini adult, may look superficially cool, calm, and collected most of the time, but underneath he or she is highly strung and can't handle emotionally fraught situations.

The same advice applies if your child was born with Moon in Gemini. The Moon is the indicator of our emotional response throughout life, and in childhood it's very much on the surface of our personality. Like Sun in Gemini, Moon in Gemini children are sociable and quick to learn. But they're also tense, and perhaps even more tightly wired. If you detect a quiver in the voice and a rise in the pitch, it's a clue that they're not coping with a situation. It's important not to pressure them, and to know when to just let things drop.

Clear and calm communication is everything to Gemini children. They need to know that they have the right to express their point of view. Make your discussions respectful, two-way conversations, give them the right of reply, and there shouldn't be too many impasses.

Talking of two-way conversations, have we mentioned the Gemini addiction to the telephone? That begins early, too. Offer them their own telephone line for their thirteenth birthday, combine it with a lesson in practical living skills by attaching the proviso that they get a part-time job to pay the bill, and they'll probably be only too willing to go along with the deal. They may even have thought of it before you. Already you can see signs that Gemini wants to be free to go their own way and do their own thing.

Gemini starts young in all sorts of ways. Early sexual experiments may have as much to do with curiosity as with hormones. Geminis often manage to escape the big parental talk on sex, because when their parents finally pluck up the courage, they're met with disdain . . . "Oh, that . . . is that all? I know all about that already." There is an astrological joke going around in which one seven-year-old Gemini says to another seven-year-old Gemini: "I found a condom on the patio." His friend says, "What's a patio?"

Restless by nature, Gemini children benefit from a home with enough rules, routine, and structure. They need it to ground them. But at the same time, it has to be a home where they're not going to feel cosseted, suffocated, overly supervised, or questioned about every coming and going.

Like everyone, Geminis are bound to make their share of the mistakes of youth. Yet their cool head and quick thinking will save many a day, and rescue them from many dicey situations while they're stretching their wings.

When you see that they are ready to fly the coop, it would be a big mistake to try to clip the wings on those mercurial heels. If you have created a happy, welcoming home, and cultivated a friendship based on trust and honesty, you can be sure your Gemini will fly back often.

BORN UNDER GEMINI

Queen Victoria	King George III
Salman Rushdie	Morgan Freeman
Errol Flynn	Henry Kissinger
Peter the Great	Wallis Simpson
Johnny Depp	duke of Edinburgh
M. Scott Peck	Boy George
Steffi Graf	Jessica Tandy
Patrick White	George Bush
John Wayne	Donald Trump
Marquis de Sade	Frank Lloyd Wright
Thomas Hardy	Paul Gauguin
Clint Eastwood	Newt Gingrich
M. C. Escher	Josephine Baker
Bob Hope	Paul Eddington
Allen Ginsberg	Christo
Sir Laurence Olivier	W. B. Yeats
Miles Davis	President Sukarno
Brigham Young	Bugs Bunny
Colleen McCullough	

CANCER

June 22–July 23

69

Ruling planet

MOON

Without feelings we cannot make de-
marcation between justice or injustice, truth or untruth, good or bad.

Tenzin Gyatso, Fourteenth Dalai Lama—born July 6

THE CANCER NATURE

"Look at the Moon . . ."

Is there anyone who has never, at some time, been moved to utter
these words? For when the Moon rises, so do our feelings, our long-
ings, even our fears. At night our intuition is sharper and our imagination soars. Night is the time to reflect on what is, what has been,
and what might be . . .

Worshiped by poets and lovers since the beginning of time, the
Queen of the Night shines into the corners of our psyche that lay
hidden during the day. We are all affected by the rays of the Moon.
In astrology the Moon represents our emotions and imagination, a
different experience for each of us according to where it's placed in
our personal horoscope. But for people born under Cancer, the sign
of The Crab, her influence is supreme. That's because the Moon is
the ruler of Cancer.

Cancer is the first of the three signs of the element of water. Along
with the other two, Scorpio and Pisces, Cancerians are particularly
open to vibrations or sensations that are quickly translated into feel-

ings. Cancers are sensitives, and their intuition is strong. Which is why so many decisions Cancerians make in life are based not so much on how they think but how they feel. They are subjective by nature. In the previous sign, Gemini, we learned how to communicate by relating to each other on an intellectual level. Now, in Cancer, we are ready to express our feelings and to explore our emotions.

As the first and primal water sign, Cancer's emotions are felt on an almost raw level. Their young hearts are open, receptive, and vulnerable. Sensitive Cancerians have an instinct to protect themselves and their feelings from the harsh onslaughts of the world. Like The Crab, which they take for their symbol, Cancerians believe they would not survive the swirling tides were it not for their protective shell and a safe, quiet rock pool to scuttle away to. That's why they invest a lot of effort in creating a private sanctuary. Home is truly where the Cancerian heart is.

Cancer well deserves its title of the homemaker of the zodiac. From a young age they give precedence to building and feathering the nest. Cancerians are always much happier when they have a home they can call their own. It makes them feel safe, and a respected and valued member of society. As the years go by, Cancer will put more and more money and a great deal of creativity and imagination into building a bigger and better nest. Whether it's a palace or the classic Cancerian dream cottage with roses round the door, it must be a private space away from the hurly-burly.

The Moon is also the planetary indicator of home and domestic life, and our day-to-day needs and comforts. Cancerians shine at taking care of creature needs. With Cancer, things simply get done. The car is serviced. There's always food in the fridge and clean clothes in the closet. The cats get vaccinated and the children get picked up on time. Bills are paid and the tax return is mailed off promptly. By and large, Cancerians are brilliant at managing their homes and their time. In fact, they're pretty marvelous all round at managing their lives.

Sensitive and emotional, they may be, but rarely do Cancerian emotions undermine their ability to get organized and stay organized. At least not for long. Immediately after a blue mood—which is something Cancerians are prone to—they'll start polishing the silver, dusting the books, or scrubbing the kitchen floor as a means of wiping away the tears. All performed to the cathartic melancholia of Mahler (a Cancerian, naturally) issuing from the stereo. Getting the house in order is the best therapy for Cancerians. It's the outward sign that they're getting their inner house in order.

Don't assume, though, that the Cancerian belief in domestic bliss makes them reluctant to deal with the cut and thrust of the world.

Quite the contrary. Cancerians are acutely aware that the best way to acquire all the comforts and security they want is precisely by being out there in the workaday world. How else are they going to afford the good life, if not by earning a good living?

Money may not buy happiness, but for Cancerians it sure is a big down payment. Even if they happen to be born rich, they'll be prepared to work hard to get richer. And richer. Just like Henry Rockefeller, who inherited the oil fortune made by his father, J. D. Both father and son were born under the sign of The Crab. The truth is, few signs can come close to Cancer in shrewdness with money. People are often surprised when they first discover the business acumen of such a soft, sensitive soul. Perhaps they don't know that besides being a water sign, Cancer is also a cardinal sign.

The day when the Sun enters Cancer is the longest day of the year: the day of the northern summer solstice. It's the time when the crops are ripening and the fruit is heavy on the trees, a time of fecundity and ripeness. This was the day for the midsummer rituals that ensured fertility of earth, man, and beast.

As the second cardinal sign of the zodiac, Cancer is linked to Aries, Libra, and Capricorn. Being born under a cardinal sign means being born with a "go for it" attitude and the drive to back it up. Have you ever watched a crab move in to get its claws around a desirable object? It can be extremely illuminating. Keeping its goal constantly in sight, it moves sideways or even backwards a little. Suddenly any timidity or fear evaporates as it races to grasp the prize tightly in its claws. It's quite an insight into how the cardinal quality manifests in the not-always-so-gentle, not-always-so-self-effacing Crab. And a lesson in why no one should ever make the mistake of underestimating Cancer. Not ever.

In Julius Caesar's account of how he conquered Britain, he left us the immortal phrase *Veni, vidi, vici* . . . "I came, I saw, I conquered." Caesar was a Cancer. How cardinal can you get?

Sun sign columns tend to paint a picture of Cancer as a sweet, sensitive, sentimental, home-loving sign, leaving little space to tackle the tough side of The Crab. Every sign has its own priorities. And Cancer's priority is to obtain the funds that will provide a home and security. Money is what builds the protective shell of The Crab. Indeed, Cancer equals and sometimes even surpasses Taurus in its uncomplicated interest in money.

Taurus is the quintessential earth sign. There is, in fact, an astrological link between Cancer and Taurus that gives them a lot in common. That link is the Moon. The Moon and the Earth are, of course, intrinsically linked. The Moon dictates the rhythms of life on our planet, affecting not only the tides of the ocean but also our personal physical tides, including fertility and our moods.

The Moon has many mystic and mythological names. One of them is Fortuna, also known as Dame Fortune or Lady Luck. Both Taurus and Cancer often seem blessed by Fortune in that they are either born into a materially secure family, or given the means to create their own riches. Yet neither sign is inclined to fully trust to luck. Neither likes to gamble or take risks because they are aware of how fickle "Lady Luck" can be, and how she and the tides can turn against the unprepared or the unprotected at any time.

Using a style touching in its simplicity, American writer Pearl Buck (born June 26) wrote about the Cancerian respect for Lady Luck in one of the best-selling novels of the twentieth century, *The Good Earth*. It's the story of how Chinese peasant farmer Wang Lung was forced by severe drought to leave his land, and see his family turn into scavengers and beggars. Later, through a blessing from Lady Luck that was as sudden and unexpected as her blow, Wang Lung was given a second chance to go back to his land and start over again. But this time he left nothing to chance. He had learned the lessons about the cruel vagaries of nature, and the shifting sands of good and bad times. He and his wife worked their fingers to the bone to ensure that when fortune turned again, their storerooms would be full.

In mythology the Moon is also known as Artemis, Diana the huntress, Selene, Phoebe, or Hecate the crone. In Egypt she was called Isis. Many names, each with its own story. Yet all these Moon goddesses are ultimately one and the same. Each is simply a different dimension of the lunar principle—the female principle.

Do you know a Cancerian man or two? They're usually every bit as sensitive, caring, and domestic as Cancer women. Even the most macho of Cancer males has a well-developed female side to his nature. His anima is strong, and women relate to him well. The Cancer man often has more women friends than the men of other signs, and is generally just as involved in running the home and raising the children.

Cancer is the sign of mothering. In all its glory and all its pain. Mother is, after all, our first love. Mother loves us unconditionally. She feeds us, nurtures us, and teaches us. But Mother also punishes us. Mother has the power to hurt. Or to heal. When we have her love and kindness, we feel safe and protected. Should her love be withdrawn, we can fall into the emotional abyss. Such is the power of Mother.

For male and female Cancerians alike, Mother is a figure who looms very large. Being born a Cancer, though, doesn't automatically ensure devotion from a loving and nurturing mother. It can, but Mother is usually a double-edged sword for Cancerians. Many are, in fact, dominated by their mothers and have feelings for Mother that swing between filial piety and frustration and scorn. It's not uncommon to hear of a Cancer who was tragically separated from his or her mother, or made to feel "orphaned" in some way. Such Cancerians then idealize the mother they never knew. Whatever mother card destiny has dealt a Cancer, there is always some reason in the past that explains why the umbilical cord is never completely cut.

Artemis is the name of the Moon in her role as the mother goddess. She was the twin sister of Apollo, the Sun god. When time came for their mother to give birth, Artemis, who was born first, helped her mother to deliver Apollo, and that is how the Moon became known as the protector and helper of women and children.

It's true, the maternal instinct and the urge to mother is strong in Cancer people. For some, it becomes their calling. The lifework of Cancerian Dr. Barnardo was the care of orphaned children. Child psychologist Dr. Spock had the Moon in Cancer. And Cancerian Bill Cosby has turned to writing books on parenthood.

Cancerians harbor a nostalgia for the simplicity of childhood. You see it everywhere in their homes, and sepia family photographs and corners stuffed with antiques and collectibles. Some even preserve their teddy bears and toys, and arrange them in little family groups. The children's classics are there, too. They are rarely handed on to the next generation. Rather, the collection is expanded by forays into thrift shops and secondhand bookstores to find the missing volumes. Cancer is wonderfully sentimental. They delight in the past and the old-fashioned ways, thinking of it as a time that was more simple, more solid, and more nurturing.

It is through all the Moon goddesses that Cancer is connected to women's issues generally. In our own age, there is a call to reinstate the female principles of cooperation, nurturing, protecting, and healing. All of which are now seen by women (and by many men, too) as an essential counterbalance to male-dominated culture.

The key word being *balance*. The importance of balance between male and female is symbolized in the birth of Artemis and her twin brother. Note: brother. Just as the male forces need to be balanced with female, so, too, is the male Sun god critical to the healthy expression of the female lunar nature. This is basic yin and yang. Too much of one and not enough of the other always spells trouble.

Astrology teaches us that one way every sign can feel more fulfilled is by anticipating the best qualities of the sign to come. After Cancer comes Leo, the sign ruled by the Sun. In Leo the individual becomes more expansive, and bold enough to look beyond the immediate horizons. Cancerians would benefit at times by taking on board some of the fire and spirit of Leo, and to venture out of the security package they wrap around themselves.

Leo people seek freedom to express themselves and use their talents, and they encourage others to do the same. Cancerians, on the other hand, instinctively put security before freedom and self-expression every time. They put the needs of the family before the rights of any individual. When Cancer is confronted by a loved one who dances to a different drum, the danger is that Cancer will try (even unconsciously) to sabotage the other's freedom. These are the times when the nurturer becomes the destroyer of individuality. Or when mothering becomes smothering. A happy family is a Cancer ideal, but through their tendency to be overly possessive and emotionally controlling, they have the potential to ruin what they cherish most. In this scenario, caring Cancer has moved onto the dark side of the Moon, where emotional response dominates reason, and crushes independence and individuality.

Things can look very murky when they are viewed only under moonlight. Even when the Moon is full, there are some shadowy areas that remain impenetrable. People are more easily spooked at night. But under the bright light of the Sun, the dark corners disappear, and everything can be seen more clearly for what it really is.

In the same way, Cancerians' clarity of vision can sometimes get blurred by the moonlight they dwell in. Those who can't learn to think objectively enough end up taking everything too personally, and can too easily get stuck in the emotional whirlpools of the past, and unhealthy relationships or circumstances they cannot bring themselves to end. These are the Cancers who get locked into childhood patterns and live a life addicted to safe routine.

The swinging moods of Cancer are part of astrological legend. More than any other sign, Cancerians are washed by emotional tidal waves that they have great difficulty in holding back. Even the most aware and mature Cancerians who understand how susceptible they are to the pull of their emotions are still prone to sudden shifts in mood.

Like a kaleidoscope of different colors and complex patterns, the nature of Cancer is to change from one day, even from one hour, to the next. It's often called a changeable sign, but the changeability of Cancer is quite different from that of Gemini. The Gemini individual seems to possess several different personalities, moving from being one person to another as interests and goals change. Cancerians, however, remain strictly the "one" person. They don't really change in themselves. Nor does the focus in their interests and ambitions change. It's as if Cancer is passing through different moods or different phases—just like the Moon. Rest assured, Cancerians' waxing and waning cycle always brings them back round to the same state or mood—often a little bit wiser for having gone round again.

When Cancerians are in an up phase, they're delightful to be with—warm, gleeful, fun-loving, and funny, too, in a refreshing uncomplicated, childlike way. Cancer is not the least bit self-conscious about playing a prank or acting the clown. They can be hugely entertaining, mimicking friends, colleagues, or the boss, and can have you in stitches with one of their farcical routines. Sometimes their humor borders on the vulgar. Still, always they are forgiven. The Cancerian comedian turned professional has his or her own particular stamp of humor. There's often an element of slapstick or buffoonery. It's the sort of comedy of uninhibited hoots and chortles perfected by Robin Williams, Terry Thomas, and Mel Brooks.

When their mood is up, they will welcome you into their homes with open arms. They will want to share their good cooking, not to mention a yarn or two about who's doing what, and with whom. For a friend in need, Cancer can be the personification of sympathy and understanding. They will listen patiently and intently to every detail of your suffering at the hands of your parents who don't understand you, the lover who left you in the lurch, or the boss from hell. When you pour your heart out to Cancer, you feel like you're really being heard.

Mind, you, a reinterpreted secondhand version of your most private angst may make its way back to you eventually. Cancer loves to gossip. Even well-educated, sophisticated Crabs are avid consumers of TV soaps. The bored Cancerian is quite capable of rewriting large chunks of your personal life that was not originally intended for general viewing. Be warned: You could become an episode of the days of their lives.

When they are up, they are really up. And when they are down, no one (with the possible exception of Capricorn, Scorpio, or Pisces) can get so down. Others may never hear about it. Cancer is very secretive when it comes to their own suffering. When they are heading into one of their blackest of black moods, they won't broadcast it. They just go to ground. At home, Cancerians can barricade themselves against the world by pulling the phone out of the wall and not answering the door.

What draws the cloak of darkness around Cancer is actually the same thing that puts us all down. Rejection. Criticism. And fear. Yet Cancerians seem to take the knocks more personally than most, and their reactions are more acute and more immediate. With their emotions just below the surface, even the slightest slight or curved ball can deeply upset them. Those who have ever been personally responsible for upsetting a Cancer will no doubt have been stunned at the swift and unexpected swing of their emotional pendulum.

Could such a sweet, gentle person really be this ball of shrieking rage that has suddenly turned on you? What could you possibly have said or done? Cancer in a fit of pique is not a person to be reasoned with. There's no use trying to talk sense when you are being delivered a stream of vitriol and spite. Faced with a furious Cancer, strategic withdrawal is your only defense. Just how ugly the scene could get if you don't exit fast enough is revealed in the most unattractive episode in the story of that most attractive of the Moon goddesses, Diana the huntress.

One hot day Diana stopped to bathe in a mountain pool. Actaeon, who was out hunting with his hounds, had the fatal misfortune to happen upon her at the moment her tunic fell. She felt personally violated, and all sense of reason and reasonableness left her. The fact that it was unintentional wasn't a fact at all. Revenge came in an instant. Diana transformed Actaeon into a stag and turned his own hounds on him. She didn't even flinch when they ripped him to pieces.

The moral of the story? Hurt Cancer and you can expect to get hurt. So much for all the Cancerian sweetness and light. So much for Mr. Nice Guy or Girl. In real life, a wounded Crab will go straight in for the kill. Cancer the exterminating angel operates as victim and victor in one.

Once they've let off enough steam, calm will be restored. After your first experience of this side of Cancer, you might well be waiting for an apology. Don't bank on it. Cancer is more likely to slip into the next phase, and simply act as if nothing ever happened. Many are oblivious to what a bad impression their temper tantrums make, and what devastation their personal attacks can create.

The Cancerian bad mood inevitably blows over. After a respectable passage of time, during which Cancer has deftly scuttled back into their shell, they'll pop back up in your life one day, beaming with renewed sweetness and light, making you feel that it would be far too insensitive of you to even broach that little incident of the arrow or two shot below the belt. If, however, you should happen to be treated to an action replay some time later, you'll be less taken aback. And probably less likely to forget and forgive.

Forgiving is much easier when you understand that Cancer is a deeply subjective creature who takes everything to heart. Happily, there is a solution—the solution that can be found for the most negative behavior of every sign. Namely, going as far as you can across the zodiac to your opposite sign, and building into your nature a little of the best characteristics of that sign.

Capricorn is the opposite sign to Cancer. Where Cancer is subjective, Capricorn is more objective. Where Cancer is supersensitive, Capricorn aims to stay cool and detached. Where Cancer is emotional, Capricorn is controlled and rational. Cancer can be childlike in times of stress, but Capricorn will adopt a stoic, stiff-upper-lip approach. Cancer focuses on today, tomorrow, and the immediate future. Capricorn is more far-sighted, often making calculated sacrifices in the present, in return for a bigger future.

If Cancerians can acquire something of the great Capricornian virtues of self-discipline, self-reliance, and self-control, and if they try not to allow their feelings to be the deciding factor in situations where feelings have little place, they will have gone a long way towards conquering the tyranny of their moods. Pearl Buck knew it. She said, "I don't wait for moods. You accomplish nothing if you do that. Your mind must know it has got to get down to earth." Capricorn, needless to say, is an earth sign.

Living out the cycle of their moods may be a great source of release for Cancerians themselves. But it can be extremely draining on those around them who can end up tiptoeing on eggshells, nervously living in fear of triggering another swing. Even more common than being hotly attacked by a Cancer is being given the cold shoulder. Cancer has perfected the art of the huff.

Part of the picture of Cancer's moods is turning their anger and aggression inward, onto themselves. There are a few classic variations on the Cancerian self-destruct theme.

When a Cancerian depression sets in, all their fears, anxieties, and insecurities rise to the surface and begin to feed off their fertile imagination. Fear plus imagination equals a dangerous Cancerian equation. "What if . . ." becomes a frightening proposition. "How will I cope without . . ." and "Who will pay for . . ." are the questions that chase each other around and around in their minds.

Should Cancerians ever feel that their security base is threatened, fear takes over and rules their life. It happens if a loved one withdraws affection. It happens if their work looks like it's drying up, or if they can't find an immediate solution to a financial problem. Basically it happens if they don't get what they feel they need. Then they feel like Linus without his security blanket. When Cancerians are in low spirits, they cannot get enough of whatever it is that they love so much. Deep down, it's insecurity and fear of having to go without that is at the root of Cancer's covetousness. Depression is likely to send them out to the shops where they'll buy something that they already have plenty of. It could be a vase to add to the three dozen in the cabinet. It could be a tablecloth that will go in the drawer along with all the others. It could be a new pair of shoes. It could even be five or six new pairs of shoes to add to the four thousand sitting in the cupboard back at the palace. That's what made Cancerian Imelda Marcos feel better in her moments of insecurity.

A lot of their personally destructive behavior is centered on food. Cancer connects emotional nourishment with physical nourishment. When they're feeling emotionally undernourished, the Cancerian impulse is to head for the fridge. Even the average, well-balanced Cancer knows all about the medicinal value of comfort eating. And who would deny anyone a chocolate cookie, or two, or three . . . when they're feeling low?

Most Cancerians have a delicate relationship with food. They love it. And many of them love it far too much. The Moon rules the stomach, which is why Cancers are prone to digestive problems. Anorexia and bulimia are not uncommon among the natives of the sign that is famous for its fondness for food. Cancerians gain weight easily, and controlling their eating habits can become an ongoing battle. Especially when they find themselves sleepwalking into the kitchen at 2:00 A.M. to fry up a plate of bacon and eggs because they dreamt they felt peckish. The great philosopher Jean-Jacques Rousseau said, "Happiness is a good bank account, a good cook, and a good digestion." He was a Cancer, and there aren't many Cancerians who would disagree with him.

Overeating, hoarding, and covetousness are all exaggerations of the nurturing Moon principle.

But when it operates in a healthy expression, the nurturing principle works both ways for Cancer. Cancer nurtures. And Cancer becomes the nurtured. Cancerians may be good at caring for themselves, but they are also brilliant at eliciting support from others. People somehow feel that Cancerians are genuinely deserving, and that they're the sort of people who should be treated with kindness. You rarely find a Cancer who goes without for too long. Somehow they never seem to be the one to be made redundant when the ax falls at work. They always seem to be the one who finds the best apartment. And parents, especially mother, step in to help them through lean times.

Maybe this type of Cancerian luck has something to do with Jupiter, the planet of opportunity and material good fortune. Astrologers say that Jupiter is exalted in the sign of The Crab, which means that Jupiter gives of his best in Cancer. Jupiter governs Sagittarius and Pisces, the signs that often attract luck to themselves by being willing to take chances. But Cancer, as we know, is no risk taker. Perhaps it's precisely because Cancer is so astute and careful with money that Jupiter can operate so well in Cancer and bring such bounty.

The most obvious way in which Cancerians gain support from others is through their warm, gentle manner. It's a sign with tremendous personal appeal. You cannot help but love them. Cancer badly wants to be liked. They find rejection of any sort very painful. Few Crabs are true renegades or rebels. In fact, Cancer is one of the most conservative signs of the zodiac. Their private moods may be inconsistent, like the Moon but their public image is usually rock-solid.

Cancers can easily translate personal appeal into public appeal. Another astrological function of the Moon is her rulership over the public. A Cancer in the public eye knows what people want, and knows how to deliver it. It makes them natural stars in any work that involves dealing with the public, such as public relations and promoting products and events.

The secret of Cancerians' success with the public has much to do with their seemingly ill-fitting blend of being both a sensitive watery sign as well as an ambitious cardinal sign intent on achieving what they set out to do. What seems an odd partnership initially is actually a winning combination in public life. The water acts as the emotional drawcard, the feel-good factor. And the cardinal quality provides the drive and the ambition.

Just as Cancerians are easily touched by others, so do they have the ability to touch the hearts of people they do not even know. The sign of The Crab has been called the sign of the common man. Cancer understands exactly what will appeal to every man, not just the chosen few. Is it so contradictory, then, that shy, private, domestic Cancer can become a public figure adored by millions who feel as if they know him or her personally.

Do you remember when the then Lady Diana Spencer first stepped onto the world stage in 1980? The press embraced her as "Shy Di," the fairy-tale princess. Shy, yes. Cancer can appear charmingly naive. But believe us, they know instinctively how to play to the gallery. Almost overnight, Diana became the world's most photographed woman, conscious of camera angles and her image. For a lackluster monarchy, she was a promotional dream come true. Although she may never have felt that she belonged to the royal family, it very soon became clear that Diana belonged to a much larger family: that of the people of England and her worldwide public. Long after the fairy-tale marriage failed to end happily ever after, Diana's face still adorned every magazine stand around the world. And her presence at charity functions guaranteed donations would pour in. When it became clear that Diana would never become queen of England, she arranged her own public relations exercise in which she declared to the world that she would like her role to be "Queen of Hearts." Diana, self-appointed Queen of Hearts, had struck on the power of

Cancer. The power of sensitivity, sympathy, and the warmth of human feelings.

Every Cancerian, whether they're in the public eye or not, has this special power.

When Diana died, the world stopped and wept. The mass grief was so extraordinary that people began to ask what it was about "the people's princess" that affected so many. Was it because of her vulnerabilities and the fact that she wore her heart on her sleeve? Was it because she gave people "permission to feel"? Was it because she personified the Cancer qualities that people clearly needed in their lives? Something Diana said in her last interview was straight from the Cancer heart: "Nothing gives me more happiness than to try to aid the most vulnerable of this society. Whoever is in distress who calls me, I will come running."

One of Diana's two sons, and future heir to the throne, Prince William, is also a Cancer. William has inherited the Cancerian sensitivity of his mother, and astrologers are already eagerly examining his horoscope and speculating about potential emotional entanglements.

When Cancerians have the reassurance of belonging, be it to a family, a company, or a nation, when they feel nurtured, supported, and loved, when they have their part to play in the established scheme of things, only then do they feel truly happy and content. And only then does Cancer feel empowered to help others. Cancerians who actively care for others—without thought of personal gain—find they're walking a road with more riches than they ever dreamt possible. This is the key to their happiness. It's a happiness that no amount of money can buy.

Cancer can be a remarkable force for healing and reconciliation. And when they can draw on those very best of the Capricorn traits of nobility, dignity, patience, and long-distance vision, their contribution can be nothing short of extraordinary.

Great Cancerians such as the Dalai Lama, Nelson Mandela—and Diana—show us, by the example of their lives, that goodness is not a question of intellect. Such fundamental moral matters as what is good or bad, and what is just or unjust, cannot be understood by cold, hard logic alone.

Cancer teaches us that a good mind is no good at all without a good heart, and that kindness and sensitivity often go a lot further than reason and rationality. As the first of the water signs, Cancer brings the importance of feelings to the fore.

We all have those moments when we "know" if something is right or wrong, even if we're not quite sure why. That's because it's the kind of knowing that doesn't come from the head. It comes from the heart.

THE CANCER CAREER AND DIRECTION

"Hi ho, hi ho, it's off to work we go . . ."

Does it seem contradictory that Cancer, the sign that has been affectionately labeled the bread and baby maker of the zodiac, is such a force in the world of business? Not really.

Don't let the soft voice and gentle manner fool you. Behind it there's a sense of purpose that's as mighty as an Aries. A determination as persistent as a Taurus. And an imagination to rival Pisces. Some Cancerians are likely to pull back and pale at the suggestion that they are, dare we say, ambitious. But if any sign is a closet high achiever, then it's Cancer. It's just that they like to keep their ambitions to themselves. Hiding the magnitude of their material goals works in their favor.

Taurus is, strictly speaking, the sign of the zodiac that "rules" money. But Cancer could certainly be considered one of the money signs. Both signs are concerned with the protecting and hatching of the nest egg. And while few Cancerians are destined to make it to tycoon status, there are many who secretly dream about it.

Their shrewdness with money and an obsession with creating a sound material base brands Cancer for success in the financial industries. Many find their direction in banking, insurance, investment, and real estate. Stockbroking also fits the bill. Strictly blue-chip portfolios, of course, with minimum risk. Unless there are indicators to the contrary in their birth chart—Mars or Jupiter rising, for example, or maybe lots of planets in fire signs—Cancer will steer away from wild speculation. They're sure to have many a splendid fantasy about what they could do with a spare million or two, but when it comes down to making a living, Cancerians are realists.

A big business, Cancer knows, often starts out as a small business. And the small family business is a familiar Cancerian theme. Keep it in the family (or at least small enough to feel like a family) and Cancer can keep a watchful eye on everything. Cancer prefers to be firmly in control of his or her own money and assets, and will ponder long and hard before handing the reins over to someone else.

One common Cancerian dream is to live off the interest from safe investments, and run a hobby business. An antiques store with a tea room attached would be perfect. Cancerians love to ferret out collectibles and curios. What nicer way to spend your days than ringing up the dollars on an old-world cash register in your own old-world establishment.

Cancer is the procurer of the zodiac. If there's anything you want and don't know where to find it, you can save yourself heaps of time by asking a Cancer. They're a gold mine of information. One

Cancerian man we know is the first person everyone turns to when they want to find laurel oil soap from Damascus, the best deal on a food processor, or frozen okra when it's out of season. No one better than Cancer to locate those domestic essentials and little comforts.

Any business relating to the home is a Cancerian business. It could be setting up a home-help company where everything from cleaning, to dog walking, to shopping is provided. Perhaps their sights are set on running a country guesthouse, or a vacation cottage by the sea in which they can create a beautiful environment for guests to rest and relax in. And what of that gorgeous new home furnishings store that's just opened up in town? You can be pretty certain it's got the Cancerian touch.

They're also drawn to any business connected with food, such as delicatessens, coffee shops, and restaurants. In the days of the friendly corner store, it was likely to be a Cancer behind the counter. This was the place where everyone passed through to buy bread, cat food, and the paper, and catch up on the local gossip at the same time.

Whether they're running their own business or working for someone else, Cancerians like to create a home away from home at work, especially if they work in a large, impersonal office environment. The same Cancerian man who knows everything there is to know about soap, food processors, and seasonal vegetables has transformed his office desk into a second home. One section is set aside as the complete home pharmacy to which all his colleagues run for aspirin, Band-aids, tissues, and indigestion remedies. Cancerians, with their sensitive stomachs, are experts on tummy troubles. Another section is allocated to survival rations such as instant soups, tea bags, and snacks for every whim. What's that steam rising from his desk? Why, his personal one-cup coffeemaker, of course.

Many Crabs build a shell for themselves at work by turning their desk into fortress Cancer. With bookshelves bowing under the weight of favorite books, magazines, family photographs, and a treasured bibelot or two, you may be hard-pressed to actually catch them working. And that's just the way they like it. Cancerians feel nervous if they're on view all the time. They like to venture out occasionally for a chat, but like always to head back to their sanctuary behind the wall of plants.

It would seem a natural assumption that Cancer is a sign well suited to working at home. Yet this is often not the case. At home the boundaries between work life and domestic life can get too easily crossed and confused. Leaving home to go out to work is very good for Cancerians. It takes them out of their shell and gives them a view of the bigger picture. Besides, being home alone, Cancerians can too easily fall into one of their famous bouts of introspection and melancholy. Generally speaking, it's far more healthy and productive for Cancer to be "out there" with others as a wanted and valued member of a team. The Cancer individual needs to feel included. They can get very upset if they feel left out. Actually, feeling excluded can be tantamount to a physical shock to their system.

At work, Cancerians are careful not to present themselves as outsiders. No matter what they really think of their boss or their colleagues, they're unlikely to reveal it—at least not on the job. It's not in their nature to rock the boat. Cancer wants to be thought of as a nice person. Being liked brings protection and security. Anyway, it's hard *not* to like Cancer. If we've said it once, we'll say it again; Cancers are liked by most everyone.

How could being so "nice" be anything but an advantage? With no conscious effort on their part, and for no reason you can easily put your finger on, Cancerians win support and sympathy. Colleagues (and that usually includes the boss) seem reluctant to ever come down too heavily on Cancerians for fear of offending or hurting them. Even when their work is not up to scratch, people are ready to make allowances. Just as Cancer is cared for by others, so, too, do people seek them out for a little TLC. Got a problem? Talk to Cancer. Soft, sensitive Cancerians are the people who make work a more human, friendly place to be.

Moon-ruled Cancerians are empathetic, kind, and tender. All the qualities that are now appreciated as essential for a productive and happy working environment. In the eighties it seemed all you needed was aggression to take you to the top. But a new philosophy emerged in the nineties, one that recognized workers as human. And if you wanted to make it, you had to be human, too.

Headhunting agencies are now testing job candidates for what has become known as EQ: emotional quotient. If you've got a high EQ, you're someone with a natural ability for getting along with others. You work out problems through tolerance, understanding, and listening to other points of view. People with a high EQ are not autocratic. Their methods are cooperative. In the new millennium, IQ will no longer be enough. IQ might get you in the door, but EQ will help you climb the promotional ladder.

Empathy, kindness, and tolerance cannot be taught. People either have EQ or they don't. Nor can EQ be learned in a weekend workshop. You don't get it by simply mouthing clichés such as: "We'll work through it together" or "How can we help each other on this?" Basically, EQ comes down to the fact that being nice, not just acting nice, gets better results.

With their people skills, Cancerians move ahead almost magically in human resources and employment agencies, where they need to listen to and understand someone's needs and match them up with someone else's.

That human touch also leads a lot of Cancerians into the healing arts. Aside from the traditional field of nursing, there is a whole new choice of natural therapies that utilize the Cancerian gift for making people feel better. Herbalism, iridology, reflexology, and aromatherapy are just a few.

In the same vein, there is the lunar connection with women and mothering. Midwifery is a classic Cancerian profession. So too, is work that involves surrogate mothering in some way. Many young Cancer women earn pocket money as baby-sitters, and go on to work as nannies. And you'll find plenty of Cancerians (as well as people who have a strong Moon in their horoscope) working in kindergartens, neonatal care, and pediatrics.

Others seek work in crisis centers where they can give hands-on help, as well as a sensitive ear to people's sufferings. They make good counselors because they instinctively know how to make others feel better. Being born under a watery sign makes them naturally sympathetic and caring. Water flows over you, washes away troubles, soothes pain, and leaves you feeling cleansed. Whether it's by saying just the right words, providing just the right food, blending just the right herbs, or massaging just the right spot, Moon-ruled Cancerians can be a remarkable force for healing.

Water-sign people are also imaginative. And we know that on some deep level, imaginative, creative work also has the power to heal. The creative process needs fire to spark it off, but astrologers believe that the water element is vital in producing something truly imaginative. As the first water sign, the artistic Cancer captures that first raw emotion, and bang! There it is, painted with one stroke of the brush, written in one word, or strummed in one chord. It may be simple, even simplistic. But whatever they create seems to have the power to evoke an instant, emotional response—one that is oh so sweet, or conversely, oh so sad.

Even Cancerians who are not professional artists love to create and collect beautiful things. The gentle arts are in Cancer territory. Cancerians are often regular patrons of craft markets, and many make quite a cozy living out of selling homemade wares, from patchwork quilts to quince jelly. Creative and imaginative work requires a certain freedom of spirit that, for Cancer, is easiest to draw on in a home environment. Dancer Twyla Tharp summed it up for fellow Cancerians when she said, "Art is the only way to run away without leaving home."

Other artistic Cancerians find commercial art, in all its aspects—

photography, design, and graphics—is a good option. Cancer is in an excellent position to create and deliver what the public will love. Remember, this is the sign that rules the public and the consumer. They are expert riders of the current wave. Rarely, though, do they swim way out into unchartered waters, or as far as the cutting edge. Cancerians would need to have a strong Uranus or Neptune in their horoscope to take their intuition a step ahead into innovation. Giorgio Armani is a Cancer. His design style is internationally recognized as what everybody wants to be seen in. Chic but conservative. Stylish but not outrageous. The proof of his widespread appeal is the extent to which his designs are imitated.

The Cancerian sense of the mood of the consumer can be put to excellent use in promotions, sales, and PR. Cancer has a feel for the marketplace reminiscent of the dealers in the souks of Marrakech. They love the exchange and bartering, and relish the time it takes over coffee and sweetmeats to arrive at the right deal. In the marketplaces of the twenty-first century, the same trusted Cancerian methods still yield results.

It's an enormous help to have the sign Cancer strong in your birth chart if you want to draw on public appeal or make it in the public arena. Tom Cruise and Isabelle Adjani are two Cancerians whose popularity stems largely from an endearing, almost innocent manner. No matter how tough or worldly the role, there's always a softness and a suggestion of vulnerability that touches the heartstrings.

Many Cancerian leaders successfully combine a direct appeal to the heart with a passionate nationalistic identification. This special combination often makes them a rallying point for mass movements.

The passionate patriotism inherent in Cancer is not confined to people. Astrologers believe that nations also fall under the influence of certain Sun signs, and that includes America, born on the Fourth of July. It's not surprising that the mass consciousness of the American people is deeply patriotic. Gemini on the Ascendant may make America the country of bright ideas and the center of youth culture. But the bedrock of the American character is solidly Cancerian. America is the land where hometown values, mother, and apple pie are synonyms for goodness, and are raised to the level of moral icons. Sentimentality and nostalgia for the past is one side of Cancer, and of America. But so, too, is the drive for wealth, and the practical, cardinal "can do" ethic.

Clearly, Cancer individuals have got what it takes to make it. Which begs the question, why then do so many Cancerians—including some who are very talented—choose to stay in the trenches. They are prepared to work for years, decades even, for large companies or the public service in humdrum routine jobs in which big demands will never be made on them, and where they can earn a respectable enough salary with a good retirement package.

Why? The truth is that many Cancerians are prepared to give up a lot in return for a secure job. Cancer is a sign that may have a hankering for the past, but lives very much in the present. As for the future, well, to Cancer, that is dubious territory. Long-term dreams aren't going to pay the rent today, thinks Cancer. And why go through prolonged denial for future possibilities that may or may not eventuate? Cancer figures this is just plain stupid. Far more sensible and more immediately gratifying to capitalize on what you have now and what you figure you can reasonably count on. Securing the present is the best way to come out ahead in the long run.

The self-absorbed Cancer tucked up in his or her own sheltered world of job, home, and family can become terribly smug. Others make the mistake of confiding to a Cancer how they aspire to doing something bigger or better with their lives, only to have the proverbial bucket of cold water thrown over them. "But what will you do? How will you live?" is the standard Cancerian response. Why so scathing of someone else's dreams? Maybe, by scoffing at others, Cancer is bolstering his or her own "superior" position. Could it be that their scorn is a cover-up for resentment of those who dare? Those who dare to mortgage the house to set up the business they've always dreamt of. Or those who dare to walk away from a safe but boring job. Indeed, anyone who dares to step out into the unknown.

Yet if someone dares to suggest to Cancerians bemoaning their lot that maybe there is a way they, too, could break out of an unsatisfying or limiting situation, they're likely to retort, "But I can't—I've got a mortgage" or "I've only got fifteen years to retirement." Sound far-fetched? No, not really. It's a lament we heard from a Cancer woman who was very unhappy in her job, and probably still is.

Cancerians' deep-seated fear that the rug could be pulled out from underneath them at any time is what makes them do all they can to cushion themselves. They fear that if they take on something too big, or more adventurous, they'll be tempting fate. And Cancer has too much respect for Fate to tempt her.

Besides, there are compensations for being content with what you have. Affordable pleasures such as being able to buy whatever you fancy, take weekends away whenever you feel like it, and enjoy the best wine and food every day. For Cancer, day-to-day comforts represent a lifestyle that is far too good to give up for something new that doesn't come with a guarantee.

We know there are lessons to be learned from our opposite sign, but there are also important traits that opposite signs have in common. Cancer and its opposite sign, Capricorn, share a desire for status, respectability, approval, and security. Yet each has its own way of achieving these things. You can no more tell a Cancer to sacrifice the pleasures of the now for something more rewarding down the track than you can tell a Capricorn to ditch his or her long-term goals and settle for bigger dollars now. No sign can change the essence of what it is. Each must be true to its own nature.

On the plus side, Cancer isn't hooked on what might be—because, let's face it, it's only a "might be." Indeed, Cancer has something to teach all of us who have ever chased after the impossible. All of us who have gone too far out onto a shaky limb, and fallen off. They have a lesson for the Pisceans, Geminis, and Sagittarians who have sought change for change's sake.

But, on the down side, Cancerians can get so entrenched in what keeps them secure and happy enough now that they kill off their own potential through fear of the future, lack of trust, and poverty of vision. The issue of opting for security and safety in the system versus making a bid for freedom and a more expansive life is a core conflict for creative Cancerians. Is Cancer the ultimate bourgeois? This question has been examined by many Cancerian writers, including George Orwell and Hermann Hesse. In *Steppenwolf* Hesse did an in-depth study of this important Cancerian theme.

It is the tale of Harry Haller, a troubled soul who wandered from town to town renting rooms in comfortable, middle-class homes. He loved the order, the cleanliness, the regularity, and even the smell of a well-run house. Yet Harry could never truly belong to this world because part of him was a Steppenwolf, as he called himself: *"A wolf from the Steppes that had lost its way and strayed into the towns and the life of the herd."*

Steppenwolf was a shy, lonely, and restless creature who waged an ongoing personal battle to tame the wolf within and live a "normal respectable life." Deeply attracted to the life of the bourgeoisie, yet destined to remain separate from it, Steppenwolf knew, in his heart, that this was a battle that could never be won. Not while his individualistic, creative, and passionate self howled for attention. A self that could never ultimately be ignored without destroying his very life force.

Steppenwolf is a story about the exquisite torture endured by gifted and creative Cancerians. It's about the suffering they endure when they trade off their individuality, their imagination, and their passion in return for the trappings of a secure, comfortable existence. If such a gifted Cancerian cannot escape, even temporarily, from the cage of mundane responsibilities, he or she is destined to swing into a regular cycle of depression, denial, and sadness.

The wolf within is something vital to the heart and soul. If it is banished forever, life would be intolerable and meaningless. Hesse explained it this way:

We see that he had in him a strong impulse both to the saint and to the profligate; and yet he could not, owing to some weakness or inertia, make the plunge into the free untrammeled realms of space. The parent constellation of the bourgeoisie binds him with its spell. This is his place in the universe and this his bondage. Most intellectuals and most artists belong to the same type. Only the strongest of them force their way through the atmosphere of the Bourgeois-Earth and reach the cosmic. The others all resign themselves, or make compromises. Despising the bourgeoisie, and yet belonging to it, they add to its strength and glory; for in the last resort they have to affirm their beliefs in order to live.

For many Cancerians, this struggle is never an issue. But for those who yearn to express their individuality, finding a resolution is an important quest.

The resolution actually lies within their own nature. Cancerians need only to remind themselves that they are one of the cardinal signs of the zodiac. And if any sign has the incentive to get up and do something, as well as the capability to restructure their lives, it's Cancer. If the spirit is willing and the urge is strong enough, it can be done. Cancerians have the financial acumen, they're born organizers, and they know what will succeed in the marketplace. Tapping into a little of the courage and faith that is just around the corner in Leo is all they need to do.

Yes, choices will have to be made. Maybe something will have to go. If they have to pull in their investments, reduce their retirement savings, and get a part-time job that covers the necessities of life, is that such a frightening idea, after all?

There are many Cancerians who would have liked to take a quantum leap into something different, but didn't because they ultimately deemed it too risky. Cancerians will never take that leap unless they reach the point where they can transcend their fear. Happy is the wise and insightful Cancerian who embraces the Steppenwolf in their soul, who feeds and nurtures the wolf, and gives him his own territory to run wild in. Unhappy is the Cancerian who pulls back into his or her shell when they could pull off the masterstroke of a lifetime.

Helen Keller, born blind, deaf, and mute, once said, "Avoiding danger is no safer in the long run than outright exposure. The fearful are caught as often as the bold." Surely, here was someone who could have been justified in spending her life within the protective Cancerian shell. Yet she became famous for drawing public attention to the rights of the disabled, and for showing just how much you can do when the desire is strong enough.

For all Cancerians, not following your heart can end up more psychologically damaging. So be bold, Cancer. You can be sure that if you are, the rest will all fall into place.

LOVE AND FRIENDSHIP

Once upon a time there was a little prince who lived all alone on an asteroid where he spent his days tending his two volcanoes and the seedlings that blew in from space. One of these seedlings grew to be a lovely rose. She took much longer than any of his other plants to bloom. The rose was extremely beautiful. But she was also extremely demanding. She wanted a screen to protect her petals and a globe placed over her at night. The prince had to pick off the caterpillars, water her, and care for her every need.

Even though he thought his rose was the most lovely thing he had ever known, the prince soon began to tire of her demands and the little ploys that kept him running around. He felt confused, and upset by her changes of mood. Not having any previous experience of roses, he decided the best thing to do was to leave his asteroid and the rose and go in search of the answer to his dissatisfaction.

The prince's travels brought him to Earth where he met a fox who taught him what he hadn't understood about his relationship with the rose. The fox told the prince that his rose was like no other rose precisely because she was *his* rose. He was the one who had tended her, kept off the caterpillars, watered her, and listened patiently to her complaints. The rose had tamed him. And, in turn, the prince had tamed the rose.

The fox said: *"It is the time you have wasted for your rose that makes your rose important. Men have forgotten this truth. But you must not forget it. You become responsible forever for what you have tamed. You are responsible for your rose."* Real love, the prince discovered, is what blooms when you give your time, your energy, and your heart to another.

And so the prince returned to his asteroid and his rose, having learned that all her little ploys and demands were of little consequence compared to the happiness and comfort they gave each other. Did they live happily ever after? Very likely, yes. You see, the prince and his rose is a story about Cancer and love. Both are Cancerians. So was the real-life creator of *The Little Prince*, Antoine de Saint-Exupéry.

"Saint Ex" was a famous aviator who met his untimely death over war-torn France in 1944. But at heart he was a boy who never grew up. He was one of those Cancerians who was an indulged child. All his life he loved to reminisce over his childhood world of magic gardens, fairies, and fantasies.

The Little Prince is written in naive style, like a children's story, and became popular in the sixties with the flower-power children who saw love as the answer to everything. Fey and a bit schmaltzy, it may be, but it nevertheless has a lot to reveal about the Cancerian approach to romance. As the fox said, *"One only understands the things that one tames . . ."* How does this "taming" process begin? The fox had an answer for that, too. *"First, you will sit down at a little distance from me . . . I shall look at you out of the corner of my eye, and you will say nothing. Words are the source of misunderstandings. But you will sit a little closer to me every day . . ."*

This is how it begins with Cancerians. Subtly. Slowly. But surely. The lunar goddess first weaves her Moon magic. Then Cancer is poised to set your heart fluttering. It takes just a twinkling of the eye. If it's true that the eyes are the windows to the soul, then the soft, gentle soul of Cancer shines through. Their sparkling eyes are often their most alluring feature. Some Cancerians have slightly protruding eyes, and they, too, seem to break down your defenses.

The Cancerian voice is equally seductive. It has a tonal quality that is soothing and pleasant to listen to. It's an atypical Cancer who talks too fast or too loud. A shy fluttering of the eyelashes and a quiet, inviting "hello," and your defenses have dissolved.

Physically, there seem to be two types of Cancerians. The tall, willowy, graceful ones, like Jerry Hall, Meryl Streep, and Princess Diana usually have an oval face. Then there's the shorter, rounder model with a moon face, the type of Cancerian who could be described as Rubenesque—a term synonymous with the appreciation of a well-padded body. Rubens obviously loved to paint beautiful women who appreciated the benefits of a hearty breakfast. He was, as you might expect, a Cancer himself.

Cancer men have a tendency to baldness. Those who have lovable receding temples at twenty-five may be totally bald by forty-five. Yul Brynner was one. It's worth noting if baldness is your biggest turnoff . . . or turn-on.

It's not caveman chemistry that you'll be initially drawn by when you first encounter Cancer. It's more likely to be those tentative signals of emotional bonding that Cancer puts out. After all, Cancer is an intuitive water sign. Their emotional response to any situation clicks into place before the rational thinking process begins. The heart speaks before the head.

If you are a sensitive, too, you will intuit Cancer's feelings that this could be the first step in a relationship that's really leading somewhere. Somewhere serious. Cancerians are not afraid to commit. How could they be, when commitment is precisely what they're looking for? In the year 2000 and beyond, you can be sure there will be Cancerians still dreaming of a nineteenth-century courtship, with a romantic wedding in sight.

Cancer is not one to indulge in a string of affairs and sexual conquests. Once the initiations of youth are passed and they've found out what it's all about, Cancer is unlikely to pursue a sexual encounter just for the "experience." Not like a Scorpio, Aries, or Gemini might. No, thank you. Cancer knows what such experiences can lead to, and how deeply a person can be hurt if they are left seduced and abandoned. Their solid self-protective instinct warns them against putting themselves in the emotional line of fire. Sexual adventures and wild times for their own sake are not what The Crab is after.

There is something a little ethereal about Cancer in love, something that nonetheless holds the promise of earthy delights to come. Their sensory perception is acute. They're very responsive to scents, and they love perfumes, aromatic baths, and essential oils filling the air. Cancer also has the gift of touch. They are wonderful masseurs, knowing just how to release stored-up tensions. In short, Cancer is an arch sensualist.

They love water. The candlelit spa scented with ylang-ylang and overflowing with bubbles and rose petals is most definitely a Cancerian sexual fantasy. Add a bottle of Moët at arm's reach, and a pair of gentle hands to wash their back, and the picture is perfect.

An important part of the Cancerian sexual dynamic is caring and being cared for, pampering and being pampered. Cancerians want evidence that they are cherished. So lovers should give some thought to the small but important things they can give them and do for them. Things like going out of your way to track down their favorite flowers, or a jar of their favorite jam, or preparing their favorite dish, will go a long way to winning the Cancerian heart.

Don't think that the fairy-tale courtship will be spoiled by talk of money, or that it could ever be too soon for a prospective partner to indicate the healthy state of his or her bank account. Cancerians will be looking for the signs that their partner has a correct attitude towards money. They're not the least bit embarrassed talking about mortgages, insurance policies, stocks and bonds, and salary brackets. This is not unromantic talk to Cancer. *Au contraire*. It's just what their heart and their head want to hear.

If they like what they hear and they decide they like you, Cancerians fall in love quickly, if not instantly. This is a moment when the emotional impulses of the otherwise self-protective Crab sweep away all sense of reason. Cancerians of both sexes find it hard to draw a dividing line between sex and love. How could they be separate? thinks Cancer. Enjoying a leisurely breakfast in bed the morning after is how it's going to be (or how it ought to be) every morning after. This is how all romantic heroes and heroines live.

Should Cancer fall overboard for the wrong person, they're inclined to suppress any misgivings they may have, believing that they can "tame" this person. A few months at the Cancer training school for well-domesticated partners is all it will take. Eventually Cancer will come to his or her senses and realize that not everybody wants to be tamed. But before a doomed-from-the-start relationship comes to an end, Cancer usually tries to tough it out for the sake of what they've already invested in it.

The Cancerian romantic ideal is to find a love with whom they can settle down in the very old-fashioned sense of the word. Someone with whom they can build a life centered on home and family, and with whom they can strive to attain all the comforts of life. A wealthy Cancer will want a city home overflowing with children, cats, and dogs, as well as a country cottage, beach house, and annual luxury holidays with the whole family in tow. Cancerians want a helpmate, someone to help them spin a cocoon around themselves, and to live with them in its warmth and protection.

The Cancerian home is sacrosanct. Comfy clutter is the decorative style favored by most Crabs. They find it therapeutic just to be in residence with their favorite belongings. Indeed, the Cancerian urge to collect can be quite extraordinary. Cancer would move from a studio apartment into a four-bedroom house, and have every wall and corner filled within the month. Why put up with the inconvenience of having only one Bang & Olufsen video player in the den, when you can have another at the foot of the bed? Cancerians are as attached to their modern conveniences almost as much as they are to their antiques. Cancer-turned-minimalist is unheard-of. You can't be a Cancer *and* a minimalist. It's a contradiction in terms.

The kitchen is the heart of the Cancer home. It's a warm, homey, and inviting place with copper pans hanging from the ceilings, jugs full of daisies, a pile of well-thumbed cookbooks, and cupboards stacked with enough supplies to withstand a cyclone. Sure, you'll find lots of healthy fruits and vegetables, and yogurt in the fridge. But open a cupboard and you're likely to have ten packages of Oreos and Cheez Doodles come tumbling down on top of you. Whatever their favorite junk food is, there'll always be plenty in the house for snacking in front of the new super screen TV.

Cancer has a wonderful way with good, old-fashioned comfort food. Not since your mother's strawberry-rhubarb pie have you felt so warm and cosseted. Living with Cancer must surely be paradise found.

Caring and totally committed to those nearest and dearest, Cancer certainly is. But isn't it curious how the nurturer of the zodiac can be downright disinterested in the welfare of those outside their closed circle. With Cancer, it often comes down to "me and mine." And as long as Cancer's me and mine are taken care of, then frankly, others can go take a flying leap. For Cancer, charity begins (and sadly, often ends) at home. When this Cancerian inclination to not give a damn about "outsiders" surfaces, people will catch a glimpse of the hard, mean side of The Crab that makes others feel left out and inconsequential. Warm, sensitive Cancer can also be remarkably cold and insensitive. All the emotional water signs are capable of being extremely cruel, cutting, and hurtful.

Cancerians generally don't cultivate a wide circle of acquaintances. Nor do they call just anyone or everyone a friend. And they certainly don't have an "open house" mentality as many Geminis and Aquarians do. Once Cancerians form a relationship with someone, whether lover or friend, they never quite relinquish the attachment they feel for that person. That person will continue to live on in some corner of their thoughts, and their heart.

Cancerians protect themselves against the hard world by constructing a moat around their castle, or nailing a "Trespassers—Keep Out" sign on the gate. Even though they do like to get out regularly and mingle with friends, Cancerians prefer for selected people to come to them, to their castle. Which is wonderful for partners who want the same. But some partners of Cancer will need to be strong in insisting that Cancer respect their space, their time, and their interests. They will need to mark out their own territory. Otherwise they may wake up one day to find the drawbridge has been pulled up and they're trapped, an emotional hostage in the castle.

Anyone close to a Cancer will at some time face the Cancerian possessiveness and will begin to contemplate the difference between nurturing and taming. And wonder whether they are loved or owned. And whether this is what you want. There are days when Cancer will moan from dawn to dusk about how much they do to "keep it all together." They'll complain and gripe about how hard they work, how much everything costs, and how everyone depends on them. But the truth is, they like it that way. When people depend on you, it's easier to control them and run things the way you want. When people need you, it's easier to think you own them, and that you've got the right to call the shots. It's a decidedly negative Cancerian trait to convert other people's dependency into their power.

Next time you hear a Cancer complaining about how much others need him or her, reflect a moment on who really needs whom.

Male or female, Cancer falls naturally into the role of mother. And you can be sure that if Cancer behaves in an overly dominant, possessive way, his or her own mother is somewhere at the root of it. For many adult Cancers, mother is always there, even if she is living twelve thousand miles away, or died twenty years ago.

Their moods are their methods of control and domination. Others are going to have to learn quickly to distinguish between when Cancerians are displaying the bona fide need we all have to be alone at times, and when they're heading for a serious withdrawal, with all communication cut off behind an invisible force field. It's as if Cancerians expect others to intuitively know why they're upset or angry. But unless they're married to a psychic, they're expecting way too much. Silent brooding or sulking is not the best way to communicate your feelings.

When Cancer holds back from expressing anger and frustrations, the floodgates are inevitably going to burst open at some time. A Cancerian mood often precedes some kind of guerrilla attack. This is the dreaded moment when all those repressed hostilities pour out at once. It's fast and it's furious. When Cancer's emotions explode, you might like to bear in mind that Mike Tyson and Leon Spinks are both "sensitive" Crabs, because you could find yourself confronting your very own Rocky. (Yes, Sly is a Cancer, too.)

Actually, an occasional bout of tears and hysteria brings enormous emotional relief to Cancerians. But while it may be a release for them, the cumulative effects can be ruinous to a long-term relationship. Cancerians seem to regard their displays of temperament as acceptable on the grounds that they were "upset." Maybe they don't think about how deeply they can upset others. They want others to sympathize with them, but how can others sympathize when their own feelings have been torn to shreds?

Too many Cancerian outbursts, too many stored-up resentments, and too many emotional leg traps can feel like a form of slow Chinese water torture. Drip drip drip over the years can leave others wet and cold. It's no one specific incident, no one particular drop of water— but all the incidents, and all the drops together, that can put an end to a Cancer's relationship.

It can come as an awful shock to Cancer if, after twenty-five years of marriage, his or her partner walks. This is exactly what happened to one Cancerian woman we know, a successful gallery owner with everything going for her: children, house, BMW, and a loving Capricorn husband. Or so she thought. Until one evening he quietly, calmly informed her that he'd thought it over carefully and was moving out. Ms. Cancer was stunned. He wasn't running into the arms of another woman. What possible reason could he have for wanting to leave such a comfortable home and loving family?

When Cancer's girlfriend was summoned to the rescue, and the discussion turned to how and why it happened, the reasons came out. "I was a bit hysterical, I suppose. I did go a bit over the top at times. Well, who wouldn't? He's so insensitive!" cried Cancer. Here is a lesson to all Cancerians. It is important to broach any relationship problem directly and honestly. It is also important not to react to every little issue emotionally. Try to be as objective as you can.

Breaking up is hard for anybody, no matter what sign he or she is born under. But many Cancerians go through a personal hell if they ever have to finish a long-term relationship. The emotional wrench from their partner is tough enough, but dismantling their whole material base that they have invested so much of their person in makes it simply all too much to bear. That's why when Cancerians fall in love, they intend it to be for keeps. They are devoted partners who don't call it quits for no good reason. Cancer believes that love takes time, patience, and effort to cultivate. Commitment is about being responsible for the other person, and putting up with the occasional grumble, bad mood, or misunderstanding.

This is what the little prince had to learn before he could return to live happily with his rose. The prince and his rose needed each other. They loved each other. It's really quite simple.

The world's most successful writer of romantic novels, Barbara Cartland (born July 9), taps into this Cancerian ideal. The ideal that true love lasts forever. She concludes every one of her stories with the same lines: "They found love, real love, the kind of love that comes from God. The love that lasts for eternity."

Eternity is a long time for love to last. But if you're a Cancer, or you're in love with a Cancer, you may wonder if eternity is long enough.

THE CANCER PARENT

Mum's the word. The magic word for the Cancer parent.

Holding her little one in her arms, the Cancer mother positively radiates. All that is gentle and heartwarming about motherhood is felt in her heart and shines on her face. At last, she feels, she has arrived. She has joined the club. "This child needs me," thinks Cancer. "We need each other. We are bonded forever."

Cancer parents of both sexes are terribly sentimental. Cancer men are every bit as concerned and involved with the business of child care. They like to fuss. Indeed, many Cancerian fathers are often seen by their children as the "mother" of the family. They are not the type of men who try to evade the chores on the grounds that they don't know how to heat up a bottle, or that they've never gotten the knack of diaper changing. What the Cancer man does already know, he'll make it his business to learn. Why? Because he is genuinely interested.

Single Cancer women, as they get older, become acutely aware that their biological clock is ticking louder and faster. Their desire to have a child is strong, and so is their belief in the traditional family unit. In creating a child, Cancerians create the emotional focal point for the rest of their lives. Their involvement with their children can be so consuming that other important people may tend to be pushed aside, including friends and sometimes even their partner.

Some Cancerian women make motherhood a full-time career. But after the congratulations cards have been pasted in the baby book, the ambitious, career-minded side of Cancer begins to weigh the advantages of returning to the workforce, and maybe leaving baby in the hands of a well-chosen nanny.

Cancerians insist on nothing but the best for their child. No expense will be spared for the apple of their eye. The best education, nice clothes, and a large, comfortable home with room for swings, slides, wading pool, dogs, hamsters, and guinea pigs all cost money. And that's why many find themselves modifying their stance on ideal motherhood. The picture of Mom rushing out the door, clutching briefcase and mobile phone, to make that money is most definitely one image of the Cancerian mother. Quite a few get so hooked on making money, and keeping their career, that they can end up paying lip service to motherhood.

But the majority of Cancerians are the most mindful of parents. They never fail to pick up on coughs and wheezes and are the ones who notice when their child is reluctant to go to school or has lost a bit of his or her bounce. Caring Cancer waste no time in getting a sick child to the doctor, or making an appointment to talk to the teacher. They always remember when the school report is due, and what marks Junior got for mathematics last time. There's little that escapes their attention.

Cancerians protect their young ones fiercely. It may be that their own vulnerabilities lie at the root of the Cancerian tendency to be overprotective. Any remarks about their children's behavior are interpreted as an intrusion into the privacy of the family. Cancerians feel that they, and they alone, should deal with their children. Even legitimate complaints from school or neighbors can be taken as huge personal insults. The Crab's tough protective shell covers a very thin skin. Nowhere is Cancer's possessiveness and protectiveness more evident than in their relationship with their children.

Cancerians believe that they are as dedicated as parents could possibly be. And who would argue that in many ways, they are? Children of Cancer rarely go without anything. They are the children who bathe in the milk of human kindness, who know they are cherished.

Being very possessive of loved ones means that dependency versus independence inevitably emerges as a big issue for the Cancer parent. How do you give your children the loving attention they need, but still give them enough space to develop into mature, independent human beings? A lot of the time, what Cancer parents might think is best for their children isn't necessarily what their children know is best for them. Cancer can be very emotionally dominating. In extreme cases, Cancer mothers and fathers can become so controlling of their children's lives that their children cease to be able to make up their own minds. The truth is that some Cancerians secretly hold on to the notion that dependence is not such a bad thing, after all.

Constant fussing, fretting, and worrying may well be evidence that you love someone. But it can become invasive and tiring for those on the receiving end. Living with—and learning from—a parent who tends to respond emotionally to every little drama is bound to have a long-term effect. Talking calmly and rationally to a child about the dangers of coming home alone, for example, is far more effective than a torrent of tears and wailing.

Children, as they get older, find it excruciatingly embarrassing to be fussed and fretted over in public. Cancer parents may do well to pause before rushing up to the school at the merest suspicion that everything is not perfect. And they may need to stand back if their fifteen-year-old 'child' falls in love with an eighteen-year-old. Especially if that fifteen-year-old is born under a fire or air sign. Try to let them work it out for themselves, Cancer. Learn to pull back a little, and trust that your children won't run away from home and become delinquents or dropouts. Far from it. They will love you all the more for respecting their feelings and acknowledging that they've got their own lives to live.

Few signs can come close to Cancer in creating a warm, loving home environment. Children of Cancerians remember being tucked into bed with their teddy bear. They remember fondly the family picnics and the visits to Grandma.

When they grow up, children of Cancer will be grateful for a parent who was sympathetic to all the knocks and bruises of childhood. The parent who knew the value of cooking their favorite dinner after their school exams. The parents who went to so much trouble to locate the latest toy that all the stores had sold out of, or the rare collectors' album they knew would make the child's birthday a special one.

These are the things that children remember, and it's why, as the years go by, the bond between Cancer parents and their sons and daughters stay so strong..

THE CANCER CHILD

Cancer child. Moon child. There, beaming up at you from the cradle, is the winner of every beautiful baby competition. Cancer babies are positively cherubic. They remind you of the little cupids and cherubim smiling down from the clouds in Renaissance paintings. This is the baby who brings out the cheek pincher in every grandma, the baby your friends will actually beg you to let them mind.

Just the fact of being born under the sign ruled by the Moon is evidence enough of the strong attachment that Cancerian children are going to develop with their mother. The bonds of love that start at the breast will last a lifetime. Cancer is the sign in which the imprint of early maternal conditioning is the deepest. Everything that the mother of a Cancer child does will have a lifelong effect.

Cancer children are very loving and affectionate. They are also deeply sensitive. Much of the same applies to children born with the Moon in Cancer, no matter what their Sun sign. The Sun sign personality will begin to emerge more clearly, as it does for all of us, as we grow out of infancy. But in our earliest years, our Moon sign shines through very strong. The Moon is in its own sign when it's in Cancer. And someone born with a Cancer Moon will display strong Cancerian characteristics throughout life. Moon in Cancer people of all ages are very emotional. In times of stress, there are usually floods of tears and temperamental outbursts.

It's obvious that a child who is so strongly attached to Mother and family is going to need a little extra encouragement to peep over the edge of the nest. Anything that encourages Cancerian children's independence is good because they may be a little reluctant to make those first sorties out from under Mother's skirts, and may need a little extra push in stepping out into the big, wide, unknown world. That is, unless they've got one of the extrovert signs such as Leo, Sagittarius, or Aquarius on the Ascendant.

The Cancerian tendency to fret and worry starts young. If Cancer is given the secure base in life that begins at home, he or she will become one of those Cancerians who is enormously successful in worldly life. But note, this is not a child to be dropped off at summer camp without lots of discussion and reassurance beforehand. Nor a child to be minded by someone he or she doesn't know. Cancerians don't cope well with having independence forced upon them. Parents will need to tread a fine but not impossible line between giving them the warm, safe cocoon that they need and the closed, insular, overprotected existence that they definitely don't need and that will stifle their development.

Mind you, a lot of what the Cancer child needs isn't necessarily what the Cancer child wants, or tries to get. Sweet, sensitive, and cherubic, Cancer may be. But the Cancerian shifts in moods start young, too. Without training and discipline, he or she could easily become the child in the supermarket throwing a temper tantrum because Mother said no to a bag of potato chips. Important advice to parents of Cancer children; Don't give in. Don't let the histrionics embarrass you into grabbing the chips.

Cancer children wrote the book on "parent taming." They've got built-in knowledge of the dynamics of emotional control. Your little angel is taking the first steps in nagging and manipulation. Cancer children can be strong-willed and determined. They're going to grow up to be ambitious people who will want to be liked. So they'll soon learn that being nice gets you a lot further.

Cancer is, by nature, possessive. They cling tightly to people and to places. Too many family upheavals or house moves will unsettle them. Cancerians become terribly attached to their things, too. Signs of covetousness are going to show up as soon as they're old enough to understand what it means to own your own things. "It's mine" might be a phrase parents will need to keep an ear out for. Sharing is an important early lesson for Cancerian children.

Cancerians are equaled only by Taureans in their love of family traditions. Birthdays and Christmas with the whole family give them a wonderful sense of belonging. They love the rituals. When the tree comes out, little Cancer is in heaven. If you reserve for them the special task of putting the star on top, you'll be creating a memory that will never fade. Every year, cards are written, gifts are wrapped, the turkey is roasted, and delicious smells emanate from the kitchen and fill the house. And then, finally, Christmas dinner is served. Oh, joy and bliss. Peace on Earth, and peace at home.

The family table is, for Cancer, the underpinning of a contented life. Parents will never have to worry that their little Cancerian doesn't eat enough. These are not the children who don't have time to eat their lunch at school, or need to be cajoled into finishing what's on their plate. In fact, the opposite usually applies. Cancer children love their food. The only exceptions are likely to be those tense, anxiety-ridden times before exams and school shows when the Cancerian nerves make it impossible for them to keep food down. Cancers, young and old, suffer from butterflies in the tummy.

There is a series of English children's books about a make-believe Cancerian devotee of food called Billy Bunter, the fat schoolboy anti-hero who is notorious for doing absolutely anything to lay his hands on any "interesting comestibles." Somewhere in every one of the Billy Bunter books, Billy screams, "Gimmee!" at the sight of cakes and sticky buns. Yet Billy is beloved by generations of children—and adults—who secretly relate to him. He is, after all, only human. Is Billy Bunter a symbol of the naked, unashamed desire for comfort and gratification you see in the Cancer child? Beware the gimme factor in *your* little Cancer.

One real-life Bunter we know had his whole school talking about his coup at the school fundraiser. Having spied a plate of glorious cupcakes with a price tag of one dollar, seven-year-old Cancer thought, "Bargain!" and promptly handed over his dollar. The woman running the cake stall did not have the heart to tell him that the price of the cakes was one dollar *each*, not one dollar per plate. Not with that little Moon face flushed with anticipation. Half an hour later, Cancer was sighted demolishing the last crumb. Twenty-two cupcakes (yes, twenty-two) is no mean feat. Not even for a Cancer. A tall tale, you may think. But a true one.

Let the story of the cupcake kid be a lesson to parents of Cancer that healthy eating habits are created young. You don't want to produce a classic case of the plump Cancer child who becomes the plump Cancer adult. Remember, childhood conditioning means everything to a Cancer, and that's why many Cancers carry food hang-ups through life.

Teach your Cancerian to eat slowly and to stop when they're full. Tell them about how it takes twenty minutes for the stomach to fill up. Otherwise, you could have a little Cancer cherub flapping his or her angel wings in vain, trying to get off the ground.

Cancer is such a family-oriented individual that they don't so much fly the nest as extend the nest. A Cancer son or daughter is unlikely to emigrate to Tasmania, or anywhere so far away that it will prevent family get-togethers. Why would they when the most important things in life are close to home? Like Mother's kitchen, and that unforgettable smell of roast turkey. And, of course, the thought of one day lifting up their own little angel to put the star on top of the Christmas tree.

BORN UNDER CANCER

Louis Armstrong	Henry Thoreau
Pamela Lee	Dave Allen
King Henry VIII	Colin Wilson
Sir Edmund Hillary	Elisabeth Kübler-Ross
Tom Hanks	Frida Kahlo
Robert the Bruce	Pierre Cardin
Sir Edward Elgar	Marcel Proust
Harrison Ford	Lord Louis Mountbatten
O. J. Simpson	Ken Russell
Kathy Bates	Emmeline Pankhurst
Canada	Ernest Hemingway
New Zealand	Dennis Lillee
Franz Kafka	James Cagney
Homer Simpson	Nancy Reagan
Carl Lewis	Donald Sutherland
Ringo Starr	Kenneth Clark
The Sultan of Brunei	Edgar Degas
Antonio Gaudí	Rembrandt van Rijn
Edward, Duke of Windsor	Winnie the Pooh
Ross Perot	Courtney Love

LEO

July 24–August 23

♌

Ruling Planet

SUN

Effectiveness of assertion is the alpha
and omega of style.

George Bernard Shaw—born July 26

THE LEO NATURE

It is the source of light and heat, and the giver of all life. It is the Sun, the star at the center of our solar system.

In astrology the Sun rules the sign of Leo. And like their ruling star, Leos shine. The star of the zodiac exudes a natural warmth and radiance that draws people in, like moths to a flame.

When you call someone a star, you think of him or her as someone with presence. Someone whose impact can't be explained by looks or talent alone. You know it has a lot to do with force of personality, but there's still something extra that's hard to define. Call someone a "star" and everyone knows what you mean.

Even ordinary Leos (mind you, that's a contradiction in terms— Leos would never consider themselves ordinary) have their own measure of star quality. It shines especially bright in those off-duty times when people get together to have fun and enjoy themselves. Leo can turn an everyday event into a happening. Whether you're meeting your Leo friend for a coffee, or catching the bus together to go to work, a rendezvous with Leo is always a memorable moment in the day. One thing is certain; Leos are impossible to ignore.

This is the Leo style. It's not glamorous (although many Leos are very glamorous), and it's not presentation, because there are lots of unkempt bohemian Leos who've still got style. Nor is it dependent on fashion. If it were, anybody who wears designer labels would have style. You can't teach it and you can't buy it. Style is an individual thing that comes from within. It starts with attitude. And Leos have got that attitude. Style, as George Bernard Shaw said, is asserting yourself effectively. Anyone can assert him or herself, but only those who are effective have got style wrapped up. From alpha to omega, from A to Z.

Unfortunately, it's sometimes hard to define the difference between asserting yourself effectively and hogging the limelight. Leos can come across as so self-assured, so confident and assertive, that some people are bound to think they're just arrogant, dominating, and opinionated. And yes, most Leos *are* all these things, at least some of the time. It's not too hard for Leos to overwhelm, or even intimidate, the merely human with the force of their personality. Most people feel warmed by the rays of the Sun, but there are some who get burnt.

In all cultures, the Sun is a dynamic, life-affirming principle. It's the yang of yin and yang, the active, positive, and energizing force. Everything revolves around the Sun: the Earth, the Moon, and all the other planets. For thousands of years the Sun has been associated with kings and rulers. In ancient Egypt it was worshiped as the god Ra, and the pharaohs were hailed as the sons and daughters of the Sun.

The symbol for the sign of kings is The Lion, the king of the beasts. His impressive mane sets him apart from the other big cats and makes him appear even more grand and imposing than he really is. The astrologer's shorthand, or glyph, for Leo is the sweep of The Lion's mane. Some say it's the kink of the Lion's tail, complete with the little tuft of fur at the end.

The mane of the human lion is a very important part of the royal regalia. Leos spend an inordinate proportion of their grooming time on their hair. A bad hair day for a Lion could mean a cancel-everything week while they find a new hairdresser and get their hair, and their ego, back in shape. The male of the species often sports a beard and identifies so strongly with his facial hair that he comes close to developing a Samson complex. Oh, to see the king of the beasts practicing the art of facial topiary, snipping and shaping his beard and mustache. This may be your first little insight into the vanity of the Lion. Leos are very proud and terribly conscious of the image they cut.

Royal coats of arms are adorned with lions, and the sign of The

Lion is always strong in the horoscopes of royalty. Have you ever noticed that coronations, royal weddings, and presidential inaugurations take place at noon? At noon the Sun is at the zenith where it shines down on the event from the highest point in the sky. It's no secret that royalty—and presidents—have long sought the counsel of astrologers, who advise that this is the most auspicious hour to be crowned or wed. If you want a reign or a marriage that brings the blessings of the Sun, including success, glory, and acclaim, book the cathedral for twelve noon. If you want your new restaurant, shop, or any new venture to have a built-in success factor, sign on the dotted line or open the doors at noon.

Every Lion has a regal manner when it's called for and a taste for a touch of pomp and ceremony. They love opportunities for display and ostentation. Gala occasions are few and far between these days. More's the pity for Leos, because from time to time they need to dress to the nines, head for the swankiest venue in town, and have a ball. It was those ancient royals who invented the banquet. Leos can be wonderfully baroque. Their taste for grandeur is rivaled by none, and can reach operatic proportions.

Perhaps their appetite for the full and rich life stems from the fact that Leo is a "high summer" sign. They're born at the time of year when everything is lush and full, the fruit is dripping from the trees, and the grain is heavy on the stalk.

Pleasure, creativity, and romantic love are all ruled by the sign of Leo. As the second fire sign, Leo has been handed the torch from Aries and continues to run with the same fiery qualities of passion, idealism, and desire for personal achievement and recognition. Leo inherits its energy, high spirits, forthrightness, and extroverted nature from Aries. The Lion's journey is a heroic quest like the Ram's. Both feel compelled to make their mark and create something in their own right. But Aries is more of a Lone Ranger, more overtly competitive and aggressive. Leo is no less ambitious or driven than Aries, but Leo is destined to develop his or her individuality in relation to other people. For Aries, approval comes ultimately from themselves, whereas The Lion is more dependent on approval—sometimes, it seems, even adulation—from others.

Generous of spirit, mind, and purse, they despise anything petty, mean, small, narrow, or dreary. Unaspiring, unimaginative, limited people are incomprehensible to Leo.

In the wheel of the zodiac, Leo, the sign of the Sun, follows Cancer, the sign of the Moon. The first Sun god of Greek mythology was Helios, who drove his golden chariot across the sky from dawn to dusk. But when the Olympian gods ruled the world, the beautiful and talented Apollo became identified with the Sun. Apollo was the twin brother of Artemis, the Moon. He was the second-born. Sun follows Moon. Leo follows Cancer. There are sound astrological and psychological reasons why this is so. Cancer is drawn back to the past. Leo looks to the future. Cancerians are inclined to act unconsciously; they're strongly informed by their childhood conditioning. Home, family, where you come from, and who you belong to is a very large part of who they are, and color the decisions they make in their lives.

But it is Leos' destiny to step away from the conditioning of their past in pursuit of a more independent life. Most Leos can't wait to grow up and assume responsibility for themselves. As they mature, they make the very conscious decision that they're not going to be held back by any hang-ups from the past that will prevent them from becoming an individual in their own right. When they take this forward-looking stance, they discover that the potentials of life open up before them.

Leos believe in the power of the individual. And they figure that no one can become an individual or break free from the ties that bind without developing strength of will. Or without hope as a guiding light. Will and hope, Leo has in abundance. In fact *will* and *hope* are key Leo words.

Our will is shaped largely by our fathers, and always there's an important issue with father in the life of a Leo. Just as mother is the stronger influence for Cancer, father is the parent who dominates the psyche of young Leo. Connected to their father is Leos' drive to prove themselves. Of course, there are as many variations on this theme as there are Leos. Some Leos have great respect for their fathers. But there are just as many for whom respect is mixed with a cool ambivalence. Perhaps father was unencouraging at a critical time or ignored the aspirations of their Leo son or daughter. Maybe father had unreasonable expectations. Whatever the cause, the result is that many Leos are critical of their father and feel that he has no reasonable claim on the loyalty he demands. Loyalty and trust are big issues for Leo.

You hear many stories of Leos working their way through college, intent on pursuing the career of *their* choice, not their fathers'. Or even a Leo who elopes with the love their father disapproves of. It's a hard psychological knock, but it can be instrumental in pushing Leo out onto a path of independence. Whatever the details of the scenario, the building of the strong Leo will has begun. And the foundations have been laid for the Leo belief in self-reliance.

There is an episode in the story of Apollo that is about making a conscious break from your past in order to fulfill your destiny as an independent individual.

In ancient Greece the people of Delphi lived in terror of a large female serpent called the Python. Apollo became hero of the day when he freed the people from the Python by shooting it with an arrow. The Python is the symbol of the power of the unconscious mind, the strangulation of the present and future by one's past. We all sense that we've got to kill off the Python if we're going to move forward. But this is something that Leos *know* they must do because once the Python is slain, it no longer has the power to rule or terrorize.

Yet none of us can kill off the python of our past completely. Because it has a powerful force, it must be respected and allowed to live on in some way. After Apollo had slain the Python, he erected a temple over its lair on Mount Delphi to be tended by a priestess called the Pythoness or the Delphic Oracle. In this way Apollo was acknowledging, as Leos must, that the way to move forward is not to deny our past, but to deal with it and put it in its correct place.

"There is no coming to consciousness without pain," said psychoanalyst C. G. Jung (born July 26). Becoming an individual in one's own right and achieving self-realization is the essence of Leo. And it was at the core of Jung's work.

When Leos clear the way for an independent, mature life, their self-confidence blooms and the true force of their personality shines through. They have prepared the ground for living a creative life in the broader sense of the word. Leo is the sign that rules creativity and self-expression. Few signs (Capricorn and Scorpio are probably the exceptions) are so admiring of the self-made man, or people who have the creative imagination to make something more of themselves, and who strive to be successful in their own right.

Who better to guide you to living a creative life than the most civilized and cultivated of the gods, Apollo, who rules the arts, music, self-expression, pleasure (not to mention divination and medicine)—in short, the god who was the all around golden boy of Olympus.

The Sun is the focal point in any horoscope. The Moon and all the planets have an important function, but the first thing that astrologers always look to when they begin to analyze a horoscope is the Sun. The Sun and the aspects made to it from the other planets show the individual's capacity for self-realization in the outer world. When you understand the significance of the Sun, you understand better the meaning of Leo.

As interested as they are in the arts and as admiring as they are of artists, being born under the sign of Leo doesn't mean that every Lion is destined to paint, write, sing, or become an actor. Creativity in its true sense is an act of self-assertion, of impressing yourself as

an individual on your world and creating something—anything—
that can be attributed to you. It *could* be painting a picture, writing
a song, designing a dress, or going onstage. But it could equally be
staging a wonderful dinner, inventing a new game for the children,
or knitting a wildly challenging sweater. It could also be creating a
business. Leos are famous for their organizational and managerial
skills. When a new department or a new branch of the company is
planned, call in Leo. The place will soon be humming with the bustle
and friendly enthusiasm that Leo generates so well.

Part of the Leo creativity is simply living a life with style. Some
Leos become famous for that alone. The name of Jackie Kennedy
Onassis is still synonymous with style. Regal Leonine Jackie was
America's answer to royalty. Her signature style of Chanel suits,
pillbox hats, and dark glasses was copied everywhere, proof that
imitation is the sincerest form of flattery. A friend of Jackie's once
said she gave him the best advice he'd ever had when she told him,
"Just make sure you keep your hair cut and your weight down."

Jackie made *herself* her own creation, the Jackie O style. Some
would say that her friend and fellow Leo, Andy Warhol, did the
same in his own inimitable way. Whether Warhol will eventually be
remembered more for being Warhol, or for his pictures of cans of
soup, remains to be seen.

Asserting yourself, attempting to do something genuinely creative,
and aiming for the stars obviously involve putting yourself—and
your ego—on the line. But Leos will do just that. They're courageous
and they're bold. And more important, they're prepared to work
very hard to get there.

They soon learn, however, that not everyone will applaud their
efforts. There will always be people waiting to trip them up and pull
them down. The openly ambitious Leo quickly discovers the "de-
tractor factor." So often is Leo admired. But adulation also spawns
envy. In fact, some Leos positively seem to invite enemies by the
strength of their personality, the size of their ego, and the Olympian
scale of their ambitions. Leo superstar Madonna (born August 16)
said, "I will never get used to the hostility that comes from fear and
envy. That basic human desire that most people have to see another
person fail."

Does Leo deserve this? Is this antagonism the product of those
small, mean minds and cold hearts that Leos despise so much? Does
it come from people who are not prepared to put in the hours and
the energy that making your own success often demands? Whatever
Madonna's critics might say about her, no one could deny that she
works hard.

Hard work is not a dirty word to The Lion. Far from it. This is definitely not a person who expects something for nothing. Leos are among the hardest workers of the zodiac. On one condition, that is. That they love the work they do. Leos cannot be content with just a "job." They cannot separate who they are from what they do. A boring job with no scope for self-expression and limited potential (even if it pays well) can destroy the Leo soul. Leos are idealistic; they need to believe in what they're doing.

They also need in some way to be running the show. Leo is too commanding a personality to be an underling for long. Leos who know their nature know they need a large measure of autonomy and authority. They like to manage, they do not like being managed or closely supervised. In short, Leo wants to be the boss. Or at least wants to have someone they can boss around. Even if it's the boss.

An important ingredient in Leo success stories is the fact that Leo is a fixed sign. The passion, energy, and idealism of fiery Leo are what create the ambition and the drive, but being fixed as well makes Leo the most centered and stable of the fire signs. Like the other fixed signs, Taurus, Scorpio, and Aquarius, Leo has the determination to hang in there and see jobs through to the end. Being both fixed and fiery gives Leo the astrological credentials to maintain a grueling pace for protracted periods with humor and dedication. Passion plus perseverance is a pretty fantastic formula for success. So long as their hope and their vision of what their hard work is leading to stay burning, Leos will work twelve hours a day for months on end if that's what it takes. Their tough persistence is often why they achieve while others who are equally talented don't.

Once Leos have given their word, they will move heaven and earth to deliver, especially if their reputation is at stake, and more especially if others depend on them. There's a great sense of noblesse oblige about the sign of kings. The life of T. E. Lawrence, the "uncrowned King of Arabia," is one such Leo story of loyalty, commitment, pride, and idealism. Could the passage from unassuming Oxford scholar to soldier organizing the desert Arabs into a victorious army have been made by anyone other than a Leo? The popular image of Lawrence as a proud noble figure in flowing white robes sitting atop a camel, or making a sweeping entrance into a room full of the important and powerful, is somewhat assisted by Peter O'Toole as Lawrence in the movie *Lawrence of Arabia*. In spite of differences in physical appearance (Lawrence was five foot two), O'Toole carried off the role wonderfully. He's a Leo too. (This sort of synchronicity happens so often.) When politicians in distant lands prevented Lawrence from honoring his pledge to install Faisal, his brother-in-arms, as king of Arabia, Lawrence took it as a personal betrayal and a deep wound to his pride. He had given his word, and that means everything to a Leo. All Leos have at times been too trusting and too idealistic, even naive. It's simply not in their nature to be devious or double-dealing.

We are all capable of going to extremes in our own Sun sign way. The Leo extreme is an obsessive pursuit of glory. All fixed signs can push determination to obsession. And all fire signs can fan their flames into a burning desire to get what they want at any cost. But pride is often the final catalyst in a Lion's undoing. If Leo is motivated by the sort of overweening pride and glory seeking that was regarded by the ancient Greeks as such as serious failing that they gave it a name of its own—*hubris*—then he or she can become the most arrogant of beasts. Somewhere on the extreme dark edge of the Leo nature lies megalomania.

There are times when others are quite justified in accusing Leos of suffering from a Napoleon complex. It's entirely appropriate considering Napoleon was a Leo. His armies may have marched under the banner of republicanism and the brotherhood of man, but Napoleon was no democrat. When it was deemed to be politically convenient, he jumped at the suggestion of becoming emperor and even arranged to be crowned by the pope in the Cathedral of Notre Dame so that his coronation would be more splendid than that of the kings of France. Just as the pope was lifting the crown over his head, Napoleon seized hold of it and crowned himself. Could this be the ultimate historical image of Leo megalomania? As Napoleon himself said, "From the sublime to the ridiculous, there is only one step." Napoleon was one of those Leos who pushed pride and glory too far, and met his Waterloo. Believing that their strength of will and their right to rule are all they need to overcome any opposition can be Leos' greatest error.

History records a long list of Leo dictators: Fidel Castro, Benito Mussolini, Simon Bolivar, et al. Even your everyday Leo can turn into a small-time dictator—though they would prefer to think of themselves as a benevolent dictator. When they're being pushy and domineering it's because they know what's best for themselves—and everyone else. It's all in a good cause, so that makes it all right. People are often willing to let Leo play this role because they *are* so brilliant at organizing everything (and everyone) around them. And anyway, who's going to be bothered putting up a fight against such a force? So many times, friends, partners, and colleagues find it easier to take the line of least resistance, and just laugh the whole thing off as another little Napoleonic episode.

But when Leos sweep everyone else up in their wave of enthusiasm, and expects them to play the supporting roles to their obsession, it can lead to problems. All fire signs are risk takers. They're easily lured by the promise of big returns. Leo's success rating is high, but not all Leo ventures succeed all of the time. Some Leos can take a lot of people down with them in battles that are doomed to fail. Leos can dangerously overestimate their potential and blindly believe that their will is strong enough to achieve anything they set their sights on. There are plenty of Leos who, like Icarus, flew too close to the Sun.

It's all very admirable to want to achieve and aim for the top, provided you remain in touch with reason and what can reasonably be done. Astrologers hear many stories from partners, friends, and colleagues of Leos who were expected to wait in the wings while their Leo lived out his or her passions.

The weaknesses of each sign are always illuminated by its opposite sign. And for Leo, that's Aquarius. Where Leo is strongly individual-oriented, Aquarius is more group-oriented. Aquarians aim to get along with others on an egalitarian and democratic basis. Moreover, Aquarius is an impersonal air sign, and finds it easier to detach emotionally and look at a situation in a more cool and objective manner than Leo.

If Leos can draw on some Aquarian detachment, if they can consciously put a little more space between themselves and the object of their passions, then reason can reign and they'll find they're not beleaguered by great (and sometimes unreal) expectations.

Noble and positive Leos are very aware of the need to cool their passions, step back occasionally, and review their goals. They're also aware—sometimes too aware, at their own expense—of their responsibilities to others. Personal satisfaction is very important to Leo. But Leo is a spiritually generous sign. At their best, they're magnanimous and are genuinely keen to share the rewards that come from their hard work.

So how does this Leo capacity for hard work sit with their reputation for laziness? You may have read about how Leos like to wallow in self-indulgence and spoil themselves rotten. Is it all untrue? No. There are interesting contradictions in every sign, and this is Leo's. The truth of the matter is, they can be both workaholics *and* dedicated decadents.

Since the pleasure principle comes under the rulership of Leo, when Leos say "enjoy," it's not just a formula, they mean *enjoy*. It's why so many Leos actually work in the pleasure and leisure industries.

When they feel the need for a bit of creative self-indulgence, they'll shop for all their favorite treats in preparation for a day of almost total immobility spent reclining in a fluffy bathrobe on the couch with smoked salmon, chocolates, champagne, and a pile of magazines all at arm's reach, blissfully tuned out to the medical warnings about the dire effects of high cholesterol and inertia. It's called luxury. And Leos need regular doses of it, believing as they do in its therapeutic effects. The first person to say, "Peel me a grape" must have been a Leo.

If there's some spare cash, Leos may choose to do their indulging in lavish surrounds. A day at the local "sanctuary" being pedicured and pampered into an altered state of consciousness, or booking themselves into a ten-star hotel just around the corner to be waited on hand and foot, sleep in till noon, and loll around in their whirlpool—if only for the weekend—is not something that Leos will torture themselves to justify. As they see it, they've earned it, they're paying for it, so they're entitled to it. And who could disagree with that?

The laid-back Lion takes some beating. Even a Pisces would have trouble rivaling Leo's taste for total self-indulgence. But don't think that when Leos are doing absolutely nothing, they're achieving nothing. A lot of Leos (and Pisces for that matter) claim to be at their most creative when they're horizontal. One of the most industrious Leos, Henry Ford, said, "Exercise is bunk. If you're healthy, you don't need it. If you are sick, you shouldn't take it." He understood that being both idle and hardworking is no contradiction, at least not for Leo.

Leo aims to lead a civilized life, and wants to experience all that a civilized society has to offer: art, theater, beautiful clothes, adornments, comfort, fine food, and wine. Especially wine. A good meal without a good claret is not an entirely civilized occasion as far as The Lion is concerned. And a good meal with far too much good claret is a common method of Leo transcendence.

Leo figured out early that the 1980s ethos of working hard and playing hard is a nonsense. How can it be "play" if it's hard? Now, there's a contradiction in terms if ever there was one, thinks Leo. The fact that people spend their leisure time at the gym "working out" implies it's not something they do for fun. And having fun is something that Leo excels at.

Indeed, the Leo sense of fun is one of the positive sides of this Sun sign that's always mentioned but rarely given its due credit. The Leo understanding of the importance of pleasure and play has much to offer to counter the current fad that play is something you have to work at. Sure, they're often described as the life and soul of the party, but Leos know that playing and having fun go deeper than just dressing up, spending money, and partying all night. In an age when stress has become the demon in our lives, Leo has an instinct for knowing when kicking up your heels and letting loose is the best medicine.

Dancing round the den because you feel like it, having a swing in the playground on your way to the shops, or singing along to the car radio (and who cares what other drivers think) can be an incredibly healing force—precisely because it serves no purpose except that it is fun. Fun is something you have when there is no pressure to perform or compete, and that in itself would be enough to qualify play as time well spent. Yet play does actually have a purpose. It's a precursor to self-expression. We even talk about "playing around" with ideas to see what comes up, and we know that children who don't play enough don't grow up to realize their full creative potential. Adults who think that you need an excuse to play are short-changing themselves on happiness and strangling their creativity and originality. The important thing about play is to think of it not as achieving anything, but rather as something you do for its own sake because it makes you feel good. Leos know that play has a lot to do with freedom. And Leo, The Lion, was born to be free.

Childish? No. Rather, child*like*. Children also come under the rulership of Leo. Certainly Leos, with their warm, affectionate, and playful nature, seem to have an easy rapport with children.

Like a child, theatrical Leo is not afraid to play the buffoon. Wacky redhead Lucille Ball was uninhibited about playing the fool, and *everyone* loved Lucy. Steve Martin is another Leo who makes being crazy so entertaining. Leos love to poke fun at self-consciously earnest and serious types. Being silly from time to time shakes up the neurons and inspires the creative thought that helps you think and act independently. And it's the people who can think creatively and act independently who will be less likely to get swallowed up in our conformist corporatized computerized society.

The value of original thinking is likely to become an increasingly important issue in the high-tech world of the new millennium. Neptune, the planetary indicator of trends in human affairs, enters Aquarius in 1998, and continues to highlight the Aquarian influence up to 2012. Much is written about the Aquarian connection with humanity and the brotherhood of man. Yet Aquarius is an intellectual sign with a scientific bent. And in the immediate future we're going to witness an explosion in all forms of technology, computerization, and robotics.

But as we know, every sign of the zodiac can only operate at its best if it reconciles itself with the principles of its opposite sign. Aquarius, you recall, opposes Leo. There will come a time in the near future when the forces of Leo will rise to the fore to balance off the Aquarian thrust. What backlash can we expect?

The principles of Leo will act as an antidote to the excesses of the Aquarian influence that our world has just stepped into. The Aquarian individual can too easily accept the impersonal group mind-set. Leo, we know, doesn't run with the pack. Leo stands for the power of the strong, self-willed individual.

It's curious that at the beginning of this Aquarian episode in global history came the relaunching of a film that deals with the theme of the machine versus man, the power of the group versus the spirit of the individual. And, of course, the eternal theme of the battle between good and evil.

Luke Skywalker is the young, idealistic hero of the film *Star Wars*. The moment Skywalker receives the telepathic message from his mentor Ben Kenobi is a triumph of the Leo ideals. Fighting a life-and-death battle that he clearly cannot win by technological means, he is told, "Turn off your computer and trust your feelings." At this point Skywalker assumes his true power by having faith in himself as an individual—something that a machine cannot do. In the end Skywalker wins, not with strength of numbers or the aid of computers, but with goodness as his motivating force, and strength of will as his weapon.

To every Lion on Earth who seeks the freedom and satisfaction of a creative life way beyond an "ordinary" existence, the message is clear. May the force be with you.

THE LEO CAREER AND DIRECTION

get your name in LIGHTS
get it up there in
8 ½ x 11 mimeo

Leo, above all else, wants recognition. The Leo Corp., Leo & Sons, or Starring Leo all sound good to the Leo ego. And yes, they'd like to get their name up in lights, as Leo poet Charles Bukowski said, but Leos will be happy so long as they're doing something they can pour their heart into, something they really love.

Leo is not one to plod on in a safe, routine job for long. Indeed, it's not at all advisable. The caged Lion becomes restless and tetchy. The Lion needs to be able to roam free and fulfill the Leo urge to create something out of nothing.

As the sign of personal creativity and self-expression, the most satisfying thing Leos can do, careerwise, is in some sense give birth to their own baby. Nothing makes proud Lions prouder than seeing what they have created from their own talent, hard work, and determination.

Leos don't expect financial support from their family or wait for parental approval. They're quite prepared to make their own way in life. One enterprising young Leo woman we know told us how she was cross questioned by her family when she was packing to depart for the big city to set up her own hairdressing salon. "Why would you want to go when you can get a good job here and save yourself a lot of hard work and trouble?" asked her grandmother. "Because I want more," replied Leo. Now, two years later, she owns her own salon and is planning to open a beauty clinic. "I would never have forgiven myself if I hadn't tried," is something you often hear Leos say, regardless of whether their ventures work out or not. Lots of small-time players aspire to becoming big-time players. Leos don't just dream about it, they do their utmost to make it happen.

The Lion is greatly helped in his or her ambitions by being born under a fixed sign. They're willing to shoulder a very heavy workload for long periods if that's what it takes to get what they want. Fire gives them their energy and enthusiasm. And the fixed quality of Leo makes them capable of intense prolonged focus.

Few signs have such staying power. And there are few with such fabulous organizational skills. Leos are natural-born managers. They're brilliant at getting a system, an office, or a team up and running . . . and keeping them up and running. Born to rule, leadership fits The Lion like a long velvet glove.

The king of beasts want to be the boss. Giving directions and getting people organized come naturally. On the whole, it is the Leo calling to lead, not follow.

Nevertheless, Leos are very capable of working with great devotion for somebody else on the proviso that it's somebody they respect and admire. Having said that, Leos must still have opportunities for autonomous decision making and organization. They can make excellent personal assistants, for example. All the better if there's a touch of glamour and prestige attached to the job. A big name helps, too. Working as the right-hand man or woman to an important and powerful person is definitely a Leo type of job. Though there are sure to be times when the boss will turn to Leo and ask, "Who's the boss?"

When Leo is at the helm, people are happy to take orders from someone so friendly and approachable. The Lion leads by example. They themselves are indefatigable, and their passion for the job is catching. Leo lives by the principle that respect goes both ways. They are always accommodating of individual needs and idiosyncrasies, provided they know that employees are committed and hardworking. Leo bosses are not clock watchers. So an occasional long lunch may not even get a mention provided Leo knows that you come up with the goods. If you need extra time off to recover from a bad bout of the flu, Leo will be the very soul of kindness and understanding. Mind you, he or she will probably courier you the unfinished reports on your desk so you can work on them in bed. Loyalty is everything to a Leo. And anyone who is deemed deficient in loyalty could soon find themselves looking for another job.

The Leo belief in the divine right of kings is matched by their sense of noblesse oblige. If it weren't, they would never get away with their dominating ways and occasional displays of arrogance which, by the way, they never feel they need to apologize for. Leos have high standards and expect total professionalism. They loathe mediocrity and second-rate performances. Sycophants, hypocrites, fumblers, inadequates, and anyone who beats around the bush can drive Leo to new heights of despotism. The benevolent dictator can be horribly patronizing and critical of those of their subjects who can't get it together. And the little Napoleon lurking in every Leo is bound to make an appearance from time to time.

The often dictatorial Lion actually has a strong social conscience, and is passionate about politics and social justice. They love to instigate a hot political debate, and are keenly interested in who's pulling the strings in politics, which policies are not working, and what should be done to change things.

In the lion's den of politics and public life, Leo is as comfortable and at ease as Daniel. It's not only their warmth and their presence that make them such a drawcard, it's their finely tuned sense of decorum and protocol. Leo is never awkward in any social situation. They'll look you straight in the eye and never flub their lines. Exactly the kind of people skills needed for the highest levels of leadership.

Leo Bill Clinton (born August 19) has Libra on the Ascendant. (The combination of Leo Sun and Libra Ascendant is a successful one for politics and business.) There are moments when President Clinton looks and sounds very much like a Libra. Libra is the sign of reconciliation and cooperation symbolized by the scales of justice. Clinton's pledge in his 1996 inaugural speech was to reconcile the racial divisions in America. Only time and history will tell whether the president with the pleasing, cooperative image will be remembered for social reform. But in spite of his Libra Ascendant, there's no mistaking his Leo Sun sign shining through in these words from his inaugural address: "America demands and deserves big things from us, and nothing big ever came from being small." The president in office at the end of the twentieth century is an unabashed idealist, making his bid for Leo greatness at a time when the world is looking for inspiration from its leaders.

Leo leaders *are* inspiring. Whether as president of the United States or president of the local PTA, the combination of high ideals and personal charisma is a winning one. Others may be equally capable, but much of Leo's success comes from the ability to project a larger-than-life personality.

The rays of the Sun cast light on everything it shines down on. In fact, people born under any sign who have the Sun in a dominating position in their birth chart radiate a noticeable extra force of personality. If you were born at dawn, your Sun is very strong because it falls on your Ascendant. It's as if you are a surrogate Leo. You belong to that special group of naturally forceful people who were born at the time of day when the first rays of the Sun light up the horizon. People often think of you as someone with that Leo star quality.

Many movie stars have the sign of Leo prominent in their horoscopes. Moon in Leo is particularly common: Elizabeth Taylor, Barbra Streisand, and Judy Garland all have it. Film is an industry that satisfies many of the Leo needs—creativity, the glamour of show biz, and the possibility of recognition, glory, and rewards. There is no bigger stage on which Leo can perform.

You can't imagine a Leo ever saying, "I wouldn't know what I'd do with a hundred million." Leo the manager would manage it well. Leo the big spender would have no trouble spending it. Leo Mae West once said, "I've been rich and I've been poor, but rich is better." It sounds like something that other Leo grande dame, Madonna, would have said if Miss West hadn't said it first. Still, the latter-day star did say, "I won't be happy until I'm as famous as God." That's a heck of a lot bigger than 8 ½ x 11 mimeo.

The Leo touch has turned many a filmmaker into a movie mogul. In fact, "movie mogul" is practically a Leo title by definition. Frankly, it's impossible for a Leo production to be too big. A Cecil B. De Mille epic is still a metaphor for anything larger than life. Let's just say the image of Moses in the guise of Charlton Heston descending the mountain bearing the Ten Commandments is about as Leo as a Leo production can get. De Mille could not have been born under any other sign. Also born under the sign of The Lion are Dino De Laurentiis, Jack L. Warner, Robert Redford, Dustin Hoffman, and Arnold Schwarzenegger. And Alfred Hitchcock, who always made a cameo appearance in his movies. Such a talent behind the camera couldn't resist turning the lights on himself, if only for a split second. Last but not least, Samuel Goldwyn and the roaring MGM lion. Coincidence?

If there's no production that's too big for Leo, then there's no job too glamorous either. It might not be going too far to say that a horoscope without a strong Leo input can never really attain true glamour. Fashion icon Coco Chanel was a Leo (complete with the Leo arrogance and sense of superiority). She is reputed to have said of fellow Leo Yves Saint-Laurent, "Saint-Laurent has excellent taste. The more he copies me, the better taste he displays."

It's only natural that many Leos gravitate towards fields providing luxury and indulgence. Fashion itself attracts many. They design, they manufacture, and they open boutiques. Hair design, makeup, and perfume—just about anything that makes people look good and feel good—are all Leo vocations. Astrologers believe, incidentally, that France is also ruled by the sign of The Lion. The country that raised fashion and food to the status of pure art and called them *haute* couture and *haute* cuisine certainly fits the Leo profile.

The pleasures and theater of the table are Leo territory. Fine foods and wine scarcely fall into the luxury category for Leos. More like basic requisites for living. You could say Leo has a very "French" attitude towards food and wine. It would be a miserable life indeed without a well-cooked, well-presented meal accompanied by a bottle of the best red—preferably two. Have we mentioned Leo's particular fondness for the grape?

You see, with Leo, luxury is more than a way of life. It's a philosophy. *Everything* must be presented and savored in the right context, as a whole package. The food must be fabulous and so must the decor. The ballgown must be a work of art, and you can't arrive at the ball in anything less than a limousine. The holiday must be exciting and you should travel with only the best line of luggage. It all comes back to style. "Life itself is the proper binge," said American chef Julia Child. A Leo, of course.

The convivial, genial Lion is a natural host. It's a role that brings out the performer in every Leo. You'll find plenty working in hotels and restaurants. But don't expect to find them running a fast-food outlet, a drive-through sandwich shack, or a backpackers' hostel. Their taste is for the lavish, never just the basics. The challenge of renting a bare concrete floor and four walls and turning it into a "venue" spurs Leo into action. They'll soon be proudly serving the best arabica coffee with the best *tarte à la fraise* in town, and adorning the walls with the work of local artists.

Anything that provides leisure and pleasure is Leo ground. At one level, the impresario is a classic Leo image. But there are a lot more Leos running chic bars and managing bands.

Jobs in which they play center stage themselves are perfect for Leos. It could be product promotions, job training, lecturing, or public relations. Being a natural performer is one reason Leo is a sign attracted to teaching. Their idealism is another. Leo teachers are not afraid to show their students that they have strong opinions. Life is there to be seized, to be enjoyed, and the way in which Leos encourage their students to make use of their talents always leaves its mark. The Leo classroom is never a dull, dry, or boring place. Their sense of fun, their enthusiasm, and a gift for theater ensure that. Years later, Leo teachers are remembered by their ex-students as inspiring role models.

Leo is a gambler by nature. And we're not talking about blackjack or roulette. We mean stocks and bonds, futures and commodities, the money markets, and big-time wheeling and dealing. Speculation of all sorts comes under the Leo banner. But there are bound to be times when Leo's boldness turns out in retrospect to be a foolish excess of self-confidence. Their "I can do anything" attitude can leave them dreadfully burnt.

Combine that boldness with their trusting nature, and you can see how easy it is for Leos to get ripped off. The gambler in Leo can be seduced by what promises to be an exciting venture. They can't resist the magic combination of a business that is creative and clever and dangles a multidollar carrot in front of them. Many Leos have got themselves into the classic Leo bind of sinking themselves so deeply into a business venture that they find it hard to give up when the writing on the wall reads "Get out now, it's not working."

Fixed signs are fantastic at maintaining focus and hanging in there when tenacity and determination are necessary. But when things aren't working out, they're not so good at being able to pull out and look at new prospects if that's what will save the day. Obsession can sometimes grip all the fixed signs in a state of immobility. Add the Leo pride to the equation and it all makes for a potentially disastrous scenario.

Forcing an issue way beyond the point where it should be forced—no matter how strong, determined, and able they are—can lead some Leos to their personal undoing. And it's even more destructive if that obsession takes other people down, too.

There's a story about proud, willful obsession and its terrible consequences that could be read as a Leo object lesson. Herman Melville, the author of *Moby Dick*, was born under the sign of Leo, and Captain Ahab, the hunter of the great white whale, is a character who had fallen into this negative Leo mode. You remember how Ahab had lost his leg in the hunt for Moby Dick and had set out across the seas in a maelstrom of pride, fury, and obsession in search of the whale. When they sighted it, the voice of reason finally came from Starbuck, the chief mate, who pleaded with Ahab to give up the impossible: "Vengeance on a dumb brute! that simply smote thee from blindest instinct! Madness!" But, of course, Ahab was mad.

Mad with the idea that his will was strong enough to do anything. Ahab could not relent. He could not bear the idea of giving up, and in his downfall he dragged a crew of innocent men down with him.

Moby Dick is, of course, a very dark tale. But even ordinary, perfectly reasonable Leos discover that pride so often comes before a fall. Many Leos have had the experience of having to accept that there are circumstances in which their great force of will and personality, not to mention hard work, don't always win out. The "I'll show them" credo can work for or against you. Proving yourself at any cost is not proving anything other than arrogance and a capacity for self-undoing.

When Leos are behaving in their brash, superior, superconfident manner, it's usually a signal that their confidence is on the wane. Leos can put on a very convincing act at covering up a fear of inadequacy. Bravado is a telltale sign that The Lion is secretly distressed that things aren't going well.

It would be utterly wrong to advise a Leo to sit on the sidelines and not "go for it." After all, as the sign of the creative individual, it is The Lion's proper destiny to venture forth with courage and determination when others timidly hold back. Naturally, Lions are only human and are at times fearful that they can't live up to the expectations they put on themselves. The point is not whether they win or lose, but that they give it their best shot. The Lion *must* try. Because it is The Lion's boldness and daring that is often the very key to their success. Truly secure and successful Leos are the ones who have realized that drive and confidence are always backed up by a certain circumspection and restraint. A little modesty also goes a long way. All of which are the prime virtues of Virgo. Virgo is the sign that follows Leo. Leos, like every sign, can enhance their own best qualities by trying to integrate a little of the best of the sign to come.

Our opposite sign, you recall, is the other important pointer as to how we can bring out the best in our own sign. Aquarius, the sign of humanity, believes in the strength and the power of people working together.

When Leos hold on to their own strong belief in the power of the individual, and also become aware of the impact that one human being has on the welfare of the whole group, then they're fulfilling the Leo destiny. To make a personal contribution to the grand scheme of things is immensely satisfying to a Leo.

The first man on the Moon, Neil Armstrong, was a Leo. Perhaps he didn't realize it, but his words struck the exact chord of the Leo Aquarius axis: "One small step for man, one giant leap for mankind."

LOVE AND FRIENDSHIP

Leo rules okay. And why not?

When the Lion king decrees that a good time will be had by all, you can mark your summons to attend as a day to look forward to. In any circle, Leo is the instigator of events big and small—office lunches, reunions with friends, Christmas Eve drinks—just about any occasion that's cause for celebration.

No one, but no one, entertains like Leo, and when they throw a party, it can involve a cast of thousands, with Leo in the leading role. The Lion is friendly with many people. But true friends are another matter. Leo has a special reverence for close friends. The bonds of friendship that Leo forges are often the strongest and most enduring of his or her life.

People know their Leo friend will assist in times of trouble, and not just mutter words of sympathy. Leo doesn't say, "I'd love to help you if I could." They don't make excuses on the grounds that they've got a lot going on right now, or a temporary cash-flow problem. Leo will swing into action and organize a rescue operation.

The Lion is equally thoughtful with the little gestures of kindness and consideration that revive your spirits when you're down. If your relationship has fallen apart, Leo will take you out to lunch once a week for months to cheer you up. When you're sick, they'll send flowers if they can't get there themselves. They'll even call your favorite restaurant and have a small banquet delivered to your door. When you know that there's not going to be one Valentine card in the mail for you, you'll be cheered by the big heart emerging from the fax machine drawn by your Leo friend.

But be prepared, a Leo friend who gives total loyalty and dedication expects nothing less than total loyalty and dedication in return. Friendship is a serious business for Leos. They have no time for fair-weather friends. Trust means a lot to Leos. They figure if you can't trust someone you call a friend, who can you trust?

One of the many things that people love Leo for is that they have enough generosity of spirit not to lecture you when you've done something stupid and brought your troubles upon yourself. Later on there may be plenty of philosophical reflections on what lessons you should have learned from your experiences. Leos may be good at handing out advice (too good at times), but they're also good listeners, and often provide a weekly counseling service for their friends.

When Leos are having a bad day themselves, feeling down, grumpy, and unsociable, they always seem to be able to pull themselves together and rise to whatever the occasion demands of them, presenting a brave and happy face to the public. They're very conscious of not appearing weak. Leo believes that the show must always go on.

Leo the sharp social observer doesn't miss a trick when it comes to people's mannerisms, social acumen (or lack of it), style (or lack of it), and talent (or lack of it). They note, and they judge. If you're not as quick as they are to pick up the tab or open your purse, or if you leave the party without saying good-bye, don't think it will go unnoticed. We remember one occasion when a Leo organized a luncheon in an elegant Chinese restaurant for a new colleague. For all his sterling qualities, the guest was sadly lacking in social graces. He arrived unshaven in a crumpled shirt with a crystal and a shark's tooth dangling from his neck. The guest was well known for his belief that past-life therapy was the answer to any and all of his problems. After a couple of hours of forced and awkward conversation during which the new colleague consumed twice as much as everyone else (in spite of his embarrassing technique with chopsticks), Ms. Leo turned to her friend and said, "It's pity he doesn't spend as much time and money examining *this* life as he does his previous lives."

Beware the Dorothy Parker type of Lion in your midst. Anything you say is likely to be edited and replayed for his or her own theatrical benefit. Leo can be a penetrating social satirist. They can be terribly scathing, dropping memorable aphorisms about people's idiosyncrasies. And they're also among the most merciless detectors of people's flaws. How do they get away with it? By being so thoroughly entertaining, that's how. And by being the leading authority on who does what, how, and with whom.

Perhaps this is why Leo is sometimes labeled a snob. But this is a superficial misconception. People are too quick to interpret the Leo displays of superiority as snobbery. How could anyone with such a big heart really be a snob?

Leo would hate to be called a snob. Unlike a Capricorn, Taurus, or Cancer, Leo is singularly unimpressed by a person's background or pedigree per se. Remember, this is the sign that believes in the merit of the individual. Dismissing someone for having no style, no talent, and no class may be a Leo foible. Yes, they can be condescending at times. But they certainly won't write anyone off simply because that person comes from the wrong side of the tracks. Leo looks for the worth in the individual and couldn't care less about where someone comes from or where they went to school.

We know one real-life version of *Lady and the Tramp* involving a Leo lady who observed a homeless man discreetly rummaging for scraps in the garbage bins outside her apartment. Rather than give him a handout, which she thought might offend his pride, she took to leaving packs of sandwiches on top of the bins every evening. Leos are just too human to be snobs.

One accusation that they do deserve is that they are opinionated. Of course, Leos' *own* opinion on this is that they are strong people with strong opinions. Indeed, hearing one of them expressing these "strong opinions" may be the first clue to others that they are in the presence of a Leo. They love engaging in a hot debate on who's making a mess of foreign policy, or delivering a monologue on what's wrong with the politicians today. The Leo body language speaks loud and clear. Assertive, energetic, and dynamic, with an air of nobility (some would say self-importance). The single Leo femme fatale emits "come hither" rays that can either magnetize men or send the less courageous running for cover.

Leos love jewelry. And Leo women usually wear twice as much gold and glittering gems as anybody else. As for the dress, well, that's a little harder to define. As one Leo clotheshorse described her wardrobe: "I've got everything—next to my Gucci and DKNY, there's my vintage lace skirt from Oxfam and my new seventies flares." The Leo woman is not afraid to go for something on the edge of flash trash, the extra inch of thigh or cleavage. Leo will dare to be bare. There aren't many who get up in the morning and reach for the first T-shirt that comes to hand. It's an uncomfortable revelation that many are still harboring a politically incorrect attachment to their fur coat. Who knows? One day they might take a trip to Moscow in the middle of winter and get the chance to wear it again. Happily for Leos, diamonds are inorganic and are still a girl's best friend.

Leo men also work hard at creating the right image. There's an unmistakable type of supremely confident Leo man with a cock-of-the-walk manner. Think of Mick Jagger strutting across the stage, flicking his fringe in time to the beat, and you get the picture.

Leos of both sexes are arch romantics. How could it be otherwise when they're born under the sign of romance? The heart is the part of the body ruled by Leo.

Curiously, however, the male Lion is not the most active hunter in the jungle. In fact, he's quite happy lying in a tree, catching the breeze and waiting for the lionesses to bring home the dinner. The Leo man is less predatory than an Aries or a Scorpio, for example. Still, he easily accumulates a circle of adoring females. Not all of whom, it should be said, have serious designs on him.

If you *do* have serious designs on a Leo man, here is your best strategy. Prove that you are his match—socially, creatively, and intellectually—all the while allowing him to sweep you off your feet. It can be tricky. So it helps to know that Leo is extremely susceptible to flattery. But be careful—they hate to be fawned over. Ah, but to be told they're absolutely fabulous by someone they think is absolutely fabulous, well, that's a genuine compliment, isn't it? Make him feel like he's one in a million, but do it so cleverly that you're not perceived as a pushover.

If you're a man in pursuit of a Leo woman, the method is much the same. Pull out all the stops. It's never ever too early with Leo to make the grand romantic gesture. Send flowers (big, bright, and lots of them) and boxes of chocolates (please note boxes, not box), pronto.

The first date? This is your big opportunity, and if you don't get it right, it could be your last. It's probably a cliché, but with Leo it's best to go for the big first-date number. No casual cups of coffee after work or three weeks of preliminary chats on the phone first. No long philosophical strolls by the duck pond dining on take-out spring rolls and rice balls à la Aquarius either. No, no, no. To Leos this is evidence that you don't regard them as important enough to warrant a formal date. Even worse, it's evidence of stinginess, the ultimate Leo turn-off. Would-be partners of a Leo can eliminate the nonsexist notion of going dutch from their consciousness.

The formula is quite classic and quite simple. A splendid dinner in a top restaurant, followed by a show. Leos love the performing arts. You can't go wrong with opera, ballet, or a Broadway hit. To really make an impact, get expensive seats. The most expensive seats if you can. Don't agonize over whether you could be overdoing it. Leos won't feel the slightest bit embarrassed. Nor will they suspect you of having a hidden agenda. As far as Leos are concerned, spoiling them rotten from the start is a token of the respect and esteem you already hold for them.

The same Leo lady who left sandwiches for the tramp gave one nugget of advice to her daughters: "Never marry a mean man." The merest suspicion in Leo's mind that a suitor is a tightwad at heart will lead to instant dismissal.

This most definitely does not mean that you've got to be made of millions to win a Leo's heart. Leo values the riches of love far more than money. University students, struggling artists, poor musicians, and undiscovered geniuses will not be turned down on the grounds that they're flat broke. All they have to do is show their true colors by sharing generously what they have. If Leo knows that you're temporarily down on your luck, he or she will be delighted to share a pot of homemade spaghetti in your studio apartment.

The point is that whether you're dining at the Ritz or on a picnic blanket, love will not bloom for Leo without romance. Even your quieter, more restrained Leo (and they do exist—maybe they have Virgo on the Ascendant or the Moon in Pisces) has romantic fantasies of either playing one of the three musketeers . . . or being seduced by one of the three musketeers, complete with the velvet cape, the long sweep of the feathered hat, the silk gowns, and the perfumed handkerchief. The age of chivalry has never ended for Leos. In their hearts they yearn for the *Wuthering Heights* type heroine, the swashbuckling hero, and the great romantic adventure. (Dumas and Emily Brontë were both Leos.)

Love and romance live eternal in the Leo soul. But being born under the sign of romance is no astrological guarantee that Leo romances will always run smoothly. Leo is an idealist. And romance by definition is an idealistic notion. Indeed, in affairs of the heart, Leo is one of the signs most susceptible to falling into the chasm between romance and reality. For a sign renowned for managing people and worldly affairs so well, Leos sometimes have a problem managing their love life. Every sign has its interesting little contradictions. And this is one of Leo's.

Leo in love can be too trusting, far too generous, and more than a touch naive and gullible. And, like all fire signs, Leo tends to rush in where heroes and heroines fear to tread. Many young Leos get badly burnt by love.

They can be too eager to be swept up into commitment, figuring that loyalty and devotion will conquer any misgivings they may have, and that everything will fall into place, including sexual compatibility. Often, though, it doesn't. In later years Leo graciously puts this down to a learning experience in which they discovered that romance is not the same as sex, and adoration and mutual respect are not the same as compatibility.

Loyal Leo will stay and try to make things work. Indeed, if a relationship is *not* working, it's very hard for them to admit it and say enough is enough. If Leos don't bale out when a relationship is already past its use-by date, there's the possibility that they'll slip into the routine, uninspiring sort of life they despise so much. Anyone in an unsatisfactory relationship is capable of switching off sex and transferring his or her passion into work. The modern Leo version of "Not tonight, Josephine" isn't "I've got a headache." It's "I've got a backache." Which is perfectly credible—even if it isn't entirely true—since Leos are prone to back problems.

At difficult moments in a relationship, Leo, like all fire signs, will come out fighting. The Leo superiority complex is at its most superior when Leo erupts into one of their sudden angry outbursts. If you're on the receiving end, you will be admonished, told what's wrong with you, and given a sound dressing down. At such moments, everything you've ever read about the dictatorial, dominating Leo will come true before your eyes. Even in the best of relationships, Leo's little typhoons are bound to sweep in occasionally.

Should Leo be faced with the undeniable fact that the person they've pinned their heart on is not the person for them, then normally optimistic, happy Leo can get as dark, down, and depressed as any other sign. Dorothy Parker, who had her own fair share of failed romances, had some witty Leo words of wisdom on this.

> *Guns aren't lawful,*
> *Nooses give,*
> *Gas smells awful,*
> *You might as well live.*

The flame of hope never burns out in the Leo heart. In love, as in life, Leo bounces back. And most Lions are rarely alone for long. Like a magnet, they'll attract a new love scarcely before the tears have dried from the last. Leo aspires to life à deux.

One of the very best things about a relationship with Leo is that you'll have a loyal and reliable mate who values your differences. Leo will gladly enjoy the best that life has to offer, but is also prepared to tighten their belt and live cheerfully and frugally in two rooms if that's all you can afford. Having your own modest nest (while you raise the deposit on a bigger and better nest) is preferable to postponing togetherness. Anyway, Leo will love the challenge of creating a palace out of two bare rooms, and you won't feel like you're living in reduced circumstances at all. Mind you, Leo doesn't plan on suffering reduced circumstances for long. Leos need to know that the two-room palace will soon become a ten-room palace.

Leos are not the type to become emotionally dependent on anyone, but they won't mind if you need to lean on them from time to time. Few signs are such a tower of strength to a partner. They'll shoulder financial responsibility for both of you if necessary, and not remind you of it. They'll encourage your interests and career. And they won't tell you you're crazy when you say you'd like to leave your job and do what you've always wanted to do. Leo respects those who want to better themselves, and who have the courage to try and turn their life around.

For a sign that values loyalty so much, it's understandable that Leo can be a little prone to jealousy. Partners of Leos are advised not to make the mistake of proving they've still got what it takes by flirting with another. What matters to Leos is that *they* know that they've still got what it takes. Save your flirting for them. With Leo you must never let the romance wither and die. Tell them they're gorgeous. Every day. Show them that you desire them as much as the day you met. Don't assume that Leos, with their supreme air of confidence, don't ever need their ego stroked. In fact, in personal relationships, Leo possibly needs a great deal more ongoing affirmation of their desirability than most others.

Keeping your Lion happy and purring can be a touch demanding for partners at times. The role of leading man/lady comes so easily to Leos that they're bound to forget the principles of domestic democracy when it suits them. A quick quip about being a bossy boots is usually enough to pull Leo back into line. With The Lion, it's a case of strength meets strength. If you don't show your own strength of will, you could find you're forever marching to their tune. (And then they'll turn on you because they think you're a wimp.)

Norman Schwarzkopf is a Leo, and there's a Stormin' Norman waiting to emerge in every Leo. Anyone living with a Leo has felt at some time that life at home resembles a military operation, with Generalissimo Leo in charge. It's hardly a formula for domestic bliss if you have to defend yourself when overbearing Leo is stomping all over your psyche in hobnail boots. Without some planets in a water sign, Leo can be a touch insensitive, and could possibly take the prize as the most unsubtle sign of the zodiac.

When Leo decides a little action is in order, it will be instantly communicated, one way or the other. Leo has a bit of a problem with phrases like "Would you mind . . ." or "I'd like you to . . ." If you're not handed direct verbal orders, there are other indirect (and more creative) ways Leo will tell you what he or she wants you to do. You're a bit behind on your share of the housework? Leo will be vacuuming outside your bedroom door at 6:00 A.M. No matter that it's a Sunday and your only day to catch up on sleep. The dishes haven't been washed? Leo will risk breaking the Royal Doulton, crashing and bashing at the kitchen sink to get you away from your favorite TV show. You could be in a state of psychological warfare by now. The Leo strategy is to create terminal guilt in you, and to get you to surrender. What Leos don't realize is that they may win the battle, they may even win a few battles, but they risk losing the war. This is a reason some partners of Leos decide it's ultimately best to defect.

However, when Leo is in the mood to conquer and occupy the chaise lounge with a pile of magazines, you may well wonder where Stormin' Norman went. Don't worry, he's only on R and R. He (or she) will be back.

Happily, partners of Leo don't have to give in or give up. Leos are born to lead, to manage, and to organize. It's part of their role in the natural order of things. There are plenty of happily married Leos whose partners have negotiated a peaceful solution. We know a Gemini man who's been devoted to his Leo for twenty years. He's perfectly willing to let her play the boss because she's genuinely so good at running the show. But deep down she knows that he tolerates her playing the boss, and he knows that she knows he's every bit her equal in every way, and can certainly stand up for himself when he wants to. By letting her play boss enough of the time, he's acknowledging and respecting her nature. This in turn feeds her respect for him. It's all a bit of a game really, letting Leo play at king or queen.

It's quite simple really. When there's give and take in a relationship, when there's mutual respect and lots of love, then Leo can rule . . . and it's okay.

THE LEO PARENT

Picture the scene. A distinguished elderly Leo gentleman is taking a dip in the sea when a small boy comes swimming towards him. But just as he is about to reach the gentleman, he turns and begins to swim back. The man calls out, "What is it you wanted?" "The other boys bet me a shilling I wouldn't be brave enough to duck you," panted the boy. "But I can't do it . . . They've won." "Nonsense," says Leo. "It's easy money. If you wait a moment while I get my breath, I'll let you push my head underwater." A short while later the boy collected his shilling.

The elderly Leo who could still remember what the little triumphs of childhood felt like was none other than George Bernard Shaw. It is well known that the old man who looked like a biblical prophet had a way with children. All Leos have.

What attracts children to Leos and Leos to children is undoubtedly their sense of fun. Children pick up on the friendly, uninhibited signals coming from Leo, and respond with the same. No matter how "important" Leo might be to other adults, with children there's never the sense that Leo is unreachable. They're never condescending or patronizing. On the contrary, Leo has a natural affinity with the openness of young minds.

Parents born under the sign that so values strength of character and individuality are obviously going to want to foster that in their child. Leos will be determined that their children get the best all-around education. A Leo parent knows you can never start too early providing the civilizing and socializing experiences that a child needs to grow up to be a confident, independent person.

Leos will enjoy exploring the world of museums, art galleries, and theater with their children, and will take them to the local Lebanese restaurant for their first experience of Middle Eastern food, to the New Year festival in Chinatown to see the dragon, and to the Russian ballet when it comes to town. On all occasions Leo will be guiding his or her little one through important lessons in manners and etiquette. How to answer the telephone, how to speak properly to the waiter, and which knife and fork goes with what.

It won't be all cultural and cerebral, though. The circus and the amusement park will be high on the list. And it's debatable who will enjoy the Big Dipper or the Ghost Train more—parent or child.

The Leo parent will be especially keen to instill initiative in his or her children. If Junior loves animals, Leo mother or father might have a friendly word at the local pet shop and ask if their child could help out sometime. Leos are firm believers in work experience. All fire-sign parents are big on encouragement. Any hobby or subject that their child displays an interest in won't be ignored or passed off as a silly stage.

Few signs get such a thrill from giving, and seeing a little face light up at the sight of a special gift. Leos will go out of their way to procure toys that will stimulate their children or simply anything they think they'll like. Even when those children have children of their own, many a Leo parent is still the thoughtful sender of imaginative little surprises. A beautiful book here, an exotic trinket there, and always postcards from everywhere.

Leo, the manager mother or father, will have their children's lives pretty well organized, covering all bases from choosing the right school to making sure that their name labels are sewn in their clothes. This is the parent who always seems to be on top of things.

They will be there when problems arise at school or disputes break out with friends. But they won't be smothering in their efforts to guide. Because Leos are very much their own person, and because their own life is generally busy and full, they won't interfere unnecessarily or become unhealthily engrossed in their children's lives. Never do Leo parents attempt to live their lives through the lives and the achievements of their children. One of the wonderful things about Leo parents is that it truly doesn't matter to them whether their child wants to be a plumber or a prima ballerina. What is important for Leos is that their children are happy at whatever they do. Leos will try to give their children the best start in life, but accept that they must find their own way and make their own decisions.

On the other hand, Leo is a sign that does not tolerate weakness. The Lion genuinely believes that the main reason people don't achieve what they'd like to achieve is that they don't try hard enough or long enough. But sometimes Leos don't take into account enough that their children may not have inherited their own vast reserves of strength, endurance, and confidence. Some signs are not as well equipped, astrologically speaking, to pit their will against the world.

What Leo can't abide is people who give up. Even the child who phones in tears asking to be taken home from camp will quickly get the message that demonstrations of lack of backbone are embarrassing and unacceptable. Perhaps Leo should pause to think about whether the child was ready for camp. Just because Leos couldn't wait to bolt out of the door at age seven doesn't automatically mean that their offspring will want to do the same.

Leos may expect their children to also inherit their famous bounce back. They can become too obviously impatient should their child come down with a virus and be confined to home at an inconvenient time. Leos are terribly stoic; they have little patience when they themselves are sick, and frequently get out of bed and back into full swing before they've recovered. Could it be that Leo can't help feeling that it's a bit of a burden (and a little bit boring) to stay at home and play nurse? Leo might never say the words, but the implication that someone should "pull himself together" is clear. Children of a Leo are bound to have some cause to remember when their parent seemed so wrapped up in his or her own life that they felt they were playing second fiddle.

It's very difficult for a Leo in any personal relationship not to overmanage and overcontrol. In other words, to become pushy and bossy. Let's be frank, the Leo urge to organize can be a fond—or not so fond—memory that many children of Leos have. We know a Leo mother who used to draw up menus for the family camping vacation and pin them to the tent flap. To be asked to say precisely what you want for breakfast, lunch, and dinner every day for the next week when you've gone camping to escape clocks and schedules, well, it can feel a touch regimented. Could this Leo mother ever understand that her strict meal schedule defeated the whole purpose? Years later, the children still recall—far more fondly now with the passage of years—the "relaxing" vacations. Mother's menus are now remembered as an amusing little idiosyncrasy.

Camping vacations and trips to museums aside, the most enduring gift that Leos give their children is the gift of love.

What all grown-up sons and daughters of Leos remember most of all is that they were blessed with a loving parent. As the years go by, they realize that simply by being so warm, kind, and affectionate, their Leo mother or father has left them the most important legacy a parent can leave.

THE LEO CHILD

A star is born.

You sense it from the start. And you know it for certain when little Leo is big enough to open mother's box of beads, or when they starts singing into a hairbrush pretending it's a microphone, and the long drapes in the living room are turned into stage curtains for Leo's little performances. At any moment you can expect a head to pop out and announce the title of their latest production.

Leo children need to be given opportunities to dress up and put on a show. They're the perfect choice for flower girls or ring bearers at a big wedding. Every little Leo girl needs at least one princess party dress. And every Leo boy needs a full-length mirror to make sure his pirate gear or his sheriff outfit sits right and looks good.

Most children with Moon in Leo are going to display the same theatrical tendencies, perhaps even more so, because the Moon is a very strong influence in our earliest years. Parents who have a Moon in Leo child may wonder if they've got a budding Oscar nominee on their hands, so strong is the early confidence and charm of Moon in Leo children. A five-year-old with Moon in Leo is already someone with presence and charisma.

There are lots of creative fantasies being played out in that bright little brain. Lion cubs have secret dreams of what they will do when they are grown-up and famous. At an early age, Leos already believe that they're special, and born to stand out from the crowd. Living with an up-and-coming director/producer/actor could get a little taxing. Sure, they'll get their fair share of setbacks and disappointments in time. But crushing the Leo child's hopes and dreams would be unforgivable.

The Leo pride is also evident young. Pride can be a double-edged sword. Not enough applause and appreciation of their talents can damage their ego. Too much, on the other hand, is going to create the overblown pride that trips them up. It won't be long before precocious little Leos discover not everybody is as captivated by them as their parents.

Leo, the leader of the gang, will emerge soon enough. This is a youngster who's all for liberty and fraternity, but mustn't be allowed to forget equality. Any early signs of dominance, especially with siblings, may need to be nipped in the bud.

There are some Leo children who are shy and stand back from the spotlight. Maybe the quieter, more reserved little lions have the Moon in Capricorn or Pisces. Don't think, though, that they're any less creative or aspiring than the more extroverted and boisterous ones. Or that they don't need every bit as much encouragement—if not more—for their Sun sign to shine through. All Leo children, but especially the less extroverted ones, will be dreadfully hurt if their parents fail to turn up and glow at the school play or awards assembly.

It's never too early to introduce your Leo to the big wide world and all the wonders it has to offer. Such inquiring little minds will devour the hustle and bustle of markets and the thrill of the circus, and will love wandering through grand galleries and museums, or spending a day visiting a stately mansion.

Young Leo is a fast learner in the lessons of social dynamics. Remember, this is the sign of kings, and the heir apparent knows it is his or her duty to learn the dos and don'ts of social mores. Leo children don't buck authority just for the sake of it. If young Leos don't see the point of what they're told to do, they won't be blatantly defiant. Nor will they whine and wail until they get their way. But you can bet they'll quietly go their own way anyhow. This is the first step towards being your own person.

You're bound to find yourself embroiled, sometime, in a test of wills, and there will be occasions when strong words are clearly called for. But it's important not to ever embarrass a young Leo in front of other people, and never put them down or drop a remark that will damage their growing pride.

With each passing year, Leo's personality is going to shine brighter and brighter. When they grow up, no one will be as proud of their own achievements as a Leo. No one, that is, except the parents of a Leo.

BORN UNDER LEO

Amelia Earhart	Gary Larson
Robert Mitchum	Alfred Lord Tennyson
Helen Mirren	Davy Crockett
Aldous Huxley	Annie Oakley
Martin Sheen	Danielle Steel
Percy Bysshe Shelley	Hulk Hogan
Queen Elizabeth, the Queen Mother	Christian Slater
Princess Margaret	Patrick Swayze
the Princess Royal (Princess Anne)	Mata Hari
Sean Penn	Shelley Winters
Whitney Houston	Danny La Rue
Pete Sampras	Rosanna Arquette
Omar Khayyám	Alan Whicker
Mark Knopfler	Henry Moore
Sandra Bullock	Louella Parsons
"Magic" Johnson	Top Cat

VIRGO

August 24–September 23

♍

Ruling planet
MERCURY

Are you in earnest? Then seize this very minute.
What you can do, or dream you can, begin it;
Boldness has genius, power and magic in it;
Only engage and then the mind grows heated;
Begin and then the work will be completed.

Johann Wolfgang von Goethe–born August 28

THE VIRGO NATURE

Are you in earnest? If you're a Virgo, it's a rhetorical question,

To be earnest is to be serious and sincere. It's to be committed to what you set your heart and mind to. And impassioned by something you believe is worthwhile, and worth doing well. To be in earnest is all these things. And all these things are what it means to be a Virgo.

Virgos know that once they begin, "the work will be completed." It could be signing up for a degree that will further their career. It could be putting the company's accounts in order when nobody else can make sense of them. It could even be rescuing a garden and having lavender, daisies, and parsley blooming where previously there were only weeds.

Everyone knows that you've got to start somewhere. This is no Virgo secret, but Virgo understands better than anyone that only when the first small details are taken care of can the big picture begin to fall into place. As one Virgo psychologist puts it to his patients who complain that they're falling apart under the stress of too much to do in too little time, "You *can* eat an elephant. How? You take one bite at a time." Built into the Virgo nature is the means to start—and finish—what they put their mind to. Their conscientiousness, their reservoir of self-discipline and quiet application, take them far. And they're top of the list when it comes to efficiency.

As the sixth sign, Virgo follows Leo. It is the Leo path to find an outlet for self-expression, with the quest for individuality being a major issue. Virgo continues that quest but also brings in the values of modesty and restraint. Virgo people do not have the strong Leo desire to stand out from the crowd, nor do they possess such an obvious need for applause and approval. Virgo finds greater rewards in a job well done, in a home well run, and in a life in harmony with the values of society. Virgos rate themselves by how effective they are in attaining their goals. And Virgos *are* effective, because it's a rare Virgo who makes the mistake of aiming for an unreachable star.

That doesn't mean that Virgo is any less ambitious than other Sun signs. Fulfilling their ambitions, though, does not mean seeking fame and glory. Often the opposite is true. Modest Virgo knows that there are definite advantages to staying out of the limelight. From the sidelines Virgo can retain a clearer perspective and is able to observe people and situations and engineer things in his or her favor.

In the wheel of the zodiac, earth always follows fire. After the explosion of energy and ego in every fire sign, there is, in earth, the natural swing back to caution. All the earth signs, Taurus, Virgo, and Capricorn, are concerned with the practical, material realm. And in our world, that translates into money and security. Taureans, born under the first earth sign, are more likely to be satisfied with their lot. Once Taureans have acquired enough material security, they readily accept the status quo and have no burning need to change it, or themselves. Where Taurus is happy to symbolically putter around the house and garden, Virgos want to open the garden gate and take a walk down the road where they can view themselves in the context of the wider world. How do I fit in? asks Virgo. What can I do to improve myself, my environment, and my prospects?

Virgos are not content—as Taureans often are—to regard money and security as the primary goal of life. All Virgos need to have the sense of autonomy that comes from earning their own living, and even if they are wealthy, they want to feel they're making some contribution of their own. They might not be as overtly materialistic as Taurus, but financial self-sufficiency is most definitely crucial to their happiness. This is why they place so much store on working hard and staying healthy. Virgo knows that body and mind are inextricably linked, and when you look after the body, the mind can operate at maximum efficiency.

The traditional planetary ruler of Virgo is Mercury, the clever young god with wings on his heels who was the messenger and aid-de-camp to Jupiter, king of the gods. Mercury's domain is the world of ideas, words, communication, and commerce. Like Geminis, who are also ruled by Mercury, Virgoans are interested in a wide variety of subjects and are quick to seize on new concepts. Always reading and always learning, Virgo is as alert, perceptive, sharp, and often as witty (though in a drier, more sardonic sort of way), as a Gemini. Yet Gemini seems to be more purely mercurial. It is, after all, an air sign. And air *is* the element of the mind. In Virgo the electric current of Mercury is firmly earthed. On the whole, Virgo shows more intellectual rigor than Gemini. The flighty "don't pin me down" traits of Gemini are absent. The earthiness of Virgo adds a large dose of practicality and common sense to their thinking.

Most Virgos come across as eminently sensible individuals, and unless they have an extroverted sign on the Ascendant, they're quiet and reserved, sometimes shy. But behind the gentle manner and the clear, lovely eyes there is the hint that all is not entirely calm in the Virgo mind. Signs of worry and anxiety peep through the surface. The effect of highly strung Mercury gives many Virgos a restless, sometimes nervous disposition. In spite of their efforts to maintain a calm exterior, their minds are constantly mulling over problems and probing for answers. Virgo has a tendency to worry if things aren't just "right." Perhaps a guest insisted on washing up and did such a bad job that Virgo was just itching to get into the kitchen and do it properly. Maybe a glaring spelling mistake slipped into the report that Virgo was responsible for putting together. How will they ever live it down? These things hang around in the Virgo mind. They plague them even to the point of giving them knots in the stomach.

In Virgo, Mercury reveals his discriminating and discerning side. Virgoans have an extraordinary gift for analysis and excellent powers of observation, which serve them well in many fields and in many ways. No sign scrutinizes and analyzes like Virgo, and no sign surpasses Virgo in their ability to sort through details and create order out of chaos. They don't miss a thing. For this reason, they can't help being critical. It's simply part of their discriminating nature. From their point of view, there's nothing wrong with criticism if it leads to improvement. Other people, though, are not always as rational or as meticulous as Virgo, and not everyone deals well with Virgo's criticisms—spoken or unspoken. These people can take some solace in the fact that Virgos are ten times harder on themselves than on others.

If there's a better way of doing something, Virgo, the perfectionist of the zodiac, will try to do it. They'll remake, remodel, rectify, recycle, and refine. In fact, they'll redo anything again and again until it's right. And they won't hesitate to make really radical changes if that's what's needed. But Virgo is not a revolutionary or a rebel. By and large, Virgos, like all earth signs, are conservatives who are respecters of the rules and regulations. They don't seek to overthrow the existing system, rather to improve it from within.

Virgo is also a mutable sign. It shares with Gemini, Sagittarius, and Pisces an inborn flexibility and adaptability. All mutable signs are open to change. But because Virgo is earthy and circumspect, they never rush headlong into change for change's sake. Virgo is no risk taker. They take their time to assess all the factors very thoroughly first. By the same token, Virgo has a great talent for sensing opportunities and knowing whether something has a good chance of working out. They can be as quick as any sign to "seize this very minute."

Being both mutable *and* earthy makes Virgo adaptable and open to change, yet practical and not one to leave things half done. It's a mighty strong formula for success. What quiet Virgo can achieve with this combination is remarkable.

Possessing Mercury's highly tuned senses, they quickly and accurately pick up signals and vibes coming from other people. Consequently their sensitivities are easily assaulted by people who are insensitive, vulgar, ill mannered, or coarse. Likewise, they are sensitive to injustice, pain, and suffering. Virgos are charitable in the true sense of the word. Charity is a Virgo virtue.

In 1896 Virgo Maria Montessori became the first woman to graduate from medical school in Rome. For ten years she worked in hospitals teaching hygiene (and that's a Virgo profession if ever there was one). But Montessori's destiny lay in the realm of education. Moved by pity for the poor, neglected children of the city, she began the work that she is remembered for. From a small room in a tenement house with forty dejected children she described as "closed flowers," Montessori went on to develop her teaching methods that have influenced education systems throughout the world.

No one believed that Montessori's efforts in that first humble room would ever come to anything. It seems to be a common story at the launch of so many Virgo ventures. But as Goethe said, "Boldness has genius, power, and magic in it." Besides, Montessori was motivated by more than Virgoan compassion. True to her Sun sign, she had shrewdly calculated what could be done with those children. Inspired, she wrote, "I set to work like a peasant woman who, having set aside a good store of seed corn, has found a fertile field in which she may freely sow it. But I was wrong. I had hardly turned over the clods of my field when I found gold instead of wheat." The gold that Montessori discovered was in the children who opened up and, for the first time in their lives, began to learn. The gold was the proof that her ideas worked.

Interesting, is it not, that Virgo is the sign of the Alchemist. So many positive Virgos are true alchemists, refining base metal and turning it into gold. Like magicians, they can transform the ordinary into something precious through faith and hard work.

The first rule in every Montessori classroom is the Virgo dictum "There's a place for everything and everything has its place." She understood, as Virgos do, that outer and inner order (order in your environment and order in your mind) is a prerequisite for self-discipline. And that the fruit of self-discipline is freedom. Self-discipline and freedom are complementary, not contradictory. Virgo is blessed with the knowledge of this great truth.

But emphasizing the need for order and working in harmony with others and your environment, Montessori was simply working with the natural laws. Virgos aim to work with the laws of nature, not against them. They have the conviction that "natural is good" and that doing things the natural way is the best way. *Holism* is a word we have adopted to express the idea of living in harmony with the natural laws. The wisdom of Virgo is the wisdom of holism.

Nearly two hundred years ago there appeared a story that everyone knows, but the deeper meaning of which is not so well understood. It's called *Frankenstein*, and it's hard to believe that the Virgo author of this strange and macabre tale was a sweet nineteen-year-old girl, Mary Shelley, wife of the romantic poet Percy Bysshe Shelley.

Dr. Frankenstein was a student of natural sciences who penetrated into the darker zones of magic and alchemy. Spurred on by the desire to possess the illicit power to create life, he discovered a method by which he could bring to life a monster of his own creation, a hideous replica of a man made from pieces of human bone and tissue retrieved from graveyards and morgues. The story has become such a part of our culture that the name of the creature's maker, Frankenstein, has been given to the creature himself.

But at the moment of the electrical animation of his creature, Frankenstein is struck with a terrible revulsion for what he has done. He flees his laboratory, hoping that his mistake will die with the monster. But when he returns, the monster has escaped. Reviled and rejected by the humans he encounters, and totally alone, the monster becomes so consumed with bitterness and revenge that he murders everyone that Frankenstein loves—his family, his best friend, and his bride. He accuses Frankenstein of being the cause of his loneliness and implores him on the grounds of moral obligation to relieve his suffering by making him a female companion, promising to disappear forever if Frankenstein agrees. Frankenstein's conscience is torn. He has to concede that his monster has a valid point, but it is his sense of moral duty to humanity—not the creature—that stops him. In a vain attempt to hunt down and destroy the creature, Frankenstein dies a desperate and broken man.

Years later, Mary Shelley wrote of the vision that inspired her timeless classic: "I saw the pale student of unhallowed arts kneeling beside the thing he had put together. I saw the hideous phantasm of a man stretched out, and then, on the working of some powerful engine, show signs of life, and stir with an uneasy, half-vital motion. Frightful it must be; for supremely frightful would be the effect of any human endeavor to mock the stupendous mechanism of the Creator of the world."

The story of *Frankenstein* was conceived, some would say prophetically, when modern science was taking its first steps. Everyone was talking about the theories of Darwin and the experiments in electricity. *Frankenstein* is a tale about one of the greatest moral dilemmas facing the human species. It is the story of what can go horribly wrong when the laws of nature are violated. It is a Virgo tale of caution on a global scale.

Virgos comprehend that nature, morality, and survival are all connected. And this is the lesson they can teach us. Virgos are prepared to deal with moral issues, and not sweep the dirt under the carpet. When there's work to be done, Virgos roll up their sleeves and begin.

Once when Maria Montessori was seriously ill, she said to a friend, "Do not be alarmed; I shall not die; I have work to do." All Virgos feel they have work to do. This is why Virgo is called "the sign of service." Their identity is derived primarily from the work they do, and the contribution their work makes. Unfortunately, Virgo's traditional title of the sign of service is the source of a host of misconceptions, including images of Victorian servants waiting on their masters. But this is not the meaning of "service" in respect to Virgo. It's not about being servile and subservient. Not at all. Virgo's service is about pride in a job well done, about the self-esteem that comes from a reputation for delivering the goods.

Virgos need to know that they are a vital cog in the wheel, and that what they do really matters and really makes a difference. The Virgo mother does everything possible to ensure that her children are well fed, well educated, and well behaved. The Virgo journalist checks all the facts and figures and presents copy that an editor doesn't need to revise. The boss with a Virgo secretary will never be caught out with incorrect information or a missing document.

The so-called service professions of medicine, nursing, social work, and education do actually attract a lot of Virgos. But the fundamental meaning of being born under the sign of service is to work at something that is worthwhile. Think for a moment about the words *work* and *worth*. They sound almost the same, don't they? For Virgos, the ethics and morality of their endeavors count for much more than a fat paycheck or public acclaim. Not that Virgos are prepared to live forever without appreciation for their efforts. Rather they seek praise from the sources that count. In fact, Virgo would be suspicious of gushing compliments, and would worry about the motives behind them. Virgo is a person of enormous integrity who despises sham and insincerity.

Another bundle of misinterpretations about Virgo arises from its symbol of the Virgin. The popular translation of the Virgin as proper, correct, even prudish, is again superficial. What the Virgin represents is purity of purpose. She is depicted carrying a sheaf of corn plucked fresh from the harvest. The time of the year when the Sun is in Virgo is the time when we reap what we have sown, when everyone works as a team to ensure that no one will go without in the lean months ahead. There couldn't be a more earthy image, or a more fitting reminder that Virgo is a practical sign concerned with laying down stores for the future.

The mysterious glyph for Virgo has several explanations. But one of the most feasible is that it forms the initials MV for Maria Virgo, the Virgin Mary. When Christianity took root in Europe, the essence of the female goddesses of pagan mythology were largely absorbed into the one image of the Virgin Mary. Virgo is a sign linked to the whole spectrum of the female principle of caring, nurturing, and guiding, not to mention love of nature.

Astrologers have for some time been saying that Mercury, Virgo's traditional planetary ruler, does not entirely account for these Virgoan characteristics. There are hundreds of tiny bodies revolving around the Sun between the orbits of Mars and Jupiter called asteroids—little stars—although the term *planetoid* is more correct since they are not stars but tiny planets. Their significance, however, is not so tiny.

Most astrologers agree that the two biggest asteroids—Ceres and Vesta—are linked to the sign of Virgo. In mythology, the goddess Vesta was the keeper of the hearth and the protector of home and community. Her priestesses were the vestal virgins whose duty was to tend the sacred flame that kept the city safe. The vestal virgins led self-contained, contemplative lives and were respected by all.

Virgo women, and men, too, enjoy their own company and need time for themselves. Whether it's reading, gardening, or studying, there must be time for a little introspection and self-cultivation.

Ceres, the Roman goddess of the grain and agriculture, is an obvious archetype of the Virgo woman and man. She represents the productive side of Virgo. She is connected with sustenance, food, and fertility of land, man, and beast. There are suggestions that Ceres also casts her influence over Cancer, the sign of mothering and nurturing. But Virgo, by its earthy nature, is more in keeping with the consistent and grounded qualities of Ceres. Attributed to Cancer, she is familial. Ceres as a ruler of Virgo is global.

The myth of Ceres (or Demeter, as she was known to the Greeks) and her daughter Persephone throws light on an important personal issue for Virgos, namely their relationship with their mother.

Demeter and Persephone, mother and daughter, lived a peaceful life of devotion to each other. That is, until the day Persephone was raped by Pluto and whisked away to the underworld to be his queen. Demeter searched the countryside for Persephone, blessing those who gave her hospitality and laying waste to the lands of those who spurned her. The goddess of the grain in her grief caused such devastation to the land that Jupiter, with the aid of his trusty messenger, Mercury, stepped in to negotiate a settlement. Henceforth, he decreed, Persephone would spend one third of every year in the underworld and the other two thirds with her mother. And so it was that the cycle of the seasons came about. When Persephone is in the underworld, the earth lies fallow. When she emerges, fertility returns.

Many Virgos of both sexes have a binding relationship with their mother, who instilled in them a strong sense of duty and mutual devotion. So much so that the influence of father fades by comparison. In some extreme cases, Virgo's mother (maybe unconsciously) gives the message that father is irresponsible, ineffective, or even that mother and child are better off without him. Whatever the individual details, the result is that mother is definitely the parent who leaves the stronger impression on the developing Virgo personality. At some stage in their lives, adult Virgos usually find themselves responsible for the welfare of their mother. And because they are so dutiful, they often have a hard time making the psychological break away from her.

When Persephone returned to Ceres from the underworld, the bond with her mother was changed forever. She was now a mature person in her own right, with a husband and a life of her own. Many Virgos— men and women—reach the point where they have to spell this out to their mother.

Ceres, as goddess of the grain, also explains a lot about the Virgo preoccupation with food. The sixth sign of the zodiac rules health as well as work. Virgos, as well as people whose Sun falls in the sixth house of their horoscope, are very concerned with matters of health, diet, and nutrition, and often make these interests their career. Most Virgos are firm believers in moderation in all things, including food, and won't deny themselves the odd Hershey bar. But Virgo is very self-controlled. Purity of body and purity of mind are inseparable to Virgo. Quite a lot are vegetarians or vegans and experiment with a macrobiotic diet.

Yet their healthy interest in food (and who would disagree that we are what we eat) can sometimes become an unhealthy obsession. It's interesting that Virgo and Cancer—the two signs most likely to suffer eating disorders—are the signs linked with the goddess Ceres. Quite a few young Virgos have waged their own war against the "new" diseases of anorexia and bulimia, spurred on by images of superthin supermodels that started to appear in the sixties. It was Virgoan Twiggy who was the first.

Physiologically, Virgo rules the intestinal tract, in particular the small bowel where nutrients from food are absorbed into the bloodstream. Getting the right diet is important to good Virgo health. (Many Virgos are prone to food allergies and intolerances.) Virgos are not the most robust individuals, but they are often among the most healthy simply because they respect their bodies. However, there some Virgos who are altogether *too* worried about what they eat and how their bodies function, with every twinge, every passing headache, and every "off" day suspected as a symptom of something more serious.

Something else that Virgo allocates serious worrying time to is germs. Virgo probably believes that of the seven deadly sins, sloth is the deadliest. But they would like to add dirt to the list. Hygiene can become a consuming passion for Virgo. And it seems that everybody has their own tale to tell about an encounter with a Virgo on a mission to clean. If Virgo's sharp eyes haven't detected the state of decay inside your fridge, you can be sure the nose knows. Only a Virgo can identify an overripe banana at fifty paces, or how many days the toothpaste has been ingrained on your sink. When Virgo comes to visit, it's pointless to attempt to disguise your dust, dirt, grease, and grime. So either display your dirt with wanton pride, or allocate a whole day to cleaning before Virgo arrives.

Lots of jokes have been spawned by the Virgo love/hate relationship with dirt and disorder. Jokes aside, there *is* method in their madness. Maybe the jokers are lazy or just don't know what Virgo knows, that scientifically speaking, as Virgo will inform you (if you've got the courage to ask), there's an important biological link between cleanliness and survival. It must have been a Virgo who coined the expression "healthy, wealthy, and wise." Stay clean and you'll live better and longer. It's plain common sense. There's also the added bonus of looking better longer. Like their Mercury-ruled Gemini cousins, mature Virgos generally look considerably younger than their years.

The pursuit of perfection comes naturally to Virgo. But the zeal with which some Virgos pursue perfection can be positively unnatural. In any case, who can define perfection? Everyone has a different idea of what is perfect.

One famous Virgo has been "perfecting" himself for years. Michael Jackson (born August 29), whose appearance is as well honed as his shows, has the most famous remodeled face in history. And his Virgoan horror of microbes has turned him into the world's most hermetically sealed celebrity. It may not be so daft or fanatical to wear a face mask when you fly into tropical Australia in midsummer. But are mask and gloves really essential attire when you're shopping for baby clothes in a department store? Ah, but Virgos know that Legionnaires' disease could be lurking somewhere in the air-conditioning vents, so why take any chances?

The Virgo profile would not be complete without some mention of Chiron, the newly discovered asteroid that was first sighted in 1977. That's because astrologers are already proposing that Chiron is a new ruler of Virgo.

The Chiron of myth was the wise centaur, teacher of the great heroes and gods, and master of astronomy, astrology, medicine, and all the healing arts. But when he was wounded by a poisoned arrow he found he was unable to heal himself. Being immortal, Chiron could not die, yet he could not bear to live in eternal suffering, so he traded places with the tortured mortal Prometheus and found release in death.

Astrologers believe that this tiny asteroid has an importance way out of proportion to its size. In an individual's birth chart, Chiron is the indicator of the personal wounds that we all suffer in some way in our early years, wounds that never heal in maturity unless we are prepared to tend to them. Chiron insists that we confront our personal dilemmas and work on them with the solid Virgo virtues of reason, self-discipline, and compassion. The benefits of Chiron don't come automatically to anyone. Everyone must prepare their own cure. Nor are Chiron issues ever an easy matter. But resolving them is possibly the most worthwhile thing a person can do for themselves. This is why many astrologers say that Chiron is the key to happiness in every birth chart.

Astrologers also say that the discovery of Chiron at this time in our history is far from coincidental. A new body is discovered in the heavens when the time is right for humankind to absorb its significance. Chiron the healer also has a global application. Few would argue that the greatest challenge at the turn of the millennium is to heal our planet. Chiron's link with Virgo gives Virgo individuals the opportunity and the responsibility to teach all of us that our wounded planet can be healed through knowledge and concerted effort.

Does this sound all too saintly and out of this world? If doing your best to solve problems that are crying out to be solved (even if it all looks futile) is "saintly," then the answer is yes. Mother Teresa was born on August 27 under the sign of Virgo. She has become a modern icon of the finest Virgoan virtues.

Everyone knows how Mother Teresa left the comfort and cloistered safety of her convent to set up her mission for the sick and dying in the slums of Calcutta because she could no longer bear to look over the convent wall and see the suffering on the other side. She knew she had to act.

Mother Teresa often spoke about how she got far more from the people she cared for than she gave to them. You see, in helping to heal others, Virgos heal themselves. She once said, "We can do no great things. Only small things with great love." This is one of the great Virgoan gifts: the ability to jump into a seemingly overwhelming task and get stuck into it. Remember, you have to begin somewhere, and when you take care of the small things, the rest falls into place.

So often does Virgo act as a catalyst, a person who makes that initial suggestion or takes the first critical step that opens the gates of change. There is no doubt that the life of Mother Teresa is an inspiration to a troubled world. Many believe she was a saint. But even saints are only human. And all humans, Virgos included, inevitably stumble sometimes into the traps waiting for them in their Sun sign.

Once, Mother Teresa's order paid the sum of one dollar to New York City for a large vacant building in the Bronx where they planned to set up a home for the sick and homeless. The city stipulates that a building of its height must have an elevator for the disabled, and offered to pay for it. Strange as it sounds, Mother Teresa refused the offer, and the project was abandoned. Why? Because the rules of her order require the sisters to live like the poorest of the poor that they serve. To us, an elevator is hardly an indulgence, but it was rejected by Mother Teresa as an infringement of her strict rules, which demand the sisters live a life of austerity. The question has since been asked—did the rules ultimately serve the needs of the homeless that the sisters are called to serve? In the final analysis, do the rules against traveling in an elevator defeat the very purpose of the rules?

All Virgos can get hung up on rules and regulations. Sticking to the "shoulds" and "ought tos" can, unfortunately, sometimes becomes the end in itself and not the means to an end. There are some rules and regulations that undoubtedly need to be questioned, and maybe rewritten. It's a dilemma that can make Virgos very anxious and cause them to seek refuge in minutiae, covering every corner and turning over every stone when what they really should be doing is looking at the big picture.

There is always a profound relationship between opposite signs of the zodiac. Part of it is an uneasiness from seeing, in your opposite sign, the qualities that you know deep down you're short on. Pisces opposes Virgo. And while polite Virgos would never say it, most of them regard Pisceans as a bit impractical, careless, and untogether.

Pisces is a mutable sign, too. But Pisces has a great deal more to offer than flexibility and adaptability. Its position as the final sign of the zodiac means it encapsulates all that has gone before in every other sign, giving the Pisces individual a breadth of vision and enormous scope to his or her thinking.

Pisces knows that often so much more can be achieved by bending the rules a bit. When Virgos become too blinkered, too pedantic, and altogether too tied up in details and what is correct or incorrect, it's an indication that they need to take on board just a little of that Pisces gift for seeing the big picture and being able to go with the flow. Virgos have a problem with spontaneity. Perhaps it's because they're too afraid that if they stray from the rules, they'll descend into some kind of chaos.

Pisceans are the first to make allowances for human foibles and failings. It is not in their nature to be judgmental. They take into account the vicissitudes of life, and are the first to acknowledge that there are some things in life that you simply can't regulate or control.

In an imperfect world, Virgos' perfectionism can sometimes work against them. Virgos, the harsh critics, can stymie themselves and their work as well as frustrate and alienate others with their penchant for always doing things by the book. When they're in their superpunctilious mode, Virgos can get so tense and uptight that they make others tense and uptight. Then they can become obsessed with correctness, and be carping, nitpicky, and terribly draining on the people around them.

When Virgos try to force the order they value so much, they can actually end up creating the disorder they dread. It can take years for Virgo to discover that there's more to be gained in the long run by being less exacting.

The positive Virgo makes allowances for the human factor—in themselves and others. They don't push themselves beyond breaking point in work, in relationships, or in life. They know when enough is enough because they don't have unreal or unreasonable expectations. Virgo is a sign with great potential for personal happiness.

"There are nine requisites for contented living," according to Goethe:

> Health enough to make work a pleasure.
> Wealth enough to support your needs.
> Strength enough to battle with difficulties and overcome them.
> Grace enough to confess your sins and forsake them.
> Patience enough to toil until some good is accomplished.
> Charity enough to see some good in your neighbor.
> Love enough to move you to be useful and helpful to others.
> Faith enough to make real the things of God.
> Hope enough to remove all anxious fears concerning the future.

Goethe, you recall, was a Virgo. Enough said.

THE VIRGO CAREER AND DIRECTION

Virgos need to love their work. As a Virgo, D. H. Lawrence had some excellent advice to fellow Virgos: "There is no point in work unless it absorbs you like an absorbing game. If it doesn't absorb you, if it's never any fun, don't do it."

Staying long term in a job they loathe can actually destroy the Virgo soul. It can even make them physically sick. That's because work, more than anything else, defines Virgo's life. Everyone wants to enjoy the work they do, but the enjoyment and personal satisfaction that Virgos derive from their work is tied to their whole being. Some Virgos find it impossible to switch off from work when they go home. The Virgos who keep their job in perspective can manage work, home, and personal life more successfully than just about any other sign.

Time management is a new term, but it's by no means a new concept to Virgo. Making the most productive use of your time is second nature to Virgo. It's called "efficiency," and Virgo knows that you can't be efficient without self-discipline. Time management, self-discipline, and efficiency alone are enough to take Virgo to the top of the career ladder. Higher, in fact, than many of their less-organized colleagues ever dreamt they would go. But Virgo has another trump card tucked up their well-pressed sleeve. Their sharp brain. When speed and accuracy are of the essence, Virgo thinks very clearly and very quickly.

So don't be deceived by this quiet achiever. Virgos may not be as loud, pushy, or domineering as Sagittarians, and they certainly don't wait for luck to land in their laps. They might not appear as blatantly ambitious as their Leo or Aries colleagues, whose push for the top is taken for granted by themselves and everyone. And they would never dream of using sympathy as a way of eliciting special treatment, as a Cancer might. Nor would they turn up late every other day like a Gemini and expect to get away with it on the grounds that they work twice as fast as anyone else. Not Virgo.

Virgos' feet are firmly on the ground, and their heads are tightly screwed onto their shoulders. Modesty does not permit Virgo people to trumpet their own successes, flaunt their intellect, or jinx their goals by discussing them with everybody. As for tears, drama, and the "poor me" approach, well, Virgos are far too dignified and self-conscious to embarrass themselves in this way. And if you do happen to know a Virgo who is ever late for work, you can bet that he or she has got Gemini on the Ascendant or lots of planets in Pisces.

Virgos get where they want to go because they're practical, realistic, and never bite off more than they can chew. They are also one of the most responsible signs of the zodiac, and are willing to put in the hours and effort that are needed. Virgo never expects something for nothing. But they do expect credit where it's due, and the rewards that they've earned. Because Virgos constantly apply their gift for analysis to themselves, much of their success can be attributed to knowing exactly what they can achieve, and the full extent of their talent and limitations. Few signs are so honest with themselves. And none are so self-critical.

If they do find themselves in a job that's wrong for them, or going nowhere, Virgos *will* make the break, but only when the time is right. They're not ones to switch off the computer and just walk out as the other mutable signs might. Sagittarius would say, "Something will turn up." Gemini would mutter, "I'm outta here." And Pisces would simply know that they have to take a giant leap of faith and just go. But Virgo, remember, is the only mutable sign in the element of earth. Ever practical, when Virgo quits, the departure will be well timed and well calculated. It would be a rare (and very anxious) Virgo who did not have his or her financial survival sorted out beforehand.

Satisfaction is one thing, but Virgo knows that labor equals money. All the earth signs want to build the material framework of their life as soon as possible. Virgos have a secret dread of poverty and will work as hard as they can in their twenties and thirties to buy their own home and put aside funds for a rainy day. The rainy day may never come, but Virgos would worry if they were not prepared.

The Virgo person is a little like the ant in the story of the ant and the grasshopper. Do you remember how the busy ants worked all summer to provide for themselves in the winter months while the irresponsible grasshopper danced and played his fiddle, frittering away the long, hot days when food was plentiful? Come the first cold winds, when the ants were retreating to the comfort of their well-stocked larder, the grasshopper was found shivering and hungry on their doorstep, begging to be taken in. He was. But not before the chief Virgo ant had delivered a stern lecture on the virtues of hard work and self-sufficiency, and the grasshopper had vowed to be as busy and industrious as the ants next summer.

Virgo raises being busy to the level of a prime virtue. You never hear Virgos complaining that they've got too much to do, or wishing they weren't so busy. Even on vacation, there are only so many hours lying by the pool with a strawberry daiquiri that Virgo can take. If they do finish a task early, they wouldn't dream of putting their feet up on the desk and flicking through the *TV Guide*. Virgo will already have prepared a list of things to do, and waste no time in getting down to the next one.

The cartoon character of Lois Lane comes to mind as the archetypal Virgo career woman. She's gentle but tough. She's the dedicated professional career woman who likes to be praised for work well done but is quietly confident of her own ability. Cool, calm, and collected, Lois rushes back to the office with the scoop of the week, and not a hair out of place. And as for patiently holding out for Superman, well, is that aiming for the top or what? You know that beneath Lois' neat, unruffled persona lies a smoldering but controlled desire for the man she's set her sights on. An impossible dream? No, Virgo doesn't have those. Lois always knew that she would get her man.

Virgo is very conscious of maintaining a good image. They're always polite, cordial, and considerate to colleagues, whom they treat with tact and diplomacy. They are very respectful of a person's rank and standing, and have no trouble accepting authority. Likewise, the Virgo boss is not intoxicated by the power of position. They cleverly manage to achieve precisely what they want by remaining polite and considerate. And they handle people with gentle firmness when required (which is not a contradiction in terms for Virgo). Virgos work hard to achieve a position of respect, but they would have to have plenty of planets in fire signs to make them crave a high-profile, high-flying job. Most Virgos do not have the burning desire to build an empire. And when it comes to fame and glory, well, that's something you can't spend too long dreaming about, figures Virgo. Not when there's work to be done.

Modest and self-effacing, Virgos may be, but they're nevertheless acutely aware of the importance of personal presentation and what people think of them. If Virgos are not entirely confident that they've got the right look, they'll set to work getting it. And Virgo is smart enough to go to the experts for advice, if necessary. When one successful Virgo executive we know thought his career was faltering, he booked himself an appointment with the top image consultant in town. After being told that gray was not his color and that everything in stripes had to go, he braced himself in true Virgo fashion and delivered a dozen expensive suits and shirts to the local thrift shop. It hurt but it had to be done, so Virgo did it.

Far more common is the Virgo who carefully observes and assesses what gives other people that extra edge in appearance, and sets to work imitating it. It's a gradual process. First the new suit, then the new haircut and new briefcase, and before you realize it, Virgo is a changed person. It's an unusual Virgo who tries to make a distinctive fashion statement all his or her own. But they're very clever copyists of what works.

So often are Virgos seen as the indispensable member of the team, and that's exactly what they want to be. No other sign is a more disciplined worker. Virgos don't need to be supervised and are quite happy to work alone. They work brilliantly under the pressure of deadlines because they're so well organized and have covered all the details well ahead of time. Should a crisis occur, they may be churning with anxiety like everyone else, but they'll hold themselves together and stay outwardly calm. It is not in their nature to explode with anger or frustration. Actually, Virgo has a tendency to implode, usually at the cost of their own nerves.

All things considered, it would be hard to find a more reasonable and even-tempered person to work with, or work for. Virgos pull their weight and are usually the first to volunteer when others need a helping hand or there's extra work to be done. Indeed, Virgos are often the ones who work harder and longer than anyone else, sometimes beyond the call of duty. When everyone's heading off for Friday night drinks, Virgo will be reluctant to go if there's work that can be wrapped up before Monday. But while Virgo is projecting an air of selfless devotion, inwardly they could be developing a pool of resentment as they think, "Why is it always me who has to stay back and finish the job?" "Why do I feel guilty?" as their colleagues walk out the door at five.

Such dedication to the job is admirable. And there are many people who admire Virgos, but not many who can—or want—to emulate them. The truth is that Virgos can sometimes develop an almost perverse relationship with their job by investing more time and energy than is healthy. Virgo is often called the "workaholic of the zodiac." The fact is, they can become a martyr to their job. Every Sun sign has its own reasons why they can push themselves too hard. If Virgo does becomes a workaholic, it's usually because of a deep-seated insecurity and fear. Their insecurity is that they often feel they are not valued. And, like all earth signs, they fear that the ground beneath them will shift (for reasons often beyond their control) and they might lose their job.

Less conscientious or simply less career-minded individuals may find they are unwittingly comparing themselves with Virgo, and begin to feel that their own faults (which hitherto they'd been happy enough to live with) are being projected in CinemaScope for general viewing. Sometimes just having a Virgo around is enough to make you a little edgy, defensive about what you say, and just a little bit paranoid about the quality of your work. You begin to tidy your drawers, you double-check—no, triple-check—your work, and you stop leaving half-empty coffee cups on your desk overnight. You've never done these things before. What's going on here? It's not that Virgos do anything offensive or say anything rude, so why do they sometimes get people offside?

The high standards Virgos impose on themselves are almost unconsciously picked up by others. Virgo is not called the "critic of the zodiac" for nothing. Without realizing it, Virgo has a knack for being pedantic and persnickety. When Virgos are in this negative, heavy, critical mode, they can be a real wet blanket, and very inhibiting. And inhibitions are not what you need when creative or imaginative work is called for.

Just as bad as making others feel repressed and inhibited is what inhibitions and worry can do to Virgos themselves. What a shame to waste all those sterling qualities (especially as Virgo hates to waste anything) when all you have to do is switch off the worry button and be a little less earnest. Of course, that's easier said than done. But once Virgos turn their analytical ability on themselves, they don't take much convincing of the benefits of loosening up.

When Virgos are relaxed, they're fantastic at sparking off other people's ideas. Creativity flows, people become more cooperative, and there's a feeling of vitality in the air. The positive Virgo can be enormously interesting, good fun, and funny to be with. At any moment they can turn their native perception into penetrating wit. Their ruling planet, Mercury, the quick-thinking, clever god, will see to that.

Mercury the communicator leads many Virgos into work that demands an inquiring mind. Writing and education are both areas that Virgo is drawn to. Jobs requiring a wordsmith suit Virgo perfectly, which is why copywriting, speechwriting, journalism, and editing are traditional Virgo careers. The discriminating Virgo brain quickly picks up what works, and what doesn't. Refining, correcting, and perfecting are all Virgo talents. When details are everything and meticulousness is what's called for, Virgos come into their own. They zoom in on the small but important errors that others would miss.

The Virgoan ability to find the faults in something and fix them is why Virgos are well represented in repair jobs of all kinds. It could be repairing a script, but it could also be fixing a car, a computer, or a clock. There are even Virgos who make a living by improving the way that other people work. Efficiency experts, time and motion consultants, and technical specialists all need the Virgoan input.

The long haul doesn't daunt Virgo. They're by far the most patient and persistent of the mutable signs, and will toil for months, years, even a lifetime, to perfect a piece of work. As the great wit Samuel Johnson put it, "What is written without effort is in general read without pleasure." Writing a dictionary of the English language single-handed as Dr. Johnson did clearly wasn't done without effort. Nor was it done overnight. Writing *War and Peace* has become a metaphor for writing something that is inordinately long and difficult. Tolstoy, like Dr. Johnson, was a Virgo.

Mountains of facts and figures are no more intimidating than mountains of words. Most accountants have got Virgo strong in their horoscopes. So do mathematicians, scientists, and engineers. It's practically a prerequisite for anyone who enjoys working with data, numbers, and statistics. The computer software industry provides the right kind of work for many Virgos. Their logical, analytical brains are precisely what's needed for writing programs and uncovering the bugs in the system.

Research also appeals to Virgo because it involves the collating and analyzing of information. Not just scientific research but social research too. Virgos have acute powers of observation and deduction. They are natural detectives, and even those who don't ferret out information for a living can be a regular Inspector Poirot or Miss Marple. Agatha Christie, the creator of Poirot, Marple, and volumes of detective stories, was born under the sign of Virgo. So, incidentally, was Peter Sellers, who played Inspector Clousseau in the Pink Panther movies. His dry, deadpan Virgoan humor and talent for mimicry never failed.

The workings of the mind and understanding why we are the way we are fascinate Virgo. Quite a few become professional psychologists or sociologists. And nearly all Virgos are well informed amateur shrinks with a large home library, from Freud to Jung to Edward de Bono, plus a pile of paperbacks of the latest theories on positive thinking, creative visualization, and how to develop your right-brain function. Mercury ensures that Virgo will never want to stop learning. Virgos don't just read "how to" books, they write them. They're enthusiastic participants at seminars designed to improve your career and personal life. Virgos lap up any information that can be useful. What's more, they like to spread the word. Mercury draws many Virgos into education and training. The classroom is one ideal environment where Virgos can feel they are making a positive contribution to society.

The Virgo kindness often finds its outlet in nursing and welfare work. Charitable organizations can benefit from Virgo's excellent administrative skills. When Virgos know that the work they do is morally and ethically sound, they are spurred on by a tireless energy and passion.

Usefulness is paramount to Virgo. It's an integral part of their pragmatic, earthy nature that something—be it a carved antique table, an ornate fireplace, or a fragile glass vase—is more valuable if it can be used. They don't decry art for art's sake, but if something is useful as well as beautiful, then its value is increased tenfold. Virgo is a functionalist at heart and is often drawn to a career in building, architecture, or town planning. It was Virgo architect Louis H. Sullivan who gave us the motto of modern design: "Form follows function."

Too much extraneous, dust-gathering, unutilized space offends Virgo's sensibilities. Less is definitely more in the Virgo book. Few will ever embrace total minimalism, but there are plenty of Virgos who firmly subscribe to the simplistic, no-frills philosophy.

Who else but a Virgo could have given the world a pared-down, defatted reinvention of traditional French cooking? Pierre Trosgros, creator of nouvelle cuisine, did exactly that. His rationale was healthy eating, and it became fashionable at a time when health and fitness were the specials of the day. But even the health buffs are now saying that a little bit of what you fancy does you good. It's all very well taking discipline to the dinner table, but does it become self-defeating if you snap under the pressure and resort to making yourself a triple-decker cheese and ham sandwich when you get home? There are some Virgos who take their interest in healthy eating to the extreme. Quite a lot have been through a food fad or two.

Virgos' seemingly insatiable thirst for knowledge combined with their interest in health makes them obvious candidates for work in medicine and health care. There are many Virgo doctors, dieticians, nutritionists, and health specialists of all sorts. Animal medicine, too, is a field that needs the blending of Virgo's scientific mind and their quiet, calm manner. Most Virgos love animals and make excellent vets and animal trainers.

But it is the whole spectrum of alternative health therapies that particularly captivates Virgo. If healing can be achieved by natural means, then surely, thinks Virgo, this is the way to go. It comes back to the Virgo connection with, and respect for, the laws of nature. Herbalism, working with earth's natural medicines, has long been a Virgo profession. Aromatherapy is a "new" one. The intricacies of acupuncture don't faze Virgo one little bit. And a career in physical and exercise therapies such as Reiki, Feldenkrais, yoga, and tai chi can be just right for Virgo.

Virgos were among the first to shop organic, and many are now discovering there is a growing, lucrative business in producing and selling chemical-free foods. Holistic eating, holistic medicine, and ho-listic living are scarcely alternative concepts any longer. They never were for Virgo. As the trend towards holism becomes mainstream, Virgos are finding that their message of maintaining a healthy body and a healthy mind is at last being heard, and taken seriously.

The Virgo principle of the necessity of living in harmony with the laws of nature and the rhythms of the earth is at the fore of new-millennium issues. Eco-awareness is here to stay. With their abhor-rence of waste and excess, Virgos were the first to take the trouble to separate their bottles from their newspapers and appreciate the importance of recycling our limited resources. The Virgo-style ecolog-ical movement has spawned a whole new Virgo-sounding vocabu-lary. People who want to simplify their lives (just like Virgo) and get back to basics are "downsizing." Those who realize that they had a life but no lifestyle are going to search of "radical simplicity." It's not all altruistic and a question of saving the planet, though. It's also a matter of having the time to enjoy the simple but important pleasures of life. And Virgo understands that perfectly.

A global revolution has also begun in that other Virgo domain of work and employment. The whole concept of work is now being redefined as we face the fact that "jobs for everyone" as we used to understand "jobs" no longer exists. Sensible, practical, flexible Virgo is open to new ways of working and earning a living. In the trend towards working for yourself, working part-time, working from home and with local communities, Virgo has a head start.

It doesn't matter, Virgo, whether you're a writer, an ecological crusader, a social worker, or a shoemaker. Nor is it important whether you work in a restaurant, a hospital, a school, or a large office. With your self-discipline, efficiency, strong social conscience, and work ethic, all you need is to take that first step forward in the direction that you *know* is right for you. Whatever you do and wherever you work, there's never been a time when your gifts are more in demand.

Every Virgo can relax in the knowledge that it's true that if you take that first step towards the heavens . . . the heavens will take three steps towards you.

LOVE AND FRIENDSHIP

When Ms. Virgo arrived at the home of her Pisces friend to spend a "lazy, do-nothing weekend," they had a lovely time. Within an hour, Virgo was busying herself in the kitchen, chatting away as she chopped vegetables and washed the dishes. By the end of the weekend, Virgo had reorganized the pantry, planted the herb garden, mowed the lawn, taken out the garbage (and hosed out the garbage cans—Virgo never does anything by halves), and attacked numerous other tasks, large and small, that were crying out to be done.

Initially her Pisces friend felt—as any host would—embarrassed and a little bit ashamed. It's easy to feel lazy, even slightly incompetent, when a Virgo is around. Somehow you can't help making comparisons between their total efficiency and your apparent total lack of it. But Ms. Pisces, who knew a thing or two about astrology, understood that because her friend was a Virgo, she was happiest when she was busy. Idleness is not a natural state of being for Virgo. The idea of "enjoying doing nothing" for more than an hour or two is alien to their nature. Even when they're not at work, they like to be working on something and feel that they're being productive. Needless to say, Pisces looks forward to her Virgo friend's next visit.

Like rare gems, Virgo friends are treasured by those who share their conviction that true friendship is all about honesty, mutual respect, and an exchange of ideas. Because Virgos are such interesting people, they usually find themselves a circle of stimulating friends. And because they're people of integrity, you can count on a tried-and-true Virgo friend when you need help. Help with preparing an important dinner party, help with your tax return, even help with renovating your bathroom. How is it that Virgos know so much about the tax laws, and the secrets of making tiles stick? Simple, they've read books on it.

Virgos make a point of knowing about those utilitarian things that make everyday life run smoothly. A veritable fount of information, Virgo is always hungry for more knowledge. Many of us may *think* about doing something to improve our mind, our health, or our career prospects, but Virgo is the one who will get up and do it.

No wonder Virgo seems so together. From the first meeting you know this is someone reliable, someone sensitive but not swayed by irrational emotion. Someone gentle but strong. Someone open to new ideas but not gullible. Virgos aren't out to draw attention to themselves, but it would worry them terribly if they thought they were creating the wrong impression. "Was I too quiet? Was I too assertive? Should I have said something? Did I say the right thing? Am I wearing too much cologne?" When it comes to fretting, Virgo takes first prize. It drives them crazy (and sometimes others as well) if something is not just 'right'.

Usually, though, Virgo *does* manage to get it just right. Well mannered and often good-looking, even Virgos who are not strikingly beautiful always have something comely and appealing about them. Your Virgo friend is never going to embarrass you with rude or inappropriate behavior. In fact, Virgos pride themselves on their propriety. The Virgo woman is a real lady in the old-fashioned sense of the word. And the Virgo man is hardly ever guilty of behavior unbefitting "an officer and a gentleman." Think of Virgo Richard Gere in the movie and the image comes to life. Indeed, some Virgo men are so respectable-looking, you may find yourself suspecting that there's more behind that clean-cut image than first meets the eye. And you could be right. We all have our secrets, and darker corners to our psyche. Virgos do a very good job at keeping theirs under wraps.

Virgos try harder than most to remain master or mistress of their emotions, so much so that they're often thought to be lacking in passion. Every Virgo reading this—and every lover of a Virgo—knows that nothing could be further from the truth. So how did this misconception arise? Perhaps too many people take the symbol of Virgo the Virgin literally. There *is* a kind of purity of spirit about Virgo men and women. *Wild* is certainly not a word you would normally associate with Virgo. They even hold back from too much "coochycooing" in public. As for indiscretion and outrageousness, they have no place in the Virgo concept of passion and romance. It is their nature to be prudent.

But prudish, Virgo is not. Nor disinterested. The reality is that beneath the cucumber-cool exterior there smolders a very sexy person with depths of passion just waiting to be unleashed on the right person at the right time. The mere mention of sex symbols Sophia Loren, Claudia Schiffer, Sean Connery, Keanu Reeves, and Hugh Grant should permanently quash any notion of Virgo as cold and unresponsive because they're all born under the sign of The Virgin.

So is Lauren Bacall. Do you remember the scene in *To Have and to*

Have Not when she walked out of Bogart's room saying, "If you want me, just whistle. You know how to whistle, don't you? You just put your lips together and blow." How could he resist a woman who knows her own mind, is nobody's fool, and gorgeous at that?

If you're whistling, hoping to attract Virgo's attention, be smart and prepare yourself for the Virgo selection process. Because you can whistle as loud as you like, but if you don't get top marks on the Virgo scorecard, you probably won't be heard. In intimate relationships Virgo seeks someone of similar ilk. This is a sign that feels more comfortable with a partner who shares their own tastes and beliefs. Sure, they'll have a colorful friend or two who don't mirror every one of their ideas, but when it comes to the most important person in their life, Virgos wouldn't want to settle down with anyone *too* different. Virgo studies the reports that reveal that relationships last longer when partners share the same values and tastes, come from the same social background, and are similar in temperament. Virgo takes those reports to heart.

As for looks, trim, health-conscious Virgo is not going to be attracted to someone carrying twenty pounds too many. Virgo must never be allowed to wonder when your jacket was last dry-cleaned or notice that your shoes are scuffed. They won't be even remotely interested in someone whose clothes scream "Look at me!" If you want to make a serious impression, leave that orange and purple striped shirt or that red Lycra minidress with the plunging neckline at the back of the wardrobe. On the whole, Virgo prefers to dress simply, without too much adornment, too much makeup, or too much of anything. Virgo knows that beauty comes from within, not from Max Factor or a coat hanger.

Ideally Virgos would like to be able to hand over a questionnaire on the first date, but even *they* realize that would be pushing it. Still, there are questions that Virgo needs answers to. Questions that run along the lines of: Which magazines do you subscribe to? How often do you visit you mother? Can you fix a fuse? How often do you replace your toothbrush? Do you prefer to bathe or shower? Do you belong to Greenpeace? Do you have health insurance, disability insurance, homeowner's insurance? Any other insurance? What book/books are you currently reading? Have you ever been overdrawn at the bank? If so, why?

Virgo is clever and tactful enough to extract this sort of critical personal data without a prospect feeling like they're being given the third degree. Only those with marked psychic ability will pick up on what's going on, and be aware that unless they quickly conceal any faults, their file could be stamped "unsuitable."

Basically, Virgo wants assurance that you are health-conscious, environmentally aware, kind to animals, and careful with money. Speaking of money, Virgos are not looking for someone to financially support them. Virgo is one sign that will happily support a partner provided he or she believes that you're working hard towards positive goals that will bring a better life for the both of you. So don't worry if your career hasn't taken off yet. This in itself will not put Virgo off. Many a Virgo has worked to put a partner through school. What Virgo is scrutinizing is your attitude. Right from the start, they want some certainty that you're going to pull your weight in the relationship.

When it comes to that all-important first date, for goodness' sake, make sure you turn up on time. Virgo is a stickler for punctuality, and you could blow it before you even arrive. If you're planning on eating out, choose carefully because your eating habits will reveal a lot about yourself and your lifestyle. You need have no fear about taking them to that Chinese Taoist place. Virgo will love it because it's healthy and they will no doubt be able to fill you in on the nutritional and philosophical theory behind it all. Flash and fancy five-star restaurants do not necessarily make a big impression on Virgo, who is more into good, simple, unpretentious food at a price that's easy to swallow. That's all very well if you share Virgo's preference for health-conscious, money-conscious dining. But if you appreciate the spiritual benefits of feasting on a first rate meal complete with chocolate cake and liqueurs, then you may be dating the wrong Sun sign (unless, of course, you've already checked that your Virgo has lots of planets in Libra, or Pisces, or maybe Cancer on the Ascendant). We know of one Leo woman who was asked out for dinner by a Virgo man, and was horrified to find herself ushered into the local Hare Krishna cafeteria where she "dined" on lentils, brown rice, and yogurt, for which the gentleman left a donation at the door. Warning—there are some Virgos who are so careful with their money, they've been accused of keeping mothballs in their wallet.

As for things to do and places to go, Virgo's interests are wide and varied, although it's safe to say, the more cerebral, the better. Galleries and museums are a good choice. The opening night of an exhibition or a lecture given by a celebrated speaker would appeal to Virgo. The best way to get to a Virgo's heart is through their brain. Which does not rule out less intellectual activities. All earth signs are nature lovers. The park or the botanical gardens are locations where you can get to know Virgo better. Wherever you go, your task is to give Virgo the opportunity to evaluate you and come to the conclusion that you are someone they want to get to know better, too.

There are plenty of people who let their hearts rule their heads and live to regret it at leisure, but Virgo can run the risk of letting their heads rule their hearts. Romance, by definition, is not a rational affair. And Virgos feel a little uncomfortable with the notion of being swept off their feet by a romantic fantasy. Maybe it's because deep down Virgos are more susceptible to romance than they would like to admit. All earth signs, Virgo included, want to know from the outset that their romance has a solid base in reality. And reality means finding a partner who doesn't shy away from commitment. Virgo is the most idealistic of the earth signs, sincerely believing in together forever, et cetera. But it's pretty difficult to be both an idealist *and* a realist. Most Virgos run into trouble if heart and head collide.

It is often the Virgo experience to spend too long in an early relationship with someone who seems so right at the time, but turns out to be so wrong. Yes, they scored ten out of ten on the questionnaire. They buy a new toothbrush every three months and they've never been overdrawn at the bank. They've got the right job, the right image, and the right attitudes. Having secured a neat life package, the future looks set for young Ms. or Mr. Virgo and partner. Yet something seems to be missing. Is it passion?

Many Virgos grew up in a strict home where children knew their place and knew what the rules were. As a result, they become very adept at a young age at repressing their emotions in return for approval. In intimate relationships problems can arise through Virgo's tendency to impose such rigid discipline on themselves that they begin to cut off from their feelings. Too much self-discipline becomes self-denial. So many Virgos over thirty have stories to tell about an awakening that happened once they turned their famous powers of analysis on themselves. When they make the link between their parental conditioning and their relationship problems, Virgos often realize that they have fallen into the social trap of sacrificing emotional and sexual fulfillment for the "right" person and the "right" situation. But once "the light goes on," as one Virgo we know expressed it, you'd be surprised how quickly and definitively they make their exit. Virgos need to learn to trust that what they *feel* is as valid as what they *think*. And that they have the right to listen to their heart as well as their head.

On the surface, Virgos seem to handle the business of breaking up as efficiently as the rest of their affairs. If they make a sudden departure, it may look cold, heartless, and detached, but in all fairness to Virgos, it has to be done this way because this is not a sign that recovers quickly from ugly, emotional scenes. They need the self-protection of a clean break. Virgos do not make ill-considered decisions of any kind, and they plan carefully beforehand so that when the time comes, there is no question that they're making a mistake or that they'll agree to a reconciliation.

Because Virgos stay young and attractive longer than most, it's not at all unusual to hear of them making up for lost time with midlife amorous adventures, often with lovers years younger than themselves, and discovering that love is better the second time around.

Love and contentment bring out the finer sides of every Sun sign. Virgo will excel at making your life together the good life. They gain enormous pleasure from giving of themselves to someone they love. Your home will be spotless, you won't run out of vitamin B, and you'll never have to dash out before breakfast to buy milk when Virgo is at home.

When Virgos are in love, they're geniuses at creating domestic bliss. They are not stay-at-homes, and neither do they have the urge to keep up with the Joneses or live in a lavish mansion and decorate it to death. But they must have a happy and peaceful home for their sense of well-being.

When harmony is missing in their home life, they tend to slip into the habit of finding faults in others. They can easily turn into nervous fussbudgets who won't let others relax and just be themselves. Partners of Virgo know that they won't be able to sneak in a pizza between meals without Virgo noticing and disapproving. Virgo's disapproval may be unspoken, but it will be clear. How can you enjoy that extra hour in bed on Sunday morning when you know that it's your turn to scrub the bathroom and your Virgo is itching for you to get started? How can you possibly roll over and go back to sleep when visions of bathtub grime invade your dreams?

It must be said, there are some Virgos who do not know where love of cleanliness and order crosses the line into unnecessary fastidiousness. When does a germ buster become a compulsive cleaner? When does noticing what needs to be done become noticing what doesn't need to be done at all, or at least not right now? Anyone living with a Virgo has their own amusing story to tell about Virgo's unhealthy interest in dust and dirt.

On the whole, Virgo is not someone who is difficult to live with. It's not in their nature to want to dominate the household or play power games with their partner. In fact, most Virgos are devoted to happiness and harmony in the home. They may be a little overly fussy and fastidious at times, but you can be sure that they're setting themselves high standards, too.

Astrologers believe that the sign following our own holds certain qualities that we need to try to consciously acquire. For Virgo that means looking to Libra and the Libran belief in the value of pleasure and relaxation. Librans don't need a reason to indulge themselves.

But indulging is something that many Virgos don't do often enough. Librans have no trouble putting their feet up and enjoying the good things of life. Nor do they feel compelled, as Virgos sometimes do, to shoulder a heavy load alone. As the sign of partnership, Librans understand only too well that a relationship is about sharing responsibilities. When Virgos incorporate just a little of these more easygoing Libran traits, they find that life—and love—run more harmoniously.

The Virgo man or woman has enormous capacity to work for and achieve lasting happiness. When Virgo says, "I love you," you know that it's for real. And in this mixed-up, muddled-up world, real love seems to be a rare commodity. "I'm getting married in the morning . . ." sings the lucky person who has captured the Virgo's heart. May we remind them of the last line of the song: "Just get me to the church on time."

THE VIRGO PARENT

Have you ever been in the supermarket and winced at the scene of a harried and harassed parent trying to placate their screaming offspring? It's enough to put you off parenthood for life. Then you join the checkout line and there in front of you is the perfect picture of the model family, making civilized conversation while they wait their turn. Suddenly parenthood looks appealing once again.

What's their secret? It could be that the patient, unruffled parent of the neat, well-behaved child is a Virgo. If that's the case, there's a good chance that the child is a Virgo too. Perhaps the child has Moon in Virgo, or Virgo on the Ascendant. In any case, he or she is bound to have some planets in Virgo because Sun signs, like red hair and green eyes, run in families.

Every parent dreams that when baby arrives, everything will go according to plan. Many dream, but Virgo stands a good chance of pulling it off. Virgo will have read the latest literature on pregnancy and birth, and will stun the obstetrician with a correct diagnosis of exactly what stage her labor is at, and provide a pretty accurate ETA.

Back home, the nursery is fully equipped, waiting to swing into action. Rarely does Virgo confuse a hungry cry for a tired cry. The Virgo parent will also have boned up on mothercraft, and should the baby happen to cry a few minutes longer than usual, Virgo won't panic. He or she will gently and competently do whatever has to be done to comfort and soothe.

As for what baby eats, health-conscious Virgos will religiously examine the contents of everything they buy. They prepare the best-balanced meal ever to grace the inside of a lunch box—though there's a risk that some of the more puritanical Virgo parents may try to impose their own strict eating habits on their children, only to find that they've got a rebellion on their hands, or worse still, a child who is developing a complex about food. Fortunately, most Virgo parents lead by example, and their children grow up learning that junk food is not totally evil unless you have it too often.

Virgos won't want their children to grow up to be carbon copies of themselves. Because they respect children as individuals in their own right, they're very conscious of encouraging a child's personal development. Responsible Virgos take the time to teach their children how to tie their shoelaces, run their own bath, blow their nose properly, and generally help them to help themselves wherever possible, and as early as possible. Only Capricorn is as adamant as Virgo in their determination to give their children practical living skills. The children of Virgo know how to prepare themselves a meal, how to run their own bank account, and which bus to catch. Good old-fashioned manners are never out of fashion as far as Virgo is concerned. The child of a Virgo will answer the phone politely, and knows the difference between a soup spoon and dessert spoon.

As soon as their children are ready, Virgos will be eager to introduce them to the rich world of books that they loved so much when they were young. It's quite likely that Virgos will still have safely stored away their own train set or dollhouse and be looking forward to dusting them off and spending many happy hours with them again.

The right school—from both the academic and philosophical point of view—is a major concern of Virgo parents. They will be very involved in their children's education but not constantly knocking on the teacher's door. They know when not to interfere, and leave it to the experts.

Virgo believes that a little work experience goes a long way, and that you can never start learning about work too young. They will proudly take their children on a conducted tour of the office to see how everything works, and let them help out by sharpening the pencils and doing the photocopying. Children of Virgo are also encouraged to join in grown-up conversations and to make their own useful contribution to running the home. It won't be playacting or the nominal washing up of a cup or two, either. The child will be assigned a task that genuinely helps.

The children of a Virgo will never miss a dental checkup or run late for their music lessons. They may not have every new toy that they ask for—they won't be spoiled—but they will certainly have everything they need. Virgo never squanders money. Consequently, children of Virgo learn restraint and the Virgo art of living well but modestly.

As for matters of right and wrong, the lessons that Virgo parents teach are frequently unspoken but nevertheless crystal-clear. Their children know that there are lines which must not be crossed. The Virgo parent is not particularly tolerant of any extracurricular activities that are deemed unwise or improper. A Sagittarius or Pisces parent might be a little more philosophical when they learn that their fourteen-year-old has been caught smoking behind the gym. Or when they overhear a telephone conversation they wish they hadn't heard detailing what took place after the school dance.

But all in all, it's pretty hard to fault Virgo as a parent. Steady as a rock, they're anxious to teach their children what they need to know to get on in life, and give them a sense of safety and security. Does this remind you of anyone? How about Maria from *The Sound of Music,* hired fresh from the convent to care for the seven children of Baron Von Trapp. Maria couldn't possibly be anything but a Virgo. Wonderfully resourceful and imaginative, she turned faded curtains into playsuits, and made physical exercise fun, skipping up the mountain with guitar and troupe in tow. Singing is good for the soul as well as the lungs, as Maria knew. And she was irreplaceable when it came time for heart-to-hearts on important matters such as the birds and the bees.

Put Maria into a time machine (H. G. Wells was a Virgo too), turn the handle, stop the dial at the year 2000, and you've got thoroughly modern Maria, the archetypal Virgo mother. Sensitive and sensible.

This is the mother who can get her kids out from in front of the TV and convince them that kicking a ball around or going to dance classes is more fun. The mother who can dress her children immaculately on a budget, and who won't leave them to find out about the facts of life for themselves.

Virgo will create a warm and secure family home. And should the time come to pull up roots and move, then adaptable and organized Virgo will make an adventure out of it. Over the Alps went Maria, the baron, and all the children, making the best of a difficult situation—because they knew it was all for the best.

Incidentally, the land they fled to is believed by astrologers to be a country (yes, countries have Sun signs too) ruled by Virgo. Switzerland. It's a place where neatness, cleanliness, and efficiency reign. When Maria and all the children go to the supermarket, you just know that everyone will be delighted to see them. What shopkeeper wouldn't be? Seven hungry children to feed. And not one of them out of line.

THE VIRGO CHILD

If your baby was born under the sign of Virgo, you can thank your lucky stars. Or was it your clever astrological foresight? Because from the time little Virgo can talk, you will be wondering whether it's your imagination or whether he or she really is more cooperative, more polite, and more bright than all the others.

Being born under a clever, quick-thinking sign that also loves peace and order means they soon figure out that being good has distinct advantages. These are not the type of children who are given to tantrums or attention-seeking performances. But don't think that they don't know what they want. It's just that these are children you can appeal to on the grounds of reason when you don't see eye to eye.

No one could fail to notice little Virgos' burgeoning curiosity. From an early age Virgos are ready to discover what the world around them has to offer. They love to visit interesting places and meet stimulating people, soaking it all up and fast forming their own ideas and opinions.

But if there are too many comings and goings in the home, Virgo children get easily distressed. And they can become quite edgy if they don't get enough precious quiet time alone. They like to be left to tend to their own business. There's always something to be sorted out, put into boxes, or moved to a different spot where it works better. It's a form of therapy for Virgo, and it's a message for parents of young Virgos—don't take it upon yourself to rearrange their things, and don't assume that any piece of paper covered in scribbles is rubbish. If it were, Virgo would already have filed it in the waste-paper basket. It could be a prototype for a new bicycle or an architectural blueprint for a playhouse. Virgo children are blessed with the ability to enjoy their own company, but remember, Virgos are communicators, and they also need the regular company of like-minded little friends to talk to and play with.

Erstwhile child actor McCauley Culkin is a Virgo. And if ever a child, for one reason or another, should find him or herself "home alone," then Virgo is probably the one who would cope the best. The Virgo child will know what to do and whom to phone, and won't go hungry. In the movie, young Virgo home alone had no intention of leaving his safety in the hands of fate. Instead, he applied his ever-practical Virgoan mechanical ability to constructing elaborate booby traps to ensnare the baddies.

In more tranquil moments, little Virgo is a genius with complicated do-it-yourself model airplanes that would drive the average adult (unless, of course, they're a Virgo, too) to the brink of a breakdown. They have fantastic powers of concentration as well as the discipline to complete that five-thousand-piece jigsaw that they asked you to give them for their birthday. Buy them embroidery kits, construction kits, tool kits, and craft kits, and they'll never get bored or demand to be entertained. Since Virgo is generally keen to learn to read, books must be top priority.

Virgo accepts that rules are made for good reasons. And you rarely need to tell Virgo children something twice, provided what you've asked them to do is reasonable. Explain to them once why they can't swing from the balcony, and they won't try it again. Tell them they can pick up things and look at them, but they must put them back. Virgo children are easy to house-train. Which means their parents don't need to pack up the Wedgewood china and roll up the Persian carpets.

If this sounds too perfect and doesn't entirely fit your Virgo child, it's because personality is a complex thing. Boisterous Virgo children do exist, but they've probably got Sagittarius or Aries in the Ascendant, and even then they won't be *too* boisterous. If they're not especially meticulous, they could have Cancer in the Ascendant. Does your Virgo child like to hold center stage? Check his or her Moon sign and see if it falls in Leo or Aquarius.

By the same token, no matter what your child's Sun sign, if they were born under a Virgo Moon, then they'll be thrifty, well-organized, and unhappy when they're not up and doing. Children with either Virgo Sun or Moon are practical little people. They intuit that the sooner they learn how to make their own bed, wash their own socks, and conquer the mysteries of making toast, the sooner they'll acquire that Virgo security that comes from being able to take care of yourself and manage your own affairs.

Something that might cause some tears and tension is Virgo's tendency to be a fussy eater. Parents of Virgo need to give special consideration to their child's diet, because Virgo is often sensitive to particular foods. Try to avoid additives and chemicals, and aim for as natural a diet as possible. It may be a general principle of child raising these days, but with Virgo it can be a necessity.

Speaking of things natural, young Virgo loves puttering around the garden carrying out nature studies on the life cycle of the bugs. Young Virgo botanists will want their own shelf in the shed and their own plot for their first crop of tomatoes. Virgos love animals. Cats and dogs, guinea pigs, hamsters, and rabbits will all find a way into your little Virgo's heart and (despite their reputation for an obsession with hygiene) into their bed.

School shouldn't present too many problems. Virgos generally can't wait to get there. This is not a child you'll have to drag out of bed in the mornings. Because they're so attentive, inquisitive, and eager to please, they are a teacher's delight—except on those annoying occasions when they fly in the face of their otherwise self-effacing profile by pointing out that someone has slipped up. That Pierre is the capital of South Dakota, not North Dakota. And that the first railway was built in 1825 and not in 1835. Could these be early signs of the Virgo tendency to exasperate others by getting bung up on details? Virgos like people to know that *they* know. An important part of their self-esteem is based on being smart and having the answers.

Most Virgo children are not out to win and annihilate the competition. Rather they are more likely to yield and concede. But it won't be long before Virgos see that others take advantage of their deferential nature, and they begin to feel resentful if they're always at the back of the line. Parents and teachers may need to encourage Virgos to put themselves forward and say they'd like to go first sometimes.

Because little Virgos seems so mature and responsible, it can be tempting to let them assume more responsibility than is good for them. The Virgo child may actually need to be encouraged to play.

When Virgo grows up and introduces you to their first boyfriend or girlfriend, it will pay to show a little Virgoan propriety yourself and play the whole thing low key. Cool Virgo can become very uncool if there's too much parental interference in personal matters. Rest assured you can trust your Virgo teenager not to become infatuated with the wrong type and ignore their studies.

There will be many moments when you'll feel justifiably proud to be the parent of a Virgo child. And there will even be times when you wonder how on earth you managed before Virgo came along. Who's that knocking on the bedroom door? Why, it's your Virgo child. He's just turned seven and already he's bringing you your morning cup of tea. He hasn't spilled a drop, and the toast is just the way you like it.

BORN UNDER VIRGO

Buddy Holly	Harry Connick, Jr.
Grandma Moses	Maurice Chevalier
Roald Dahl	Bill Murray
Stephen King	Queen Elizabeth I
Patsy Cline	Prince Harry
Van Morrison	Chrissie Hynde
Lily Tomlin	Charlie Sheen
Ivan the Terrible	Kate Millett
Zandra Rhodes	Jeremy Irons
Jimmy Connors	Anne Bancroft
Otis Redding	Lenny Henry
Elvis Costello	Peter Falk
Confucius	Cass Elliot
David Copperfield	Cinderella
Larry Hagman	

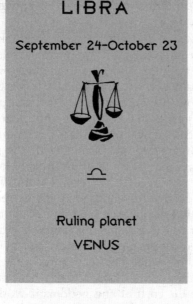

LIBRA

September 24–October 23

Ruling planet
VENUS

Give peace a chance.

John Lennon–born October 9

THE LIBRA NATURE

Imagine a world without conflict, without poverty or ugliness. A world where the sun shines every day and the flowers bloom. If it sounds like a dream, that's because it is. We know that we can have no idea of summer without winter, and that black would not exist without white. And that the notion of peace exists only because we have conflict. We live in a world of opposites. Libra is born with the keenest appreciation that there are two sides to everything, and that life is full of contradictions. Obtaining equilibrium is difficult, but it is Libra's role to try. This is the essence of Libra, the sign of balance.

Libra's symbol of The Scales of Justice is often seen carved above the doors of courts of law, where evidence is weighed without prejudice. People born under the sign of The Scales are very concerned that things should be fair, and will put in more effort than most to keep everything in their life—especially their relationships—in balance. Librans have a special gift for bringing opposing forces together to find a resolution.

Conceding that your opinion is not the only valid one and appreciating that everyone is entitled to their point of view are the first steps towards peace. And they're the steps that Libra is the first to

191

make. Libra believes in, and practices, give and take. There is no one more willing to compromise and cooperate. This is why Libra is called the sign of the negotiator, the diplomat, and the peacemaker.

Mohandas Gandhi was a Libra. He has become a human icon of the fight against injustice and inequality through peaceful means. By bringing together parties in conflict and getting them to talk, he tried to get them to focus on what they had in common, not what held them apart. History records his struggle for the rights of outcasts, his fasts to try to get the British to grant India independence, and his efforts to convince Hindus and Moslems to reconcile their differences. Nonviolence and passive resistance were his weapons. The little Mahatma firmly rejected the label of saint, but Mahatma means "a great soul." Today, half a century after his death, Gandhi is revered as a saintly figure loved by people of all races and religions.

Libra offers us their belief that peace can only be achieved through peaceful means. Libran writer Gore Vidal, whose penetrating eye and razor wit lay bare the corrupt and hedonistic world of governments and high society, once said, "I have noticed in history that every war ends in settlement. Why not have the settlement without the war?" It's a question that begs to be answered not only by the leaders of a world in conflict, but by men and women living everyday lives, fighting everyday battles.

Why are Librans so understanding of everyone's point of view? Because Libra is the sign that rules relating to others. The zodiac is a symbol of the cycle of the evolution of the soul. In the previous sign, Virgo, it was the task of the individual to learn how to be self-reliant, and the meaning and the value of service to others. Now, in Libra, the major lesson for the individual is to learn the importance of relationships.

For Librans, the emphasis is on achieving balance and tranquility through relating to significant others. A husband or wife is usually the "significant other" in most people's lives. Certainly the spouse is the most important person in the life of a Libran. This is why Libra is the sign of marriage. No Sun sign is so utterly single-minded in its mission to secure a lifelong mate. In their working lives, too, they often seek partnership. The benefits and advantages of working with others are so obvious to Libra that they wonder why anyone would want to go it alone. It's a rare Libra who chooses to operate as a lone ranger.

Of course, we all find ourselves alone at times. But Librans feel somehow incomplete when they are alone for long. It's as if their scales have tipped and lost balance. If they tip far enough, Libra can fall into depression and anxiety. "It's not fair," thinks the malcontent single Libran who looks around and sees happy couples everywhere.

But Libra, who understands that everything has its opposite, ought to know better than anyone that togetherness can't really be appreciated unless you have spent some time on your own.

There is so much to be learned from opposites. In astrology, too, our opposite sign always shows us the virtues that we can cultivate to make our own sign work better for us. Aries opposes Libra. Aries is the first sign of the zodiac, the sign of self-awareness and independent action. Other people are, of course, important to Aries, but their own needs come first. In Aries their strong sense of self is at the forefront of all decisions in life. There are many Librans who need to adopt a little Aries-style self-assuredness and be more of their "own" person.

Moreover, Aries never has a problem making decisions. Libra does. Being blessed (or cursed) with the ability to see all sides of any situation means Libra often becomes confused, even overwhelmed, by options. To Libra, arriving at the right decision means making a choice based on what seems like an infinite number of possibilities. And then what of the consequences? Libra can't help thinking, "If I apply for this job, I'd have to spend two hours a day in traffic, so it would be logical to move. But I really like this apartment, I've finally got it just the way I want it, and there's no guarantee that I'll find somewhere as nice. Maybe I'll just stay here and look for another job closer to home. But that job is such a good career move, and it pays so well . . . I could probably afford a house with a garden. Wouldn't that be lovely. Hmm . . . maybe not. It's common knowledge that houses are almost impossible to find in that area . . ." Once Libra has made up his or her mind, the worst thing anyone could possibly say is, "Are you sure?" Watch Libra start to run through it all over again.

In attempting to arrive at a "balanced" decision, no one prevaricates and procrastinates like a Libra. Aries would think about it for three minutes and decide. Aries are firm believers in the idea that "he who hesitates is lost." Okay, in hindsight the decision might not have been the right one, but they would be confident they could rectify the mistake with another quick decision. Librans are inclined to spend so long weighing all the pros and cons that they can become so beset by indecision that they get stuck, and unable to move in any direction.

Opposites can never merge. Librans can never think or act exactly like Aries, nor is it their destiny to do so. But adopting some of the virtues of our opposite sign is just about the most helpful thing we can do for ourselves.

It's precisely because they can see all the ramifications that Libra understands that there is often no such thing as the right or wrong choice. Let's face it, very few things in life *are* black and white. There are many shades of gray, and Libra knows the advantage of choosing gray, of following the middle path. On the playing field of life, Libra prefers to take center position where he or she can skillfully and safely kick the ball around somewhere in between defense and attack.

In discussions on politics, religion, and all the heavy issues, Librans like to place themselves on safe, neutral ground. People feel that Librans understand their point of view because they usually do. It's a wonderful ability that helps Libra get along with others so well, and is one reason why Libra is so popular on the social scene. Master of the art of social interaction, Libra's name is at the top of everyone's guest list. A successful dinner party or office social probably wouldn't be so successful without Libra, who can be Prince or Princess Charming. The consummate exponents of civilized conversation, Librans know exactly when to speak and when to listen. And they never put their foot in their mouth as those other great bon vivants, Sagittarians, usually manage to do. Yet, like Sagittarians, they can always be relied upon to entertain and amuse. When Librans speak, what they say is intelligent, well expressed, and peppered with clever witticisms and metaphors that captivate even the most jaded sophisticate. Their facility with words, the way they achieve a stylistic balance between the poetic and the pithy, earns Librans intellectual credibility. It can also earn them the reputation of deliberately using their erudition and vast vocabulary to impress.

Libra is the second sign in the element of air: the element that rules the mind, ideas, and communication. Listen to the Librans you know when they speak and you'll notice how they're keen to present a balanced perspective, always striving for objectivity and impartiality. Their sentences are full of phrases like "On the contrary . . ." "Look at it from her point of view . . ." "Nevertheless . . ." "Putting that in perspective . . ." Libra deftly tosses the discussion back and forth, constructing an even-sided debate, and preventing one party ever getting too hot under the collar. Libra would hate to be considered biased or out of line in any way.

Mind you, there are times when their efforts to remain impartial and politically correct make you wonder if they have an opinion of their own. You find yourself tempted to ask, "Will the real Libra please stand up?" But this *is* the real Libra. Because in the final analysis (as Librans would say), it is the role of their Sun sign to find a balance.

Rarely do Librans fail to make a good impression. Not only eloquent but also elegant, they're very aware of the fact that people *do* judge by appearances. And they're prepared to spend a lot of time and effort, not to mention money, on getting the right appearance.

Like Aries (opposite signs also have a lot in common), Libra is urbane, sophisticated, and gives plenty of thought to personal presentation. If you want the name of the best hairdresser in town, ask a Libra. If you want to know where to buy designer labels at discount prices, Libra has a list. Libra is possibly the only person who flings open the doors to his or her dressing room (yes, Librans often have an entire room consecrated to their clothes, not a meager closet) and sincerely laments, "I haven't got a thing to wear."

Beauty, in all its manifestations, is essential to Librans because theirs is the sign of aesthetics. To live surrounded by beautiful things and to create beauty are all part of that fundamental Libran search for balance and harmony. According to the ancient Greeks, truth, beauty, and goodness were the great virtues. And it is Libra who comprehends so well the link between them. You cannot have beauty without truth, nor beauty without goodness. Beauty is an integral part of happiness.

If they're faced with drabness, banality, and ugliness for any length of time, it can disturb the Libran nature to the point of making them seriously depressed. This is why Libra has more than just a taste for the beautiful. They have an instinct for what makes the beautiful beautiful. Librans never need to consult an interior decorator or read books on how to put style into their home, their wardrobe, or, indeed, their life. They just *know* whether the curtains should be silk or velvet, whether cobalt blue will work better than indigo, and why carrots and beans look (and therefore taste) better than broccoli and beans. The magic component in all concepts of beauty is the Libran word: *balance.* Blessed with a finely tuned sense of proportion, symmetry, juxtaposition, and contrast, they know exactly what looks good where.

Designer Terence Conran has defined the Libran style. Through Conran's Habitat, his international chain of houseware stores, Conran brings simple, unadulterated beauty into every home. You know you can't go wrong with a Habitat couch or teapot. Conran's highly successful business is based on the concept that by living simply and aesthetically, you create an air of well-being and your whole life is better for it. It's more than style. It's lifestyle.

Conran also has the Libran gift with words and has written several glossy books on how anyone can live more aesthetically. He says, "Design really does matter, because if people are satisfied with their home life they feel comfortable, pleasant and relaxed. If their friends come into their houses, coo with admiration and say, 'You've done a wonderful job here, how clever you are,' it adds to the pleasure of life. I can't think of many easier ways to improve your life."

For people who seem so confident in their sense of style, it's curious how many Librans wait in expectation for others to "coo with admiration" over their fashionable stainless steel industrial-look kitchen, or their divine antique Chinese medicine chest they keep their jewelry in. Libra beams when guests marvel at the Mulberry Bavarois with Almond Crème Anglaise that they whipped up from the recipe in *Larousse Gastronomique* (the French edition, of course). When Libra is around, it's not hard to begin to feel desperately plain by comparison. Why, even the dishes their cat dines from are more gorgeous than the ones you eat from at home. So why is it that people who are so sure of their taste need so much affirmation and approval from others? Being born under the sign of opposites inevitably makes Librans look around and compare themselves with others. Most Librans are heavily into comparisons.

The Libran love of beauty and pleasure in all its variations is bestowed on them by their ruling planet, Venus, the goddess of love and beauty. Libra shares Venus with Taurus, a sign that also loves pleasure and the good things in life. But Taurus is a fixed earth sign, and Taureans are more traditional in their likes and dislikes. Taurus doesn't care too much for the vagaries of changing fads and fashions and what's "in." In airy Libra, Venus becomes intellectualized and operates through the mind and the eyes. She is elevated to the realm of *concepts* of beauty that are, by definition, never constant. Librans are receptive to shifts in trends, which is why they have such a feel for fashion and design.

There are many Librans with exquisite taste who can create a stunning Zen room on a shoestring budget, or run up a fabulous couture gown on their home sewing machine. Libra can be an inspiration to us all in the times when paring down and simplicity is a virtue, even a necessity. But total devotion to the beautiful things in life can be an expensive business. Librans want only the best—the best in style and the best quality. It costs dollars to buy the Aga stove that's not only an integral part of the French provincial look, but also makes it blissfully easy to create the perfect soufflé. Classy cars don't come cheap either. And Librans tend not to trust cosmetics or lotions that haven't got the reassurance of a hefty Parisian price tag.

Donna Karan is one quintessential Libran designer who has cleverly capitalized on designing the prescribed "must haves" of a contemporary lifestyle. DKNY beeswax candles come in every subtle shade of cream and brown, and DKNY mineral water can satisfy your thirst for about four times the price of any other water. At that price you feel you really ought to do something with the bottle. You can't just toss it in the garbage; it would feel like a moral transgression. Why not take a leaf out of Conran's book and place two vermilion tulips in it and position it just so on the windowsill. It makes such a nice little composition, and besides, everyone will know what brand of mineral water you buy.

It's extremely important—often too important—to Librans what others think of them. If they've got it and they've made it, they want everyone to know they've got it and they've made it. They seem to get a buzz out of eliciting a little envy in others. Some Librans, it must be said, can be dreadful snobs. Most of them, though, are witty enough to recognize this little potential peccadillo that they have, and cleverly send themselves up.

Libran Groucho Marx (born October 2) had his own memorable way of dealing with snobs. With his Groucho-style wisecracks, he was the genius satirist of the self-important, the hoity-toity, and the would-be somebodies. Social climbers had every reason to blush when Groucho said: "I wouldn't belong to any club that would have me as a member."

Libra's efforts to impress and acquire a "lifestyle" can cost them heaps. Other people's gold credit cards have been known to turn green with envy at the attention that Libra's cards receive. The fact is that Libra is one sign that finds it dangerously easy to spend more money than they should, or more than they've got. We're all prone to a bit of bona fide retail therapy at times, but Libra's love affair with Bloomingdale's and Neiman-Marcus can turn into a tortured romance.

Sarah Ferguson, Duchess of York, is one Libra who is reputed to have overspent to the tune of millions when her marriage to Prince Andrew was on the rocks. By her own admission, she discovered that home-delivered luxuries from Harrods' food hall, and extravagant holidays on the ski slopes of Europe, were an effective antidepressant. That is, until the bills arrived. Credit where it's due, though, Fergie has publicly pledged to work to pay off her debts. Pleasure-seeking Librans can stun their critics with the speed with which they can swing into action.

Here's another paradox of Libra. The sign ruled by sweet, indulgent Venus, that is so good at deferring to others and so much loves their pleasures, is such a force to be reckoned with in the world of business. Libra is one of the four cardinal signs of the zodiac. And cardinal signs go all out for what they want in life. Libra may not be as assertive and aggressive as an Aries, nor as savvy with money as a Cancer, nor as shrewd and calculating as a Capricorn, but being the gentle go-getter and the quiet initiator of the zodiac is often the very key to Libra's success.

In the tricky world of politics and the cutthroat atmosphere of corporate boardrooms, Libra is often flying high. The professions, particularly law, are prestigious fields in which Librans can wield their native wit and charm to their great advantage. Remember, Libra excels at interaction with people. In the tough arena of public life, the Libran manner is often what gives them the edge. It has been said by many before, but it's worth repeating: Libra is the iron fist in the kid glove.

The Iron Lady herself, Baroness Margaret Thatcher (born October 13), is a ladylike Libra who has displayed her cardinal qualities on the world stage. Who would ever dispute that Thatcher knew precisely what she wanted, and was prepared to stand her ground to get it? Much of Thatcher's fighting spirit and lust for power can be attributed to her Scorpio Ascendant. But Thatcher also made excellent use of the Libran Venusian touch. Think back to the occasions you've been intrigued by impeccably mannered Mrs. Thatcher on the TV news annihilating her opposition with clever caustic retorts, all the while smiling benignly. Libra's aptitude for verbal comebacks can cut to the quick, and leave others looking stupid and inarticulate. Libra is hardly ever at a loss for words, which is clearly a major asset in the political world as well as in the politics of everyday life.

Did you ever notice how, in midattack, Mrs. Thatcher would cock her head to one side, holding her chin at a polite and deferential angle, before she fired a verbal bullet? It's a typical Libran affectation. The great Libran wit and social observer Oscar Wilde was clued in to it. There's a line in *The Importance of Being Earnest* where arch snob Lady Bracknell says, "Style largely depends on the way the chin is worn." Watch the Librans you know and you'll notice that when they turn their head to the side and tuck their chin in, it's a sure signal that they're preparing to let you know, in no uncertain terms, who's got the upper hand.

The typical Libran is well proportioned. You'll search hard to find a Libran with a nose that's too large or a mouth that's too wide. And if you find one, he or she might have a Sagittarius Ascendant. The Libran face is often classically beautiful but not necessarily striking unless you count the dimple in the chin that deepens when they smile. And when Librans smile, they can charm the most hardened cynic.

Indeed, appearancewise, Libra has much to thank Venus for. It's a sign that seems to have more than its fair share of physical beauty and grace. They're generally slim and well proportioned. Rita Hayworth, Catherine Deneuve, Cheryl Tiegs, Michael Douglas, and Luke Perry were all born under the sign of The Scales. But so were Meatloaf, Luciano Pavarotti, Dawn French, and Chubby Checker. Venus was a goddess with an appreciation of the pleasures of the table. Librans share their love of food (especially sweets) with Taureans. These are the ones who belong to that group of Librans whose bathroom scales are forever swinging up and down. As Oscar Wilde said, "I can resist almost anything except temptation."

Astrologers believe that, besides Venus, two of the larger asteroids, Pallas and Juno, also cast their influence over Libra. Pallas and Juno occupy the space between Mars and Jupiter, together with hundreds of other tiny heavenly bodies that orbit the Sun, just like the large planets.

Pallas and Juno were in the top rank of the hierarchy of classical goddesses, which makes Libra the only sign to be ruled by not one, but three of the female heavyweights of mythology. Juno (Hera to the Greeks) was the wife of Jupiter. She was the goddess of marriage and childbirth, and in everybody's personal horoscope Juno represents the desire to find a mate, even though, interestingly enough, Juno's own marriage to the king of the gods was not all Olympian bliss. Jupiter was notorious for his extramarital affairs, but when Juno said, "for better or for worse" she meant it. It's true that Librans of both sexes will put up with more than most to stand by their man . . . or woman.

The reason they do is that everyone born under Libra looks to their spouse for a large part of the meaning of their life. The Libran woman still prefers to take her husband's name when she marries, and always marks the "Mrs." box on forms, never "Ms." Male or female, the Juno-oriented Libran provides the invaluable support to their partner that is often indispensable to the partner's success, and Librans themselves often gain through the position of the person they marry. Eleanor Roosevelt was a Juno-type Libran. She had political acumen in her own right, but could she have used it had she not been Mrs. Roosevelt? Marriage and derived status often give Libran women power. Libran men, too, seem better off when they're married. They consciously seek a well-heeled, well-presented partner who will be seen as an asset.

Pallas was an ancient warrior goddess whose story and name became fused in mythology with the goddess Athena. The Greeks worshiped Pallas-Athena as the goddess of wisdom. (The Romans called her Minerva.) Pallas-Athena was skilled in war, but unlike Mars, the male god of war who reveled in the action and bloodletting of the battleground, Pallas-Athena never got her tunic dirty. Instead, she armed herself with tactics. She was the supreme strategist, quiet literally the "brain child" of her father, Jupiter. Legend has it that she was born a fully grown woman out of his head. She was Daddy's girl, Jupiter's favorite, the only child who could wrap him round her little finger. It's a hint that most Librans have a better relationship with their father. Emotions between Libra and Mother are often strained.

Brain, not brawn, is the preferred Libran modus operandi. The Libran skill for careful plotting and planning can leave even Scorpio and Capricorn for dead. Libra may hate confrontation, but that's not to say that "peace-loving" Librans are so passive that they won't fight. They do fight. In their own way. The Libran way is to try to talk people round to seeing things their way. This is how they can never actually be accused of being aggressive. By looking as if they're meeting you halfway, it puts you in the position where you feel compelled to compromise. And so it is that they cleverly maneuver you in their direction. With Libra, it can be hard to figure out where compromise ends and manipulation begins.

Pallas-Athena was crafty in both senses of the word. As the patroness of architects, sculptors, spinners, weavers, and artisans of all sorts, she, too, is connected with the aesthetic dimension of Libra. Her particular talent was her ability to perceive patterns. Librans are often exceptionally gifted in the decorative arts. They can take something ordinary—a room, an office, or a piece of fabric—and turn it into something extraordinary. The concept of the city as a gracious and peaceful center of civilization comes from Athena. To Athens, the city that bears her name, she gave the gift of the olive branch, the symbol of peace. True to Libra, Pallas-Athena found herself doing a balancing act between devising winning strategies on the one hand and creating a peaceful, cultured, and civilized life on the other.

In the battleground of politics, Margaret Thatcher, the polished tactician, surely personifies the Pallas-Athena type of Libra. No matter how feminine they look—and they always do—Libran women can equip themselves as well as any man for worldly life. It's an interesting aspect of Libra that the women have a very well developed animus, the male side of every female personality. And Libran men, likewise, have a strong anima. Their female side is well developed and they relate well to women. Thanks to Venus and Athena, Libra men and women are both blessed with an affinity for beautiful things.

Sometimes the pursuit of beauty for beauty's sake can become the raison d'être of a Libran's life. The philosopher Friedriche Nietzsche was a Libra. He went so far as to say, "It is only as an aesthetic phenomenon that existence and the world appear justified." Nietzsche knew how art and beauty were Libra's healing balm for the vicissitudes and the ugliness of life.

Oscar Wilde knew it too. He wrote a story about the perverse pursuit of the beautiful and how it can become a dalliance with narcissistic self-obsession. Every honest Libra will recognize a little of themselves in the character of Dorian Gray, a beautiful and impressionable young man who lived a life of idle luxury in Victorian

London. When the decadent Lord Henry Wotton advised Dorian to stay young and beautiful because that was all that mattered, Dorian took it so much to heart that one day, before a portrait of himself, he uttered an invocation declaring that the portrait should bear all the physical signs of his sins and aging, so that he himself would never grow old.

And so it was that for two decades, Dorian never looked a day over twenty-two. But with every passing year his deeds became more hideous, and his life more shallow, as he descended into the soul-destroying world of sham and vanity. With no truth or goodness to back up his beauty, he drifted aimlessly from one entertainment to another, from one salon to the next, destroying one person after another—his sins all the time accumulating and always transforming the picture. But the pleasure and self-adoration he thought was the meaning of his life ultimately brought him only suffering because deep down he comprehended the vanity and futility of his existence.

Like a Greek tragedy, *The Portrait of Dorian Gray* could not have had a happy ending. Dorian murdered the friend who had painted the picture and then tried to destroy the painting. But when he thrust a dagger into the portrait, which had grown more and more grue-some over the years, it reverted to its original beautiful image. And Dorian, in an instant, was struck with the effects of all the years of his vanity, shallowness, and evil. He lay dead on the floor, a wizened, loathsome-looking old man. Was Lord Henry to blame for the de-struction of Dorian Gray? Or did Dorian bring it on himself? Maybe, as so often is the case with Libra, the truth lies somewhere in the middle. "There's nothing that can cure the soul but the senses," says the cynical Lord Henry at the beginning of the story. But he balanced it off by saying, "And there's nothing that can cure the senses but the soul." The senses and the soul feed each other. Both must be nourished. Librans who want to maintain their equilibrium would be wise to reflect on this.

By living only to satisfy the senses, Dorian Gray lost touch with his soul and became the classic Libran dilettante. The Libra who devotes his or her life to pleasure, who dances from one party to the next, who spends too much time deciding whether to buy the blue suit or the black one, is trapped in an unbalanced and precious exis-tence. Librans often have a reluctance to delve too deeply into the depths of life and ponder on what really motivates them. The super-ficiality of having lovely things and a relationship that looks like it's sailing along smoothly (even if it isn't) is a major weakness of this sign.

Librans have the dubious ability to be able to tell themselves that something is working just because they think it ought to be. They also convince themselves that if it *looks* right, it is right. They can become so focused on outer peace that their inner peace gets eroded as they try to whitewash over the ugly, the unwanted, and anything that is too difficult to deal with. But what price peace? Ultimately Librans find little peace if they suppress for too long the reality of an undesirable situation.

Some of the solutions lie in the following sign, Scorpio. Every sign of the zodiac benefits from preempting a little of the virtues that are going to be developed in the sign to come. Scorpio is an emotional water sign. Airy Libra sometimes runs the risk of not *feeling* emotions but intellectualizing them instead. What's more, Scorpio people are penetrating. They cannot help but plummet the whys and wherefores of life in their desire to understand what makes themselves—and others—tick. It's not an easy thing to do, but Scorpios feel it's some- thing that must be done. It's a Libran tendency to take the easy route every time and to avoid the heavy issues. The result is that they can put themselves through misery in order to avoid honest examinations of themselves and their relationships.

The positive Librans who look inside as well as out manage to cut through the superficialities of life and come into an intellectual class all their own. This is when Libra becomes a sign of truth, the kind of truth gained through the perspective they are justifiably famous for. These aware Librans are the keenest, most insightful observers of society and are a civilizing influence on us all. They provoke us to think about how we relate with other human beings. They are the Gandhis, the Wildes, the Nietzsches, and the Gore Vidals of the world.

In his novel *The Judgement of Paris*, Vidal does a retake on the original myth that taps into the essence of the Libran dilemma, that of weighing all options and arriving at the right judgment. In the classical myth called "The Judgement of Paris," the hero Paris was summoned by Jupiter to judge which goddess—Athena, Juno, or Venus—was the most beautiful. It was a hard choice, and it was made even harder by the bribes each goddess offered him to judge in her favor. Athena promised Paris victory in battle. Juno promised him political power. And Venus said she would give him the most beautiful woman in the world. Paris did what any normal young man with an eye for beauty might have done, and promptly declared that Venus was the most beautiful. The most beautiful woman in the world, it turned out, was Helen of Troy, and she was already mar- ried. The rest, as they say, is history. Paris abducted Helen and started the Trojan war.

In Vidal's version, Paris is transformed into Philip, an agreeable young American on a sojourn in Europe to "find himself." He meets three women, each of whom vie for his affections. At the end of the story, just as you think he's going to do what the original Paris did and opt for the dazzling beauty—and if not, then surely the woman who could open doors for him into the world of power and politics—Philip surprises you and chooses Sophia, the quietest and plainest of the three. Is it no more than coincidence that the victor is called Sophia? Sophia means wisdom. That beauty is more than skin-deep is an important lesson for Librans. The modern Paris had learned what the mythological Paris had failed to grasp. The right choice is often not the easy—or obvious—choice. For ultimate harmony and happiness, choice must be based on substance.

Truth requires a wisdom that the Libran clear-thinking can attain. But it means you've first got to sift through the contending voices inside yourself and make peace with the warring factions in your own mind. Gandhi said, "The only devils in the world are those running in our own hearts. That is where the battles should be fought."

All Librans who seek that peace that comes from within, and who have sorted out their own devils, discover the depth of their Sun sign. They find harmony for themselves, and bring perspective and understanding to the eternal human issue of how to live with others. These are the Librans who are then in the position to ask others to give peace a chance.

THE LIBRA CAREER AND DIRECTION

With such a good head for business, Libra has got what it takes to get ahead.

"A great advantage I had when I started The Body Shop was that I had never been to business school." So said Anita Roddick, who proved that she, too, had the Libran head for business. What began as a one-woman shop in Brighton, England, selling simple beauty preparations has become a global business with hundreds of stores around the world trading in eighteen different languages.

Librans can instantly see the business potential in a creative idea. All the better if that business is built on something to do with beauty or beautiful things. All the better still for Librans if it's based on truth. Roddick's business philosophy is to "marry principles with profit." It's a philosophy that is the source of The Body Shop's success.

On the one hand you could say that by exposing the ugly truth about the beauty business, Roddick performed a service to women. She exposed the hype of the cosmetic industry, and revealed exactly what percentage of a fifty-dollar face cream goes into packaging and advertising, as part of her own publicity. On the other hand, you could say that in true Libran style, Roddick cleverly turned the knowledge that women will always be prepared to part with hard-earned cash for beauty products to her advantage, and cashed in on the trend for simple products that look and smell gorgeous. She herself is a very skillful promoter . . . as Librans are. The Body Shop had no formal advertising or marketing department, but it's number one when it comes to effective communication.

Librans are born under a business-oriented cardinal sign, and they're highly motivated to get out there and achieve their goals. All the cardinal signs have a self-propelling ambition. Although Librans—who want so much to get on with everybody and have everybody like them—cleverly cloak that ambition in the spirit of cooperation and a charm and sweetness that come naturally.

Libra is a people person. They have a wonderful way of getting people on their side and would never knowingly do anything to alienate their colleagues. This makes Libra a terrific team player. They always work best in groups; working alone for extended periods gets them down. Harmony and equilibrium in the workplace are everything in a Libran's work. If their work or their workplace, for whatever reason, is unharmonious or has lost its interest value, then all that cardinal ambition goes, temporarily, out the window.

As an air sign and a communicator, Libra likes to talk. What's more, they're very good at it. Not just social chitchat (although they're very good at that), but getting an exchange of ideas flowing between people.

There is one profession that always tops the list in the astro-career directory for Libra. It's diplomat. Career diplomats most certainly need the Libran touch, but any job that relies on the gentle art of diplomacy is a Libran job. And there are many of those. Receptionist, maître d', flight attendant, public relations consultant, all need to be able to handle people tactfully. These are jobs that require you to put aside your personal views when necessary, don a crocodile smile, and be cheerful and helpful (even when you don't feel like it). In short, to be someone who's nice to do business with. No one can do this as well as a Libra. It's why they're so successful in sales. Like their airy cousins Geminis, Librans can sell just about anything. But the more beautiful, fashionable, and sought-after the product, the better they'll be at it. There's no trickery on their part when they themselves have the conviction that what they are selling is desirable and therefore (at least to Libra's way of thinking) indispensable.

Other people sense that Libra is someone who understands their position. Because it is their nature to reconcile and pull people together, they make excellent mediators and troubleshooters, and are generally suited to any job in which their task is to sort out conflicts between people or groups. On the factory floor or at the highest level of international affairs, it's the same basic principle: getting people to see the benefits of making peace with their enemies. If anybody can find the common ground between people and open the doors of cooperation, it's a Libra.

Archbishop Desmond Tutu has earned himself a reputation as a very effective mediator. As head of the Truth and Reconciliation Commission in South Africa, it is Tutu's task to assess the crimes committed under apartheid and to try to achieve justice. For years he has been working to bring opposing forces together in that skillful Libran manner. Others watching from afar are not privvy to the sheer hard work, the intellectual demands, the political maneuvers, and the diplomacy. But what they can see is Tutu's Libran smile. He positively beams. When Librans smile, it's as if the whole world really does smile with them. The Libran charm and affability take them—and their work or their cause—a long way. It makes them very likable people.

People are often surprised to discover that gentle, genial Libra is the sign that rules enemies. But it's all part of relating to other people. And that means the people who are both for and against you. Libra rules "open enemies," to be precise. Astrology distinguishes between "open" and "hidden" enemies, the latter being ruled by Pisces. Open enemies, as the name suggests, are your competitors, your critics, your rivals, and, on a larger scale, the political opposition. Open enemies are the ones who make no secret about whose side they're on.

There are many men and women with Sun in Libra or who have a Libra Ascendant who do well in politics. At least in the political arena you generally know who your enemies are.

Libra is a sign connected with the largest group of people of all— the public. Any position that involves face-to-face interaction with the public, and taps into public attitudes or communicates information to the public, is a Libran domain. Spokespersons for corporations and government departments, for example, publicists, and media present- ers all need the Libran touch. Television reporters Bryant Gumbel and Barbara Walters are both Librans. So, too, is the market re- searcher who invites you to sample a new brand of coffee, or the receptionist who greets you when you enter a hotel.

Astrologers have long noted that people whose Sun is in Libra or whose Sun falls in the seventh house of their horoscope (which is the house of Libra) have a special knack for relating to others on a person-to-person basis. And because they are good at listening and giving objective advice, they often make a career in the Libran professions of counseling, advising, or consulting. You find them working as marriage counselors, beauty consultants, and home relocation specialists.

Human resources, too, is a field that's perfect for Libra. They can circumvent the personality tests, the forms, and the résumés, and zoom in on exactly which person matches which job. They're also good at matching up one lonely person with another "with a view to a permanent relationship." Who better than a Libran (someone born under the sign of marriage) to run a successful dating service?

The learned professions, especially law, attract a lot of Librans. Justice and fair play are, after all, what Libra is about. There is a less apparent reason why Librans choose to go into law. The planet Saturn is in its exaltation in Libra, which means that Saturn functions very well in this sign. The rules and regulations that bind society together come under the auspices of Saturn. Status-conscious Saturn, the ruler of Capricorn, is the planet of material gain. And you often find the professional Libran, and Capricornian, in high-status positions in corporations or government bureaucracy.

So often Librans' success is derived from pooling their resources and efforts with others. They always see the advantage in partnership. It's extremely common for people born under Libra, or with a Libra Ascendant, to go into business with their spouse. Librans will never accept that business and pleasure don't mix. Since they feel more comfortable working side by side with another person, why shouldn't business and pleasure mix? Partnership, for Libra, holds the promise of greater rewards, and there are plenty who go into business with a friend or a relative.

Librans are very aware of equality and want everyone to pull their weight. It's as if they carry a pair of portable scales in their pocket so they can instantly tote up who put in more hours today, who did the paperwork last week, and whose turn it is to do the washing up. Libra can't help making comparisons. And they get very rattled if their scales tell them that their partner is not as committed as they are. But because Librans believe in keeping the peace and compromising, [including when compromise is not called for,] they tend to bottle up their gripes, which inevitably turn to resentment and surface—as resentments must—in an uneasy tension. Libra has the capacity to keep on working as if everything is just fine and then suddenly snap and pour out all their stored-up resentments. It can come as a shock to others who have become used to working with an amenable person. What happened to cooperation?: Where did the harmony go?

People who work closely with a Libran can find themselves starting to watch their words, and are careful to be seen to be doing their fair share. It can be a bit of a psychic burden to be forever on guard. Curiously, Librans can be so intent on everyone being equally productive that often they end up being counterproductive.

Another foible that Librans are prone to, and one that perplexes their colleagues (until they understand what Libra is all about), is that they seem to hold back on decision making. Libras like to hedge their bets. Their ability to see all sides to a question can confuse them, as the pros and cons run around in their head, making it agony for them to make up their minds. Part of that agony is their reluctance to bear sole responsibility for important decisions. It's another reason why they prefer not to work alone.

Many Librans are fortunate enough to be able to turn the flair and artistic talent that Venus endows them with into a career. And thanks to their auspicious relationship with materialistic Saturn, they have an excellent chance of making money from it. Venus and Saturn make an unbeatable combination for someone who wants a career in any of the arts, but especially in design and decoration. All those lovely things that fill the glossy magazines are either made, bought, sold, written about, photographed, or publicized by Librans. *Elegance* is a Libran byword. You certainly won't find them making any deviations into froufrou or cheap imitations.

The gift for visual aesthetics is possibly at its zenith in Libra, who has an instinctive eye for line, form, texture, and color. Coordination comes naturally to Librans. What goes with what is one quandary they never have to endure. You'll find them working in art galleries and gift and flower shops. And there are many window dressers and stylists who were born under Libra.

It hardly needs to be said that fashion is an industry made for Librans. It's a field in which they can bring to life all their creative ideas, with the added status of being able to mix with the beautiful people. Ralph Lauren epitomizes the Libran style. His classy casual wear looks simple, but it whispers status. Studied chic is the Libran stamp. Surely it is Libra heaven to be able to spend your working hours surrounded by divine fabrics, creating new designs and producing your own works of art.

Every level of the fashion industry—running a boutique, or buying for the big stores, or modeling—is well populated with Librans. Libran men and women move well, and they carry clothes well. They don't have to learn to glide along the catwalk. The classic Libran face has even features and good bone structure that enable them to project whatever look is in. Every Libra—no matter what field he or she works in—is fashion-conscious and aware of the importance of how much dress and looks count in the working world. Walk into any large office, select the most elegant people in the most fashionable suits, and ten to one they're Librans.

In fashion or in any artistic endeavor, Libra has a sharp eye for what will sell. People are often quite surprised that soft-spoken Libra is a dynamite accountant, and can whiz through figures and calculate costs, income, overheads, and profit percentages while others are still tapping away on their pocket calculators.

It must be said that Libra has a taste for easy money, and no compunction about marking up an item 300 percent. If people want it, they'll be happy to pay for it, thinks Libra; nobody's forcing them. Libra will do a fantastic job of persuading you that a Navajo blanket or a bottle of Egyptian rose water is exactly what you need.

Where Librans work, and what it's like, are terribly important to their whole well-being. They simply cannot function in ugly, noisy, or uncomfortable surroundings. It's an assault on their sensibilities to be cooped up in a dingy office with rows of gray filing cabinets, harsh fluorescent lighting, and an ancient air-conditioning system groaning in the background. Librans get depressed in a soulless and soul-destroying environment. Like their opposite sign, Aries, they are prone to migraine headaches. And if the migraines become more and more frequent, it's a definite sign that Libra needs to bail out.

Most of us, at some time, have found ourselves in that transitional period between a job we hate and finding a new job that's right. The Librans' response to being stuck in an incompatible job with incompatible people is not to grin and bear it as Virgos or Capricorns might, nor is it to leave as soon as they've seen the writing on the wall as Geminis would. Rather, Librans keep on working in a halfway zone in which they're not giving their best, but are not able to bring themselves to leave. Should Librans find themselves in this scenario, they need only remind themselves they are born under a cardinal sign and can initiate just about anything once they put their mind to it, including the launching of a new chapter in their working life.

Even when they're perfectly happy in their job, Librans have bursts of concentrated effort alternating with slack periods. Catch them on a day with their feet up on the desk, chatting on the phone about where to meet for lunch, and it's not hard for people to form the opinion that they're lazy. For all their business acumen and their need for approval, Librans sometimes let their cover slip, and you can clearly see the Libra belief that there's nothing wrong with taking things easy. Yes, Libra can be very self-indulgent and, on occasion, just plain lazy. If their job is making them miserable, Librans will have trouble summoning the motivation to get out of bed and get to the office on time.

The pursuit of beauty and harmony is central to the Libran path in life. It may be that they are content to make their home a harmonious and relaxing place to be in. Libra might take up painting, or go to evening classes to learn Japanese cooking, gilding, or creative writing. All Librans need an outlet for their artistic inclinations. Expressing themselves artistically is something they feel compelled to do.

For those who make a career in the arts per se, their passion for their medium drives them to produce work that sets them apart as innovators. These are the Librans who have such a strong conviction of the value of their work that they would rival Aries for drive and self-assertion. Annie Leibowitz is one artistic Libran who has become as famous as the celebrities she photographs.

Genius touches each sign in its own way, and the way it touches Librans is to give them not only a passion for their work but the gift for creating work that people can readily relate to and appreciate. Libran writers have this sort of genius. Think of Harold Pinter, Arthur Miller, P. G. Wodehouse, Clive James, and Melvyn Bragg. So many of them build their success on their skill as clever, cynical, and very entertaining social observers. Libra's eye into the windows of the rich and famous—and the ordinary—expertly analyzes the dynamics of society, the serious, the silly, the pompous, the sublime, and the ridiculous. Libran writers and artists chronicle popular culture, revealing the good and the bad for public viewing.

Born under a sign connected with public appeal, they do very well in anything that is created for the public. And they always seem to hit the mark. This makes them well recognized and well recompensed for their work. As Leibowitz says, "I have been at this for twenty-six years. I do know what I'm doing . . . and they have to pay me for that." Librans know what they're worth.

No one should ever underestimate their sharp brain, their way with words, and the clever way they get people onside. Behind the likable, cooperative, and sociable Libran you know is someone who knows exactly where he or she wants to go in life, and has a well-formulated plan on how to get there. It's called ambition. Though in typical Libran style, it's wrapped up so beautifully with grace, and tied up with such lovely words, that you might not at first even suspect it's there. But don't be deceived, it is still ambition.

LOVE AND FRIENDSHIP

"This is the One," says the voice on the end of the line jolting you into consciousness at 1:00 A.M. It's your Libra friend who couldn't wait any longer to tell you all about the wonderful man or woman they've just met.

When Libra says, "This is the One" you can be certain that Libra is already running the big day past their imagination. Should it be a sumptuous church wedding or city hall? Morning or late afternoon? A sumptious big bouquet or an understated bunch of freesias?

If you're a friend of Libra, you may think you're experiencing déjà vu as you find yourself mumbling the same things you said last time Libra met "the One." "It's early days . . . Give it a little time" or "Don't rush into anything." But of course, you know that Libra will. For people who have so much trouble making up their minds and are renowned for a lengthy weighing of the pros and cons, Librans sure don't take long to make up their minds about love. Should the object of their desire show signs of not committing as quickly as Libra would like, then Libra will spend many anxious hours plucking the petals off daisies . . . "he loves me, he loves me not" . . . and you can expect a few more midnight calls.

For Libra, every first date has the potential for permanent nuptial bliss. It's a clear message to those thinking of dating a Libra (and who wouldn't when an unfairly high percentage of Librans are drop-dead gorgeous?) that this is someone who doesn't take a light or casual approach to relationships. Easy come, easy go is not their style. That's because so much of the meaning of Libra's life is invested in finding and nurturing a committed partnership. Libra is, after all, the sign of marriage.

Librans are never entirely happy living the single life. They feel like they're in limbo until the One appears. It's as if there's some kind of void in their life and they become preoccupied with thoughts of how and when they're going to meet the right person. As luck (or their stars) would have it, Librans are never without a partner for long. If a relationship begins to sour, they always seem to have someone waiting in the wings. They are notorious, in fact, for jumping into a new relationship before the previous one has been put in the Ex-File.

For all their rational and objective understanding that marriage is a social institution, Librans cannot renounce their belief in "true romance." Marital bliss is still the Libran ideal. There's nothing that worries them more than statistics that show divorce is still on the increase. And nothing that delights them more than the thought of being one half of a happily married couple. There are many Librans who feel that their life is really going to take off once they're married. And often that happens very young. At least the first time around. Oh yes, just having faith in marriage doesn't guarantee any special protection against those disturbing statistics.

It's very common for Librans to settle down with their high school sweetheart. So keen are they to become an "item" and avoid what they can't help regarding as the social stigma of being single. Aloneness is often the same thing as loneliness to a Libra. If they don't marry young, most Librans look for a roommate. They like to have someone around and are unhappy living alone.

If you live with a Libra, you can expect the place to be a hub of social activity. Librans throw the best parties, with the best food, the best music, and all the details thoughtfully planned. They know lots of people and cultivate an interesting circle of friends. They're expert at initiating lively conversation, and they've always got a good story up their sleeve. When Librans decide that they're going to have a good time, they do. Venus, their ruling goddess, makes sure of that. She gives them carte blanche to indulge every whim and fancy.

If you feel like hitting the town, or if you just want to go somewhere interesting, Libra is the person to go with. They know all the best spots. Libra figures that you could be alone forever if you're not prepared to get out and meet people. "I'm in with the in crowd," sang Bryan Ferry. He's a Libra, so he ought to know. It's important to Libra to be in with the "in crowd" because frankly, they seek a prestige partner. Radicals and revolutionaries (they've no desire to make it in the establishment), scruffy types (or even people sporting cheap plastic wristwatches or the wrong label on their jeans), and high school dropouts (unless they've dropped out to make their fortune) won't get a second glance. Since Libra adores artistic people, painters and poets won't be dismissed out of hand so long as they can prove their credibility. Quality means everything to Librans, and on the whole they're pretty discerning about who they will or won't date. There are some Librans for whom no one seems quite good enough.

Does this sound like the Libran you know? Okay, so this is another one of those little Libran paradoxes. The person who can come across as cool and choosy is also the person who starts to feel a little desperate when dateless. At this stage, any relationship looks better than no relationship.

Friends of Libra have amusing stories to tell about Libra's various "Ones," even if they lasted less than a week. Librans so much want to believe that each new love is right for them that they can become overly eager to please. At the bottom of Libra's efforts to fit in and be liked is a need for togetherness and an abhorrence of domestic disharmony. The origins go back (as these things usually do) to a childhood in which Libra was distressed by hostilities, spoken or unspoken, between his or her parents. Many Librans are born into homes where mother and father are a mismatch or were often at loggerheads when Libra was growing up. Young Libra may have felt that peace was a fragile and precious commodity, and they quickly learned not to do anything that might upset the precarious emotional balance at home.

Consciously or unconsciously, Librans do have the tendency to mold themselves into the sort of person they think the other person wants them to be. We still remember one Libran woman who was dropped by her sophisticated law-student boyfriend on a Monday, and was in the arms of a bright young yoga teacher by Friday. Within a week, Miss Libra had switched from *cordon bleu* cooking and elegant Italian shoes to lentils with yogurt and Indian sandals. To all appearances she had been through some mysterious personality makeover. Maybe she had. There are some Librans who are prepared to make radical changes to their lifestyle in their attempts to convince the man or woman of the moment that they are the One themselves. Should it not blossom into true love, Libra comes to realize what his or her friends suspected from the start: namely that the only thing that they had in common was that they were both single and both wanted to be in a relationship.

Another insight that friends of Libra are bound to have at some stage is that when love is in the air, friends come second. In these liberated times, Librans are still capable of phoning a friend to cancel dinner because they've got a date. "I know you'll understand . . ." says Libra tactfully. And of course, friends do understand, at least once or twice. To be so reasonable and accommodating in their relations with people generally, yet so susceptible in affairs of the heart, is yet another Libran contradiction.

Libra is an air sign, and all air signs live more though their minds than through their feelings. Perhaps that's why Libra plays the politics of relationships so well. They often gain the upper hand by not directly asserting themselves but by appearing to do exactly the opposite. In disagreements, Librans always make a point of showing that they understand the other person's point of view. Remember, it is their nature to be conciliatory and cooperative. "I'm on your side, I know what you're going through," Libra reassures you. All the while, Libra is moving closer towards getting what they wants. How can you make a stand against someone who's being so nice? Libra seems to make confrontation impossible. You feel you ought to go along with them, and in the end you find yourself agreeing, or at least compromising. Later you may think, "Hang on, this isn't what I wanted or what I planned," and you realize Libra has gently maneuvered you into doing things their way. It's very clever. Sometimes, though, Librans are too clever for their own good. They can turn people off, and then genuinely wonder why.

To get an idea of how far they can push the power politics of relationships, study the movie *Dangerous Liaisons*. It's based on the novel by Pierre de Laclos. (Only a Libra could have written it.) Of course, not many Libran liaisons get as dangerous as the ones in the story, but quite a lot could be labeled "tricky liaisons." When Librans are intent on sealing the relationship they've set their mind on, they can be as predatory as their opposite sign, Aries.

Jim Henson, creator of the international star Miss Piggy, was a Libra. So, too, is the lady herself. Who could forget Miss Piggy, decked out in pearls and gorgeous gowns, ingenuously batting her eyelashes and declaiming, "Pretentious, *moi?*" Notice her affected preference for the French. Somehow "me" sounds less self-centered when you say it in French. More romantic, too. Like the Libra that she is, Miss Piggy is not prepared to give up on Kermit. With her trotters firmly clasped around his neck, she's forever trying to get him to come to his senses and realize what he's missing out on. Did anyone ever tell her that frogs and pigs don't make a good match? Well, that's no reason not to try, at least not to a Libra. She's willing to become more like a frog if that's what it takes.

When Librans fulfill their most cherished dream of finding togetherness, security, and happiness in marriage, then nothing is too much trouble. Librans want to give their all to another. Even if it means giving up something else in their lives.

There's a myth about what Librans are prepared to relinquish for the sake of love, in which Venus plays the vital role. Atalanta was the beautiful heroine who was the equal of any man in hunting and in battle. Her father was urging her to marry, but Atalanta was reluctant. She declared she would only marry the man who could outrun her, so certain was she that there were none who could. The penalty for losing was death, yet many suitors tried, and lost. But one of her admirers, Hippomenes (who was no great athlete), was more determined than the rest, and he prayed to Venus for help. His prayers were answered. Venus gave him three gold apples, which she instructed him to drop in Atalanta's path during the race. When Atalanta saw the gleaming golden apples cast before her, she stopped to pick them up. Her split-second pause gave Hippomenes enough time to win the race. How Libran of Venus to think of the distraction of beautiful things. And how Libran of Atalanta to be so impressed by Hippomenes' ingenuity that she was converted from confirmed spinster to loving wife overnight. Atalanta may have lost a footrace. But she gained a husband.

Libra puts their relationship with their partner before anything else, including career, friends, or family. Not that personal interests, career, friends, and family don't matter to Libra. It's just that their relationship is always their number one priority.

There is no bigger day in a Libran's life than The Big Day. If you receive an invitation to the wedding of a Libran, you know it's going to be an event not to be missed. We recently attended the wedding of a Libran publicist who, every day of her working life, was impressing clients, winning new business, and efficiently directing a staff of twenty. She organized her wedding in the same way. Libra knows that a good show needs a good producer. Preproduction schedules, postproduction schedules, briefing the relatives, briefing the bridesmaids, were all handled with cool Libran aplomb and executive expertise.

None of the guests expected, however, that the businesslike bride, a woman whom they knew to be an accomplished public speaker, would be rendered speechless when the time came to say "I do." So overwhelmed was she by the magnitude of the moment that the guests were momentarily left hanging there, wondering if it was possible that Ms. Libra was having second thoughts. But no, sighs of relief were audible all round when the bride summoned enough strength to nervously squeak her vows.

Librans may believe that marriage is made in heaven, but they're the first to accept that it's lived out on earth. Once married, they're prepared to put in a lot of maintenance work. Librans are the people who tell you, "A good relationship takes effort, and marriage is something that has to be worked on." The Libran wife or husband will make home a haven to return to even if it's a one-room flat. It will be as splendid as the bank balance allows since every Libra is an interior decorator at heart, and even those on the tightest budget will have linen tablecloths, lovely wineglasses, and a dishwasher. Libra can turn a dingy bathroom into a statement of style by artfully placing a loofah next to a cake of oatmeal soap and one divine flawless seashell. Life with Libra is domestic and aesthetic bliss par excellence. Libra knows that sex, too, is an art form and that marriage begins and ends in the bedroom. They make very attentive lovers who are only too aware of the dangers of taking their partner for granted. There are a multitude of reasons why the partners of Librans will never forget how lucky they are. Many, indeed, will wonder how they ever lived before their Libra came along.

It's quite easy for Librans to become so identified with their spouse that they begin to see themselves only as one of a pair. You can tell this is starting to happen when the first-person singular pronoun vanishes from their vocabulary. Libra becomes allergic to the sound of "I" and replace it at every opportunity with the royal "we." Perhaps they don't realize that people *do* notice, and that some are even a little put out by not being able to have a conversation with Libra alone. Even when their partner is not present, you have the impression that you're talking to two people, not one. It can be even more tedious when Libra can't come to a decision on his or her own, or without saying something like, "Let me check with my better half and get back to you." Learning to be your own person is one of the biggest challenges for people born under Libra.

It is frequently the destiny of Librans to gain enormous advantage from marriage precisely because they are born under the sign of partnership. Yet contained within that advantage is the potential to lose their own identity. Codependency is a classic Libran trap.

Some would say this is what happened to John Lennon when he married Yoko Ono and became the world's most famous codependent house husband. Lennon's dependency on Yoko was so all-consuming that she became his life, and he felt powerless without her. The dynamics of the John and Yoko relationship are better understood when you know that he was a Libra and she is an Aquarius. He fell in love with her instantly. "When I met Yoko it was like when you meet your first woman. You leave the guys at the bar." Yoko's account of the beginning is "I mean, what happened with John is like, I sort of went to bed with this guy that I liked, and suddenly the next morning, I see these three in-laws standing there" (Paul, George, and Ringo, we assume). Aquarians, of all people, need their space. They have a horror of any relationship that is too cloying or looks like it's getting too serious too soon. History records that through several separations and reconciliations, John and Yoko played out their own version of *Les Liaisons Dangereuses*.

In times when making a commitment to another seems to have become a difficult thing to do, Libra, above all others, is able to make that commitment. Happy is the person who is looking for a lasting, loving relationship and falls in love with a Libra. Because a lasting, loving relationship is exactly what Libra is looking for, too. When you turn to Libra and ask, "Will you still love me when I'm sixty-four?" Libra will smile and say yes. You, too, can smile in the certainty that they mean it.

THE LIBRA PARENT

Children are part of the ideal of home and marriage. So when the first baby is born, it's the icing on Libra's cake. But Libra knows that when two become three or four, the relationship between mother and father will inevitably be changed. And Librans will do their utmost to keep those changes to a minimum, and try to ensure that their spouse will never feel neglected.

Insistent as Libra is that home should be a well-run and tranquil place, everything for baby will be set up, ready and waiting. Libra will put great thought and effort into creating a wonderful nursery for baby to come home to, and will take delight in making it look like a feature from *House Beautiful*. You can be sure, though, that it's just as important to Libra that it's functional.

The Libran household is not one where guests will trip over toy cars left on the doorstep. You won't find mountains of diapers, buckets, and bottles cluttering up the place. There's a strict limit to the disorder, chaos, and clutter that Librans can live with. They will design an efficient system of shelves and cupboards for those buckets, bottles, and toys, and their children will be taught to keep things in their place. And for Librans, that's as soon as they can do it.

Librans are very mindful that children need to be trained to do things correctly from the beginning. They believe that it's their role, as parents, to be a civilizing influence.

They will give a lot of attention to the right food, the right stimulation, the right amount of sleep—all at the right time. Librans manage to keep the ordered, harmonious life that they value so much by creating an ordered, harmonious life for their children. They know that everyone will be happier and healthier for it.

Because Librans are keen to keep all their relationships running smoothly, they will make it clear to their children that the channels of communication are always open. And that problems are never so bad when they're shared.

All air-sign parents teach their children to read young, and Librans will actively encourage their children to share their own love of the arts. Their children will grow up knowing that there's a wonderful world of art, music, and stories waiting to be explored.

There are few pages in the etiquette manual that won't have been covered before Libra's child turns five. Children of Libra are unlikely to have the bad manners and unruly behavior that make them impossible to take anywhere. The Libra parent is prepared to put in the time and effort to train a toddler not to put their elbows on the table, not to forget their pleases and thank yous, and not to interrupt when others are speaking. Children of Libra still write thank-you notes to grandparents and aunties for their birthday presents. Libra is also concerned that their children should speak well. They'll be quickly taken to task for mumbling and muttering, and told to speak clearly and finish their sentences.

When it comes to birthday parties, the ones staged by a Libran parent will be the talk of the kindergarten. Few people are as creative and inventive as Libra. One Libran grandmother we know was always summoned to organize her grandson's parties. For his fifth birthday she made a troupe of hand puppets and staged a show that had every child—and adult—enthralled. It was a hard act to follow,

but she did it. The following year she came up with the original idea
of a piñata. In Australia, ten thousand miles from Mexico, no one
even knew what a piñata was. But she'd seen pictures of them, and
decided it would be great fun. Indeed it was. So much fun that
piñatas became a popular theme at children's parties all around
town.

Libra is never short of ideas for fun things to do and interesting
things to make. Children of Libra don't grow up without learning
how to sew, knit, and paint. The Libra mother usually has some kind
of creative venture of her own going. It's a great preventive for the
baby blues. As an air sign, Libra can't bear to be trapped in tedium.
That's why, dutiful as they are, many Librans will consider returning
to the workforce, and will apply their executive business brain to
restructuring their life to accommodate children and job. You can be
sure that any interruptions to a Libran home will be kept to a minimum. And as for those precious early years with their children, well,
quality time is not an empty cliché to Librans. They will have organized the time for special one-on-one attention.

Let's face it, when you've got children there are some things that
just *can't* be predetermined. The unexpected always happens sometime. And Libra's delicately balanced scales are easily upset when a
crisis inevitably occurs.

Perhaps the three-year-old has come down with the measles on
the very day the family is booked to go on vacation. Or maybe the
baby-sitter has her own crisis on her hands, and cancels ten minutes
before Libra is due to walk out the door to leave for a business
meeting. Every parent has these horror moments. Positive Librans
will quickly regain their balance and swing into their well-organized
backup system. But what will throw them is the cumulative effect.
Libra, the good manager, doesn't manage very well should the responsibilities and the crises pile up too high and too quickly. If Libra
gets overwhelmed, they tend to get depressed and offload those responsibilities onto their partner and family.

Libra has such definite ideas about how home and family should
be that one of their greatest challenges will arise should they have a
child who turns out to be a throwback to great-grandfather, perhaps,
who was an Aquarian and notorious for his willful ways. Or maybe
an uncle who was an Aries with an Aries Ascendant, and uprooted
his family ten times in ten years in pursuit of his latest ventures. The
child who is seen as too independent or simply too different can
cause Librans many headaches, and plunge them into one of their
famous bouts of indecision in which they toss and turn all night
wondering what on earth they're going to do about it. Does Junior
need to change schools? Should they talk to the pediatrician? Would

it be best to just ignore the whole thing and wait for him to grow out of it? You can be certain that Libra will try hard to choose the course of action that has the best chance of keeping the peace and harmony in *everyone's* lives.

What the Libra parent gives his or her child is the great advantage of growing up in a home where order and calm are respected as essential elements of life. Even more important, the child of a Libra will have the security of a mother or father who is not only deeply committed to their partner, but believes in keeping the family together. And in this day and age, that's a pretty good start for any child.

THE LIBRA CHILD

Okay, we know that every baby is beautiful, but when the relatives come to visit and say, "What a beautiful baby," this is one time they sincerely mean it. It's not just that Libra babies look beautiful, they have a beautiful nature too. So even-tempered and so placid. "Is that a smile?" you ask yourself when you haven't been home from the hospital a week. With a Libra baby, it could very well be.

All parents want their children to grow up to be happy, fulfilled human beings. The best help a parent can give their Libra child is to provide them with a peaceful and harmonious family home in which emotional dramas are avoided wherever possible, and disagreements are resolved by talking things through. Libran children need an atmosphere that is conducive to emotional equilibrium. Libra is a sensitive sign. It's something that's very important to keep in mind, because little Libra's well-being is so tuned in to their surroundings. Try not to allow disturbances or physical chaos to disrupt the home. If you're considering embarking on a five-year home renovation project, you can't expect your Libran child to take the rubble, dust, paint cans, and general mayhem in their stride. Try not to stray too far from regular mealtimes and bedtime, either. All children like an ordered routine. But Libra needs it more than most.

The same applies to children born with their Moon in Libra. Our Moon sign represents our everyday needs and our emotional response to our family environment. The Moon supports us in times of stress. So the first thing that people of all ages with Moon in Libra instinctively do when they're under strain is to buy a huge bunch of flowers and go home to restore some inner peace and tranquility.

Both Moon in Libra and Sun in Libra children benefit from being encouraged to create beauty in their surroundings. It could be that they have the urge to redecorate their room. Get them the color charts and the wallpaper and show them how it's done. Let them cultivate their own window box, or hang their own works of art on the wall. Beauty in all forms is medicinal for Libra.

Libran children get a lot of pleasure from playing house. Little Libran girls will be thrilled if you present them with a dollhouse with all the fittings and furniture for them to arrange and rearrange a thousand different ways. A box full of your old clothes, hats, and jewelry will keep them amused on rainy days. They'll spend many happy hours parading in their latest creation and take great pride in showing off their princess or buccaneer look.

Libra is a child that is going to feel deprived without a couple of special party outfits. Remember they're going to grow up to be the adults who keep the fashion stores in business, and from a young age they can be quite insistent about what they will or won't wear.

With Libran children it's extremely important to lay the groundwork for their interest in the arts. Music lessons, art lessons, drama classes—whatever they show an interest in, encourage it. Their talents may turn out to be far greater than you could imagine. Give serious thought, too, to dance classes if they haven't already been requested. Libra will simply love the social participation and being part of a performance. A beautiful ballerina is what every little Libra girl, at some stage, wants to be when she grows up. Dancing is also good physical exercise. On the whole, Libra is not a sign that is fond of tough competitive sports. Even many of the boys would rather do dancing than race around a basketball court if they had the choice.

Libra children are always well liked, both by other children and by adults. They instinctively know how to fit in socially, and you won't have a hard job on your hands teaching your little Libran how to get on well with people. With a Libran child, your own social life won't go down the drain, and you need not fear that you will become one of those parents whose friends only invite you over when you can get a baby-sitter.

Having said that, it's important not to push your Libran child into a room full of strangers. They don't take well to noisy gatherings where there are dozens of unknown faces. Librans like familiarity. And they like to know that Mother or Father, or someone they love, is there. The Libran child who feels secure is rarely an attention seeker, and is well behaved and compliant.

One grown-up Libran told us how he is still haunted by the memory of something that happened to him when he was seven. Along with his brother and sister, he was dropped off at an amusement park for the day while Mother went to work. They'd been there three hours when his older sister noticed that he hadn't moved from the tree trunk he was sitting on. It turned out that as soon as he'd arrived, he'd ripped his pants. Mortified with embarrassment and fearing that all eyes would be focused on him and that other children would laugh, he preferred to sit out the whole day alone on his log. It's enough to bring tears to your eyes. What this true-life story reveals to parents of Libran children is that they should never underestimate their children's sensitivity. And how important it is to Librans that they're never put in embarrassing situations or made to feel the odd one out.

Yet parents must also be careful not to wrap up little Libra in cotton wool. Not that Libra will complain if you do. Far from it. Already Libra is showing a taste for the easy life. But life's not like that in the big wide world. And Libra children are going to need a little nudge to extend themselves and test the waters of their independence—boys included. If anything, Libran girls are more extroverted and assertive than the boys. They'll never be tomboys (unless they have Aries or Sagittarius on the Ascendant), but neither will they want to stay home and bake cookies. As for the boys, you mustn't give them a complex just because they're quieter, more gentle and artistic, than the other boys. Don't make your Libra son feel like he's a sissy if he takes special interest in his clothes, wants to read your cookbooks, or spends time getting things just right in his room. As Librans grow up, they're going to develop more and more their taste for gracious living. Never forget they're going to need it as their anchor in a hard and aggressive world. Nurture it.

Above all, the most important thing you can do for your Libran child is to maintain an atmosphere of peace and cooperation between people in the home. Even quarrels between siblings will upset them. Disagreements, though, are a fact of life, and Libra should be given early lessons in how to handle conflict resolution. It's a special Libran gift and it's going to be very useful in their working lives.

All air signs are ready to read at an early age. Point out the A's and the B's, and before you know it, they'll be reading stories to you. When they start school, they'll impress their teachers straightaway. Libra children are alert and articulate. And they'll be very proud when they bring home their A-plus compositions.

Socially, Libra children grow up fast. It will be no time at all before their little admirers will be dropping in to ask if Libra can come out and play. Librans, likewise, will go through a series of infatuations before they're fifteen. Try not to look too surprised (and whatever you do, don't laugh) when Libra, age twelve, comes home and tells you that he or she is engaged. Don't be alarmed either at the volume of Valentine cards pouring through your mailbox every February. Just let those first romances run their course. Be prepared, though, for the trauma of the first big breakup. When Libra hits the first trough in the learning curve of love, it's going to leave a lasting impression.

Handle this properly and you'll be helping them to handle their adult relationships. If Libra learns from you that relationships are precious and need to be nurtured, you will have given your child perhaps the best thing you could. Because having a happy home and children of his or her own will one day be the greatest source of happiness in your Libra son or daughter's life.

BORN UNDER LIBRA

Alfred Nobel
Jesse Jackson
Jean-Claude Van Damme
George Gershwin
Clark Gable
Horatio Nelson
Sebastian Coe
Cliff Richard
William Penn
The People's Republic of China
Vienna
Martina Navratilova
Sting
Lee Iacocca
Paul Simon
Oliver North
Christopher Wren
Arthur Miller
Bela Lugosi

Susan Sarandon
Mickey Rooney
Sigourney Weaver
Bruce Springsteen
Walter Matthau
Bob Geldof
F. Scott Fitzgerald
T. S. Eliot
Thor Heyerdahl
Jimmy Carter
Linda McCartney
Ronnie Barker
Felicity Kendall
Christopher Reeve
Olivia Newton John
Brigitte Bardot
Dwight D. Eisenhower
Sleeping Beauty

SCORPIO

October 24–November 22

♏

Ruling Planets

PLUTO AND MARS

Love, and do what you will.

Saint Augustine—born November 13

THE SCORPIO NATURE

What's out there? For a long time astronomers suspected that there was an unknown force at the far edge of our solar system. They figured that whatever it was, it must be big because it had the power to affect the orbits of Uranus and Neptune. But when the mystery planet was eventually sighted in 1930, they were amazed to discover that it was actually very small, the smallest planet of all. It was named Pluto, after the god of the underworld.

It wasn't long before astrologers were describing Pluto the same way—very small, but very powerful. Nor was it long before they gave Pluto rulership over Scorpio. The distant "hidden" planet that was the last to yield its secrets fitted perfectly with the nature of Scorpio.

Until Pluto was discovered, Mars was the sole planetary ruler of Scorpio. Mars, the god of war, also has rulership over Aries. And Scorpios are every bit as driven and dynamic as Aries. When their passions are ignited (which is often), Scorpios will fight. And when it comes to ambition, they can leave Aries for dead. Both have a healthy ego. But on the whole, Aries people are more direct and up front. What you see is what you get. Not so with Scorpio.

This is a complex sign, and there's always more to Scorpios than meets the eye, which doesn't make it easy for others to know what they're really like, let alone what they're thinking. And that's just the way Scorpio likes it. They prefer to play their cards close to their chest. Scorpios love mystery. And they are only too aware of the power that comes from being a little mysterious themselves. Mind you, Scorpios are pretty expert at finding out whatever they want to know about others.

Scorpio is the sign of the investigator. It is their instinct to probe, to uncover the facts and find out what lies beneath the surface . . . of everything and everybody. They want to know what makes people tick. But even more, they want to know makes *themselves* tick. Scorpios are heavily into self-investigation, and they're not afraid to put themselves under the microscope.

The one thing Scorpios cannot conceal is their penetrating gaze, though they may try. These are the people who wear dark glasses on cloudy days. They know that they sometimes make people feel uncomfortable, as if they are under that Scorpio microscope. It's true, Scorpios can be very intense and confronting. But lesser mortals who aren't daunted by the intensity will be drawn, wondering why Scorpio is so interesting and intriguing.

From your first encounter you'll realize that this is not someone who wastes too much time on idle chitchat. Scorpios can't show interest in the superficial for long. They want to get down to the fundamentals. And in no time at all, you find yourself telling Scorpio about your first formative love affair, your philosophy of life, and your most private aspirations that, up to now, you've only ever confided to your best friend. In spite of their slightly guarded, sometimes aloof manner, Scorpios have the empathy that allows people to express their deepest and most heartfelt thoughts without feeling embarrassed or awkward.

Once engaged in deep and meaningful conversation, Scorpios will drop just sufficient snippets of information about themselves and their own experiences to keep *you* fascinated, and you'll mean it when you say, "We should talk some more."

Know that you are now under the spell of Scorpio. Scorpio has seduced you, and we don't mean it literally (although that's always a possibility), with something you can't quite define. It's called magnetism, and there's no defining that. The hypnotic attraction that Scorpios exude is not what you would associate with a scorpion. But this sign, with all its complexities, has other symbols that have been in use since ancient times: the wise and wily serpent, the eagle that is free to soar on the winds, and the phoenix, the mythological bird that was cast dead upon a fire and rose again from its ashes. Scorpio people, too, have that magic ability to rise again from the ashes of their disappointments. It is one of their greatest strengths.

As the eighth sign of the zodiac, Scorpio follows Libra. Yet the gap between these adjoining signs seems like a chasm so far as personality and their outlook on life is concerned. The wheel of the zodiac is a symbol of the evolving human soul. In Libra, the individual must learn the significance and the value of relating harmoniously with others. In Scorpio, he or she is given the task of looking within for answers. Libra, the sign of beauty and balance, doesn't care to look too deeply into the darker zones of the emotions and the subconscious, whereas Scorpio feels absolutely compelled to explore them.

How appropriate, then, that the modern ruler of Scorpio should be the planet named after the god of the underworld. Draped in sable robes and seated on his subterranean throne, Pluto is the awe-inspiring gothic figure of mythology. Consider the way he obtained a queen to share his kingdom. He came up from beneath the earth, seized Persephone, the goddess of life and vegetation, ravished her, and carried her away to live with him in Hades, the land of the dead. But Persephone only lived with Pluto for one third of every year. The rest of the year she remained in the world of the living. Her regular comings and goings symbolize the cycle of the seasons, the inexorable cycle of life and death, growth and decay.

The Greeks built no temples to Pluto. Perhaps they dared not risk incurring his wrath. You see, Pluto is the lord of the dead, and understandably, he's not a god you'd ever want to take chances with. Guarding the entrance to the long passage leading down to his underworld sits Cerberus, the ferocious three-headed dog who prevents the living getting in, and dead souls getting out. Here in Hades, the rivers of woe, fire, and wailing join the sacred River Styx, across which the Ferryman transported the souls of the dead to have their deeds weighed up by the judges who sat by the throne of Pluto.

Death, rebirth, and the laws of karma come under the domain of the sign of The Scorpion. There are very few Scorpios who are not interested in the possibility of reincarnation and who do not think about karma. In the smaller, more everyday meaning of death and rebirth, Scorpio is a sign that accepts the wisdom of letting go. They know that some things in life must end—relationships that are no longer happy, or jobs that don't satisfy the soul—in order to move on. In this profound sense, Scorpio is a sign of growth.

Opening a new door often means having to close the one behind you first. We all, at some time, have to renounce something that no longer works for us. But Scorpio people do this more willingly than most, and with more consciousness of what they're doing. Hillary Clinton may have made light of it when she said, "Life is like a hairstyle. You just keep changing it until you find something that works." But you can be sure that as a Scorpio, she meant it in all seriousness. Don't think, though, that this means that Scorpio walks away when the going gets tough. Quite the opposite is true. Scorpios are extremely tenacious individuals, and when they find something (or someone) with the promise of fulfillment, they won't let go easily. In fact, Scorpio will hang on tight when many would have given up.

That's because Scorpio is a fixed sign. They share with Taurus, Leo, and Aquarius the ability to focus their energy and keep their sights on a goal. Scorpio can plow through a tremendous volume of work while others are still getting their heads around it. Their perserverance is truly enviable. But ultimately Scorpio will not benignly accept an unsatisfactory status quo. Should it become clear that a job or relationship will never work out, and hanging on is futile, they *will* make the break.

Appropriately, Scorpios are born at the time of year when the chill winds blow the last leaves off the trees prior to the onset of winter. Vegetation is dying off, the nights are becoming longer and colder, animals are going into hibernation, and people want to hurry home. Death has been called the last taboo. In our culture, people draw back from looking at death. Perhaps this is why, when Pluto emerged from the underworld to move among the living, he wore a magic helmet that made him invisible. The lord of death is not a pretty sight. But then, Scorpios' interests are not limited to the pretty and the "nice" things of life. It is part of their destiny to penetrate the darkest and most mysterious realms of life, and the soul.

Like Pluto, Scorpios need to pay regular visits to their own personal underworld. Time spent exploring their psyche is time well spent for Scorpios. It may look like Scorpios are brooding just for the sake of it, but the Scorpionic "brood" is their way of having a psychological workout, of processing information, examining their motivations and desires, and working through why they feel the way they feel. Scorpios actually *need* these episodes for their well-being. Only after pondering in private do Scorpios feel equipped to make the changes they feel they have to—changes that are sometimes so dramatic they are better described as transformations.

Transformation is in fact a key Scorpio issue. From time to time, Scorpios reinvent themselves, like a serpent that slithers under the safety of a rock to shed the skin it has outgrown. Scorpios' psychological purges are, in essence, an act of purification. By dumping the dross, they are actually embracing the life force itself, knowing that there can be no new life without death. This is an awesome truth that Scorpio does not recoil from.

Major shifts in a Scorpio's life, whether in career or relationship, are accompanied by deep-seated personal transformations as well. They even look different. They may cut their hair, toss out their wardrobe, or give up smoking, all of which are the outer manifestations of changes within.

Everyone recognizes Rodin's statue *The Thinker*. This is the perfect image of a Scorpio lost in thought. Whatever he's thinking about, you know it's something heavy. When you think of Rodin, you also think of his other great masterpiece, *The Kiss*. The theme is equally Scorpionic. Rodin was a Scorpio, and sex is also a Scorpio issue. A certain love affair, even a brief encounter, can act as a catalyst that triggers an important turning point in a Scorpio's life. It's also a particular phenomenon of this sign that at the time a Scorpio child is born, or when a Scorpio gives birth, there frequently occurs simultaneously the loss of a loved one.

The metaphysical mysteries of sex, birth, and death come under the sign of Scorpio. So universal are they, and so fundamental to our existence, that we call them the rites of passage. People in every culture have created rituals around these experiences, and everyone is touched and transformed by them. But with Scorpios, these experiences are often more dramatic, and intensely felt.

Scorpio also rules those unseen forces that we call the occult. *Occult* means "hidden from view"—from the view of most people, that is, but not from the view of Scorpios, who have a healthy respect for magic and the powers that originate in the subconscious mind. Books on telepathy, divination, and the supernatural are to be found in almost every Scorpio's library.

Scorpio is a water sign. And all water people have an intuitive sort of intelligence. They just *know* when something is right or wrong, good or bad. Water is the element of feelings and emotions. Like Cancer and Pisces individuals, Scorpios are sensitive and imaginative. But Scorpio is the most intense of the water signs. They soar on the wings of their victories, and feel their disappointments deeply.

Scorpios are very proud and dignified people, and most of the time their intense emotions are kept firmly under control. It wouldn't do to let people see how vulnerable they really are. But Scorpios are no less sensitive than Cancer or Pisces. It's just that there's no mistaking when Cancerians are happy or sad; they express their emotions as they feel them. Scorpios are not as tearful as Cancer—but they *do* cry. Nor are they as overtly sympathetic and gentle as Pisces—but they *are* kind and they can be very gentle. It's all there . . . under the surface.

They are also extremely passionate. How could they not be when they feel so intensely? Scorpios don't feel anything by halves, nor do they do anything by halves. "All or nothing" is their motto. So it's hardly surprising that they've acquired themselves a reputation as extremists, for better and for worse.

It's interesting that this is the only water sign symbolized by a creature that does not dwell in water. A tropical poisonous arachnid is not the sort of animal you would want to keep as a pet. And you may be justified in wondering how it is that The Scorpion is the popular symbol for a sensitive water sign. Has someone made a mistake? No, think it over for a moment. A sensitive person ruled by the god of war. War? It can sometimes feel like war for those on the receiving end of the stinging Scorpio tail—or rather, tongue. Everything you've ever heard about how Scorpio can turn vicious in a flash when wronged or offended is true, and it's probably the main cause of the bad press that the sign has received. They are expert at directing verbal razor blades that cut to the quick. At such times they may say things they regret, but unfortunately the damage is sometimes so great that it can't be undone. At the end of the glyph for Scorpio there's a curve with a sharp pointed arrow. It's a silent reminder of the sting at the tip of the tail, and a warning to tread carefully around a Scorpio.

Because Scorpios are sensitive and intuitive and because their investigative minds are eternally roaming for information, they approach situations from two directions simultaneously; the intuitive and the rational. This gives them a fantastic edge in perceiving people's real motivations and the dynamics behind what's going on. From this perception comes knowledge. And knowledge, as every Scorpio knows, is power.

If sheer willpower has anything to do with manifesting your dreams, then Scorpio is the sign that can achieve just about anything they set their minds to. These individuals are blessed with great strength of will. They're also tough and robust, with the physical strength to act on their passions. And when motivated by a sense of purpose, no sign acts more forcefully, or is such a force to be reckoned with. Conversely, when they're uninspired, they can't feign interest.

Relationships that hold no passion cannot hold a Scorpion. It is the sign of erotic love. In the previous sign Libra, the sign that rules marriage, the emphasis in relationships is on the social union between two people. Scorpios are more concerned with the physical and spiritual union in which two become one. They are fascinated by the mystical dimension of sex, and are in search of the ecstatic.

Orgasm is a Plutonic experience. It's even called *la petite mort*—the little death.

The meanings of birth, sex, and death, sex, death, and birth, are all interconnected, and are all grist for the mill in a Scorpio's mind. Scorpio even rules the organs of reproduction and elimination.

It's possible that Scorpio's reputation as the sexiest sign of the zodiac is not unjustified. But what has been misinterpreted in popular astrology is the Scorpio connection with sex. It does not mean that Scorpios are constantly on the chase or have an overactive sex life. Frequently the opposite is true. It's not uncommon for Scorpio men and women to alternate between periods of lots of sex, and no sex at all. Scorpios understand the value and power of celibacy. What it *does* mean is that single or spoken for, satisfied or otherwise, the meaning of sex is a subject always worth contemplating. Scorpios are rarely promiscuous. Yet there are many (whether they would be willing to confess it or not) who at some stage have taken a walk on the wild side.

Lots of Scorpio men and women struggle with desire. Scorpio Saint Augustine found himself embroiled in this struggle. Desiring intensely to embrace the spiritual life but finding it hard to renounce the pleasures of the flesh, he appealed to God, "Give me chastity and continence, but not yet," and became every Scorpio's favorite saint.

Thankfully for the rest of us, not all Scorpios are walking bombshells, sexpots, or studs who have to fend off hordes of hopeful lovers. Though when they're in the mood, Scorpio *will* pull out the slinky, show-it-all number, and use it to superb effect. But even in jeans, sweater, and work boots, they still somehow manage to be sexy. It's as if sexiness is part of their whole being. Is this the source of their famous magnetism? Even when sex is not on the agenda, Scorpio has the ability to project a sexy, magnetic vibe that can be very powerful and sometimes quite unnerving to others. Most Scorpios are only too aware of the power that sex can wield.

Certainly there is no shortage of sexy Scorpio movie stars to prove the point: Demi Moore, Winona Ryder, Goldie Hawn, Meg Ryan, Loretta "Hot Lips Houlihan" Swit, Ethan Hawke, Tom Conti, and Roy Scheider are just a sample. There are plenty of magnetic Scorpios who are far from classically beautiful and would be thought quite ordinary if it were not for the glint in the eyes and the hint of wicked possibilities. Bob Hoskins, Danny De Vito, Richard Dreyfuss, and Whoopi Goldberg all prove that the Scorpio sex appeal is about attitude. Scorpio Katharine Hepburn hit the mark when she said, "Plain women know more about men than beautiful ones do." The same, of course, applies to plain men.

Sex is important to Scorpio, but bigger, much bigger, than sex is love. Fiery, passionate Mars may rule Scorpio, but remember, it is a water sign. Scorpios may need a lot of privacy, but they don't want to be alone forever. They long to form a close, loving relationship, and delve as much into the meaning of love as they do into the meaning of sex. Since the two are entwined, it can all become very complicated indeed in Scorpio's mind.

Deep down, Scorpio—like their opposite sign, Taurus (opposite signs have much in common)—wants to create a warm and secure family. But not just any family will do. That's because, more often than not, their childhood experience of family life was not an entirely happy one, and they have memories of incidents in which they felt misunderstood, lonely, or were thought of as willful by their parents. And let's be honest, Scorpios *can* be willful and headstrong. Often, though, their parents had problems with their own relationship, and young Scorpio's needs came second.

Fortunately for them, Scorpio is not a sign to passively accept that "what will be will be." They are superconscious of trying not to get into a rerun of their parents' problems, and are very keen not to repeat their own mistakes. Scorpios hold to the belief that we all have the power within ourselves to repudiate the patterns of the past and transform our lives for the better.

For all their self-examination, though, it's not uncommon for Scorpios to become so obsessed by someone that they urge him or her to tie the knot without delay—only to find the knot fast unraveling. Like Scorpios Julia Roberts and Lyle Lovett, whose quick wedding was followed by an even quicker divorce. Here's a revelation about Scorpio that you'll never hear from them: Mr. or Ms. "I'm so Hot but I'm so Cool" Scorpio really can't wait to find the right person and take that walk down the aisle.

To succeed in love and in life, Scorpios don't need to go to creative visualization workshops. They can deploy willpower like a magus. First comes the thought "I desire" and Scorpio's imagination clicks into place. Then the intellect takes it up and turns it around and around as Scorpio thinks "I could." If it feels right, Scorpio takes it on as a mission to be accomplished, and does it with such energy and focus that it has a very good chance of becoming "mission accomplished."

Pluto is the planet of power. He makes many Scorpios powerful people and he rules many powerful things; oil, plutonium (of course), and all the riches under the earth. Pluto always plays a part, astrologically, when there are shifts in the planet such as volcanic eruptions and earthquakes. In human affairs, his power pushes the collective thinking towards radical change, which is why he's instrumental when revolutions are in the air. With Pluto, there is never any going back. The changes he brings are irreversible. As you would expect, Pluto is a major player in politics. A large number of presidents and prime ministers were born under Scorpio, including Theodore Roosevelt, James Garfield, Charles de Gaulle, François Mitterrand, and Indira Gandhi.

Pluto is notorious for his role in subversive and secretive activities. Joseph McCarthy, the man behind the communist witch-hunts during the Cold War, was also a Scorpio.

The former Soviet Union is believed by astrologers to have been ruled by the sign of Scorpio, and it makes sense when you consider that this huge state was born out of a revolution (November 17, 1917). The all-powerful Czar was murdered, only to be replaced by the all-powerful communist party and the KGB. Millions lived in fear of the gulags and the knock on the door in the middle of the night. Many years before the planet Pluto entered Scorpio in 1983, astrologers were predicting that the Soviet Union would fall apart in 1989–91 prior to a rebirth, in true Scorpionic style.

The United Nations was also "born" under the sign of The Scorpion, on October 24, 1949. At first it seems right that the body set up to transform a war-weary world should be Scorpionic. Unfortunately the power of the United Nations' Scorpio Sun is astrologically "thwarted" by a lack of strong aspects. Without some sort of new charter—and new horoscope—the United Nations will never be able to fulfill its purpose of changing the world. It's food for thought that Mars in the U.N. horoscope makes an *exact* conjunction with the United States' Moon in Aquarius, the sign of humanity. In other words, any assertive action taken by the U.N. on behalf of humanity will be supported by public opinion in America.

Pluto power also means money. Big money. Which is why Scorpio is associated with corporations and multinationals. Scorpio and Taurus are the money signs of the zodiac, and both are well aware of the relationship between money and power. Taurus, more specifically, rules personal income and property. As practical earthy types, Taureans want money in the bank and will turn their back on the possibility of big returns in order to know that their money is safe in their own hands, and their security is inviolable. But Scorpios' financial sights are set on more distant horizons. Scorpios won't say no to bold ventures, at least not until they've heard the details. There are many aggressive traders in stocks, futures, and commodities who are Scorpios, or whose horoscopes have the Scorpio input.

As Scorpio is the traditional sign of "goods of the dead" and "joint monies," legacies and inheritances are Scorpionic matters. Getting their fair share of the family fortune, or battling over alimony and property, is often a thorny issue in a Scorpio's life. And then there's taxation. Scorpio rules that too. The temptation not to reveal all is too great for some Scorpios. More than one prominent Scorpio has toppled from his (or her) pedestal after an encounter with the tax man. Spiro Agnew wasn't the first, and he won't be the last. But it ought to be a warning to Scorpios. They may be born under the sign least likely to get away with a few little white lies about their travel expenses, or the three million they made on the stocks bequeathed to them by Uncle Harold. There are *some* things that even Scorpios shouldn't keep to themselves. The laws of karma, as Scorpios ought to know, cover money.

But if Scorpio is going to come asunder over money, it's more likely to be caused by something far more simple than cooking the books. Ambitious Scorpios have important lessons to learn about when to rein themselves in. The all-or-nothing Scorpio philosophy can be extremely dangerous where money is concerned.

The fact is, Scorpios are daring. At times they are too daring. Some would say rash, because the temptation to take big risks when they pick up the scent of big money can be too much to resist. And if it's an enterprise of their own creation, if it's something that completes that sentence beginning "I could . . ." then they'll be prepared to take really big risks. For all their power of visualization, their intuition and force of will, Scorpios are capable of overshooting the mark dreadfully, and suffering big losses.

Which brings Scorpio to the lessons that we all have to learn from our opposite sign. Taurus would shudder at Scorpio's big-time ambitions, and would be highly skeptical about just how much imagination, willpower, and applied energy can actually achieve. While Scorpios will never be convinced (nor should they be) that the Taurean supercautious approach to money is the right one, if they can, nevertheless, acquire enough of the Taurus-style caution and conservatism, and keep on the right side of their bank manager by not mortgaging the house and the kids to finance their "grand scheme," then they will avoid the financial black hole that many of them fall into at some stage. The Scorpio relationship with money—or to be precise, money and power—can get quite tortured at times. There are few who do not dream about the extraordinary life they could have (and the extraordinary things they could do) if they struck a bonanza.

Scorpio, remember, is an extremist. At the other end of the Scorpio spectrum of extremes are the high-flying Scorpios who go through a period of repulsion for money and materialism, and try to transcend them altogether. The romantic idea of trading in briefcase and BMW for surfboard and Jeep, and heading for a shack on a remote beach and living incommunicado, is very attractive to Scorpios who have lost their passion for what they're doing. Others might intimate that Scorpio will never amount to anything more than a beach bum ever again. How wrong they could be. Resurrection is always in the cards. Don't ever make the mistake of thinking that Scorpio is a has-been, because he or she can always rise like the phoenix from the flames with a new passion or a new project with every last detail worked out during their "beach bum" interlude.

There are many Scorpios who have begun something huge with an indispensible period during which they ponder in private, and plot and plan. As a boy, Bill Gates (born October 28), founder of Microsoft, used to spend hour upon hour in his parents' basement, sometimes refusing to come out to eat. The story goes that his mother once called out in exasperation "What are you doing?" and he shouted back "I'm thinking—have you ever tried thinking?" Gates' parents promptly packed him off to a psychiatrist. One wonders what they might think of his "thinking" now. The Scorpionic focus is sometimes too much for others to fathom. Yet without that intense focus, Gates' Scorpionic transformation from computer nerd to one of the richest and most powerful men in the world couldn't have happened. Gates' power of concentration is legendary. In the early days, even taking time out to shower or sleep was regarded as a distraction. Now he prides himself on what he calls his "seven hour turnaround." No more than seven hours elapse between leaving the office at night and the time he arrives back in the morning.

Gates has explained how his passion for computers began: "I realized later part of the appeal was that here was an enormous, expensive grown-up machine and we, the kids, could control it." Notice the key Scorpio word. Control. Scorpios want to extend their control over every part of their life. Gates has built a $50 million high-tech home where he has total control of his environment. In Gates' home, people pin an electric monitor to their clothes which connects them to the computerized "brains" of the house. Gates describes it like this "When it's dark outside the pin will cause a moving zone of light to accompany you through the house . . . as you walk down a hallway you might not notice the lights ahead of you gradually coming up to full brightness and the lights behind you fading. Music will move with you, too . . . a movie or the news will be able to follow you around the house. If you get a phone call, only the handset nearest you will ring." If this isn't an example of a Scorpionic fascination with power and control and what lengths they will go to get it, then what is? Where most of us might lose interest and settle for dimmers on the light switches, and TV sets in the den and bedroom, not Gates. In Scorpio tradition, he was determined to push his vision as far as it would go.

No sign can match Scorpios when they are passionately absorbed. Then their application to the task at hand is formidable. But there is a big difference between staying power and hanging on to the bitter end. That fabulous Scorpio focus does have a flip side. It's called obsession. Sometimes they don't know they've crossed the divide between passion and obsession. Sometimes they do, but they still can't stop themselves. It's as if they must live out their obsession and see it through to its inevitable grand finale. They can obsess over just about anything—a project, a person, a plan, or a problem. In every Scorpio's life there comes a time when they have to face their own limitations and the restrictions imposed by reality and common sense, and accept that just *wanting* something to be is not enough to make it work. The fact that you can't have total power and control over everything is perhaps Scorpio's most important lesson.

Should Scorpios ever feel that the power to direct the course of their life has been eroded, they can become the dread Scorpion of the zodiac that people are well justified in steering clear of. At such times Scorpio plunges into angry, morbid, depressive moods that can scare off the most loyal of friends. We're not talking about one of those "normal" Scorpionic introspective funks they need to pull their thoughts and their act together. Oh, no. This is much more. This is something akin to what the mystics call "The Dark Night of the Soul." All Scorpios have had a black weekend or two when they draw the blinds, take the phone off the hook, put organ concertos on the CD, and descend into their personal underworld. All manner of self-destructive activities are creatively explored as they subsist on a diet of cigarettes, whiskey, coffee, and toast spread with huge helpings of despair and angst. In their darkest hour Scorpios become deeply mistrustful and angry with others and themselves. The normally strong and ambitious Scorpio becomes insecure and stuck in a state of paralysis. Someone peeping through the blinds would never guess, but what Scorpio is actually doing is searching for a way out of his or her quandary.

The Scorpion is the only animal that will sting itself to death if it can see no way out of a threatening situation. It suggests how important it is to Scorpios not to live a life under somebody else's control.

There are some Scorpios who put themselves through protracted periods of slow self-destruction in order to lose themselves and anesthetize their psychological pain, and that's quite different from the odd black weekend. Even your average well-adjusted Scorpio has flirted with alcohol or drugs, though genuine substance abuse is an ingredient in only the most tragic tales of Scorpionic depression. It's like Scorpio poet Dylan Thomas (who drank himself to death) said: "Do not go gentle into that good night . . . Rage, rage against the dying of the light." Instead of "raging," may we suggest that Scorpios copy the words of another great Scorpio, Albert Camus, and pin them above their desk: "That which doesn't kill me makes me strong."

When Scorpios emerge from one of their dark episodes, always they are stronger than before. But in order to emerge rejuvenated and reborn, and move on to the next stage, they must purge the past and shed an old layer of skin. It comes back to that most fundamental of Scorpionic issues, death and rebirth, endings and beginnings. Positive Scorpios do not resist killing off the decayed and the outworn in their lives. They understand their own nature well enough to know that if they do not make way for the new and the life-affirming, they risk living on in a sort of half life, feeling like one of the living dead.

The vampire story *Count Dracula* has held a chilling fascination since Scorpio Bram Stoker, wrote it a hundred years ago. Horror stories, like fairy tales, make confronting unpleasant truths approachable. The story of Dracula never ceases to enthrall because it touches some deep part of our psyche. It is a story about the futility of trying to cheat death and the horror of living a half life. And as such, it is a Scorpio story, and carries the message that Scorpio can teach everyone. It warns against a becoming a "monster" trapped in the tragedy of a meaningless existence. And there is nothing more hideous to a Scorpio than that.

Life is a series of deaths and rebirths. Everything in nature is constantly changing, and new life can only come after death and decay. Scorpios know this. It's not only the mysterious and the macabre that make vampire stories so compelling. It's also that, almost contrary to rational thinking, we feel some kind of pity for these "monsters" that tried to achieve immortality, and ended up neither dead nor alive.

At the end of the story, Professor Abraham van Helsing (alias Bram Stoker—Bram is short for Abraham), the enigmatic occultist and vampire expert, helped defeat the powers of darkness in the form of Dracula by driving a stake through his heart and cutting off his head, thereby releasing him from his half-alive, half-dead existence.

So often Scorpios are accused of being hard, cold, and ruthless people with no feelings. Nothing could be further from the truth. Get to know a Scorpio and you'll discover they feel things extremely deeply, and that they know that it is far kinder and more humane (and far less cruel) to let go of people, places, and priorities if that's what will ultimately bring happiness.

It is Pluto who gives Scorpios the power to transform their lives. And Mars who gives them the energy and the passion to "do as they will." As for love, well, that's possibly the greatest mystery of all. And you know there's nothing Scorpio loves more than a mystery . . .

THE SCORPIO CAREER AND DIRECTION

One Scorpio woman who has become a household name decided when she was young that she was not going to be a nobody forever. Years before she got her big break, she wrote herself a letter that was a Scorpionic affirmation of her worth. She wrote, "This is the beginning of your life, for She who is and is not yet," and made a pact with herself that she would open it when she felt she was on the brink of success. That moment came when she heard Johnny Carson say, "Please welcome Roseanne Barr!" And everyone did. In the following six minutes Roseanne realized her affirmation—instant fame and recognition as an iconoclast, a new type of comedienne who was unafraid to take the banality of everyday life and throw it straight back in your face.

Note Roseanne's giveaway Scorpio word—*yet*. Like many ambitious Scorpios, Roseanne knew, long before her success on "The Tonight Show," that she had the power to go on to bigger things. Having the odds stacked against them never stopped Scorpios. When their goal is firmly set, they've got their famous willpower and buckets of determination to drive them to that goal. And they're tough. If this combination is what true grit is, then this is the sign that's got it.

Where some people might spend a lifetime paralyzed by the unfairness or injustices of the past, Scorpios can take their anger and resentment and transform them into a laser beam sharply focused on whatever it is they want to achieve. They are simply brilliant at turning adversity into opportunity. What Roseanne had was the guts to tell it like it was, and make the unlovely irresistible. Scorpios don't sweep the dirt under the carpet, they lift up the carpet and take a good long look. By turning the life of a "normal" dysfunctional family into compulsive viewing, Roseanne was exploiting her own experience. And Scorpios are very good at that.

Scorpios want to be writer, director, and executive producer of their lives. It's terribly important to Scorpios to feel that the control is in their hands and that they are the ones calling the shots over their life and their career. They will, however, happily work under other people's direction on the provision that they are trusted enough to be given a certain amount of autonomy, and are left alone to get on with the job. Scorpios don't like to be supervised and need to be able to do their own thing. They usually don't function at their best in a large team—unless, of course, they are in charge. That idea sits very comfortably with Scorpios. Leadership is something they assume quite naturally.

Underlying the Scorpio drive—which is second to none—is a nagging feeling that they have to prove themselves. Even if they've never admitted it to themselves (though many have), Scorpios have an "I'll show 'em" attitude. They want recognition. This does not mean they're fame freaks or desperate for glory and glamour; rather, that they want the career notches on their gun that will not only give *them* personal satisfaction, but also raise the eyebrows of those who couldn't see that they had it in them. Success is Scorpio's best revenge. Revenge for what? you may ask.

Many Scorpios have memories of their big dreams and ideas being dismissed as unrealistic. One Scorpio man we know was "affectionately" nicknamed "Bonkers" by his father, who obviously thought he had a few neurons loose. Despite the fact that he's now managing a successful business, and has proved himself to be far from bonkers, the name has stuck, much to his continuing chagrin. You see, unlike the opposite sign, Taurus, young Scorpio's aspirations frequently do not gain instant parental approval, which means that some spend several years in a kind of personal wilderness figuring out what they want to do, and suffering a crisis of confidence in the process. For such an ambitious person with a strong ego, feeling that his or her career is "on hold" can be extremely testing. It's hard for Scorpios, who so much want their life to have purpose, to go through a series of jobs while they're searching for their métier.

You also hear stories of Scorpios who have a very clear idea of what they want to do but, know too, that they can't do it . . . yet. We were once told by a Scorpio woman that she always knew she was going to be a sculptor, but she also knew that it would take time. And how in the fifteen years that she held down her nine-to-five job to support her three children and pay the rent, she never lost sight of her vision. Others might have. But not the determined Scorpios who know where their path lies. As soon as the children had finished school, Ms. Scorpio enrolled in art college and began the career she'd always dreamed of.

The urge to empower themselves is practically a basic biological drive in Scorpios. Once Scorpios settle on a career, very little will be allowed to pull them off course. Scorpios hooked on their work are a veritable powerhouses. They are, as you would expect for someone born under the sign of power, attracted to jobs in which they've got a certain degree of clout, or the power to influence large groups of people.

The scent of power draws many Scorpios to politics and the corporate world. They've got a natural executive ability and are good organizers, possibly because they're good delegators. Scorpios know how to streamline operations to get maximum results from time and energy. Sweeping a new broom through inefficient and run-down operations is something they do exceptionally well. If your organization has just been taken over by a Scorpio who tells the staff that it's business as usual and nothing is going to change, don't you believe it.

Scorpio's nose for business is an intuitive thing that can't be learned at business school, and it's worth more than an M.B.A. from Harvard. Another big advantage for anyone climbing the corporate ladder is knowing when to speak out and when to keep quiet. Scorpios can be relied upon to keep industrial secrets. But their biggest secret of all is the size of their ambition. If they're not already agreeably installed in the corner suite on the twenty-sixth floor with the water view, you can be sure it's not far off in their master plan.

Scorpios are marvelous strategists. They even formulate strategic plans for things like how to get round the supermarket as quickly and effectively as possible. So you can imagine how much plotting and planning they apply to something as important as their career.

Two thousand years ago in China, the master Sun Tzu (who is believed to have been a Scorpio) wrote a little book called *The Art of War*. It could just as well have been called *The Art of Life*, so relevant is it to achieving your goals and dealing effectively with others. The book has always been widely read in the East, where inscrutability was invented, and it now lies in the top drawer of the desks of politicians and powerful men and women all over the world. We recommend it to all Scorpios—and to anyone who'd like to get a grip on how the Scorpio mind works. Almost every sentence in this little classic is a Scorpionic quotable quote, but the best known is "To win without fighting is best."

To win without fighting requires skills that Scorpios intuitively employ anyway, including the ability to be thoroughly inscrutable. It's being smart and subtle enough to figure out how to get people to move in the direction you want them to move in, and do the things you want them to do, without them even knowing they're doing it. It's getting the right intelligence and deploying guerrilla tactics. And it's keeping both your own troops and your enemy under your control. That's the way an ambitious Scorpio wins without fighting.

Finance is a field that naturally attracts Scorpios. There are many working in banks and accounts departments. And among financiers, investment advisers, insurance brokers, and taxation experts, you'll find a high proportion of people born under the sign of The Scorpion.

Television and advertising are other arenas in which Scorpios can walk the corridors of power, work with big budgets, and be part of something influential. Many choose to direct their energies into the power of the written word. With their penchant for ferreting out information, investigative journalism suits Scorpios perfectly. But anything that involves unearthing the facts, the dirt, and secrets is ideal work for Scorpios with a literary bent. They dig deep and they never give up easily. Their fixity gives them the tenacity to stay with jobs that require patience and in which the results are slow to materialize.

Jobs that demand secrecy and an ability to work alone can't be done without the Scorpio touch. You can be certain that spies, detectives, and investigators of all types have planets in Scorpio or Pluto strong in their horoscopes. There's no need for a lie detector when there's a Scorpio on the scene. Scorpio can spot a scam or a sham a mile off.

An element of intrigue and mystery appeals to Scorpios. Any job in which you never quite know where your investigations will lead gives Scorpio a little frisson of excitement. These are the people who watch "The X-Files" and seriously wonder how you go about applying for the sort of job that Mulder and Scully have. Since the occult is ruled by Scorpio, it's hardly surprising that many psychic consultants, astrologers, and numerologists are born under the sign of The Scorpion.

Is there a Scorpio who can honestly say that they're not even slightly intrigued by the idea of past lives? This is not someone who rules out anything without investigation. Mind, body, and spirit are all connected, as Scorpio knows. And many have actually consulted past-life therapists, though it's unlikely they would ever tell you about it for fear of being labeled a kook or a weirdo. Scorpio believes it would be more foolish not to at least keep an open mind on these matters. If there's *any* information that can give Scorpios the edge and extend the boundaries of their personal power, they'll want to know about it.

Scorpios love to probe. They are the diggers and delvers of the zodiac. Forensic science fascinates them. So do the discoveries of archaeologists and paleontologists. Captain Cook and Christopher Columbus were both Scorpios who "discovered" what were believed to be "new" worlds. Every schoolchild knows that Columbus wouldn't take no for an answer when he was trying to raise funds for ships, and how he talked (and probably charmed) Queen Isabella of Spain into giving him the *Nina*, the *Pinta*, and the *Santa Maria*.

From the large to the infinitely small, Scorpios are well suited for work in scientific research. Reproduction is a specifically Scorpio issue. It may, on face value, seem correct to assume that Scorpio the investigator would be at the forefront of new research into human reproduction. But Scorpio, remember, is an emotional and passionate sign. Depersonalized reproduction—sperm banks, IVF clinics, and cloning—may well be the subject of some scientific Scorpio's probing exposés.

Especially fascinating to Scorpios are the workings of the mind. Pluto's underworld is a metaphor for the subconscious mind. And Scorpios' interest in human behavior, and what makes one person different from another, makes psychotherapy a Scorpio field. They do not accept that the way something is, is the way it has to remain, and are prepared to work hard on their own psyches, and help others to do the same. The sign of transformation knows that insight precedes transformation and breakthrough. Scorpio does not shy away from the tough psychological stuff. Few signs are able to cope with the drama of cathartic emotional release as well as Scorpio.

Since sex is a Scorpionic issue, sex therapy is obviously in Scorpio's territory. Sigmund Freud was convinced that most of our problems had something to do with sex. His Scorpio Ascendant certainly points to his interest in sex, but his Sun falling in the opposite sign of Taurus is revealing in view of his refusal to accept that the spiritual side of life is important to mental health. To Freud the Taurus, everything came down to the practical and commonsensical. He is a good example of how the Ascendant is an important indicator of career direction, but how the Sun sign is the true essence of who we are.

Sex researcher Shere Hite is a Scorpio. And so is feminist writer Naomi Wolf, whose book *The Beauty Myth* attacks the accepted "wisdom" that you have to be beautiful to be sexy or to be valued. The book asks people to consciously rethink unconsciously accepted attitudes. And it succeeds. Incisive Scorpios are expert at dissecting fallacious thinking to expose the truth. Because Scorpios understand the insidiousness of the power over mass thinking, they have a grasp of how the mass mind can be swayed, and when people are being collectively hoodwinked, duped, and lied to. As Wolf says, "The Big Lie is the notion that if a lie is big enough, people will believe it."

Those eternal Scorpionic issues—sex, birth, and death—are often the themes of the work of creative Scorpios. Controversial Scorpio photographer Robert Mapplethorpe shocked the artistic establishment with his pictures of the body that might be considered pornographic if it weren't for their striking beauty.

Pablo Picasso was also born under the sign of The Scorpion (October 25). Everyone knows about Picasso the cubist, Picasso and *Guernica*, and Picasso and his blue period, but what most people don't know is that Picasso was also a prolific producer of "pornographic" drawings. At the end of his life when he was becoming obsessed with mortality, Picasso turned to drawing female genitalia. The link between birth, sex, and death, beginnings and endings, surfaces again and again in Scorpio's art.

Picasso, by the way, was as jealous as any Scorpio lover could be. It's said that he once locked his mistress in the studio when he went out to buy the croissants for breakfast. Apparently she was as susceptible to the opposite sex as he was. Picasso painted until he was ninety-one. But not even his longevity could account for his vast volume of work. Like many gifted Scorpios, he was totally absorbed in his passion. When Scorpios love what they're doing, they seem to be able to tap into an almost supernatural source of energy.

All Scorpios have a kind of high-tensile energy that requires some physical outlet. It's why jobs that demand a high degree of physical energy or muscle power suit a lot of Scorpios. Warlike Mars, Scorpio's traditional ruler, leads many Scorpios (like Mars-ruled Aries) to work in the military. Because they're more patient than Aries ever could be, and better able to extricate themselves from sticky situations, they're particularly suited to work in bomb disposal and ballistics, which require steely control.

A whole lot more Scorpios are found working in the construction industry. From bricklayers to foremen and engineers, they love being able to throw themselves into big, physical projects. The business side of real estate development is also appealing. Pluto, you recall, is connected with everything underground. So it's not unusual to find Scorpios working in plumbing, mining, and oil exploration. The opportunity to blow things up and get paid handsomely for it, is most definitely appealing to Scorpios. This is your original Demolition Man. You know, the guy who can't wait till the weekend when he can tear down the shed at the back of the garden and rebuild it. Scorpio kids are the ones who get a bigger thrill than the others from watching a twenty-story building collapse like a pack of cards.

Deconstruction and reconstruction in any field is always interesting to a Scorpio. In medicine they are drawn to the more dramatic, intense areas such as trauma and surgery. Paramedics, who need a cool head and speedy reactions, often have a strong Scorpio input in their birth charts. One reason medicine is the career choice of so many Scorpios is that you need to be both tough and sensitive to be a good doctor. On top of that, Scorpios are intrigued by the minute mechanical workings of things. Plastic surgery and microsurgery are considered modern miracles. And Scorpios love the idea of participating in a miracle. Being instrumental in restoring quality to a person's life taps right into Scorpio's primal urge to transform.

Alternative therapies, too, capture Scorpio's imagination. Anything that involves a psychic or metaphysical element is food for thought for Scorpio's hungry mind.

When Scorpios do work that they love, the effort and energy they pour into it is astonishing. But not everyone can, or even wants to, operate at Scorpio's level of intensity. Scorpio on a roll is so enthused and works with such fervor that other people are easily overwhelmed by the force field he or she emits. If Scorpio thinks that their colleagues can't hack the pace, or that they are weak and ineffectual, then it's distinctly possible that the problem lies with Scorpio. They can, at times, be terribly draining to work with. For all their sensitivity, Scorpios can be very intolerant of less driven types. And for all their famed ability to keep their thoughts to themselves, this is something they're incapable of concealing. The knitted brows, the deep sighs, the disapproving frown, and the sullen silences give them away. Is it so surprising that people are put off and try to keep their distance? Some Scorpios, let's face it, can be so heavy going that people have been known to go to some length to shield themselves from their psychic emanations, erecting fortifications consisting of bookshelves and plantations of palm trees to protect their space and their nerves.

Frequently Scorpios' feelings of alienation are of their own making. There are some Scorpios who have a knack for making things dramatic and problematic when they need not be. They also seem to get an almost perverse gratification from playing devil's advocate in what would otherwise be a straightforward discussion about policies and procedures. The zeal with which they insist that things be done their way is bound to bring them into conflict with other strong individuals who have different opinions. Some Scorpios are agitators just for the sake of it. Or at least that's the way it looks. They can't bear to just let something drop, or let it be. They must force the issue. It's hardly surprising that these Scorpios cease to be asked to join the lunchtime crowd. May we suggest they head for the nearest bookstore in search of The Art of War.

People who work with such Scorpios often sum it up by saying they're "difficult." Seldom are they described as that nice, easygoing person everyone likes and who gets on with everyone. But when a Scorpio shows signs of being difficult, resentful, and angry, it's a sure symptom of job dissatisfaction. Scorpios cannot put up a civil front for long when they're unhappy at work.

Basil Fawlty, the tragicomic proprietor of "Fawlty Towers," the most dysfunctional hotel in England, is one of these Scorpios. He's the archetypical Scorpio who obviously hates his job. Everywhere that Basil goes, disaster follows. Everything that Basil touches falls apart. We never learn what it is that Basil yearns to do. You get the impression that he's one of those Scorpios who hasn't figured it out . . . yet. But we do know that hospitality is not his true vocation and that he's miserable, and he gets some kind of twisted pleasure in making other people—including the hotel guests—miserable, too. Clearly Basil has a monumental Scorpio attitude problem. He pushes rudeness as far as rudeness can go. He's brittle, sarcastic, and downright offensive—except when one of the guests turns out to be someone he thinks is powerful or important. Then watch Basil's offensive manner instantly turn into an oily reptilian smile. When Basil's wife, Sybil, calls him a "brilliantined stick insect" in a pique of exasperation, does she realize how close she has come to identifying Basil as a Scorpio?

The character and the hilarious misadventures of Basil Fawlty could only have been created and played by a Scorpio. John Cleese is a master of black, sardonic Scorpionic humor.

Scorpio is a sign that is not afraid to take big steps to make big changes. Scorpio actor Will Rogers once said, "Why not go out on a limb? That's where the fruit is." The tragedy of Scorpios like Basil Fawlty is that they get locked into resenting the fact that they're a nobody and hating themselves for being too afraid to go out on that limb. But when they do seize the courage and do it, Scorpios will wonder why on earth they didn't do it much sooner.

As for the Basil-style belligerence, some of the solutions to that lie in the next sign. It would be sinful to advise anyone to act contrary to their Sun sign nature. Besides, Scorpios never ask for advice, and they're none too good at taking it when it's given gratis. But it would be remiss not to suggest to Scorpio (may we?) that, like the rest of us, they, too, can benefit from considering what the sign to come has to offer. In Scorpio's case, that means Sagittarius.

What Sagittarius offers Scorpio is a lighter approach to life. Sagittarians are much more open than Scorpios. People feel that they know where they stand with Sagittarius. If Scorpios could be just a little less intense and secretive when there's no need to be, they would not come across as so paranoid and prickly. Sagittarians can be every bit as successful as Scorpios at getting their own way. But because they're more friendly and approachable, and because they don't make any secret about what they're after, they don't have Scorpios' tendency to make people wary and suspicious.

Having said that, there is possibly no sign—Sagittarius included—that has Scorpio's capacity to produce consistently and under pressure. Sure, there may be a drama or two, and some tense moments along the way, but the focus and passion that Scorpios pour into their work can be wonderfully contagious. Scorpio can be the most stimulating and inspiring of people to work with.

Without that famous Scorpio focus and passion, would Christopher Columbus have persisted in his dream, obtained his ships, and sailed off into the unknown? Would Roseanne Barr be one of the most successful names in television? And would Bill Gates be the richest man in America? Probably not.

The next time you catch Scorpio staring into space with a strange, faraway look in their eyes, don't think they're lost in a dream. They're not lost. They're just working out the details of how to make that dream come true.

LOVE AND FRIENDSHIP

"There were nights when he took a deal more rum and water than his head would carry; and then he would sometimes sit and sing his wicked, old, wild sea-songs, minding nobody . . . People were frightened at the time, but on looking back they rather liked it; it was a fine excitement in a quiet country life."

Like Robert Louis Stevenson, the old sea dog from *Treasure Island* must have been a Scorpio. Every Scorpio man and woman knows that a little mystery does wonders for your interest value.

It must be said from the start that a relationship with a Scorpio is not all smooth sailing. Scorpios are not the kind of people who are into superficial socializing. They don't feel obliged to get along with everyone, and they don't particularly care if they're not liked by everyone. This is definitely a sign that enjoys its own company. Most Scorpios have one or two true soul-mate friendships—friendships that they deeply cherish because they know how blessed they are to have them.

Like still waters, Scorpio's feelings and emotions run deep. A Scorpio friend is a faithful confessor and confidant, someone you can talk to about absolutely anything. Trust is inviolable so far as Scorpio is concerned. So when you say, "This is strictly between us," you can be certain that it will be. A heart-to-heart with a Scorpio friend is often just the therapy you need to off-load a few problems and wrestle with your hang-ups. Scorpio will be the very soul of understanding, but be prepared to hear the truth, the whole truth, and nothing but the truth. This is not the sort of person who will hand you gratuitous platitudes like "Oh, you poor thing" or "It must have been awful for you." Nor will he or she insult your feelings by saying, "Oh, I'm sure they didn't mean it," and advise you to forgive and forget. Actually, forgiving and forgetting is something that Scorpios find very hard to do. At times they are too honest, even to the point of being brutally honest. But when your Scorpio says, "Yes, you did the right thing," you'll feel a whole lot better knowing he or she genuinely means it.

Just because Scorpios have periods when they steer clear of the social whirl doesn't mean that they're not interested in having a good time. Quite the contrary. They're always open to stimulating conversation and a good meal (the spicier and tastier, the better—never serve a Scorpio bland food). Take Scorpio to the latest production of *Othello* or to a film that's creating a huge controversy. They're into drama and won't mind seeing something a bit heart-wrenching, even on the first date. The opera's always a winner. But don't try to drag them along to the umpteenth revival of *Beauty and the Beast* or *Oklahoma*. They like their entertainment—like their friends—to be a little bold and a little unusual.

Quiet "together" times spent with a lover or a close friend, and doing what looks like very little, is what Scorpio likes doing best of all. They enjoy searching, intimate talks. A good bottle of port by a roaring log fire is a Scorpio favorite. So is sitting on the back porch on a hot summer's night looking out for shooting stars and identifying the constellations. That's always inspiration for Scorpios to get started on some of their favorite topics: the origins of the cosmos, what's out there, the meaning of life, and all that . . .

Most everybody knows that Scorpio is the sign that rules sex. And yes, it's true that they're very interested in the topic. But not a lot of people know that Scorpio, being a water sign, is a romantic. Just because they don't wear their heart on their sleeve and aren't comfortable with token sentimental gestures doesn't mean that they don't want genuine displays of affection. Too many people assume that tough, reserved Scorpios aren't into romance. Big mistake.

Scorpios of both sexes are very aware of the power of their sexual projection. The single, available Scorpio may appear cool and faintly disinterested, but don't let that fool you. Unless they're fully committed to one of their celibate, asetic monk phases, which are part of the ebb and flow of Scorpio's sex life, they're open to possibilities, trust us. Maybe it's because they keep reading in the magazines that Scorpios are so sexy that many of them are conscious of not coming across too strong or too obvious. The "come on" signals may be very subtle at times. But if Scorpio wants to get to know you better, rest assured you *will* get the message.

Plain or utterly ravishing, short and fat, thin and tall, Scorpio is undeniably magnetic. Not all the women look like Scorpios Morticia Addams or Cruella De Ville (but they can if the mood takes them). And not all Scorpio men look like they've stepped out of a Romany caravan (but it's surprising how many actually do). The eyes have it. They're attractive, penetrating, and more than a little disconcerting. The nose is another clue to identifying a Scorpio. Many Scorpios have a slightly hooked, Roman nose.

Underwear as outerwear could only have been created by a Scorpio. So if you spot the C.K. elastic above the jeans, and if the hips have got an easy rhythmic swing to them, then you can safely place your bets on this person being a Scorpion. Calvin Klein even named his perfume after that great Scorpionic state of mind: Obsession. Coincidence? Not likely.

A relationship with a Scorpio is really only to be prescribed for those who like their medicine strong. The little Miss Muffets who suffer from arachnophobia might be advised to steer well clear of Scorpions. There are, after all, eleven other signs to choose from. Scorpions, spiders, and snakes are scarcely the most cuddly of creatures. But they *are* mesmerizing. The serpent, remember, is one of the symbols for Scorpio. And it was the serpent in the Garden of Eden who persuaded Adam and Eve to sample the forbidden fruit from the Tree of Knowledge of Good and Evil. He was the symbol of temptation, the instigator of the original loss of innocence, and aeons later, the serpent still whispers in Scorpio ears. Even the most apparently straitlaced and conservative Scorpios have a lust for experience.

When a Scorpio is in the grip of an intense attraction, the imagination and the pheromones slip into overdrive. Other people may wonder what on earth it is that Scorpios see in some of the objects of their desire. And it's true that Scorpios' desires sometimes seem to defy logic, or at least inferior imaginations. Their choice of lover may be blatantly unsuitable, but that never stopped a Scorpio. There's always one chapter in a Scorpio's personal history about a fatal attraction, a love affair that was doomed from the start but was impulsive, compulsive, and, in hindsight, sexually healing.

Everyone has fantasies. But there would be few Scorpios who could honestly say that they haven't tried to live out at least one of their fantasies. It's an old-fashioned line, but having their wicked way is still something Scorpio males (and females) want to do. Some Scorpios' bedrooms resemble a film set. Not the "Las Vegas pink satin sheets on a heart-shaped bed" variety, more the "bedouin tent with miles of drapery, Persian carpets, and wall-to-wall plumped-up cushions" sort of boudoir. A cathedral's worth of candles and incense is also a popular theme. But so, too, is the back-to-basics primordial rock at the secluded end of the beach. One thing's for sure; the uninspired need not apply. Though the uninitiated can.

When Scorpio is on the brink of a love affair, he or she chooses one or two very different plans of attack. On the one hand, there's the simple, direct "we both know what we want" approach. Scorpio is definitely into the split-second seduction that leaves the trail of clothing from the front door to the couch. But don't worry, speed doesn't rule out technical prowess. Fast, it may be, but gross, fumbling, or artistically inept, it is not. Scorpios are intuitive, almost telepathic, in such matters. So they won't deploy this tactic unless they're 99.9 percent sure of success. They're less willing than some other signs to put their ego on the line and risk the pain of rejection.

The alternative approach is one of those Scorpionic sex power games that you've been warned about. In this scenario Scorpio gets to exploit all the complexities and deviousness at his or her disposal. You could call this the "agony and the ecstasy strategy." Visualize the excruciatingly careful mating dance of two Scorpions jockeying for position and power, poisonous tails precariously poised overhead. It's a very tricky business that could turn nasty at any moment.

Scorpios are ever aware of the advantage of not laying all their cards on the table. Indeed, the more a Scorpio wants a relationship to work, the more guarded and the more self-conscious they are. And the more likely they are to hold back for as long as possible before making their intentions clear. Sometimes they hold back for so long that nothing ever happens. Their strategy is to get the other person "on the boil" and keep him or her simmering until they're absolutely sure that when *le moment critique* arrives, there's no possibility of getting no for an answer. In a strange sort of way, this is proof that the tough, inscrutable Scorpion really is a vulnerable creature in matters of the heart.

Scorpios are the consummate players of the power politics of sex. They can be dreadfully manipulative. So exactly how long the "will we or won't we" can be tolerated by others depends on the health of their ego, and probably on what Sun sign *they* are born under. A Gemini, for example, would lose interest. A Capricorn (who loves to be in control every bit as much as a Scorpio) may give Scorpio a good run for his or her money. But when Scorpion meets Scorpion, that desert dance could go on forever.

Yes, you're being tested, but Scorpio is also testing his or her own feelings. It can all get very twisted, especially if Scorpio—and many Scorpios secretly do—turns to the oracle at every new development. Were you careless enough to reveal your date of birth to Scorpio? No doubt it slipped out innocently when you were telling them how you threw a fantastic party for your birthday last month. Well, Scorpio is probably at home right now working on that information and getting the lowdown on you. Scorpios are among the first to rush to a soothsayer seeking confirmation that you are as serious as they are. And they're also likely to be consulting their cards or their runes for a day-to-day update on what's going on in your mind and where it's all leading to. Scorpios can never be armed with too much information.

One Scorpio woman we know was generous enough to give us the inside story on what to do should you find yourself engaged in this Scorpio-style Mexican standoff. Her advice to anyone lusting after a Scorpio is to take the enemy by surprise. "Use guerrilla tactics—attack is your best defense." When you catch Scorpio unawares and unprepared, you're more likely to get their true response.

Sometimes Scorpio uses sex as a means of control. And that can include withholding sex. Control is such a big issue for Scorpios in every aspect of life, but it's particularly important to them to feel that they have control over their love life. That's because they've experienced how easy it is for them to *lose* control when they fall in love. They know how all-consuming a love affair can be for them, and how when love walks in the door, there's a very good chance that their brains will fly out the window.

It's extraordinary how such an otherwise focused, dynamic, and ambitious sign can so easily lose focus and put the rest of their life on hold while they're in the thrall of a love affair. The fact that romance and reason often don't make good bedfellows can be a terrible personal dilemma for Scorpios. They want to experience passion, yet they know it's going to throw them off kilter. The Big O— Obsession—is always lurking around the corner.

Clearly this is not someone to flirt with. When a Scorpio is in love, he or she is a devoted partner who sincerely believes that love can last forever. They take love and marriage very seriously, and place great store on fidelity.

One of the most tender and moving love stories of mythology, the story of Orpheus and Eurydice, reveals the depth and endurance of the Scorpionic kind of love.

Orpheus was blessed with the gift of playing the lute so beautifully that it touched the hearts of all, man and beast. When he married the beautiful Eurydice, there was never a couple more in love or more blissfully content. But Eurydice was bitten by a snake and taken to the land of the dead. Orpheus was so bereft that he sought permission from Jupiter, the king of the gods, to go where no living person had ever been. Orpheus was prepared to face the living nightmare of a journey into the underworld to seek out his beloved.

At the entrance to Hades sat Cerberus, the ferocious three-headed dog. But Orpheus played upon his lute and Cerberus licked his feet and let him pass. When he reached the throne of Pluto he played again and begged for the return of his wife. The moment was so poignant and so heart-wrenching that time stood still. Even ruthless, stony-faced Pluto was moved to tears, and agreed to return Eurydice, but on one condition—that during their return journey to the land of the living, Orpheus must never look back.

Just as they approached the entrance and total dark turned to light, Orpheus suddenly became consumed with doubt and filled with suspicion. He wondered if Pluto had tricked him and whether the footsteps behind him might be those of a spirit, and whether Eurydice had changed during her sojourn in the land of the dead. Just when happiness was within reach, he committed his fatal mistake and looked back. Only to see that his true love was indeed there behind him, and that she was as lovely as he remembered. Eurydice stretched out her hand towards Orpheus, but before they could touch, she was pulled back down into the vortex of Hades.

The tale of Orpheus and Eurydice is a story about the power of Scorpio love. Orpheus' love was so strong that he came close to obtaining the unobtainable: a return from the dead and a cessation of time. Even Pluto showed just how compassionate he could be.

Anyone who has ever read the story of Orpheus and Eurydice must have thought, "If only he hadn't looked back . . ." And that is the crux of the Scorpionic matter. Trust. And suspicion. As strong as the Scorpio love may be, there are many who, like Orpheus, struggle within themselves against suspicion and fear. Will my beloved change? Will my love ever leave me for someone else? Scorpios can become so jealous and so tormented with thoughts of whether love will last that, like Orpheus, they risk losing all in a moment of weakness.

Orpheus failed to learn the lesson of trust. During his journey back from the underworld, the control over Orpheus' future happiness was not in his hands. He was in no position to call the shots. Scorpios sometimes have a problem accepting that they can't always be in control of everything.

In a long-term relationship with a Scorpio there will inevitably come a time when who's calling the shots will be an issue. Scorpios know how to look after number one. When they can safeguard their own interests and simultaneously respect someone else's need for personal power, they're on the fast track to happiness. Scorpios hate to be possessed, but they are possessive. If they feel that their personal power is blocked, they get frustrated and are prone to sudden violent eruptions of emotion.

A Scorpio in a bad relationship will hang on, but not forever. When Scorpio comes to the conclusion that it's all over, then he or she very rarely commits the mistake of looking back. Should, however, Scorpio be spurned, dare we say ditched, by the one they love, they find it well nigh impossible to bury the hatchet. All's fair in love and war as far as a rejected Scorpio is concerned. Remember this is the emotional water sign that is ruled by the god of war. The wounded Scorpion can contemplate acts of creative revenge that are so ingenious that the recipient may never suspect the origins of his or her misfortune. Scorpios don't entirely dismiss voodoo dolls as silly souvenirs from Haiti. Every astrologer's advice to ex-lovers of Scorpios is to try not to end the relationship on a discordant note. Try to swallow your pride, resolve your conflicts, and, if possible, stay friends. If you can do this, you will have a wonderful, loyal friend for life.

Scorpio needs a partner who is a strong person in his or her own right. Someone who doesn't try to control Scorpio, but at the same time is not subservient. A good dose of humor and imagination helps, too.

Partners of Scorpio may occasionally have to put up with a few scowls from that Scorpio sea dog from *Treasure Island*. But is there anyone who has never dreamt of discovering buried treasure? If a Scorpio loves you, you will discover just that. The love and devotion of a Scorpio are the kind of riches that last a lifetime.

THE SCORPIO PARENT

Long before they find their true love and settle down, most Scorpios have dwelt on what it would be like to have children of their own. Daydreams about baby scorpions scuttling around the house are not unusual, even for the male of the species. The whole process of procreation fascinates them.

Scorpio women look forward to becoming "great with child" and can develop an almost scientific preoccupation with baby's development during the various stages of pregnancy. Come the day their first child is born, it will probably be the biggest day of their life . . . ever.

For a Scorpio, creating a child of your own can be so important that there are many who feel that it's part of discovering the meaning of life. Certainly, it's an important part of the meaning of Scorpio's life.

For a sign that is such a power to be reckoned with in the workaday world, Scorpios can be terrible softies when it comes to children. The way Scorpio parents cherish their little ones comes from somewhere very deep, and something very instinctual. They pride themselves on being responsible and protective parents, and apply their sharp eye to every aspect of their child's growth. No talent and no trouble will go unnoted. A child who has an obvious gift for rhythm will promptly be enrolled in music classes. You never know, you could have a prodigy on your hands. Likewise, if their seven year old is still wetting the bed, or isn't keeping up at school, the Scorpio parent will be determined to find the solution.

Scorpios are eternal students of the human mind and the Scorpio parent will be very concerned that their child receives the right kind of conditioning. If anything, Scorpio, the amateur psychologist, might even worry too much about every little thing that their child sees or hears, and whether it could have a negative long-term effect.

Busy as they usually are, Scorpios understand the need for system and regular routine in a child's life. They believe in meals, bath, and bed on time, and never put the reminder note from the dentist aside, thinking it can wait a few more weeks.

As far as education and leisure activities are concerned, they take their responsibilities very seriously and will go without the extras in life themselves in order to give extras to their children, such as the better school that costs more. In fact, more or better of anything that they think their children deserve. And let's be honest, that sometimes means more than their children need. Many Scorpios are adoring and indulgent parents.

Scorpios know all about exercising control through staying cool, calm, and collected. But for all their attempts to be the perfect parent, it's hard for Scorpios not to do the Scorpionic thing and blow a fuse every now and again. They'll never be able to keep a permanent lid on their strong emotions and their forceful personality, so there are bound to be some occasions when all that belief in correct conditioning—and teaching by example—evaporates in the heat of the moment.

One Scorpio mother we know has kept the first drawing her son brought home from school. The topic for the art lesson was making a picture of Mommy. When Mommy was presented with a portrait of herself as a witch, complete with warts and long, pointed hat, and seated astride a broomstick, she saw the funny—and somewhat revealing—side of it. She knew that she had her moments when she could have earned herself a part in *Macbeth*. "Double double toil and trouble; Fire burn and cauldron bubble," she now jokes to her son as she stirs the soup. "You've invited a friend for dinner? No problem. I'll just throw in another bat wing and a couple of newts."

The Scorpio father, too, may occasionally resemble a dragon who fumes and roars around the place, but the odd trauma or two notwithstanding, the Scorpio parent can be surprisingly laissez-faire in matters of discipline. As Scorpios see it, nothing—and no one—has the right to stand in the way of their relationship with their children. Not even their partner. There may well be a few disagreements over discipline and who knows best. Never forget, Scorpio is a stubborn, fixed sign, and when Scorpios are adamant about anything, it's hard to shift their opinion. For some reason, Scorpio parents seem loath to come down hard on Junior's bad table manners or backtalk. Perhaps it's because Scorpios are so aware of what repression can do that they would hate to feel that they could ever be held responsible for doing some repressing of their own. We've all got a few hang-ups we're carrying around from our childhood. But the Scorpio parent may well go overboard to ensure that those hang-ups are not passed on.

They might be a little overdominant and overprotective at times, but at heart, Scorpio is devoted to the concept of a secure and loving family life, and will not hold back on love and affection.

Many parents say, "I'm happy so long as you're happy doing what you want to do." But Scorpio is a sign that really means it. They will encourage their children to follow their own path in life. Scorpios who so much want to follow their own passions, are very aware that their children have the right to do the same. They will try not to flinch when their seventeen-year-old informs them on graduation day that his future is settled—he's going to travel the world playing in a (still unknown) rock band. Scorpios will quickly put on a brave face and be enthusiastic and supportive. But their heart will sink a little as they realize the day has come when their "child" is leaving home. However, Scorpios know that no matter how far their "children" may roam, the bond between them will remain so strong that nothing, including distance, could ever change that.

THE SCORPIO CHILD

"There was a little girl who had a little curl right in the middle of her forehead. When she was good she was very very good. And when she was bad she was horrid."

Could this be a description of a little Scorpio? It's true that Scorpio children can be so very good that you'll wonder whether, by some lucky error, the stork has delivered you an angel.

Scorpios grow up fast. By the time they are seven or eight, they'll be showing maturity beyond their years and wanting to join in grown-up conversations and activities. You can trust them to assume their own small share of household responsibilities; in fact, they'll relish the feeling of independence and importance that responsibility brings.

All water-sign children intuitively know when you're a bit down, and can be wonderfully tender and understanding. Scorpios are not silly crybabies or complainers, and they're not emotionally clinging. Indeed, they'll appreciate it if you respect their need for time and space of their own. And it's unlikely you'll be called upon to provide constant entertainment.

Little Scorpios are curious and adventurous and they hate to feel hemmed in. They'll happily organize their own expeditions to the bottom of the garden, and create their own secret magic world under the willow tree where no one can see them. If it's your dream to have a wise child you can trust and who doesn't need to be constantly supervised or fussed over, then perhaps you should plan for your baby to arrive in late October or November.

But like the little girl in the nursery rhyme, Scorpio children can sometimes be such a challenge to their parents that you'll be left wondering at times if the stork delivered you a hell's angel. Angel or hell's angel, the Scorpio child can be both. Remember, this is a sign of extremes. And there are bound to be a few little apocalyptic moments that will test the most stoic and patient of parents. There is no baby bible that can prepare you for the intense glare of little Scorpio standing his or her ground. *Defiance* requires a new definition when practiced by a Scorpio child. So arm yourself for an occasional battle of wills. Scorpios are stubborn and they rarely genuinely give in. They may *pretend* to acquiesce and yield to parental authority, but Scorpios are great believers in the fact that you can lose a battle and still win the war. They've probably temporarily retreated to rethink their strategy and regroup their forces in order to approach the issue from a different direction.

Once Scorpios set their heart on something, no amount of appealing to their sense of reason or their consideration for others will persuade them to drop it. There will no doubt come a time when Scorpios learn, for the first time, one of their biggest lessons: namely, sheer force of will won't necessarily get you what you want. Better they learn this sooner than later. If little Scorpio makes it clear that there will be no peace if the promised excursion to the amusement park is postponed because it's pouring with rain, they may need the experience of going anyway and having such a miserable time that they think twice before trying to force your hand again. From the parents' point of view, it might be worth suffering a wet afternoon at the "amusement park" to make sure that they've digested this valuable lesson.

Firm and consistent discipline is a must. But so is consistent affection. For all their self-assertive ways, never think that Scorpio children are any less sensitive than the others, or need any less reassurance of your love. It's just that they're not as effusive or schmaltzy as many children, and even at an early age, they're suspicious of insincerity.

The same applies to children who are born with the Moon in Scorpio, since the Moon sign has a lot to do with parental conditioning. Mother especially seems to come under the Scorpionic scrutiny. Grown-up Scorpios will tell you how their relationship with their mother has had a few ups and down over the years. Sometimes it was close and at other times they felt the need to keep their emotional distance. All the messages mother puts out, spoken and unspoken, are received and filed away by her Scorpio child.

In fact, there's very little that the Scorpio child fails to pick up about anything. Even a raised eyebrow, let alone a raised voice, will catch their attention. So if you must have "words" with your partner, do it somewhere else altogether where there's no possibility that little Scorpio can overhear.

Parents of Scorpios can avoid a lot of misunderstandings if they realize that Scorpio is essentially a private, secretive sort of person. Even young Scorpios have their introspective periods. It's simply their way of getting themselves and their thoughts together. Never violate their personal space or belongings. And don't worry if they show little enthusiasm for group activities. Scorpios of all ages prefer the company of a few close friends rather than hanging out with the whole neighborhood.

They're physically strong and active children who are drawn to solo sports such as swimming or cycling rather than team games. Scorpios love the sea, and a trip to the beach will be one of their favorite outings.

They'll also love anything magical and mysterious. Don't be surprised if your little Scorpio declines the offer of a pony ride at the village fete, and surreptitiously slips away to join the line outside the fortune-teller's tent. Fairies, witches, ghosts, and goblins are never out of fashion with Scorpio children. We know an adult Scorpio who has read *The Lord of the Rings* three times and who rushes home from work when they're showing reruns of *The Lion, the Witch and the Wardrobe* on the children's hour.

You need have no second thoughts about taking little Scorpio along to the grandest events and the most solemn and serious places. They love the somber and studious mood of big libraries with their carved banisters and mountains of books. At Christmas you can take them to the midnight service in the cathedral and they won't fidget and whisper to you, "When will it be over?" Scorpios' sense of drama and occasion needs little encouragement.

Speaking of drama, you may be in for some as soon as Scorpio becomes old enough to take an interest in the opposite sex. That is, if you ever get to hear about it. The facts of life must be handled discreetly, but *must* be handled! Private Scorpio is going to be most reluctant to join in any "let's have a talk about it" sort of conference. Better that you leave the right book in the right place where nosy brothers and sisters won't find it, but Scorpio will. And they will. Besides, Scorpio has long since scoured your library when you were out, located your volumes of D. H. Lawrence and Harold Robbins, and read all the scintillating and saucy sections.

Try to be patient and understanding, but not intrusive, when your Scorpio is dealing with one of those important turning points that occur in every Scorpio's life. The fact that they've quit college and come to no decision yet about what they're going to do doesn't mean that you've got a dropout on your hands. Keep in mind that Scorpio is a purposeful, ambitious sign and they *will* get their act together. They don't need any hassling or pushing from anyone since they do a very good job of that on themselves. Show them, instead, that you're always behind them in whatever they choose to do. Your loyalty, understanding, and support will be amply rewarded.

Sensitive Scorpio never forgets who stood by them and who was there for them. And they will never fail to return the love and loyalty you give . . . and be there for *you* in the future.

BORN UNDER SCORPIO

Grace Kelly	Francis Ford Coppola
Prince Charles	Marie Antoinette
Sam Shepard	Rock Hudson
Diana Dors	Jawaharlal Nehru
Charles Bronson	Marie Curie
Sylvia Plath	Billy Graham
Larry Flynt	Vlad the Impaler
Georges Bizet	Joan Sutherland
Klaus Barbie	Diego Maradonna
Captain James Cook	Pelé
Charles Atlas	Richard Burton
Lulu	Robert F. Kennedy
Helmut Newton	Kurt Vonnegut, Jr.
Martin Scorsese	Ricki Lee Jones
Peter Cook	Burt Lancaster
Cleo Laine	Joni Mitchell
Edmund Halley	Bryan Adams
Hedy Lamarr	Henry Winkler
Feodor Dostoevsky	Jodie Foster
Kevin Kline	Batman
John Keats	

SAGITTARIUS

November 23–December 21

Ruling Planet

JUPITER

Bring me my bow of burning gold,
Bring me my arrows of desire,
Bring me my spear, oh clouds unfold!
Bring me my chariot of fire.

William Blake—born November 28

THE SAGITTARIUS NATURE

To think Sagittarius—think big.

Think of the big opportunity . . . something that every Sagittarius expects. Think of the big time . . . something they all dream of. The big picture . . . something the broad and open Sagittarian mind can grasp in an instant. And, of course, the Big Break . . . something that a Sagittarian is always ready for because no sign has such faith in sheer good luck as Sagittarius.

Next time you're around a Sagittarius, observe and you're sure to discover for yourself just how easily the word *big* falls from his or her lips. Listen out for *great*, too. Sagittarians have great expectations. They dream up great schemes which they are sure have great potential. And what is a great concept? Simply the way a Sagittarius describes the latest big idea.

Could it all be something to do with the fact that the ruling planet of Sagittarius is Jupiter, the giant of our solar system? At 318 times larger than Earth, all the other planets put together still do not equal its size. Jupiter also spins faster than any other planet. Start watching the Sagittarians you know, and you'll notice how they always seem to be on the move, and ready to head for wherever the action is. Even when they're relaxing with their feet up, their bodies contain a latent energy that you sense will spring them up and off the couch at the promise of anything profitable or interesting.

In mythology, Jupiter was the king of the gods. The Greeks called him Zeus and established his reputation for action and adventure. His position as king came with the executive celestial right to impregnate myriads of desirable maidens, both mortal and immortal, with or without their consent. King Jupiter was an eager lover and a prolific father, but his constant pursuit of amorous adventure is really a symbol of the fundamental Sagittarian desire to be free and unfettered. They need to be able to cast their seeds of enthusiasm for life. Jupiter's seed never fell on barren ground—those desirable maidens all got pregnant. The stories of his adventures and conquests reveal to us that the ideal Sagittarian life is one in which they can pursue their passions and their interests with few holds barred. The way a Sagittarian sees it, life can only be rich and full if you keep restrictions to a minimum.

It's only to be expected that the Sagittarius child will be the first to climb the garden fence, or the first to stand on the beach, look out to the horizon, and ask, "What's that line between the sea and the sky?" Their innate sense of wonder and their nonstop questions are bound to send their parents rushing off to invest in a set of encyclopedias. Sagittarians are broad-minded individuals who are unwilling to accept the limitations of the culture, class, race, or religion into which they happen to have been born. Not for Sagittarians to be fenced in by their roots or their background; the tedium of a narrow, predictable life is not for them. Born under the influence of mighty Jupiter, planet of joy, optimism, and good fortune, Sagittarians figure from a young age that they were born to be happy and born to be free. Another name for Jupiter is Jove. And from Jove we get the word *jovial*. It's a Sagittarian word and a good way to describe these happy, optimistic people.

As the ninth sign of the zodiac, Sagittarius follows Scorpio. The wheel of the zodiac is the cycle of the evolution of the soul. In Scorpio, the individual gains personal power through exploration of the depths of the psyche, the emotions and the occult mysteries of life. In Sagittarius, the individual is now ready to disseminate that knowledge in their own fiery enthusiastic way.

Like the other fire signs, Aries and Leo, Sagittarians are extroverts. But as the last of the fire signs, it is their role to apply their energy and enthusiasm to interests encompassing the broadest possible scope. Sagittarians are forward looking people with expansive spirits who don't want to be limited by anyone or anything.

This is why Sagittarius is the sign of the philosopher. And why it rules religion, metaphysics, education and universities. Traditionally it was called the sign of the higher mind. Sagittarius is also the sign that rules adventure, foreign places and long distance travel. Do you remember the person in your graduating class who worked two after school jobs for years so they could take off to see the world the day they wrote their last exam? It's very likely that he or she was a Sagittarius. And do you recall if that same person was the one who always took the lead in heated classroom debates on social and political issues? Sagittarian travels are also travels of the mind.

The Sun enters Sagittarius as the northern winter sets in. This is the time of year when the daylight hours are few. In ancient times it was when people used to sit around the fire and listen to stories and legends passed down through the generations.

Most Sagittarians are great readers with a deep respect for knowledge and scholarship. For many of them, their most treasured possession is their private library, which they've lovingly built up over the years. They're literary omnivores, and you'll find Spinoza and Solzhenitsyn sandwiched between the glossy art books and their pile of well-thumbed guides to the caravan routes of Morocco and Mauritania.

Born under the sign of travel and foreign places, many Sagittarians seem to find good fortune abroad or even in dealings—personal and professional—with foreign people. The sign of Sagittarius or the planet Jupiter is dominant in the birth charts of expatriates everywhere. To live or study abroad at some stage in their life is an opportunity that comes the way of many Sagittarians. But most important for Sagittarians is that they are always the traveler, never the tourist. Sagittarians don't just want to pass through, they want to stop, savor, and experience whatever the journey brings their way.

Sagittarians roam far and wide. But not necessarily physically. For every one that can't wait to get to the airport, there are just as many who are content to stay at home in the comfort of their favorite armchair with all their books and treasures around them, and roam the Net. The reclusive poet Emily Dickinson was a Sagittarius who scarcely traveled any farther than the town she lived in all her life. If you know one of the quieter, more restrained, stay-at-home Sagittarians, it's likely he or she has Taurus or Virgo on the Ascendant or maybe Moon in Cancer.

Sagittarius, along with its opposite sign, Gemini, forms the axis of the zodiac that rules communication and education. Both Geminis and Sagittarians are eternal students who never stop learning and, as others sometimes complain, never stop talking. It's just as well they usually have something interesting to say.

When Sagittarians have struck on a new idea or discovered a new theory, it's just about impossible for them to keep it to themselves. What fun would that be? Far more exciting to share it, and toss it around with their friends. There are some Sagittarians, it must be said, who can get carried away on the combination of a brilliant idea and the sound of their own voice.

The young Sagittarian is advised to pursue a higher education. Not only for the career advantages but also because a Sagittarius needs to learn to argue logically and reason well. These are people who love to engage in philosophical debates, and a Sagittarian mind that is well trained is guaranteed to reduce the volume of hot air that listeners would otherwise be forced to endure.

When Sagittarians can combine physical and mental travel, they are on their most fertile ground and feel most fulfilled. Indiana Jones did it, and became a modern Sagittarian archetype image. The physical challenge, the companionship, and the call of the open road are all important elements in the Sagittarian journey. Many philosophical Sagittarians are searching for their own grail.

The religious impulse (in the broadest sense) is strong in this sign. In the sixties many young Sagittarians in search of adventure and enlightenment followed the hippie trail to Kathmandu. And their descendants can be found today camping along the road to Glastonbury, making the pilgrimage to the Gothic cathedrals of France or the mysterious temples of the East.

Get philosophical with Sagittarians and you're likely to find that their spiritual journey has led them through a veritable smorgasbord of meditation groups, ashrams, and personal-awareness workshops. The Bhagwan Shree Rajneesh, perhaps the most flamboyant and memorable of modern gurus, was himself a Sagittarian. And so was his promise of spiritual enlightenment through the pleasures of the senses and having a good time.

When Neptune, the planet that dictates the flavor and fashions of the times, occupied Sagittarius between 1970 and 1984, there was a proliferation of mystics and gurus. But Neptune decreed another shift in the collective mind-set in 1984 when it moved on into conservative, status-conscious Capricorn. Right on cue, the yuppie was born. Corporate philosophy took over, and shoulder pads and power dressing replaced Indian beads and gypsy dresses. The nostalgic will never get a rerun of the seventies. But in 1996 Pluto, the planet of transformation, entered Sagittarius, where it will remain until 2008. Astrologers are expecting quite a revolution in orthodox religions throughout the world.

There are many Sagittarians among the traditional clergy. But Sagittarian priests, rabbis, and ministers are naturally liberal by inclination. Again, it comes down to the Sagittarian urge to move spiritually and intellectually beyond conventional boundaries. Outmoded dogma and strict orthodoxy are not for them. Yet, curiously, a love of ritual, with all the attendant pomp, ceremony, and dressing up, can be very much to their taste. Perhaps that's because they understand why and how rituals and symbols fill an important need in people's lives.

Sagittarius is called "the sign of the prophet." *Prophet* and *guru* are larger-than-life labels that have been attached to quite a few famous Sagittarians. Nostradamus, the great French seer, was born on December 5. As futurists, modern-day Sagittarians are fascinated by prophecies about the future of the world, and the people who make them.

One prophet of the new millennium, Arthur C. Clarke, is a Sagittarian. When *2001: A Space Odyssey* first appeared on our movie screens, it captured the imagination of the world. Decades have passed. Satellites now orbit the earth, space probes are moving to the far edge of our solar system, and scientists are sending signals into outer space in case there is something or someone out there that can answer. HAL is so much closer to reality than we could have believed three decades ago.

3001: The Final Odyssey was the obvious sequel. The story takes place on the moons of Jupiter, Sagittarius' own planet. Coincidence? Perhaps. In 3001 we finally encounter alien life, cyber warfare has erupted, and a microchip is able to download human life. Given his track record with 2001 and other stories, it behooves us now to take very seriously indeed Clarke's visions of the future.

Clarke believes that science fiction writers, by virtue of their foresight and imagination, have an important role that goes beyond the spinning of fantastic tales. He says, "By mapping out *possible* futures as well as a good many impossible ones, the science fiction writer can do a great service to the community. He encourages in his readers flexibility of mind, readiness to accept and even welcome change—in one word, *adaptability*; perhaps no attribute is more important in this age." The italics, by the way, are his, not ours. But he has pinpointed some key Sagittarian words. *Possible*—Sagittarians sincerely believe anything is possible. They are, perhaps more than any other sign, always open to possibilities. And as for *adaptability*, that is undoubtedly one of their main assets. Sagittarians have that flexibility of mind and the readiness to accept change that Clarke advocates. These are virtues that Sagittarians share with Gemini, Virgo, and Pisces, the other three mutable signs. To be mutable means to be adaptable and willing to move with the times.

It's interesting that Clarke, being born under "the sign of religion," describes himself as "a militant agnostic." Yet his latest epic speculates on the nature of God. In Clarke's vision of the far distant future, our descendants call religion a "psychopathology." They look back on our era of 2001 (in which the followers of competing creeds slaughtered each other over meaningless points of doctrine) as one of the most barbaric in human history. Maybe we can take some consolation in the fact that, according to Clarke, all the evils we suffer now—such as crooked politicians, overcrowded prisons, inadequate education, starvation, and war—will no longer exist.

Clark is keen to alert us to the moral questions that are emerging from the technological and space age. As he points out: "One cannot have superior science and inferior morals." Sagittarians are very interested in questions of right and wrong, and are great supporters of moral causes. Indeed, some Sagittarians have causes like other people have hobbies. But wouldn't the world be a better place if we all took a leaf out of their book, if we got up and actively supported the causes we believe in? Sagittarians apply the same zeal to saving the forests, demonstrating for human rights, and Greenpeace as they do to wrestling with the search for the meaning of life.

Many Sagittarians leave money to their favorite cause, passing over any undeserving grandchildren, nephews, or nieces. They like the idea of endowing their old school with a scholarship bearing their name, or being remembered as a patron of the arts. Seriously rich Sagittarians are often inclined to philanthropy.

Sagittarian Andrew Carnegie donated hundreds of millions of his fortune made in steel to classic Jupiterian interests. Everyone has heard of Carnegie Hall, but how many know about The Carnegie Hero Fund, The Carnegie Endowment for Internal Peace, The Carnegie Foundation for Advancement of Teaching, and the Carnegie libraries? Carnegie led an all-Sagittarius life. True to his Sun sign, he immigrated to America from Scotland and made his millions in a land far from his birthplace.

Ecological issues are close to the Sagittarius heart. Even your average Sagittarian is an enthusiastic recycler, wild-bird feeder, and planet saver. Most Sagittarians love animals. The particular affinity they have with horses and dogs is based on companionship and respect. They admire the uninhibited physical movement of animals. Maybe watching them running free and unfettered stirs up their own call to the wild.

The popular symbol of Sagittarius is The Centaur—half man, half beast. The only sign of the zodiac that is human and animal in one. This two-in-one aspect of Sagittarius makes it one of the dual signs. (The others are Gemini and Pisces.) Sagittarians are not single-minded people. Their interests are varied, and they cannot be confined for long to one all-consuming passion. On the one hand it makes them open and unlimited. But it can create difficulties when focus and discipline are required.

The human half of The Centaur is an Archer shooting his arrows of desire upward into the higher realms. The name Sagittarius is derived from *sagitta*, which is Latin for "arrow." This is the arrow that you see aimed towards the heavens in the glyph for Sagittarius, and it's crucial to an in-depth understanding of the higher purpose of Sagittarius to focus on that arrow. The arrow is the symbol of the mental energy that Sagittarians apply to the search for the meaning of life, including whether or not God exists, and if It does, what sort of God It is.

The arrow aimed high also represents the Sagittarian belief in something bigger, brighter, and better than the present. It's a symbol of that legendary Sagittarian optimism. Sagittarius is often called a lucky sign. Maybe that's because Sagittarians genuinely believe that luck is on their side. But if Sagittarians really *are* lucky—and yes, they do seem to have the knack for being in the right place at the right time, or meeting the right person who can make the right connection—is it because there is some truth to the power of positive thinking? If "luck" is about attitude, then there's no doubt that Sagittarians have got the right attitude.

You don't need to know a Sagittarian intimately to recognize the animal half of The Centaur. The centaurs of mythology were a pretty rowdy bunch. Wine and wild parties (with a couple of brawls thrown in) were the general order of the day. Moderation and temperance were not their style. Likewise, most real-life Centaurs don't feel the slightest bit guilty in surrendering to a little regular excess and self-indulgence. The centaurs were notorious for their loud, boisterous, and uncouth behavior. All except one, that is. Chiron, the wise and learned centaur, teacher of heroes and the children of the gods. Chiron himself was the son of a god. His father was the great god Saturn. The story goes that when Saturn was conducting an extra-marital affair with a nymph, they were caught in the act by his wife, Rhea. At the moment of climax, Saturn turned himself into a horse and fled the scene, which is why the child who was conceived—Chiron—was half human, half horse, and immortal like his father.

One of Chiron's special skills was the gift of healing. Yet when he was accidentally shot in the leg by one of Hercules' arrows, he found he was unable to heal himself. So painful was his wound that he begged Jupiter to grant him the release of death. Jupiter agreed and placed him in the heavens where he became the constellation of Sagittarius.

When a "new" asteroid was discovered in 1977 and named after the Chiron of myth, astrologers wasted no time working out what this new addition to our solar system meant. They suggested that Chiron, the healer, has much in common with the nature of Virgo, a sign that is very interested in health and healing. He has even been proposed as a new ruler of Virgo. For all of us, Chiron lies in the area of our birth chart—and our life—where we have personal wounds that need to be healed.

Chiron as the wise teacher centaur is also connected with the higher side of Sagittarius. All those raucous, debauched centaurs represent the lower side. Here again is the duality of the sign. That swing between the sacred and the profane, the spiritual and the physical. Sagittarians can be smart *and* sporty. Even the most intellectual of them will occasionally sit up till 4:00 A.M. in front of the TV watching a tennis match that's being beamed in live by satellite.

When a Sagittarian is in full stride, it can be poetry in motion. Sagittarians love the sensation of movement. They walk with an easy, attractive gait. Yet that ease seems strangely at odds with their reputation for clumsiness. It's true they do have a gift for tripping over your front doorstep, or knocking over a chair in the middle of a wedding speech. It's just part of the quirky charm of The Centaur.

Perhaps their greatest appeal lies in their contagious optimism, high spirits, and sense of fun. Sagittarians are indispensable at any dinner party as a raconteur to entertain the troops with their true-life tales of the unexpected, the exotic, the places they've been and the people they've met. After one glass too many of an excellent wine, however, the company may begin to show signs of being overwhelmed by too much of the power of positive thinking and long-winded sermons on their latest cause and hot topic. Should you reveal, at this stage, the slightest indication that you do not fully share their convictions, you risk being branded sexist, racist, or fascist, or merely severely limited (the latter being a very serious shortcoming under Sagittarian lore). And if you're brave enough to suggest that there might even be another side to the question, you'll catch a glimpse of an interesting contradiction in the Sagittarius personality. When they're on a roll and swept up in the tidal wave of their own enthusiasms, they turn into human steamrollers strangely lacking in tolerance for the people they have just accused of being intolerant. But dare to call *them* narrow-minded and they would be mortified. Let's face it, Sagittarians can often be a teensy bit hyperbolic. Which is not necessarily unendearing in itself—just add it to that growing list of their quirky charms.

Occasionally, however, they will strike you as being downright hypocritical, and that could be a whole lot harder to take. The truth is that their commitment is not always as strong as their rhetoric. Don't be fooled by the Sagittarian armchair activists who are more politically vociferous over the dinner table than behind the barricades.

Straightforward Sagittarians believe in being direct every bit as much as they believe in the power of positive thinking. When it comes to telling you what they think, you'll find them either refreshingly frank or horribly blunt. Honesty is a renowned Sagittarian virtue. But tact and diplomacy are not. Nor is discretion. So, friends and lovers of Sagittarians, be warned. They might be great talkers, but they are known to blab. It's not that they deliberately want to embarrass you or that they never intended to keep your secret. It's just that things have a way of slipping out of Sagittarian mouths. The trick is to be the soul of discretion yourself. Don't make the mistake of telling a Sagittarius that you've heard the balding man wearing the bow tie is the secret lover of the hostess, because everybody will know about it, including the hostess's husband, before the coffee is served.

Another mistake that's easy to make is to assume that all that Sagittarian exuberance and high spirits make them immune to depression. Don't imagine that Sagittarians never experience their fair share of setbacks, failures, and black moods. Sagittarian Winston Churchill suffered from bouts of dark depression which he called his "black dog," in spite of which he claimed he looked on the bright side of life. "I am an optimist," he said. "I cannot see the point of being anything else. I cannot believe that the human race will not find its way through the problems that confront it." Another British prime minister and another great Sagittarian, Benjamin Disraeli, was fond of saying, "Something will turn up." That's the thing—it usually does for Sagittarians. You can't keep them down for long. Their bounce-back is legendary.

Hope and faith are practically Sagittarian tenets of belief. They really do believe that if they command the "clouds to unfold" they will. Does this sound a little *over*optimistic? A little presumptuous? Jupiter may have been the king of the gods (as Sagittarians love to remind you), but he had his flaws, too. Blind faith in the future, alas, can be downright foolhardy. And an overabundance of confidence, optimism, and enthusiasm is not always a good thing.

In 1758 the French philosopher Voltaire wrote a story called *Can-*

dide that has become a classic satire on optimism. In the course of incredible life-and-death adventures across three continents, Candide and his companions experience a series of extraordinary reversals of fortune that could only be described as awful bad luck. Yet even after they are hauled back from the brink of death a dozen times, Candide's tutor, the learned but obviously stupid Dr. Pangloss, stubbornly clings to his philosophy that "all is for the best in the best of all possible worlds." As a Sagittarian, Voltaire was clearly in the best of all possible astrological positions to write a story about the madness of optimism pushed beyond all limits.

If optimism is not balanced by common sense and an acceptance of what is realistically possible, things can start to go seriously wrong—even for Sagittarians. This is the dark side of Jupiter. We see it when confidence becomes bombast, when enthusiasm turns to fanaticism, when being open and receptive looks more like being gullible and naive. Then the Sagittarian fire can all too easily flare up and burn out of control. The Archer needs control and discipline if his or her arrows are not to miss their mark and fall scattered and wasted on the ground. "The sky is the limit" attitude can transport Sagittarius into dangerous territory. Might is not always right. And the clouds do not always unfold for Sagittarius, or indeed for any sign, simply because they would have it so.

Some Sagittarians get all too easily carried away on the adrenaline rush of their own optimism. This is when the true and positive optimist turns into the opportunist, the gambler, the soldier of fortune, the con man, or even the deluded megalomaniac.

History provides many chastening examples of the terrible damage that can be wrought by Sagittarians who ride their moral high horse all over the lives of others. General Franco, the Spanish dictator who ruled for forty years, was one such Sagittarian. From Franco's point of view, his was a great cause. Yet, hundreds of thousands of people died during the Spanish civil war, so that he could succeed in his mission to keep democracy out of Spain.

Franco's life was hardly evidence of the Sagittarian open mind and broad perspective. But what it does display is how impervious to other people's suffering and opinions Sagittarians can be when they are determined to impose their way because it is *the* way. Jupiter can lead the Sagittarius individual into excesses of all kinds.

On an everyday level, too, Sagittarius can turn into a despot. All fire signs can slip into "me first" behavior. The negative Sagittarian who suffers from the "I'm all right, Jack" syndrome can be smug, self-satisfied, and insensitive. Jupiter is too often presented as a "good" planet—astrologers even call him "the great benefic." But there is nothing in astrology, no sign, no planet, that is only good or bad. Sagittarians, or people of any sign who are born with a strong Jupiter in their horoscope, can at the very least come across as somewhat pushy and overbearing at times. Others (when they're feeling generous) may describe them a "big personality" and forgive them their excesses.

Another trap that awaits some Sagittarians is gullibility. These individuals are often so keen to do something big that their eagerness can drive them to cut corners and make mistakes.

At the ripe old age of twenty-three, the world's most famous anthropologist, Margaret Mead, spent six months in Samoa researching her book *Coming of Age in Samoa.* In her book Mead described a culture where adolescents lived in a tolerant, free-love, sexually promiscuous paradise. At the time her revelations were embraced by the flower-power hippie generation of the sixties as evidence that sexual repression ought to be a thing of the past. Fifty years after its publication, another anthropologist exposed Mead's gullibility. It seems that all those years ago, Dr. Mead was duped. Her primary source of information was two young women who, in good Samoan tradition, loved a practical joke. They have since confessed that what they told Mead was all a hoax.

As a Sagittarian, did Margaret Mead see only what she wanted to see? Namely a culture where young people were blissfully free of constraints. It now seems that yes, that was the case. Her horoscope even has the classic astrological signature of the gambler and the soldier of fortune: impatient, ego-serving Mars was in conjunction with risk-taking Jupiter. Anyone (but especially a Sagittarian) born with this configuration needs to contemplate the difference between "bold" and "rash." It's interesting that Mead's birth chart also contains the mark of somebody who was *eventually* going to be made accountable. Saturn, the planet of hard work, the planet that is always waiting to trip up the careless and the less than conscientious, was dangerously close to her bold Mars/Jupiter conjunction.

Saturn is actually a very important issue for *all* Sagittarians. The virtues of Saturn are a wonderful antidote for the excesses that Sagittarians are prone to. We would all do well to study the virtues of the sign that follows our own. And Sagittarius would be wise to heed a lesson or two from earthy Capricorn—ruled by serious Saturn. Sagittarians probably think Capricorns are far too serious for their own good. But dour Capricorns are blessed with bundles of patience and self-discipline. Discipline, as any Capricorn will tell you, doesn't mean restrictions. On the contrary, discipline leads to freedom. Without discipline, life would be chaos and nothing of lasting value would be achieved. Unless Sagittarians acquire a little Capricornian-style respect for hard work and plain common sense (not to mention a little modesty and humility), they will always be prone to promising more than they can deliver. The Sagittarians who *have* integrated some of these Saturnian qualities are the ones who become the classic Sagittarian success stories.

The art of the Sagittarian life is to find an outlet for their adventurous spirit and to be able to explore their ideas—but to also keep at least one foot on the ground. Sagittarians should never suppress their sense of wonder or their sense of fun. It's what fuels their life and their achievements. It's also what makes them such exciting people and such an inspiration to others. As Arthur C. Clarke once said, "It is this sense of wonder that motivates all true scientists and all true artists."

Those Sagittarians who can marry their sense of wonder and their high spirits to practicality are bound to see much further than most. And are sure to go as far as their vision can take them.

THE SAGITTARIUS CAREER AND DIRECTION

When Sagittarian Woody Allen said, "Eighty percent of success is just showing up," he struck a note that rings true for all career-minded Sagittarians.

Few people are so willing to give something a go, and when Sagittarians turn up on the scene, you can't help but notice them. That's because they have presence and the confidence to sell themselves. You don't find many wilting violets born under the sign of The Archer.

For Sagittarius, possibilities are ultimately more important than promotions. So think carefully, Sagittarius, before you yield to pressure from nearsighted family and lock yourself into the full job-and-security package. They probably mean well when they advise you to stick at one thing, or hint that job hopping is fraught with insecurity. But do they really understand that you could never be happy in a job with no scope? And besides, can't they see, as you can, that a job for life is fast becoming a thing of the past?

Indeed, for most Sagittarians, the idea of a job for life is altogether too predictable, too limiting, and too boring. They soon become adept at reading between the lines of the help wanted ads for the jobs that give them what they need . . . room to move, both mentally and physically.

Sagittarians are always one step ahead into the future. And it's because they *are* so forward-thinking, versatile, and multitalented that they are so well placed to take advantage of the changing work scene, and even profit from it.

In the future many of us can expect to be making some kind of career shift, maybe two or three times during the course of our working lives, but this has always been second nature to Sagittarians. They are better equipped than most to cope with retraining and welcome learning new skills. Indeed, the Sagittarian versatility and adaptability look set to be very desirable career assets as we move into the new millennium.

Part-time work and job sharing suit them very nicely, leaving them heaps of time for their extracurricular activities, allowing them to make their own agendas and do a bit of moonlighting should they need any extra cash. Freelancing is attractive to lots of Sagittarians. Even the word itself taps right into what Sagittarius needs. Freedom. It's practically a sacred Sagittarian word. In spite of the fact that they have their sights set high and they love the things that big money can buy, there are a lot of clever and capable Sagittarians who steer well away from the top corporate jobs. Most are self-aware and smart enough to realize that the responsibilities attached to senior management are going to eliminate their precious freedom. They reckon there are plenty of other ways—Sagittarian ways—to pursue fame and fortune. If you know a Sagittarian who's a high corporate flyer, you can bet that he or she has some kind of escape clause written into the contract. Sagittarians like to always keep the door open.

Indeed, if you work with, or for, a Sagittarius, you've probably already noticed that he or she is rarely the last to close the office door in the evening, or the first to open up in the morning. Sagittarians hate to be chained to a desk, and the Sagittarius long lunch has been known to last for days, not hours. So it's not surprising they become excellent delegators. Sagittarian bosses are not the types to be forever looking over your shoulder, but you can be sure they want the job done. And they'll let you know in no uncertain terms if they're not happy with your performance. But they're not nitpickers, and they don't insist that everything is done by the rules. To Sagittarius, the end is always more important than the means.

Virtually any field that gives them the opportunity to stretch their minds and exploit their native curiosity is fertile Sagittarian territory. They are naturally drawn to the world of ideas and communications. But if their choice is, say, computing, then their forte is more likely to be out selling programs, rather than sitting in front of a screen all day. If it gives them the chance to make more money in a shorter space of time, all the better.

Sagittarius is the entrepreneur par excellence of the zodiac. Having the vision to see where a good idea could lead, the courage to run with it, and the willingness to take a risk are all part of the function of Jupiter. Maybe you're not a Sagittarian yourself, but if you have a Sagittarius Ascendant or if your Sun falls in the ninth house of your horoscope (the Sagittarius house), or even if Jupiter is prominent in your birth chart, then you also instinctively recognize a good opportunity when it comes your way. The Archer loves the thrill of the hunt. But they love the prospect of a quick few hundred percent profit even more.

Somewhere deep down in every Sagittarian there's a gambler. Some of them actually make a living out of it. Wall Street, the money market, stocks and options, lure a lot of Sagittarians. There isn't a Centaur who can resist an occasional flutter on the horses or the odd lottery ticket. These are the people who will put a few thousand into shares because a friend "in the know" insists it's a good bet.

Whatever their talents turn to, it's a Sagittarian career fantasy to get in on the ground floor and ride the express elevator to the top. Sagittarians dream of finding a way to circumvent the twenty-year solid grind between getting their first job and making their first million. Impatience, lack of sustained application, and, frankly, trying to get maximum return on minimum effort is one of the least attractive faces of Sagittarius. They believe you can never have too much of anything you desire, including money. Some Sagittarians can be terribly lazy and greedy.

Read any description of Sagittarius, and *generous* is a word that always pops up. It's true that the positive Sagittarian is expansive, and generosity has, by definition, a lot to do with being expansive. But when the greedy side of Jupiter klicks in, Sagittarians can become so selfishly engrossed in obtaining material gratification that you begin to question whether the magazines got it wrong and they're really not the generous spirits they're made out to be, after all.

Generosity is not the first word that springs to mind with the name of John Paul Getty. Yet he was a Sagittarian and the richest man in the world in his time. You would think that Getty was someone who had so much, he could give freely and still have whatever he wanted. But that's not the way Getty saw it. Getty was the billionaire who charged his son $20 for lunch and installed a pay phone in his home. The life of John Paul Getty is a strange, twisted story of what can go wrong in the Sagittarian pursuit of wealth. Jupiter, remember, is the planet of expansion—but also of excess. For some Sagittarians, enough is never enough. The best-known chapter in the sad personal saga of J. P. Getty is the kidnapping of his grandson. Getty spent a long time—some say too long—trying to negotiate down the ransom money. In the end, he paid up. But not before the kidnappers had cut off his grandson's ear and mailed it the family to make their point. To the greedy, wheeler-dealer Sagittarian, there is virtually nothing that is not open to negotiation.

Sagittarians are turned on by get-rich-quick schemes, and there are many who are easily deluded when they walk into that Sagittarian fantasy land of big deals and unlimited possibilities. Yet they themselves can be the smoothest, fastest, slickest talkers this side of the galaxy. And although they're often guilty of promising more than they can deliver, in all fairness, Sagittarians are more likely to fall for promises that can never be delivered. That there are times to expand and times to contract is something all Sagittarians need to learn. There will be plenty of opportunities when they can "go for it." It's knowing when to pull back that so often determines whether a Sagittarian makes it or not.

One of the all-time classic American success stories is also a classic Sagittarian success story. It's about a boy who believed in his ideas, educated himself, refused to be put off by setbacks, moved to Hollywood, and made good. Out of his rich imagination came one of the best-loved icons of the twentieth century—Mickey Mouse.

We will probably never know whether Mickey himself is a Sagittarian, but his creator, Walt Disney, was. And it's curious that at a time when Mickey's career looked like it was heading for the doldrums, Disney came up with a new role for the Mouse that was pure Sagittarius, and put him back in the spotlight . . . The Sorcerer's Apprentice. Do you remember how, in *Fantasia*, Mickey was apprenticed to a venerable old magician and left to carry out the tedious chore of carting bucket after bucket of water to fill the well? But Mickey, who couldn't resist the temptation to avoid hard work, decided to use his still-untried magic skills by casting a spell on a broom commanding it to take over the job. We all know what happened next. He got the spell only half right and it all went horribly wrong. The broom divided into two then four, and kept on dividing so that soon there were hundreds of brooms all filling the well, and the magician's laboratory was awash. Of course, there was a happy ending. The magician returned just in time to avert total disaster, and Mickey, the junior magus, had learned an important Sagittarian object lesson in why laziness doesn't pay in the end. Overconfidence often paves the Sagittarian road to failure. But confidence combined with diligence guarantees a Sagittarius success.

It certainly worked for Walt Disney. His entrepreneurial instincts were honed in France in 1918 when he made a quick buck painting fake medals on the soldiers' leather jackets. Creative, yes. Entreprenial, certainly. Disney was an inventor and promoter of ideas and stories with universal appeal. Like Disney, Sagittarians often owe much of their success to their ability to inspire and motivate others. In that typically Sagittarian way, Disney was also fascinated by the future. He even had his own vision for a futuristic city, much of which was built into Disneyland and Disney World.

Another Sagittarian—who, interestingly, was raised on a Disney diet—also worked hard, held on to his dream, and inspired the world with some of the most exciting (and profitable) films of our time. Steven Spielberg. As a boy, Spielberg financed his first films by whitewashing his neighbors' orange trees, which he still recalls earned him seventy-five cents per tree, at the rate of thirty per day. Not bad for a twelve-year-old.

Sagittarians love recounting stories about their trials and tribulations—and acts of audacity—on their way to the top. Spielberg tells how, when he was still young and unknown, he donned a suit, walked past the guard at Universal Studios, found a vacant office, and brazenly installed himself in it. There was no salary, but the point of the exercise was to get noticed and to get the people at Universal interested in him and his scripts. How's that for Sagittarius-style bravado? It's proof that Woody Allen is not the only Archer who believes that just turning up can be the most important move you can make. Sagittarians dare to do what others don't even dare to imagine.

The only problem with Spielberg's plan was that he didn't pull it off. (But you've got to give him ten out of ten for imagination and guts.) It was four years before he gave up, fired himself, and walked out. It seems that Spielberg's express elevator had gotten temporarily stuck on the ground floor. A lot of Sagittarians are destined to learn the lesson of the Sorcerer's Apprentice.

Some of Spielberg's creations are now every bit as immortal and universal as Mickey Mouse. Spielberg once said, "Since I was a little kid and first heard Jiminy Cricket sing 'When You Wish Upon a Star,' I wanted to make a movie about the song." And he did. The star of *that* film was E.T.

Every Sagittarian loves to entertain, and Sagittarian entertainers have their own unmistakable appeal. They're direct and uninhibited, and you can't help warming to them. Did Sagittarius Harpo Marx ever fail to get a smile out of you when you were down with a dose of the blues? Arch extroverts that they are, Sagittarian comedians have a gift for ribald, off-the-wall humor. Bette Midler and Billy Connolly wouldn't get away with their downright dirty jokes if they weren't so downright funny.

The Sagittarian performer has energy to burn. Think of Kenneth Branagh, who's put the fire and fun back into Shakespeare. Bruce Lee and Douglas Fairbanks, Jr., were also Sagittarians, and they both did all their own stunts.

It has been suggested that a good teacher is first and foremost a good actor. Teaching is a field that gives Sagittarians lots of scope to use the force of their personality and plenty of opportunities to perform. Add their love of knowledge and learning, and you can see why teaching is a good Sagittarian career choice. They love the atmosphere of academe. Virtually any job in an educational environment, be it registrar, secretary, or professor, will suit a Sagittarian.

As teachers, Sagittarians see their role as a whole lot more than expounding on the causes of the French Revolution or the theory of logarithms. Sagittarians don't just transfuse information, they inspire and illuminate. Thirty years on, former students still fondly remember the Sagittarian teacher as the one whose classroom was a place where they were encouraged to speak their mind and think beyond hometown mentality.

It should come as no surprise that Sagittarians are often teachers of foreign languages. This is the sign, you recall, that rules foreign places. Charles Berlitz, the founder of a chain of international language schools, was a Sagittarian. Sagittarians know that you can only really get inside a foreign culture when you speak the language.

All Sagittarians get a buzz from making the mental connection. They enjoy the company of young people, and young people relate easily to them. This is very possibly the Sun sign least likely to consent to grow old gracefully. If it wasn't a Sagittarius who coined the phrase "Youth is a state of mind," it could only have been a Gemini. Opposite signs, remember. Though when it comes to counting the wrinkles, Geminis possibly fare better. A life full of so many experiences, adventures, and indulgences can leave some Sagittarians a little the worse for wear.

Opposite signs also have a lot to offer each other. What we find irritating about our opposite sign is often precisely what we need to cultivate in ourselves. Many Sagittarians would find it beneficial to practice the Gemini art of staying cool and rational in inflammatory situations. Fiery Sagittarians are sometimes too quick to react and respond. If they could learn to stand back and be more objective and detached like a Gemini, they might be less prone to committing social and professional gaffes. Both signs are restless and gregarious, but all things considered, Geminis have got more social savoir faire, and can be very wily. Sagittarians are generally without guile. It's one of their more endearing characteristics. But being blunt and painfully honest is probably the last thing anyone needs in a delicate heated atmosphere when the collective blood pressure is rising. Observe, Sagittarius, how cleverly Geminis star in a diplomatic crisis, how quickly they charm and talk their way out of sticky situations.

Moreover, Sagittarius tend to get so caught up in the big picture and the future that they can overlook what needs to be done right now. Geminis are very good at dealing with the immediate matter at hand quickly and efficiently. It's great to be able to look ahead, but not if it means neglecting what's going on under your nose.

Publishing falls under the rulership of Sagittarius. Similarly, anyone whose Sun falls in the ninth house of their horoscope is drawn to the world of books. Writing satisfies their need to rove and roam on the mental plane. It enables them to bring their sense of wonder to life, and share their ideas and ideals with others.

Publishers and publicists both need the Sagittarian input. The opportunity to flex their entrepreneurial muscles, to get involved in the creative process *and* get in on the chance to launch a potential bestseller all at the same time is a perfect combination for a Sagittarian.

In fact, any job that requires the ability to talk one's way into a sale could be designated a Sagittarian job. Agents belong in this category. Sagittarians are born promoters. They can promote anything from rock concerts to grand opera. From the better mousetrap to pay TV. You name it, they can sell it.

For those Sagittarians who are the perennial Boy Scouts, there are many ways to make a living doing what they love doing best—hitting the road and heading into the great outdoors. Eco-tourism is a growing industry that must have been tailor-made for Sagittarians. There's also trekking, mountain climbing, and riding camels across the desert. But it's not all yaks, backpacks, and mosquito nets (as romantic as this sounds—at least to a Sagittarian). What about that indulgent streak in Jupiter-ruled people? The luxury resort is also most definitely one of their happy hunting grounds. Indeed, the travel industry generally is a popular choice for many Sagittarians. Airline pilots, stewards, booking clerks, guides, or cocktail waiters—if it takes them out into the wide world, it's a Sagittarian job. The original creator of the package holiday, Thomas Cook, was a Sagittarius. It almost goes without saying.

The sports industry is a good career option for people born under fire signs. Even your average office-bound Sagittarian is the type who organizes tennis matches after work, or the interdepartment softball game. They're active, energetic, and, of course, they play to win. Every Sun sign produces its share of sporting heroes, but Sagittarius is undeniably a "sporty" sign.

After mesmerizing the world on the cricket field, Sagittarian Imran Khan carried his sexy sports-hero image into the world of politics. Sagittarians are undaunted by the harsh glare of publicity. Television and the media are their best friends. For all Sagittarians in public life, their ability to persuade and inspire is a real asset.

Most Sagittarians feel strongly about the future of the world and the planet. For the most impassioned and committed of them, making a career in the cause that fires up their sense of justice could be the most fulfilling way of living their Sun sign. A job that combines idealism, intellect, and energy is perfect, so working for a movement that promotes peace, equality, and freedom is suitable. Greenpeace, United Nations agencies, animal welfare, environmental watchdogs, whatever . . . There's something for every ideological Sagittarian.

Sagittarians are up there with the best of them in the fight for changes that will bring a better future. But that doesn't mean they're revolutionaries. The Sagittarian way is to work within the system, to liberalize rather than revolutionize. Sagittarius always has an eye on the bigger picture.

The law is a profession traditionally ruled by Jupiter, and attracts many Sagittarians. Though astrologers believe that Capricorn (the sign of rules and regulations) and Libra (the sign of fair play and negotiating) are equally significant in directing someone towards a career in the law.

To be honest, Sagittarians are so versatile and have such a wide range of interests that there are few fields without an opening for them somewhere. In fact, Sagittarius would have to be one of the signs, if not *the* sign, with the longest list of career options.

Sagittarians move willingly with the times. They naturally look to the future. These are the gifts of their Sun sign. And for that, Sagittarius, you can indeed count yourself lucky.

LOVE AND FRIENDSHIP

Sagittarians are so friendly and so easy to talk to that it's no wonder they draw so many people to them. Few signs are as popular as Sagittarius. Maybe that's because they're unashamedly committed to the pursuit of a good time.

These people seem to know everyone, or at least anyone who's interesting. They like to hang out with the movers and the groovers. Indeed, Sagittarians can open up whole new worlds to their friends. No better person to take you to restaurants you would never have known existed, to introduce you to West African cuisine, out-of-the-way jazz clubs, and the denizens of the art world. Sagittarians get invited everywhere. And if they're not, they'll assume it was just an oversight and turn up anyway. They'd hate to miss out on anything.

Express an interest in something and they're sure to be able to introduce you to somebody who's into it, and if not, they'll lend you a book on it. If you've got the travel bug and are contemplating a trip somewhere—anywhere—chances are they'll be able to give you some valuable pointers and the address of someone you can look up. They may even volunteer to go along.

Their address book may be bursting, but the reality is that a lot of the people Sagittarius call friends are what most would call acquaintances. Possibly half of the guests at their birthday party won't be seen again for another year. No matter. Sagittarius likes to throw great parties on a grand scale, and you can't do that with six or seven people.

Forthright and demonstrative with their affections, warm and tactile, Centaurs will take you by the hand, or rather, drag you by both arms if you show signs of becoming too introspective in your corner. Too bad if you're enjoying some time out alone communing with your drink and your thoughts, and are perfectly content just taking in the scene. There's no escape for the reluctant when Sagittarius is socially fired up, and has moved from extrovert and gregarious into loud and overwhelming.

By the stage the Centaur has broken into full gallop, he or she has lost all concept of voice projection and its effect on others. If Sagittarians sometimes remind you of Foghorn Leghorn, you wouldn't be the first to make the comparison. It's a nickname we know was given to one Sagittarian woman by her colleagues who secretly hoped she would be struck down with a case of chronic laryngitis. There is a definite type of Sagittarian who manages to raise the volume by a few decibels whenever they walk into a room.

One of the most fascinating and infuriating Sagittarian paradoxes is that their passions can get so hotly engaged by injustice and noble causes, yet when it comes to real sensitivity, they are often emotionally out to lunch. If, for example, you're still feeling fragile after your stormy divorce your Sagittarian friend, albeit in all innocence, may actually inquire about the welfare of your ex, when only that very morning you were revelling in a secret fantasy about hiring a hitman. They may even tell you about the nice lunch they had with this creature from the black lagoon. Oh yes, it's not an unlikely scenario we assure you. After all, the "creature" is one of their friends, too. It's not that Sagittarians mean to be callous or insensitive, or would see this as an act of disloyalty. It's just that they're unbelievably tactless.

Sagittarians frequently fail to tune in to the needs and vulnerabilities of other people, and miss the subtle clues. For all their popularity and herds of friends, for all their warmth and camaraderie, they can be scathing of what they interpret as other people's weaknesses, and a bit wary of true intimacy. When they realize that they've overstepped the mark and left a few emotional bruises, it could be worth their while to focus their famous honesty on themselves. This is, after all, a sign that is a truth seeker. Could it be possible that the distraught, down-and-out friend who arrives on their doorstep at 2:00 A.M. with a tale of woe is in genuine need of a bit of care and understanding? Sagittarians are often guilty of assuming that someone down on their luck is a weakling, a wimp, or a loser. They seem to forget that they've had their bad days, too, and that they have had their share of tough times. There are occasions when they should resist the urge to say, "You've got to get your act together," or the temptation to deliver a sermon on the power of positive thinking.

Sometimes the full-on modus operandi is all you need to pick out the Sagittarian in the crowd. It's such a giveaway. But it's not their only ID. One visual clue is the nose. It's rarely small, and it usually strikes you as the prominent feature of the face. Then there's something in the way they move. There's a characteristically Sagittarian lope, especially in the long-limbed, lanky ones (and there are a lot of those). It's more coltlike than ungainly. Think of Brad Pitt. (He's got that typical Sagittarius boyish charm, too). Some Sagittarian men *do* walk as if they've just gotten off a horse. But they're never slouchers. They stride, carrying themselves well, head held high. Perhaps that's why they're prone to tripping over cracks in the pavement. If you're really observant, you'll notice that, short or tall, the trunk of the body is often disproportionately longer than it is in other signs. Physiologically speaking, Sagittarius rules the hips and the thighs, and there are some Sagittarians who do battle with the bulge as they get older. The women quickly put on extra weight around the bottom if they're not getting enough exercise.

If your interest in a certain Sagittarius looks like it's heading beyond a mutual exchange of books, philosophy, and beers in the backyard, the rest of the Sagittarius anatomy is not likely to remain hidden for long. Though if you're a little anxious as to whether you're reading the signals right, a good way to find out is to get Sagittarius on the dance floor. Dancing will soon enlighten you as to whether or not you're perceived as hot property. There is nothing that quickens the Sagittarian pulse more than the sight of a body in motion. As the temperature rises, try to reveal a rippling sweaty muscle or two. Sagittarians are seriously turned on by rippling sweaty muscles.

Even in sensitive matters of the heart, Sagittarians shoot from the hip. So let's do the same. On the plus side, they're up front, sexually uninhibited, and as enthusiastic as they are about everything that takes their fancy. At least you'll know where you stand. Be warned, however, quite a few of the males (and only marginally fewer of the females) appear to suffer from a Don Juan complex.

Not renowned for the leisurely courtship, Sagittarians find it almost impossible to repress their desire to get on with it. They figure life is too short to be subtle. They don't waste time with unnecessary overtures. Nor will they ponder too long on the question of should I or shouldn't I.

If you're attracted to the archetypal nature-loving, chest-beating Centaur, you won't need any reminding that The Centaur is half human and half animal, and the animal part is the part from the waist down. A Sagittarian on the hunt can be downright flashy and exhibitionist, and certainly won't think twice about making the first move (females of the species included). In love and lust, the wonderful Sagittarian impulsiveness is often the key to their success. With few if any hang-ups, Sagittarians often get what they want simply because they're bold enough to go for it. If their sights are set on somebody, nobody will misread their intentions.

Just because their approach is direct, don't assume that they're lacking in technique. Sex for a Sagittarius is a form of high art. Performance art. Something akin to the cosmic dance of an Indian god.

"Come on, baby, light my fire . . ." sang Sagittarian Jim Morrison. And what hot-blooded female could resist striking the match? There's something about that Sagittarian boldness that is undeniably sexy.

Fiery Sagittarians want the spontaneity and excitement value that they seek in other areas of life to extend into the bedroom. Mind you, don't make the assumption that love with a Sagittarian is going to be necessarily confined to the bedroom. There's a Tarzan-and-Jane streak in every Sagittarian lover. A patch of dense enough vegetation, or a stretch of deserted enough beach, are very acceptable locations. But Tarzan and Jane are also perfectly at home in the Hilton. The luxury hotel with the king-size bed, whirlpool, and champagne is all part of the Sagittarian repertoire. When Sagittarians are in full Jupiterian, self-indulgent mode, decadence takes on a whole new meaning. And to heck with the American Express bill.

Their wonderful spontaneity can, of course, land them in trouble. To Sagittarius it's spontaneity, but to other people it could be unwanted attentions. When their confidence is way up, there's nothing to lose, reckon Sagittarians. You've got to hand it to them. They're brave enough to risk rejection. Nothing ventured, nothing gained, thinks Sagittarius in love, as in everything.

The memoirs of a Sagittarian are likely to reveal more than their fair share of close but brief encounters, a taste for the exotic, and maybe one or two liaisons that were, in hindsight, perhaps a little unwise. Having said that, many an older Sagittarian with memories of sexual adventures in Bali and Berlin is probably having fantasies about doing it all over again.

You're sure to have the picture by now. When it comes to the best things in life in general, and love in particular, Sagittarians subscribe to the belief that too much of a good thing is barely enough. Though we hasten to reassure lovers of Sagittarians that when The Centaur falls in love, he or she is just as capable of fidelity as any other sign. But should the fires ever burn down to embers, then your Sagittarius will not wait too long, or test his or her conscience too hard, before looking elsewhere.

If, however, *you* should be the one to decide that enough is enough and want to make the break, be prepared for the repercussions. If Sagittarius is dumped or ditched, he or she will show no restraint in broadcasting his or her version of what went wrong, and your general sins (including your shortcomings in bed). Discretion and dignity are not at the top of the list of Sagittarian qualities. The thwarted Archer can get a great deal of satisfaction by sharpening up their wit and turning it into pointed arrows tipped with vitriol. Pointed arrows can leave deep wounds. You'll need to be thick-skinned, or leave your answering machine permanently switched on until their outrage burns out. Easygoing Sagittarians can get horribly angry and indignant if they feel they have been wronged in love.

Basically, they can be very bad losers. In spite of their philosophical nature, they're not ones to spend too much time pondering on what part *they* may have played in the breakup of a relationship. The philosopher Spinoza, himself a Sagittarian, said, "Do not weep. Do not wax indignant. Understand." Pertinent words for Sagittarians in all aspects of life, especially love. If Sagittarians can come to the understanding that a relationship is a responsibility, and realize that the ease with which they slip into insensitive, dominating behavior is not going to win them any hearts, then it could be a real breakthrough.

The Sagittarian's true mate is first and foremost a companion. They are unlikely to want to make a commitment and settle down with someone who doesn't share their interests. So if you're equally enthusiastic about discovering that there's more to life than TV dinners and spending Saturday mornings at the supermarket, if you're interested in the big issues of the day and enjoy a good debate over a good meal, then your life will be very full indeed. Sagittarius will encourage you to explore your talents and not settle for a little when you can have more. You won't feel trapped with a stick-in-the-mud who will drag you down and leave you wondering what you could have been or done if you hadn't gotten hitched.

Getting hitched, incidentally, is not something that all Sagittarians necessarily dream of doing—officially, that is. If they're living with someone they love and the relationship is going well, they may not see the point in legalizing the union. Indeed, getting them to the altar can be a bit of a challenge. There are some vow-shy Sagittarians whose minds will be racing even as they take that long walk down the aisle. When they open their mouths to say "I do," some part of their mind is thinking, "I mean I *think* I do . . . I'm sure . . . Yes, of course, I do . . . at least for now . . ." Don't worry, they *do* mean it. It's simply Sagittarius having a last-minute anxiety attack. Remember, freedom is a precious Sagittarian commodity.

The secret is to prove to them that two people *can* be committed and can still be free. Show your Sagittarius that togetherness doesn't mean that they will cease to be their own person. Sagittarians are not the clinging, possessive types. They sincerely want you to stay true to yourself, and want you to enjoy the freedom they themselves value so highly. And what greater sign of love is there than that?

THE SAGITTARIAN PARENT

And then there were three.

As enthusiastic as they will be for this great new adventure in their life, Sagittarians may need to ask themselves how long the fascination will last if their meetings, dinners, and everything else suddenly take second place to baby lotion, pureed pumpkin, and colic remedies. Perhaps they should drop a few of those unmistakable Sagittarian hints to friends and family about what they want in the way of baby gifts. They want the diaper service, not the diapers.

The birth of a child is a time when Sagittarian parents might need to transcend their natural antipathy towards the small, practical realities of life. Because there's no avoiding those tedious chores when a baby arrives on the scene.

There is always a part of every Sagittarius that never grows up. Maybe their youthful attitude is what makes it so easy for them to relate to young people, and explains why they never lose their ability to have fun. Sagittarians are friends to their children as well as parents. They're simply wonderful at building tree houses, and organizing trips to museums and fun days out. The Sagittarian father will be very keen to show what a fantastic fast bowler he is—just try to stop him. A more active, sporty father, you couldn't hope to meet. And the Sagittarian mom won't complain too loudly if a chunk of her weekend is devoted to chauffeuring the children around to sporting events, Boy Scouts, and the junior social scene.

Sagittarians will be thrilled at the first sparks of their children's creative gifts. Paints, brushes, and art materials will be promptly obtained, and their children encouraged to express any budding creative talent.

Genuinely interested when it comes to planning their children's education, Sagittarians will research all the good private schools. And if the school of their choice ends up costing more than the budget allows, then they'll just rework the budget. It's a little-known fact that Sagittarians are extremely savvy when it comes to making economies on the household expenses to pay for the bigger, more important things like books, travel, and education. What's more, they do it so cleverly that others never feel they're going without.

It's not all sweetness and light, though, for children of Sagittarians. Sagittarian parents may have to make an extra effort to contain their impatience when their two-year-old comes down with the chicken pox and needs Mommy or Daddy to be there. Most Sagittarians have little patience with their own aches and pains, believing that if they pretend they don't exist, they'll just go away. But when they have to deal with somebody else's ailments, it's not so easy to dismiss them.

All fire signs, including Sagittarius, are inclined to become the dominating presence in the home. Sagittarian mothers and fathers might need to make a more conscious effort than most to understand that their children's nature and needs are not necessarily in line with theirs, even though Sun signs are inherited and the children of Sagittarians are almost certain to have some Sagittarius input in their horoscopes. From time to time their children may feel a little swamped by their active, ebullient parent who assumes that their way of doing things are good for them, and therefore automatically good for their children.

This realization is often an illumination for the Sagittarian parent. Going off camping with all the cousins may well be a Sagittarian idea of the perfect weekend, so long as Sagittarius keeps in mind that a little Pisces needs regular Sunday afternoons to him or herself curled up on the bed reading stories to the dog. And please don't scoff, Sagittarius, if your five-year-old Cancerian son prefers to visit Grandma because she lets him roll out the pastry for the apple pies. Just think, this could be the early efforts of a future restaurateur.

But Sagittarius is flexible and broad-minded. As children turn into teenagers, the Sagittarian parent is unlikely to be overdisciplinarian or curb their first steps towards independence and freedom any more than is absolutely necessary. It's not their way to impose draconian rules or regulations on a seventeen-year-old. In fact, they are more likely than most to turn a blind eye to a few broken curfews and rebellious moments or a couple of "unusual" friends because memories of their own youth will make it impossible for them to be too hypocritical.

When it comes to supporting their children's efforts and handing out encouragement, Sagittarian parents score top marks. Their children's attempts to gain independence and do something that requires imagination and initiative will never be put down. Sagittarians won't throw cold water over their children's pipe dreams, no matter how crazy they are.

Long after they've grown up and left home and learned that friends come and go, the children of a Sagittarian will take great comfort in the fact that their first friend—their Sagittarian parent— is their best friend, and will always be there for them with open arms.

THE SAGITTARIAN CHILD

Look at that smile. Yes, we know the books say that babies can't smile until they're six weeks old, but *you* know the happy little Sagittarian that destiny has just handed you has been grinning at you since day one.

The light of our Moon sign shines very bright in our earliest years. Sagittarian Moon babies display a lot of the same Sagittarian traits as Sun in Sagittarius babies. So be ready for them, too, to be scaling the side of their crib before their less adventurous brothers and sisters. No playpen is 100 percent Sagittarius-proof, and no gate across the stairs is too high for your Sagittarian toddler. The combination of their native curiosity and their physical agility is sure to keep you on your toes. Testing times indeed.

You'll feel like you're turning into a walking, talking encyclopedia feeding their huge appetite for information. But you'd better get fit, too. Because you'll soon be pitching tents in the backyard, training for the 2116 Olympics in the local park, and rushing off to dance classes.

The legendary energy reserves of your growing Sagittarian child will continue to amaze you. There's always one more turn on the carousel, always one more shell to collect, always one more tree to climb. As for questions, well, there are thousands of those. And don't think you can escape by fobbing them off with a line like "Ask Daddy" or "Go and see Mommy—she knows all about that." Your unwillingness to intellectually engage with a five-year-old Sagittarian will be greeted with disdain and disbelief. Surely Mother and Father could not be so ignorant. Honesty, however, will be appreciated and is your way out of many sticky situations. Your best strategy is to be straight with them. Even very young Sagittarians can accept that many important issues in life are not black and white, and that there are lots of gray areas, too. They won't take you to task if you qualify your answers with "Well, nobody knows for sure, but . . ." or "Some people believe this, but other people believe that . . ." A simple "I don't know, but we'll look it up" works every time.

Make no mistake, they will hit you with the $64,000 questions long before you expect them. "Will an angel save me if I fall off a cliff?" "Will people live on Mars?" "Does God live in the sky?" Please don't think we're stretching the truth. This is a tiny sample of the actual questions we've been asked by a seven-year-old Sagittarian. So don't be caught lost for words at an awkward moment; rehearse your answers now.

The classic Sagittarian interests in religion, space exploration, and distant lands will surface at an early age. As will their fast-developing philosophy that life was meant to be celebrated.

Education, you recall, comes under the sign of The Centaur. Getting the right school is often the critical factor in putting young Sagittarians on the path that's right for them. Remember, Sagittarians are not specialists by nature, and most of them will enter fields in which the range of their knowledge and skills, rather than depth, is the key to their success and happiness. So it stands to reason that the best education for them is one that is liberal and broad, and the best school is one that gives them the longest menu of courses to sample.

Man's best friend is usually your Sagittarian child's best friend too. The relationship with their dog is special, personal, and probably at times every bit as important as their relationship with you. They're likely to ask you for a horse as well if you've got the space. And you can consider yourself lucky if, in addition to the dog, you get away with sharing your home with a dozen white mice and a cockatoo, and if you manage to dissuade them from adding a snake to the family.

Ideal birthday presents for little Sagittarians include a puppy, globe, atlas, wall charts of dinosaurs and galaxies, a stamp collection, a telescope, a chemistry set, a Superman suit, and books, books, and more books. Most Sagittarian girls are tomboys, and will appreciate a bat and ball more than a Barbie doll.

As for the birthday parties, well, they'll be grand social occasions rather like dress rehearsals for the grown-up events that Sagittarius will stage in the not-so-distant future. You will be expected to provide lavishly. Sagittarian children are usually popular and start to build their social circle early. So make plans now to entertain the entire school class. After all, when you're the natural leader of the gang, you have to live up to the obligations of your position.

Even at a tender age, their social skills are already impressive. The famous Sagittarius ability to interact with people of all ages and from all walks of life will impress you and their teachers. Their bright, open, and self-assured manner often seems to belong to someone much older.

These are not the children who need to be coaxed into being a member of the crowd in the school play. Quite the opposite. Unless they've got one of the quieter, more restrained Moons or Ascendant such as Pisces, Virgo, or Capricorn, then assuming the leading role seems to come naturally to Sagittarian children. Although, needless to say, wanting the leading role *every* time may have to be curbed.

The time may come when you have to gently but firmly explain to your little Sagittarian that he or she can't always be center stage, because other children have a right to shine, too.

This can also be an important lesson on the home front. If your Sagittarian child has brothers and sisters, you may need to put a stop to his or her attempts to dominate. Some Sagittarian children don't see anything outrageous in telling *you*—their older and wiser parent—quite emphatically what you should do. These children are not just assertive, they're fast thinkers and can be quite devious if they figure a little deviousness is what it takes to get them what they want. There will come a time when you need to tighten the reins on your little Centaur. Fail to do this when the occasion calls for it and you could end up with *enfant terrible!*

On the other hand, it would be the worst mistake to crush their adventurous spirit. As the hormones click into place, try to give your Sagittarian enough room to move. These teenagers are going to have a few escapades—with or without your permission. Okay, so they're a little bold and presumptuous at times. And they're not as streetwise as they like to think they are. But if you've armed your Sagittarian teenager with enough straight information on the realities of life (and, of course, the facts of life) and if you've taught them the difference between right and wrong, then most of them will be smart enough to sense their limits. The self-preservation instinct is very healthy in Sagittarius.

As adults, many Sagittarians maintain a certain detachment from overly close family ties. If you are too heavy-handed, narrow, judgmental, or possessive, they won't hesitate to distance themselves once they leave the nest. Sagittarians don't necessarily hold to the axiom that blood is thicker than water. They won't be bound by family opinion or family expectations just because they're family.

Treat your Sagittarian with respect. Be reasonable and honest. Give them the sense of independence that comes from being allowed to make as many of their own decisions as possible. Do these simple but important things and you will be rewarded with a son or daughter who is equally reasonable and honest.

Above all, never ever underestimate the Sagittarian need for freedom. It's in their blood and their stars. Sagittarians do not function well when they feel fenced in. Huckleberry Finn summed it up for all young Sagittarians in his parting lines: "I reckon I got to light out for the territory because Aunt Sally, she's going to adopt me and civilize me, and I can't stand it." Mark Twain was—yes, you've guessed it—a Sagittarius.

BORN UNDER SAGITTARIUS

Billy the Kid	C. S. Lewis
Jacques-René Chirac	Noam Chomsky
George Eliot.	John Milton
Henri de Toulouse-Lautrec	Kirk Douglas
Jimi Hendrix	John Malkovich
Sai Baba	Christina Onassis
Kim Basinger	Frank Sinatra
Gianni Versace	Noel Coward
Maria Callas	Ludwig van Beethoven
Joan Armatrading	Betty Grable
Ian Botham	Edith Piaf
Richard Pryor	Uri Geller
Ralph Richardson	Jane Fonda
Boris Karloff	John F. Kennedy, Jr.
Tina Turner	Tom Waits
Charles M. Schulz	

CAPRICORN

December 22–January 20

♑

Ruling Planet
SATURN

Don't compromise yourself, you're all you've got.

Janis Joplin–born January 19

THE CAPRICORN NATURE

The self-reliant self-starter. That's Capricorn. People born under this sign are among the most resourceful and practical of all. Indeed, Capricorn is often called the "sign of the self-made man." Perhaps it's because not many Capricorns are given a kick start in life, and even those who come from a privileged background greatly admire people who have made it on their own merits.

Capricorns don't sit around expecting favors or luck to land in their laps. They're prepared to go out and earn their "luck." Actually they prefer it that way. Capricorns would feel very uncomfortable accepting the offer of a free ride. They'd much rather have the knowledge that they're not dependent on anyone else's support or goodwill. Capricorns sincerely believe that *they* are their own best investment.

Few signs are able to work so hard and so long to achieve what they want. And what do Capricorns want? You've probably read that they're materialistic. Remember how Joplin sang to the lord to buy her a Mercedes Benz? Yes, they want the Mercedes, and the Rolex and the harborside apartment. And certainly they've got what it takes to get them.

But what Capricorn wants most of all is power. Temporal power. It's an old-fashioned term for a sign with old-fashioned values. Temporal power is what you've achieved when you've carved out a position for yourself in the world and you've become a somebody. Ambitious Capricorns have got a good head for business, and they're astute enough to know what they can and can't achieve.

The key to getting ahead, reckons Capricorn, is planning. Many people make five-year plans, Capricorn included. But Capricorns also have their ten-year plan and their twenty-year plan tucked away in the bottom drawer. There are even some Capricorns who have a fifty-year plan. This is no exaggeration, we assure you. Most Capricorns in their twenties have a pretty clear idea of where they want to be and what they expect to have achieved at any given point in the future. Capricorns are strategic thinkers who aim to create structure and system in every aspect of their lives. Discipline is a natural Capricorn asset. There's not a lazy bone in their bodies. (Bones, by the way, are the part of the body ruled by Capricorn.) It's yet another reason why Capricorns succeed in reaching their goals.

Some people are willing to trust to fate. Capricorn is not one of them. Daydreaming and wishful thinking are regarded as foolish indulgences and a waste of time. Capricorn Benjamin Franklin said, "He that lives upon hope will die fasting." It's not that Capricorns are totally lacking in hope and faith, it's just that they believe in having something to back up that hope and faith. Something solid and tangible.

As the tenth sign of the zodiac, Capricorn follows Sagittarius. If you think of the zodiac as a cycle of evolution, it is the task of Capricorn to take all that wonderful Sagittarian idealism and bring it down to earth. It is, after all, an earth sign. A Capricorn can be every bit as impassioned, open to opportunity, and bursting with ideas as a Sagittarian (though it won't be as obvious). But ideas and opportunities are meaningless to Capricorn unless they produce results. Capricorns want to see pay dirt. They can't bear the idea of not achieving what they know they could achieve. This is not someone who comes up with a brilliant new concept for a coffee machine and does nothing about it. If it's really that brilliant, they'll make a prototype, apply for a patent, and look for a manufacturer. Nor are Capricorns the type of people who tell everyone about the novel they want to write. They just write it. You may not even hear about it until they send you a copy for Christmas.

As the last of the earth signs, Capricorn is every bit as money- and security-conscious as Taurus and Virgo. They, too, desire to fulfill the social contract, and want to be seen as having "made it" within the framework of their society. But Capricorns have a broader social vision, and a need to focus beyond their own existence. They want to do what's right and best, not only for themselves, but for society at large. There is possibly no sign with a finer sense of personal and social responsibility.

In the wheel of the zodiac, Capricorn sits right at the top. It's an appropriate position for the sign that rules status and what we call career. Capricorn is one of the cardinal signs, which means that they need no pushing to get out of bed in the morning. Cardinal people are self-motivated, with the ability to get just about anything up and running. To be cardinal and earth combined, to be both dynamic and grounded, both ambitious and extremely practical, makes for a pretty impressive personality package.

The symbol for Capricorn is The Goat. Not just any domesticated nanny goat or billy goat, but a wild mountain goat standing alone on a craggy peak. The goat can survive, even thrive, in the most spartan of conditions. Like this tough, surefooted creature, Capricorn people have got the endurance and the quiet determination that can take them to the top of their mountain. The picture of The Goat climbing upwards is a symbol of man striving to realize his full potential. In this respect, Capricorn is the epitome of the civilized human being.

Whoever it was who said, "Life is not a dress rehearsal" must have been a Capricorn. They're never complacent or content with who they are or what they've achieved if there's still more room for improvement and even greater success. *Self-improvement and self-mastery* are Capricornian bywords. If going back to school, learning another language, or adding to their computer skills is going to help them get on in life, they'll do it. Why would anyone who has the opportunity to better him or herself in *any* way not do so? If you need to lose twenty pounds to feel better and look better, if you need to stay up all night to rewrite your university paper, if you need to economize on lunches to buy a really good suit, then it must be done. Okay, so it's not easy. But nothing ever stopped a Capricorn just because it wasn't easy. Virgo is generally regarded as the sign of the perfectionist. But Capricorn runs a close second.

Little wonder, then, that descriptions of the Capricorn personality are full of words like *authoritative, businesslike, purposeful,* and *diligent.* Look at the bottom of the list and you'll see words like *controlling, severe, dour, rigid,* even *hard* and *cold.* Capricorns take life seriously. And it's true that you can often identify a Capricorn simply by their air of gravitas. It usually goes with a dignified demeanor. In dress they favor the classic, timeless look. Understated elegance is the Capricorn signature. Capricorns have the kind of good bone structure and lean physique that carries clothes so well. They have a fantastic eye for quality, and see the right clothes as part of their investment in themselves. Capricorns know that the Chanel suit and the Hermès scarf are worth a whole lot more than fashion fads that disappear overnight.

There's no doubt that a Capricorn places great store on worldly success. But measuring yourself in terms of your achievements can be a hard act to maintain. It can also put you in a psychologically vulnerable position. If you've got such a burning desire to make something of yourself, and if you're so conscious of how you measure up against everyone else—as Capricorns often are—then it goes without saying that you can develop a fear of failure.

Capricorns are not nervous worriers or complainers (although they do enjoy an occasional good therapeutic moan with a close friend). But even the most patient and stoic of Capricorns can get very despondent if things aren't going according to one of their five- or ten-year plans, or if they feel unappreciated and are not getting the recognition they've worked hard for. Then they can become terribly envious of other people's success, money, and happiness. And deeply resentful of those who seem to get it all so easily with seemingly little effort on their part. They can't help asking themselves, "What have they got that I haven't got?"

Few will ever know just how down and depressed Capricorns get at times. That's because they have a great deal of personal pride and are very careful to hide their feelings. It's good politics and self-protection, reasons Capricorn, to keep your vulnerabilities to yourself, and under control. You have to be a very close and trusted friend before Capricorn will open his or her soul to you. When they do, you'll discover an interesting contradiction, which is fundamental to the understanding of this sign. Capricorns are often so capable, yet so plagued by self-doubt and low self-esteem.

Ruled as they are by old man Saturn, it's not surprising that Capricorns are the reliable "feet on the ground" types. Saturn is the planet of structure, discipline, and authority. He provides Capricorns with a large store of practicality and common sense. Saturn is the archetype of the mature father figure who shows you the right path, gives advices, and provides for your material needs, but who is also there to correct you if you've been foolish or broken the rules.

You can tell a lot about the influence of the father in any person's life by looking at the position of Saturn in his or her horoscope. But because Saturn is their own planetary ruler, father and authority figures are an issue of particular significance to Capricorns.

Most people shudder at the mere mention of Saturn. He's certainly had bad press as the hard taskmaster, the planet that doesn't let you get away with anything, not even the least little transgression. Clearly

they don't understand the positive side of Saturn. Any astrologer
will tell you that to have Saturn well placed in your horoscope is
just about the greatest blessing you could wish for. Perhaps even
greater than the blessings bestowed by "lucky" Jupiter. What Saturn
bestows is solid, substantial, and lasting. Sure, he's responsible for
pulling you back into line when you need it, and it's his duty to
throw a few obstacles and restrictions in your path. How else are
you going to learn the Capricornian wisdom of perseverance, econ-
omy, and restraint?

Where Jupiter expands, Saturn contracts. Where Jupiter tells you
to take a chance, Saturn whispers "Be careful" in your ear. They
represent opposite but complementary principles. For success,
achievement, and balance in your life, you need to tap into the energies of *both* Saturn and Jupiter.

Saturn was the king of the gods before Jupiter, but it was a position
that wasn't handed to him on a plate. He had to seize the reins of
power from his father, Uranus, the first lord of the heavens. Uranus
had become a dreadful tyrant, and when Saturn's mother, Gaia, goddess of the Earth, asked her son to dispose of him, Saturn dutifully
obliged. He castrated his father and assumed rulership of heaven
and the gods. And so began the golden age of mythology, that glorious and prosperous time when people lived in a well-ordered society
based on truth and justice and where there was plenty for all.

For all his strength and wisdom, Saturn fell into the age-old pattern
of repeating his father's sins, and turned into a tyrant himself. He
became so fearful that he would lose control and that his children
would one day overthrow him—just as he had overthrown his father
before him—that he swallowed them all at birth. But even this didn't
prevent the inevitable. His son Jupiter (who, it seemed, even as a
baby was singled out for special treatment) was saved by his mother.
Sure enough, Saturn's worst fears came true. When Jupiter grew up
he poisoned his father's wine so that he would vomit up all the
children he'd swallowed. Together the children of Saturn joined
forces to murder their father, and when the deed was done, they
took their places as the gods and goddesses of the new order on
Mount Olympus, with Jupiter as king.

Saturn is often depicted holding the Cornucopia, the magical horn
of plenty. It's a reminder that Capricorn is an earth sign, and Saturn
was first and foremost an agricultural god who ensured the fruits of
the harvest, the abundance of the golden age. In astrology, Saturn
represents the rewards that come from our labors, be they planting
a garden, studying for an exam, doing your best to raise a healthy
family, or working hard to put money in the bank. Saturn makes
sure that we reap what we sow. You could say he's the king of

karma. Even if they don't "believe" in karma, Capricorns are very conscious of "doing the right thing." They place great store on integrity, and wouldn't be able to sleep soundly at night if they knew they'd cut corners on their work or cheated on their tax return.

Capricorns are people who can see no rational reason why we can't live in the just and ordered society of old father Saturn. Why shouldn't we be able, through hard work and good organization, to fill the Horn of Plenty and see that the bounty is distributed fairly? asks Capricorn. Why can't we all act like sensible, civilized human beings? Is it really so hard to get our act together and get down to the business of putting things right? Surely it's harder in the long run, figures wise Capricorn, to rectify the social problems caused by injustice and inequality. There are many noble Capricorns who have devoted their lives to building a fair society based on reason, order, and justice.

Martin Luther King was one such Capricorn (born January 15) who worked to bring civil rights to all Americans. His dream was a Capricornian dream of a golden age, a "promised land" in which respect and dignity are based on individual worth, and not on race or class. King never compromised his values. He worked towards his dream in the way that so many Capricorns work towards their goals. Steadily, calmly, and with integrity and dignity. Personal dignity is something that Capricorn people value highly. They can relate to the trials and tribulations of the underdog, often because many of them have, at some stage, felt like the underdog themselves.

Capricorns are farsighted. And they have patience. Indeed, when your vision is set on a distant goal, patience is mandatory. No matter how much time it takes them to reach their goals, Capricorns will persevere. The positive Capricorn never falters or gives up in the face of obstacles that would deter less substantial types.

Yet when Capricorns have arrived at a position of status and obtained the control they want over their world, even the noblest of them can risk falling into the trap of holding on too tightly to what they've got, fearing that they might lose that control. If Capricorns become gripped in this fear, they can become extremely uncompromising and severe. It's all rationalized, in their minds, on the grounds that they are more capable, mature, and competent than anyone else. This is the paternalistic Capricorns whose decisions are not open to question, the father or mother who rules the home with an iron fist, and the co-worker who always insist on following strict procedure. Others regard them as control freaks and instinctively keep their distance. When you're intent on keeping control at all costs, it's only a short step away from turning into a despot.

The Capricorn love of temporal power can be easily abused. When

Capricorn Mao Ze Dong proclaimed the People's Republic of China in 1949, he was hailed as the liberator of the Chinese people. Chairman Mao fast turned himself into a latter-day emperor whose word was incontestably wise—and final. Under Mao, every slogan began with "Under the guidance of Chairman Mao . . ." And by the time he declared "The Great Leap Forward" (how Capricornian can get you get?), Mao had lost touch with those great Capricorn virtues of reason and patience and taking the slow, steady path to progress. It is estimated that approximately thirty million people starved to death under Mao's disastrous policies, because during the cultural revolution, absolutely no one dared to speak his or her mind to "The Great Helmsman."

Even on an everyday level, it can be all too tempting for the status-seeking, supercontrolling Capricorn to allow power and control to go to his or her head. You will occasionally meet Capricorns who have worked hard to gain respect, to make money and become a pillar of society, and yet seem disinterested in—or worse, look down—on those less successful. It's as if they've erased from their memory (and Capricorns have excellent memories) any recollection of their own humble beginnings. Some Capricorns become frightful snobs. A propensity for elitism is one of the least attractive qualities of this sign.

Astrologers believe that certain countries fall under certain signs of the zodiac. Capricorn, it is said, has a strong influence over countries with an entrenched class or caste system, such as England and India. Who else but the English could have made the Capricornian stiff upper lip a national trait?

In some pictures of Saturn, he is depicted holding a scythe. His titles include Old Father Time and The Grim Reaper. He is the one who cuts people down, not only when it's their time to die, but also when they're getting too pompous and high and mighty and need to be brought down a notch or two for their own good. That's something those Capricorns who would let position and wealth go to their heads would do well to keep in mind. Positive and truly noble Capricorns never lose the common touch, no matter how high they rise.

The Greeks called Saturn Chronos, which means Time. The value of time is something that Capricorns understand well. Ruled by Old Father Time, Time is on Capricorn's side.

Capricorns are the late bloomers of the zodiac. They may have their triumphs in youth, but with Capricorns, there's usually more, much more, to come. For many, success is hard to come by young. Some fail to find their niche. Some suffer from low self-esteem. Others are blocked by some reason or circumstance that's not of their making. But whatever the particular reason, when the rewards come—which they eventually do—in typical Capricorn fashion, they're bigger, better, and longer-lasting then most Capricorns would dare to dream of. So please note, young Capricorns: There is no need to get depressed (although we know you will from time to time) because things are not always moving forward as quickly as you would like. The poet Matthew Arnold, who was a Capricorn, once said, "I am likely enough to have my turn as they have had theirs." This is something for all young Capricorns to memorize and repeat to themselves when they feel progress is not fast enough. Your time *will* come.

The big breakthrough for so many Capricorns comes when they reach the maturity of middle age. Think of some famous Capricorns. Actor Anthony Hopkins' career didn't really take off until he was already middle-aged. And like many Capricorns, it seems the older he gets, the more in demand he becomes. Marlene Dietrich didn't find her niche in cabaret (and cabaret, not acting, was what she was really good at) until she was in her fifties. The painter Cézanne didn't hold his first exhibition until he was fifty-six. So many Capricorn people get a second and better wind later on in life. What's more, they're not "one-hit wonders." Capricorns are the stayers of the zodiac.

Quite a lot of Capricorns have become legends in their own time because, all other things being equal, they are usually very long-lived. They age well, and people often remark that Capricorns grow more beautiful as they get older. Perhaps it's due to that inner peace and confidence that come to them with age. As astrologers often say, Capricorn is old when young, and young when old. Being born a Capricorn doesn't rule out success early, but it generally brings greater successes later.

Success, as you've probably gathered by now, is a key Capricorn issue, probably because it's often earned the hard way. Capricorns are great believers in bootstrap philosophy, and admire those who have pulled themselves up by their own efforts and ingenuity, without taking any shortcuts from the path of integrity and honesty.

This Capricornian ethos was the theme of the popular children's stories of Horatio Alger, the Capricorn who became a household name in America by writing about the American ideal of success through hard work and self-reliance. The theme of every one of Alger's stories is basically the same—the hero, a poor boy, struggles against the odds and wins. Even the titles are pure Capricorn: "Struggling Upwards," "Fame and Fortune," "Plan and Prosper," "Try and Trust," "Slow and Sure."

Whoever they are, and wherever they come from, the heroes of Alger's stories always start at the bottom and end up at the top. You could easily think of them all as fine young Capricorns who remain ever optimistic and determined in the face of adversity, and are unimpressed by the trappings of wealth. Most important, they never lose sight of what they want to become. What's also Capricornian about Alger's heroes is that they always willingly deny themselves little pleasures in order to help support an embattled mother, friend, or relative. Capricorns can be extraordinarily thoughtful and giving people.

Hard work is something that is considered almost holy in Alger's stories. Yet for all their modesty and humility, his heroes crave success. They, too, want fine clothes, nice homes, and money in their pockets. When success comes (and it always does), they relish it, but they're never spoiled by it.

Alger's stories are not only about the virtue of making something of yourself, they're also about potential. A young man with potential in a land with potential can become whatever he aspires to be: a banker, a captain of industry, even president. The ability to recognize potential is a great Capricornian talent.

Interestingly, the boy's success is not *entirely* of his own making. At the point when things are looking very bleak, he always gets a lucky break. Lucky breaks, you recall, are Jupiter's territory, and when a lucky break does come Capricorn's way, he or she seizes it with both hands. In Alger's tales the break usually comes in the guise of an older man, a kind of mentor who has pulled *himself* up by the bootstraps and recognizes the worth of the boy, and gives him his first opportunity and invaluable fatherly advice.

The relationship between mentor and pupil, master and apprentice, has traditionally been a productive and important one, and it's a relationship that is coming back into fashion. Corporations are rediscovering the value of assigning young, inexperienced employees to older, experienced people who can act as guides and role models, showing them how to do their jobs more effectively, and teaching them protocol and how to dress and behave in order to get ahead.

Many young Capricorns find themselves, at one time or another, under the guidance of a mentor or a role model. If it's not someone they work with, it could be an older friend whom they admire. But it could also be a writer or philosopher whose work has inspired them and whom they aspire to be like. Whoever it is, Capricorn's "mentor" is someone who provides them with something that their parents never did.

The hard fact is that most Capricorns feel there was something lacking in their relationship with their parents. This is not to say that Capricorn has suffered at the hands of bad, abusive parents. It's more likely that one parent was physically not there through death or divorce, or was simply not there emotionally for Capricorn. Or it could be that the parents' own problems or interests consumed most of their time, leaving little to spare for raising young Capricorn. You also hear stories of the Capricorn who was one of many children, or who had a sick or handicapped sibling who required a lot of their parents' time and energy. Capricorn children never seem to be the ones who are cosseted or fussed over. Rarely are they the favorite child. Whatever the scenario, it all boils down to the Capricorn child having to tend to their own emotional needs. And what child can do that?

This is why many Capricorns seek role models and security figures outside of the family circle. Most Capricorn women are quite conscious of not wanting to be like their mothers. And as for father, well, criticism seemed to fall more easily from his lips than praise. At least that's how Capricorn remembers it. It's hardly surprising, then, that Capricorns grow up with a deep longing for approval and affection. Or that they learn to be self-sufficient and self-contained at a young age. From these early experiences comes the Capricornian fear of being dependent on anybody else's kindness and charity, and the need to be firmly in control of oneself and one's life. In times of stress they cope by donning psychic armor and putting on that Capricornian stiff upper lip rather than giving in to floods of tears and emotion.

People born with a Moon in Capricorn, too, generally experience a lack of parental nurturing, no matter what their Sun sign. Often the emotional scars are deeper in people with Moon in Capricorn because the Moon is directly connected to our childhood experiences. Moon in Capricorn people develop the same fortitude and backbone of Sun in Capricorn people, and grow up with the same determination to become self-reliant and make for *themselves* a secure, comfortable home.

It can take years for Capricorns to really come to grips with how their childhood conditioning has affected them. It explains why those Capricorns who felt the cold hand of authority as a child are determined to become someone of authority themselves. It also explains why the Capricorns who are prone to bouts of depression in youth don't come into their own until they're older.

You often read that Capricorn is a family-oriented sign. That's because astrologically, parents are ruled by Capricorn and its opposite sign, Cancer. Opposite signs are opposite ends of the same pole. They have common ground, but their way of viewing it is entirely different. Cancerians have open, uncomplicated expectations of family support. Capricorns don't. Even though Capricorns feel ambivalent about their parents, they are nonetheless very dutiful sons and daughters.

Cancerians will always be Cancerians, and Capricorns will always be Capricorns. Sun sign destiny determines that. But astrology teaches us that there are valuable lessons to be learned from our opposite sign. It's not always easy to assimilate attributes of a sign that is so different from your own. Yet that is what we can all benefit from, Capricorns included. Capricorns may be too polite to admit it, but they generally regard Cancerians as emotionally volatile and clinging. They would feel far too embarrassed to openly display their emotions as a Cancer does. But if they were perhaps sometimes just a little more affectionate and less frugal with their compliments, they would find it isn't the same thing as being immature and gushing. And perhaps they'd discover that renouncing the pleasures of the now in order to fulfill their future plans is all very admirable, but savoring the pleasures at hand has a value all its own. Cancerians can show Capricorns the importance of pausing along the way to smell the roses, and help them put worldly ambition in perspective.

Behind their reserved manner, a Capricorn is every bit as sensitive and kind as a Cancer. In fact, Capricorns respond sincerely to people in *real* need, and they can often see the suffering behind the mask of a brave face better than a Cancer can. Yet it is Cancers, not Capricorns, who are given the praise and recognition (and it's perfectly justified) for being so kind. More's the pity. Because the Capricornian kindness is the kindness that people remember. Anybody can hold your hand and say that he or she knows how bad your must feel. But not just anybody is capable of helping and leaving your dignity intact, or is generous enough to discreetly leave a hundred-dollar bill under the teapot. Capricorns give the kind of practical help that really makes a difference.

Benjamin Franklin once helped a man in need. He wrote to him, "I send you herewith a bill for ten louis d'ors. I do not pretend to *give* you such a sum; I only *lend* it to you. When you shall return to your country with a good character, you can not fail of getting into some business that will in time enable you to pay all your debts. In that case, when you meet with another honest man in similar distress, you must pay me by lending this sum to him." Franklin finishes, "This is a trick of mine for doing a deal of good with a little money. I am not rich enough to afford much in good works, and so am obliged to be cunning and make the most of a *little*."

How thoroughly Capricornian. These individuals pride themselves on making the most out of a little. And who but a Capricorn would make the other person feel good by cleverly playing down his own generosity, and making the *recipient* the trustee of an ongoing act of charity? Yes, it's very businesslike. But Capricorns also figure it's good for their karma. Remember the scythe and the Cornucopia?

Saturn presents the Cornucopia to those who have paid their dues, and who give without taking. But he's always got his scythe at hand to cut down those who take without giving.

You no doubt have the impression by now that Capricorns are serious people of substance. But if you think that means they're *too* serious for their own good, and that fun and excitement are not part of the Capricorn lifestyle, then you will be pleased to learn this is most definitely not the case.

Okay, so they're not the "laugh a minute" types, and they won't smile if there's nothing to smile about. But Capricorn people have got a wonderful sense of humor. Many would say it's second to none.

To be an object of mockery or ridicule, or to be humiliated in any way, is absolutely mortifying to a Capricorn. But gain their trust and you'll discover that they're pretty good at sending themselves up.

The Capricorn brand of humor is dry, wry, and sardonic. They have absolutely no taste for the slapstick custard pie in the face or practical pranks. Satire is their forte. Capricorns have got a sharp eye for all the subtle absurdities in human behavior. You could say it's the sign of the cynic. Perhaps it's their cynicism that saves Capricorns from becoming too hung up on respect and position. What sign better to send up the establishment than someone who aspires to be an establishment person? And who better to send up the self-important than those who want to be important? Capricorns cringe at social ineptitude, they hate brashness and vulgarity. And while they're not especially sociable, Capricorns *are* well socialized. They're very tuned in to how people—especially themselves—are perceived by others.

Capricorn comedian Rowan Atkinson has created a character out of the Capricorn abhorrence of social ineptitude. The hapless misfit Mr. Bean is so totally lacking in social skills that he makes you squirm with embarrassment. You even find yourself feeling self-conscious on his behalf. In short, Bean is an unsocialized, infantile idiot. As Atkinson says, "Children love him. But I mean, he's not a nice man, not the kind of person one would choose to have dinner with. He's self-centered and self-serving. Just a nightmare." Atkinson pulls off the character of Bean so cleverly because Bean is everything a Capricorn would most hate to be.

Were the seeds of Mr. Bean planted in Atkinson's own childhood? Atkinson was called "Doopie" and, "Zoonie" at school, and assumed it was because he "supposedly looked like an alien." Many Capricorns, at some time in their youth, feel like an outsider. Of course, it hurts. But Capricorns have the moral strength to take that hurt and make use of it. "Life's experiences bleed into your subconscious, and situations lead to create jokes," says Atkinson. This is the origin of many a Capricorn's dry, self-effacing wit. Also true to his Capricorn nature, Atkinson has an ambivalent relationship with fame, refusing to talk about his private life, which he regards as sacrosanct. Another great contradiction of this sign is that Capricorns want recognition, but they don't want the public dissection that fame brings. Fame, recognition, and other people's opinions aside, what Capricorns need to do is prove themselves to themselves.

Success came relatively early for Capricorn Atkinson (who nevertheless did not become the electrical engineer he studied to be). But it wasn't until he was in his forties that Mr. Bean went international and put Atkinson on the world stage.

Another famous Capricorn who achieved his first measure of success when he was still young is David Bowie. But now that Bowie has turned fifty, he is at the age when many Capricorns make their past efforts pay handsomely. After all these years, he has finally secured the royalties for his songs. And for all his creativity, Bowie has shown his true Capricorn colors by launching himself on the stock market. How shrewd. Yes, you, too, can now invest in "Bowie Bonds."

Born into a working-class London family, Bowie felt driven to achieve. But the money didn't come easily—or quickly. In 1969, the year of his first number one hit, he only earned two thousand dollars. True to his Capricorn Sun, Bowie is a stayer. Older and wiser, he now talks openly about his personal problems and the lack of self-confidence that dogged him (although you'd never have guessed it) for years. Looking back on his past at fifty, Bowie said, "A lot of the negativity when I first started was about myself. I was convinced I wasn't worth very much. I had enormous self-image problems and very low self-esteem, which I hid behind obsessive writing and performing. It's exactly what I do now, except I enjoy it now. I'm not driven like I was in my twenties. I was driven to get through life very quickly." Bowie was talking about himself, but he could have been talking about Capricorns the world over.

Bowie has always felt that sharing a birthday (January 8) with fellow Capricorn Elvis Presley was somehow significant. Sadly, Elvis—and Janis, too—didn't live long enough to lay their personal demons to rest. Janis spoke from the Capricorn heart when she said, "Don't compromise yourself—you're all you've got." Unfortunately, it's easier said than done. The breakthroughs that Capricorns must make are often won through great personal struggle.

For Capricorns everywhere, the key to happiness and success is understanding your past, accepting yourself for who you are, and regularly affirming that you're as good, as if not better than, everyone else. When Capricorns do this, when they push aside their fear of failure, they reach a turning point and the full strength of their powerful character can shine through. Then they enter a league that they themselves may have deep down always aspired to, but that others would not have predicted they could reach. Capricorns surprise people.

You never hear a Capricorn trumpeting his or her own talents. That would be altogether too vulgar. But when they attain their goals, they feel vindicated. One of the loveliest qualities of Capricorn is their modesty. As Bowie said, "In ten years time, when I'm playing to halls with no audience whatsoever, my contemporaries can turn round and say, 'Well, that's the reason we didn't do what you did.' But we'll see. At least I'll have the chance to see how far you can go in this life." Bowie doesn't really believe that he will ever play to an empty hall. Capricorns can be wonderfully self-deprecating.

But never doubt that Capricorns are not deadly earnest in their determination to achieve the goals they set themselves. They must, like everyone, fulfill the fundamental purpose of their Sun sign. And for the mountain goat, that means climbing up . . . and up . . . "to see how far you can go."

THE CAPRICORN CAREER AND DIRECTION

Even when Capricorns are not at work, they like to be working. In fact, the Capricorn idea of a good weekend is likely to be designing a new business card, building a computer work station, or honing a report until it's perfect. And a relaxing Saturday afternoon is spent scouring the employment pages of the newspaper (even if they're not looking for a new job) just to see what's out there and how much it pays. You can be sure that mental notes will be taken for future reference. Capricorns always like to know where they stand in the scheme of things, and how they rate.

Capricorns have no time for time wasters. They're the first to come out with the line "Time is money." Do they realize it was Benjamin Franklin who said it first? Trust a Capricorn to spread the word. They pride themselves on their dependability and efficiency, and if they say they'll deliver, they'll go without sleep, if necessary, to deliver.

All earth signs take job and money very seriously. They all know how to fit into the system and play the game according to the rules, and are careful to cultivate an image of total reliability. Like Virgos, Capricorns are invigorated by productive work. They also share Virgo's excellent organizational skills and eye for detail. But for Capricorns, detail never becomes an obsession and they never allow it to overshadow the bigger picture. Like Taureans, they've got the determination to see a job through to completion. But Capricorns never become smug or self-satisfied. When Capricorns have climbed to the top of one mountain, they'll take in the view briefly before looking around for the next mountain to climb.

Everything in Capricorn's working life is carefully calculated, and every move is shrewdly planned. These are not the types to race around the track as fast as they can in the hope that speed will win the race. Capricorns know exactly when to take a pit stop and refuel. They've worked it all out beforehand. Remember the story of the hare and the tortoise? Capricorn is the tortoise. And we all know who won that race.

Capricorns want more than a job with a good salary. They want a career. Since they're born under the sign that rules status, prestige, and worldly acclaim, how could it be otherwise? It's their nature to strive to gain a certain position in life. Fortunately, Capricorns sense that they can't rise to the top overnight. They accept that all brigadier generals have to go to boot camp first, and they're quite willing to serve their time as foot soldiers. Saturn, their ruling planet, is often called the taskmaster.

Older Capricorns often show signs of being the taskmaster themselves. They know the importance of testing someone's mettle. The Capricorn newspaper magnate is the one who insists that his son sell newspapers on the street before he takes him into the firm. And the Capricorn storekeeper will make sure her employees sweep the floor and stack the shelves before moving on to serve the customers.

Capricorns are born with the credentials for success. Whether the famous Capricorn discipline develops through the tough lessons of Saturn, or whether they've got the discipline gene in their DNA, who knows? But what is certain is that discipline is often the key to Capricorn's success. Obviously, ambition is essential. But several signs are very ambitious—not the least of which is Capricorn. (If they try to pretend otherwise, they're either lying or they were adopted, or somehow acquired a false date of birth and are not Capricorns at all.) A nose for business also helps. And Capricorns are some of the hardest-nosed people around. But ambition and brains alone won't get you as far as Capricorn plans to go if you haven't got that discipline to back them up. Discipline is Capricorn's trump card.

Around the age of twenty-nine, Saturn looms large in everybody's life, regardless of their Sun sign. That's because Saturn takes about twenty-nine years to circle the Sun, and when you're twenty-nine Saturn returns to the same point in the zodiac that it was in when you were born. Astrologers call this your "first Saturn return." At this important turning point, people sense they are on the verge of a quantum leap forward, and that the decisions they make are critical to their long-term future. And they're right. Saturn leaves you in no doubt as to whether you've been traveling on the right path. At this age people become very aware that youth has come an end and it's time to face up to the responsibilities of adult life. That's why twenty-nine (sometimes twenty-eight or thirty) is such a common age for settling down, getting married, having a first child, or making a last-ditch stand to set out on the career you always wanted.

When Capricorns reach their Saturn return, it's as if they get their first real boost of confidence. The road ahead suddenly becomes a lot clearer and easier to travel, and they can move forward by leaps and bounds. The Saturn return is a breakthrough time for all of us, but for Capricorns, it's *the* first big breakthrough.

The second Saturn return comes round at fifty-eight. It's another critical age when Old Father Time cuts down many who have neglected their health. But it can also be one of the most rewarding times in your life—especially for Capricorns who are now happily reaping the harvest of their labor. This is frequently the time when all that Capricornian planning, organization, and discipline pay off handsomely. But if you're thinking that's when The Goat will be looking forward to retiring along with everybody else, think again. While other Sun signs are enjoying mornings on the golf course and long afternoon naps in the deck chair, many Capricorns are launching a new career. That is unless they're among those who simply never retired in the first place. Retiring is not something that Capricorns ever really think about. This could be the time for anyone who's married to a Capricorn to finally be able to persuade them that "all work and no play makes Capricorn a dull boy . . . or girl."

Even at the time of the final Saturn return, at the age of eighty-five or so, there are plenty of wily, active old Goats who can still run an empire, and have enough energy left over to kick up their hooves. Take a Sun sign check on the people running "gray power" groups, and it's a pretty good bet that a lot of them are Capricorns.

Saturn is about duty and responsibility. And those Capricorns who don't hold down a paying job are usually busy being a tower of strength to others. There are many Capricorn matriarchs who have devoted their lives to raising half a dozen well-educated, well-mannered sons and daughters, and are now baby-sitting the grandchildren, running the family finances, organizing school fund-raisers, and who still find time to do charity work twice a week . . . and play the occasional game of golf.

You can spot the classic Capricorn grandma in most family businesses. She's the one in your local deli, the high priestess of the cash register who never fails to push the specials of the week: "Sundried tomatoes are only a dollar fifty a jar, or two for two-fifty—they're the best quality." Grandma remembers you came in asking for sun-dried tomatoes two months ago. The Goat has the memory of an elephant.

It's almost inevitable that Capricorns will assume a position of responsibility because they are made for authority. Being in a subservient position for too long is bound to get a Capricorn down. They're born managers. Any job that involves supervising and directing other people is a Capricorn job. The good Capricorn boss knows exactly how to handle his or her employees without being familiar or patronizing. Capricorn can spot the difference between being busy and looking busy, and is not fooled by the person who stares earnestly at the computer screen, tapping away for hours, achieving nothing.

Having said that, if you work for a Capricorn and you have made a genuine mistake, be honest, and admit it. You'll be pleasantly surprised. Capricorn won't bite your head off. Volunteer to work late and correct your error, and your dedication will be remembered. Anyone who has real difficulties, be it in their work or personal life, will receive sympathy and understanding from a Capricorn boss. What he or she cannot abide is people who can't (or won't) get their act together. Some think Capricorns are a bit stern and ruthless. But are they really? Perhaps that's the opinion of those who have failed to pull the wool over The Goat's eyes.

With their love of structure, Capricorns work well in hierarchical organization where they can climb the ladder, rung by rung. When they take their first step up, they may be outwardly suitably humble and dignified, but inwardly they're bursting with pride. Promotion is tangible evidence that they've become a valued member of the establishment. Capricorns are not interested in hollow praise, they want proof of their worth.

Many Capricorns look for a position in a large corporation or an old, established business. Government service is true Capricorn territory. They like the security, opportunities for promotion, and the scent of the carpeted corridors of old money and power. One reason Capricorns do so well in civil service is that they are, essentially, realists. They know that what should be done is, practically speaking, not always the same as what can be done. Capricorns are perfectly at home in the bureaucracy. Sir Humphrey Appleby of the TV series 'Yes, Prime Minister' is the archetypal Capricorn civil servant. And should they become prime minister themselves (and there are many Capricorns who are drawn to politics and public life) their ideals are always well tempered by the constraints of reality.

On the subject of reality, money talks loud and clear to a Capricorn. Many make the handling of monies their career. Banking, accountancy, and insurance are all popular Capricorn career choices.

Lots of young Capricorns spend a moment or two visualizing the magic words "Financial Director" or "Head of Accounts" on their office door.

In many ways, Capricorn seems to be the perfect corporate man or woman. They were the original exponents of the corporate image that has dominated the employment scene for years. Since 1984, to be exact. That was the year when Neptune entered the sign of Capricorn, staying until 1998.

During Neptune's fourteen-year period in each sign, the characteristics and aspirations of that particular sign are embraced by society at large. All of us, regardless of our Sun sign, were affected by the Capricornian "trend" in those years. It was the time when everyone wore a "business uniform" in Capricorn colors—black, dark red, or navy. Smart and conservative was in, radical and outrageous was out. As well as looking organized and businesslike, people wanted to *be* organized and businesslike. You couldn't go anywhere without your Filofax or electronic organizer and your mobile phone. The M.B.A. became almost a status symbol, and the "young urban professional" came into our language. People even stopped exercising and started "working out." This was the era when workaholism was designated a normal neurosis. In fact, no one felt embarrassed to be called a workaholic. Far from it, it was practically a badge of honor, and proved you were one of the upwardly mobile.

Capricorn people were better equipped than most to survive the years of the workaholic. You could say they were in their element. Capricorns have always been prepared to put in long hours. Astrologers would suggest that their famed ability to put in a fourteen-hour day has as much to do with Mars as it does with Saturn. That's because Mars, the planet of the ego and action, is exalted in the sign of Capricorn. When a planet is "exalted," it's in the sign of its most productive expression, and it can give of its best. That's why you won't see Capricorns rushing around wasting their energy. They spend their energy wisely. When others are flagging, they're the ones with the strength to go on.

When Mars enters Saturn's territory, the ego is strong but restrained, and the energy of Mars can be harnessed and directed where it's needed. It makes Capricorns hard and dedicated workers, and great achievers.

These are the people who always have an updated résumé in their files. They rehearse their questions and answers for job interviews, and there'll be no last-minute flaps on the day over what they're going to wear. Capricorn will have carefully pressed two or three outfits the day before, in case there's a change in the weather. The aim is to come across as cool, collected, and competent. Could there be any doubt that Capricorn is the best man or woman for the job? No. Not if you want someone who's respectful, diligent, honest, loyal, and obedient (but not subservient). A Capricorn executive told us that she adheres to an old Chinese proverb: "if you trust a man, hire him. If you hire a man, trust him." We can't be certain it's Chinese. But it's definitely very Capricornian.

On the whole, Capricorns are people who *can* be trusted. Their honesty is something that they would hate to think was ever in question. They regard themselves as ethical people and try to be scrupulous in their dealings. But a Capricorn is no pushover. They've always got an eye out for a good opportunity, and are always open to a better offer if it means taking another step up that ladder.

Owning property is something every Capricorn wants to do. There are many who are prepared to pull in their belts for years to get a mortgage. Capricorns can be very frugal while they are setting up their property portfolio. They are the champion players of the real-life Monopoly board. Many Capricorns choose a career in property, either in real estate or property development. With their love of fine buildings, Capricorns are also drawn to architecture.

There are many Capricorns in all sorts of other jobs who are busy renovating an old house or apartment in their spare time to be sold off when property prices rise. Capricorns are the shrewd ones who buy the worst house on the best street, or a run-down mansion in an undesirable area that their research tells them is going to be the next suburb to be gentrified. They don't see spending their weekends up a ladder, scraping paint off the walls, as a chore. They're not afraid to roll up their sleeves and get their hands dirty, not when they know that the visible results of their labor are only weeks away. Capricorn women are just as handy with a paintbrush, hammer, and nails as the men.

Construction is an industry that attracts a lot of Capricorns. Building, carpentry, and plumbing are not only good avenues for their practical skills, they also give Capricorns the opportunity to run their own business. And that's something that's very appealing to Capricorns in all walks of life.

When it comes to business acumen, Capricorns score top marks. This is a cardinal sign, and like Aries, Cancer, and Libra, Capricorns are good money managers and have an instinct for business. They seem to know all about corporate law and bookkeeping, and their accounts are always in perfect order. What's more, they never ignore the basic dos and don'ts in business, and always abide by the rules and regulations.

Rules and regulations are actually part of Saturn's domain. Of all the learned professions, the law is the most attractive to Capricorns.

Sagittarius and Libra are also connected with the law because both are concerned with the principle of justice. But when it comes down to the detail and the letter of the law, Capricorns come into their own, specializing in conveyancing, corporate law, family law, or trusts and wills. Speaking of wills—and deceased estates—Capricorn is, by tradition, the sign of the undertaker! Now, there's a secure occupation that will never go out of fashion.

Anything old comes under the sign of Capricorn. Antique shops with the smell of old money and beeswax are heaven on earth to a Capricorn. It's a rare Capricorn who prefers Swedish modern to English Edwardian. Measuring instruments and clocks are Capricornian specialties. Saturn, remember, rules time, and grandfather clocks are a Capricorn favorite. They love fine craftsmanship and elegant machinery. Capricorns are the parents who line up with their children to crank the handle of the first internal combustion engine at the science museum, and mourn the demise of the great steam trains.

One astrological survey revealed that Saturn was the dominant planet in the birth charts of engineers and scientists. Certainly you'll find many Capricorns in these professions. There's a mechanical bent in most Capricorns, and they've got systematic minds with the capacity for the kind of sustained thought necessary for a career in science and mathematics.

Physicist Stephen Hawking, one of the great minds of our time, is a Capricorn. In 1962 he was diagnosed with motor neuron disease and given two years to live. Is it because he was born under the sign noted for longevity that, more than thirty years later, he is still stunning us with his speculations on the origins of the universe?

In his best-seller *A Brief History of Time* (a Capricorn title if there ever was one) Hawking says, "The universe is governed by a set of rational laws that we can discover and understand." In their hearts, all Capricorns want to believe there are rational laws behind *everything*.

Hawking currently holds the same chair in mathematics and theoretical physics at Cambridge University that that other great English Capricorn scientist, Isaac Newton, did way back in 1663. Hawking actually has a few words to say about his predecessor, whom he describes as "not a pleasant man."

He outlines in his book the famous personal war waged by Isaac Newton with the German philosopher Gottfried Leibniz. It blew up over who was the first to develop the branch of mathematics called calculus. It seems that both men were working on it, quite independently, at the same time (something that often happens when new discoveries are made). But Newton was one of those extremely ambitious Capricorns who couldn't bring himself to graciously share the glory. Quite the opposite, in fact. He set out to systematically destroy Leibniz' credibility. When Leibniz died, Newton is reported to have said that it pleased him to have broken Leibniz' heart. The Capricornian capacity for ruthlessness is not one of their most endearing features.

The fact of the matter is that Newton was not the first Capricorn, and he certainly won't be the last, to put his own untrammeled ambitions before anyone or anything. Newton is an indictment of the Capricornian unhealthy obsession with career, position, and status. The story of Leibniz and Newton is a historical example of how some Capricorns lose all sense of reason and humanity in their obsession to get to the top and stay at the top. They'll show no spirit of sharing if it means that their own kudos will be diminished. And whether they're right or wrong, they always insist on having the last word. It's what astrologers mean when they say that Capricorn can be horribly egotistical. One-upmanship is, unfortunately, a game played by Capricorns whose ambition and lust for power and control are out of perspective. They will undermine and undercut colleagues, and even deflect credit from others onto themselves. For a sign that places great store on honor and honesty, how honorable is this? A Capricorn who is determined not to concede can be as insensitive as a Taurus and as vengeful as a Scorpio.

But what goes up, as Newton informed us, must come down. There's always the risk, when you rise to great heights, that you'll take a great fall. Capricorns are only too aware of how precarious life can be at the top, and they always have an eye open for potential usurpers. Do you recall how Saturn swallowed his own children to try to prevent them from taking over? Anyone who threatens Capricorn's position or authority, or who attempts to knock them down, will be severely dealt with. Think of J. Edgar Hoover and his communist witch-hunts of the fifties. Or Richard Nixon and Watergate. Capricorns, both. Capricorns, remember, are ruled by Saturn, the moral watchdog, and it behooves them to keep their nose clean.

Should Capricorns ever fall from grace, they take it very hard indeed. All Capricorns can become very fearful of being toppled, fearful that their world will fall apart. You see, deep down, Capricorns know that respectability, recognition, and control are ultimately not bankable items. And when the ego rests too heavily on anything as ephemeral as worldly status, it's only reasonable to be afraid that it could be whipped away from you at any time. This knowledge, innate in the Capricorn nature, is seen in the symbol of Capricorn when it's depicted as a Goat-Fish, not a Goat. The Goat with the fish tail represents the Capricorn consciously intent on climbing upwards, but unconsciously fearful of falling back down into the dissolving waters where its personal identity and importance will be lost. The Goat-Fish symbolizes the need that Capricorns have to strike a balance between their worldly life and the life of their soul.

The mysterious glyph for Capricorn is derived from the Goat-Fish symbol. The V section is the valley and the mountains the Goat must traverse. And the wavy line is the tail of the fish.

Not every Capricorn success story is straight up the mountain without a tumble or two. Though, as the realists of the zodiac, Capricorns will put backstops and insurance policies in place to soften the blow. Should Capricorn's career ever come asunder, they are at least patient and farsighted enough to bide their time until they can regain a foothold and start that climb up the mountain again.

If anyone can make a comeback, Capricorn can. It is a sign with the potential for extraordinary success. The positive Capricorn is well aware that worldly success alone does not necessarily bring happiness. They know what Capricorn Rudyard Kipling knew—that true happiness depends on feeling secure within as well as without. Kipling penned some very Capricornian words of wisdom on how to be successful *and* happy.

> *If you can keep your head when all about you*
> *are losing theirs and blaming it on you . . .*
> *If you can wait and not be tired by waiting . . .*
> *If you can dream—and not make dreams your master . . .*
> *If you can meet with Triumph and Disaster*
> *And treat those two imposters just the same . . .*
> *If you can talk with crowds and keep your virtue,*
> *Or walk with Kings—nor lose the common touch,*
> *If neither foes nor loving friends can hurt you,*
> *If all men count with you, but none too much;*
> *If you can fill the unforgiving minute*
> *With sixty seconds' worth of distance run*
> *Yours is the Earth and everything that's in it,*
> *And—which is more—you'll be a Man, my son!*

LOVE AND FRIENDSHIP

"Here's looking at you, kid."

When Bogie says these magic words to Bergman, it still makes you go weak at the knees. Coming from anyone else, it would be a casual enough remark. But from him, it's loaded with the promise of smoldering passion.

If you've never seen the timeless movie *Casablanca*, and you want the lowdown on the Capricorn lover, go out and get the video right now. It's the story about the quintessential Capricorn man, Rick, played by the quintessential Capricorn screen legend, Humphrey Bogart. On the surface Rick is tough, cynical, and worldly-wise. He keeps himself to himself and his past under wraps. But scratch the slightly brittle surface a little and the softness underneath is revealed. It's never obvious, at least not at the beginning, but the Capricorn lover is a softie at heart.

The Capricorn in love is not into big, flashy gestures. You probably won't wake to find a dozen red roses on your doorstep after your first date. It may be some weeks or even months before your Capricorn feels secure enough to begin to reveal his or her true feelings. But don't fret. Long after the roses have wilted and died, and the suitors who sent them have disappeared over the horizon, Capricorn is likely to be sending you bunches of irises or forget-me-nots because he's been thoughtful and observant enough to notice that blue is your favorite color.

Underneath the restrained exterior, Capricorn is a deeply sensitive sign. They don't play games and they don't flirt—at least not in the well-practiced way that a Gemini, Aires, or Libra flirts. But they do have their own subtle and clever flirtatious ways . . . for those who are subtle and clever enough to pick up on them. The one-millimeter raising of an eyebrow. That split-second eye contact that says, "I know that you know." Taking you by the arm to introduce you to someone, and letting his or her hand linger a little longer than needed. This sort of thing is Capricorn's way of flirting.

If it's a matter of true love, they'll be patient enough to take their time and be as sure as humanly possible that what you feel for them is what they feel for you. Slow and steady is the Capricorn mode. With no sudden surprises. Besides, they'd feel very awkward and embarrassed making an unwelcome gesture. Capricorns aren't ones to take rejection in their stride.

They may also take longer to reveal the depth of their passion, though there will be many occasions when you feel the heat rising. So when the time comes for them to release their feelings and unleash their lust, the sexual intensity can be very powerful, and take you by surprise. It's usually not apparent at first, but Capricorn is one of the most highly sexed signs of the zodiac, who can give Aries and Scorpio a run for their reputation. As an earth sign, Capricorns are extremely sensual.

When Capricorns meet someone they take to, they plant the seedling of affection and tend it carefully as it grows. Then, when the seedling becomes a tree and bears fruit, the relationship is all the sweeter. A Capricorn friend never lets you down or stands you up.

And, all things being equal, you can count on having a true friend for life. Having said that, should the relationship ever fall foul, should you ever let him or her down badly—even once—Capricorn won't hesitate to make a definitive cut, with any reconciliation unlikely. The Goat cannot forgive betrayal.

One of the loveliest sides of a Capricorn is sincerity. If you want an honest opinion, ask Capricorn. You'll get the truth—put gently—but you won't get told what Capricorn thinks you want to hear. They're not ones to tell you that something is pink when it's really black.

In all their personal relationships, including friendship, Capricorns seek the integrity, reliability and loyalty that they themselves give. You'll find that Capricorns don't allude to acquaintances as friends. A colleague is a colleague. An associate is an associate. But a friend is someone special you can rely on one hundred and ten percent. This is someone who will give you the spare room and provide three square meals a day should you ever be down on your luck. Capricorn feels bound by friendship—in the most positive sense of the word. Sure, they're famous for their thrift (they can be careful with money to the point of being stingy) but when a friend is in genuine need, Capricorns are there with the type of practical help that keeps your soul and dignity in one piece.

Speaking of dignity, never make fun of a Capricorn, or refer to anything that might embarrass them in company. Not because they'll blush, or burst into tears and cause you to suffer instant remorse. In fact they'll pretend they're taking it all in good humor. You could be fooled yourself into not recognizing the Capricorn stiff upper lip when you see it. Capricorns are deeply wounded if ever they're made the butt of someone else's tasteless jokes. There is some behavior that others can tolerate and even find acceptable that make a Capricorn recoil. Top of their pet hate list are the gigglers and the gushers. They have nothing but disdain for flighty, dizzy types who, nevertheless, provide them with ample material for their own biting jokes and satirical stories. Possibly no other sign perceives the absurdities of the human condition so acutely, and identifies the ironies and hypocracies of human behaviour so expertly. Capricorns excel at the deadpan sendup of Mrs. Jones' social climbing, or Mr. Wright's pathetic attempts to disguise his overenthusiasm for the new secretary. They can be the cleverest of mimics. They love to have a good laugh and be with people who can match their wit, tune in to their dark sense of humor, and give as good in return.

Music always touches a chord with Capricorns. People are often surprised to find that Capricorn loves dancing. When you're planning your first bona fide date and don't yet know your Capricorn's tastes, it's advisable to play it absolutely safe. Err on the side of conservatism. Anything too radical could be a risk that might fall very flat. So that new Mexican bean joint that you've been dying to try will just have to wait. Better to opt for traditional rather than nouveau, unless you know a new place frequented by the vanguard of the smart set that hasn't yet been discovered by the hoi polloi. Sipping cappuccinos in a gallery café and getting to know you against a backdrop of studied refinement is very appealing to Capricorns. Many are regular culture vultures, so if you know of an interesting exhibition or a "must-see" new play or opera, don't hesitate to invite them.

Capricorns will be equally impressed, perhaps more so, if you invite them to your place for a home-cooked meal. It might actually be your best move because Capricorns really do appreciate it when somebody makes a special effort on their behalf. In any case, it's a terrific opportunity to show how important home is to you. Don't think for a minute of hiding that photo of you as a child seated on Grandma's knee away in the drawer. In fact, you might like to put out one or two extra family photos, including one of your dear deceased dog. Capricorn, the secret sentimentalist, will notice any evidence that you're a sentimentalist, too.

To every Capricorn, home is a haven. It's a place where all the worries and the whirlwinds of the outside world can't intrude. In fact, home is practically sacred to a Capricorn. Owning a home of their own, putting down roots, and establishing their own family are more than just a part of the Capricorn package of worldly ambitions, they fill an important need that lies deep in their soul. Capricorns want to belong. In many cases it's because they have had an equivocal relationship with their own parents that they feel an urgency to establish a comfortable, tranquil home of their own. So if you've got your sights set on a Capricorn and your intentions are honorable, he or she will want to know that you place the same high value on having a home and family.

Capricorns hold to the tradition of respect for your elders. So when you meet Capricorn's parents, be extremely cordial, as he or she no doubt will be when they meet yours. If your Capricorn is one of those Goats who's had strained relations with his or her parents, be sympathetic and never forget that this is probably a very touchy subject. Never allow any patronizing remarks to slip out. Stop yourself before you say, "Oh, I thought your mother seemed very nice . . ." or "But your father is such an easygoing sort of man; are you sure you're not overreacting . . . ?"

Capricorns' personal feelings and opinions aside, their sense of duty will always prevail. If anyone in their family should ever need

them, then you will be expected to understand if they drop everything to run to their side. You could find yourself taking on the chore
of their grandmother's grocery shopping as well as your own. And
don't be surprised either if virtually every Sunday lunch is marked
as a family affair. Some people who are married to a Capricorn have
wondered at times how many people they're actually married to. A
Capricorn can become as locked into family structure (and family
politics) as a Cancer. As opposite signs, it's one of the things they
have in common.

Having said that, you'll be relieved to know that you can kiss
goodbye to the popular misconception of The Goat as a totally serious, family- and career-minded beast. There will be times when
"beast" is indeed the word to describe a Capricorn who has decided
to let loose and kick up his or her hooves.

The wildest festival of ancient times was the Saturnalia, the festival
of Saturn, which took place when the Sun was in Capricorn. It was
held on the shortest day of the year, the winter solstice when the
nights are long and cold, and the land lies fallow. On this day people
celebrated the coming of new light and the re-emergence of fertility
with the party to end all parties. Total abandon and misrule replaced
restraint and rules. It was the one day of the year when you could
indulge in as much feasting and frolicking as you liked—and with
whomever you liked—with no questions asked. The Capricornian
moral rectitude was turned briefly on its head. Naturally, the anticipation of the event was part of the excitement. And Saturn-ruled
Capricorns, famed for their self-control, are very good at putting
their pleasures and indulgences on hold—including sex—until the
time is right and they can enjoy them even more.

In spite of the Capricorn delight in their own personal Saturnalias,
these are not good time boys or girls who are seeking a non-stop
social life, or who can be dragged out any time of day or night.
Mind you, we do know one young Capricorn woman who seemingly
completely out of character threw caution to the wind after a good
night out with her boyfriend, and agreed to his suggestion that they
take the next flight out of town . . . to wherever that might be. It so
happened that the destination of the next flight was halfway across
the world. When they alighted in London (twenty-four hours later
and by now completely sober) she was faced with the unenviable
task of phoning her boss and trying to come up with a plausible
Capricornian explanation as to why she hadn't turned up at work
that morning. To this day, though, she's never regretted it and still
enjoys a chuckle over her "reckless adventure," even if the arrival
of the Amex bill a month later was a chastening moment. Her story
is actually not so un-Capricornian. For all their sense of responsibility

and their fundamentally conservative nature, even the most respect-able of Capricorns are likely to have had a few wild episodes of their own in their youth.

On the whole, though, Capricorns hate too many violations of their schedule. It upsets their love of order. They also dislike forced at-tempts at contrived fun, which is usually no fun at all for Capricorns. In fact, it can put them into a very bad mood. Speaking of moods, anyone in an intimate relationship with a Capricorn is going to have to deal sometime with the notorious Capricornian black moods, even though they usually withdraw because experience and intuition have taught them that there are times it's best to be alone to work things through. Besides, Capricorn would hate to be thought of as a wet blanket. They seek solace in privacy, but like everyone, they don't want to feel lonely and abandoned. It's a bit of a tricky issue for anyone in a relationship with a Capricorn. Say to your Capricorn, "I'm here if you need me." Capricorns will always remember. They never forget a kindness.

You see, Capricorns are not as strong and self-sufficient as they make out. Deep down they need as much love and approval as anyone else—and probably a whole lot more reassurance. There are times (especially when they're young) when Capricorns can feel terri-bly insecure and self-conscious, and dwell unnecessarily on any little imperfections that more confident signs wouldn't give a second thought to. Capricorns work hard to create a good image, and they're generally far more desirable than they imagine themselves to be.

Too often Capricorns are overcritical of themselves and not critical enough of their lovers. Big problems tend to arise if they play down a partner's serious shortcomings. Perhaps their own early feelings of inadequacy and insecurity allow them to fall for someone who is (for one reason or another) obviously totally unsuitable.

There's a part of conservative Capricorn's nature that is easily se-duced by the wild and the wicked. Under that composed facade is an extremely sexy man or woman who would hate to miss out on any exciting experiences. This is how it happens that Mr. or Ms. Young Otherwise Sensible and Cautious Capricorn does things that raise a few eyebrows. In middle age, some Capricorns occasionally even amaze themselves when they look back on an episode or two of their youth.

Capricorn's self-confidence improves, and keeps improving with age. Aunt Betty could well be proved wrong when she predicts that her Capricorn niece—or nephew, for that matter—is going to be left on the shelf. For every Capricorn who is fortunate enough to meet his or her love and settle down before thirty, there are just as many who make a truly happy marriage later. It seems that with love, as with so much in a Capricorn's life, the older they are, the better it gets.

When the big day does come, Capricorn is not going to opt for the hippy-style wedding in the park with the marriage celebrant in a caftan. No embarrassing "personalized" marriage vows or schmaltzy (Capricorns loathe schmaltz) proclamations of undying love. No, thank you. This is the occasion when even the most liberal Capricorn bride or groom will be transformed into the arch traditionalist. Of all the signs of the zodiac, the Capricorn male is under heavy suspicion as the one least likely to ask for "obey" to be dropped from the wedding vows.

Here's a hint of what might turn out to be a stumbling block in an intimate relationship with a Capricorn. They like to be in control. And because they're so capable, resourceful, and efficient, because they're such good all round managers and are willing to *take* control, it can be very easy for others to let Capricorns make all the decisions and run the show.

Even the most loving and well meaning of Capricorns can slip into the Saturnian tendency to impose their disciplined regime on others. When they do, partners find themselves, for example, thinking twice before they phone in to say they're having such a good time with their old friends that they won't be home for dinner. Or they may find themselves reluctantly going along with Capricorn's desire to send the children to Capricorn's old school. Question Capricorn's decision and you could be made to feel that *your* decision—or even your opinion—doesn't count.

Capricorns have their own way of expressing their disapproval. It's not the quick, angry reaction à la Aries or Leo. More like the big-chill technique. The deafening silence emanating from a disapproving Capricorn evokes the uncomfortable memory you have of standing outside the principal's office waiting to be "dealt with." You know you're in for a lecture pointing out the fallacies in your reasoning or your lack of responsibility. And you'll remember the way you felt *after* you'd left the principal's office, with your tail between your legs. Capricorns at their worst, it must be said, can be icy cold, didactic, and at times too controlling for their own good.

The masterpiece of the great French dramatist Molière is about how just such a Capricorn controller sabotaged his chance for true love and happiness. (Molière himself was a Capricorn.) In *The Misanthrope* the main character, Alceste, regards himself as a man of honor and honesty, and openly proclaims his contempt for court society with its preciousness, shallow affections, and endless meaningless conversations.

Alceste's antisocial behavior certainly doesn't win him any friends or favors. Even Celimene, the woman he loves and plans to marry, finds his misanthropic ways hard to handle. Celimene is a socially well-adjusted woman of her time who has no problem with social chitchat and performing the expected niceties of courtly life. She makes an effort to be amusing, she laughs at people's jokes (even when they're not funny) and compliments others on their appearance or their wit (even if they are frumpy or boring). Alceste, however, is of the firm conviction that if Celimene loves him, she should take his point of view and act in the manner in which he expects her to act, namely like him. He continually berates her and can't accept that Celimene has the right to be herself. When he says, "No man has ever loved as I do!" she replies, "And you certainly have a novel way of showing it! You love people so that you can quarrel with them. The only expression you can find for your passion is in reproaches. I have never heard of a lover who grumbled and scolded as you do."

Poor miserable Alceste. He is a caricature of the uptight Capricorn hung up on rectitude and righteousness. Possession, as Alceste learns (and many controlling Capricorns do learn this lesson eventually—to their chagrin), is not nine tenths of the law when applied to human relationships. If only he could have loosened up a little, he could still have been a thoroughly respectable and sincere Capricorn *and* live happily ever after with the woman he loved—even if she wasn't made in exactly the same mold as he. *Vive la difference!* as an Aquarian might advise.

Every Sun sign benefits from leaning a little towards the best qualities of the sign to come. For Capricorns that means Aquarius. One of the finest attributes of friendly, freedom-loving Aquarius is the ability to get on with all sorts of different people, complete with their various quirks and idiosyncracies. In fact, Aquarians like them all the more because of their differences. Aquarians are great believers in giving people plenty of space and room to move, whereas Capricorns tend to slip into ownership in personal relationships and try to steer their partners along the road they think they ought to travel. Perhaps they fear that if their partner is too independent, they'll lose them.

Have faith, Capricorn. Why would anyone who loves you want to walk away when you have so much to offer? Partners of Capricorn know that it's not unromantic to be loyal, reliable, and devoted. They know, too, that love with a Capricorn is one of the most enduring loves of all. And that with each passing year, it gets richer and more satisfying.

If you're lucky enough to have won the heart of a Capricorn, you can look forward to the time when you're both old and gray and all your friends have settled into their rocking chairs on the porch, because you could be packing your bags for your second, or even third, honeymoon in Paris. Remember Paris?

When you again climb the hill to the top of Montmartre (and Capricorn at eighty-something will probably still be able to climb that hill—even if those Capricorn knees are a little creaky) and walk into that little café that you came upon fifty years ago, you'll be just as much in love with your Capricorn as you were when you first met. And as you raise your glasses and toast the years that are *still* to come, you'll swear you hear the tinkling of a piano. What is that tune? Why, it's the all-time Capricorn love song . . .

> *You must remember this*
> *A kiss is just a kiss*
> *A sigh is just a sigh.*
> *The fundamental things apply*
> *As times goes by . . .*

THE CAPRICORN PARENT

Now we are a family, thinks Capricorn when his or her first child is born. And in no time at all, Capricorn will have arranged, in their own incomparable way, for the entire clan to turn up for the dynasty photo session. Mother, grandmother, and great-grandmother will all take turns at being photographed holding baby decked out in the traditional christening gown that's been handed down through the generations. And if there isn't one, then Capricorn will start the tradition.

Everyone knows that Capricorn is ambitious, with a head for business and making money. Less known is what devoted and loving parents Capricorns are. The last of the earth signs is the original earth mother . . . or father. Though even in these days of the liberated male, many Capricorn men still want to be a traditional father. They're inclined to believe that fathers ought to bring home the bacon, and that if they spend a quality hour or two on the weekends playing with Junior and imparting some fatherly words of wisdom, then that's just as it should be. Many Capricorn men are still the classic paterfamilias.

No problem is pushed aside, no need is neglected, no stone is left unturned, by the thorough and responsible Capricorn parent. They make it their business to find out which stroller is the safest and which are the brands of baby food that contain no preservatives. They're not seduced by pretty pictures in baby magazines and are geniuses at making a little go a long way. If money is short, they won't waste it on frilly trimmings for the crib, or an expensive diaper-changing table when they know the carpet can serve just as well—and could even be safer. They'd rather squirrel away the money they save in an old coffee jar to buy baby the best educational toys in six months time.

Dutiful to a tee, Capricorn working mothers are the ones you catch sight of over the fence hanging out the washing at dawn before they rush inside to prepare a hot breakfast for their children because every good parent knows that a hot breakfast is the best start to a winter's day. Capricorns would hate for people to think that they are anything less than perfect parents.

If anyone can hold down a responsible job, run an efficient home, *and* raise healthy, well-adjusted children, it's a Capricorn. How do they cope? By being so thoroughly capable, that's how. And by calling on their vast reserves of practicality. Capricorns are not the types who are given to hysteria or amateur dramatics. Should their six-year-old come through the door in tears, blood dripping from a cut finger, Capricorn will quietly and efficiently move to the medicine cabinet and mend the wound. Capricorn's whole presence is soothing and reassuring. They aim to provide their children with a sense of safety and security.

To outsiders Capricorns can come across as very controlled and reserved. But at home with their children, they can feel free to express their need to be loving and affectionate, and they'd feel deeply hurt if ever their children pulled back from hugs and kisses.

Capricorns want to create the traditional ideal of a warm and secure hearth, complete with all the comforting rites and rituals of family life. This is not the parent who is laissez-faire about children munching take-out pizza in front of the TV. Capricorn holds firmly to the ideal of the old-fashioned, home-cooked family dinner, with everyone together round the table, and no excuses for absenteeism. A table properly set and laid out makes family life very civilized, believes Capricorn. They expect their children to be dutiful about trips to Grandma's or going to church together, or indeed any place where they're seen as a cohesive family group.

Children of Capricorn will be encouraged to express their point of view—so long as it's done in a courteous, respectful manner. Capricorns believe that civilized talks are the best way to solve most problems.

Few parents are so keen to impart to their children practical living skills. We know one Capricorn single mom who patiently and systematically taught her two children how to cook for themselves. By the time the younger was eight, he could cook a very acceptable meal, wash up, and put all the dishes away. Her thinking was, "If ever I should be held up at work, I know the children will be able to cope."

Nor will the social graces be neglected either. Capricorns are likely to be fastidious over manners and etiquette. When their child answers the phone, people are pleasantly surprised to hear a little voice politely asking, "Who shall I say is calling?" If you are expecting that Capricorn gives good lessons on money management, you would be right. Self-sufficiency, remember, is a Capricornian virtue. They won't give out cash hand over fist—no Capricorn is an easy touch. But as soon as their child can sign his or her name, and can add and subtract, the Capricorn father will be proudly leading them on their first pilgrimage to the bank to open up their first savings account. And how proud Capricorn will be when their early training pays off and Junior gets his first paper run, and announces that he's worked out a budget, and should be able to bank 80 percent of his earnings.

Of course, the biggest preparation for life is education, and Capricorns appreciate this more than most. Not only do Capricorn parents carefully research schools and investigate scholarships, they are the bastions of the PTA, and quite often the president. Capricorns want to be in a position to have a say in how their children's school is run.

It's precisely because Capricorns need to have their contribution appreciated that some, perhaps subconsciously, become the *too* dutiful, self-sacrificing parent.

It's so important for Capricorn to feel in control. Discipline, that magic Capricorn word, is never neglected. Capricorn is convinced that one of the most valuable things you can teach your children is self-discipline. But it must be said there are some Capricorn parents who are so strict and disciplinarian that their efforts end up being counterproductive. Capricorns can be overanxious to keep their child away from "the wrong crowd" or "bad influences," and they could end up giving their teenager bona fide cause to turn into everything they so much wanted them *not* to become. Especially if that teenager is a throwback to the Sagittarian great-grandma who ran away from home when she was sixteen, or Great-uncle Aquarius who cultivated his reputation as a bit of a black sheep.

No matter what their Sun sign, and no matter what little problems may arise along the way, the great certainty in the lives of children of Capricorn is that their mother or father is there for them. The Capricorn parent throws a warm security blanket around their children. And in the long run, that's the most important thing anyone can do for a child.

There's only one person more devoted than a Capricorn parent. And that's a Capricorn grandparent. Capricorns genuinely look forward to the day when *they'll* be the ones seated proudly in the center of the dynasty photo with their brand new grandchild on their knee.

THE CAPRICORN CHILD

Is there such a thing as the perfect child? Of course not. But a Capricorn child could come pretty close. From the start you will appreciate this gentle child who is never such a handful or so demanding that you have to put your own interests, or indeed your life, on hold.

Capricorn children are, on the whole, very easy to raise. Obedient and well behaved, little Capricorns don't complain or whine for no reason. They are not given to foot stamping or embarrassing temper tantrums. Nor are they silly gigglers or the perpetrators of stupid pranks. They won't try and haggle extra pocket money out of you, or wear you down until you give up and buy the new robomonster just to restore your peace and quiet. Capricorns like to know what the rules are, and they're generally happy to live by them.

A structured life is very important to Capricorn children. From the very youngest age, they need a sense of order around them. They like routine and are happiest when they know that certain things—like meals, bath, and bed—will happen at certain times, and that the same people are going to be there at the same times.

By the time he or she can talk, your little Capricorn will have already worked out the social dynamics of their home, their little world, and where they fit into it.

You'll find your friends complimenting you on having produced such a well-behaved, civilized little boy or girl, and they won't mind in the least when you turn up with little Capricorn in tow. These are the children who are perfectly happy to sit with you and your friends listening politely to adult conversation, delighting you with their own contribution when asked. In fact, Capricorn children often prefer the company of adults. Many grown-up Capricorns will tell you how they hated being relegated to the kiddies' dining table at social gatherings or being sent outside to play with unknown children.

We know one six-year-old little Capricorn girl who loves to sit beside her grandfather on the verandah when his friends drop by for a chat. He's taught her to shake hands with the old gentlemen and lay out the afternoon tea on the table. Capricorns of all ages want to be doing something purposeful. Give them their own little jobs and ask them to help when there's something they can do, and it will give them the sense of belonging and contributing that's so important to Capricorn.

Teach your Capricorn practical living skills as soon as possible.

They'll need no pushing; they want to acquire them. When you show a young Capricorn how to peel potatoes and make their bed, you won't have to do it again and again. All earth signs love gardening, and it's never too early to give them their own little trowel and rake.

It's important to respect your Capricorn child's own space. They feel very uncomfortable when they're oversupervised, or smothered with excessive displays of emotion. Don't worry if they spend hours on end reading in their room, or puttering around organizing their possessions. Capricorns enjoy being alone with their own thoughts.

Capricorn children love to make useful things. They're already little functionalists at heart. So express your delight if you're presented with a pencil holder made out of the cardboard tube from the middle of a toilet roll. Whatever you do, don't laugh or show any sign that their creation is not appreciated. You *must* proudly put it on your desk. The Capricorn child is far more sensitive than people realize. Capricorns are slow to grow in confidence and self-esteem. The fact that they seem so mature can prevent people—parents included—from noticing the subtle signs of the Capricorn child's sensitivity.

Because they so much want to be approved of by their parents, Capricorn children tend to keep their worries to themselves, often suppressing their feelings and their needs. Capricorn children are not the ones who come home from school and pour out their heart to you about their troubles with math or their disagreements with other children. This is where the Capricornian "I've got it all under control" image starts. Some Capricorn children can be miserable, but no one would ever know it. Imagine, then, how easy it is for their parents to miss their fears and anxieties. Unlike their opposite sign, Cancer, Capricorn children are reluctant to put up their hands and draw attention to themselves or their worries. They fear that if they do, they won't be regarded as a "good child." Capricorns have been known to take on courses they didn't really want to, or play a sport they didn't really like, because they thought it would please their parents and because they couldn't say, "I don't want to . . ." Parents of Capricorn need to spend time finding out what their child's *real* needs are, and need to be especially vigilant in looking out for any subtle signs that all is not well in little Capricorn's world.

You have to win a Capricorn's trust before he or she opens up. The same applies—maybe more so—to Moon in Capricorn children. Our Moon signs reveals our instinctive emotional responses throughout our lives. It indicates our most fundamental needs, which is why we all fall back on our Moon sign in times of stress. Children born under a Capricorn Moon are possibly even more reticent than Capricorn Sun children in telling their parents how they feel or what they need. They are hypersensitive and easily wounded. Both Sun and Moon in Capricorn children have deep feelings and long memories. These are the children, we assure you, who will remember all their life exactly who was there for them and who wasn't.

If you're raising a Capricorn child, you'll soon realize that Capricorn's sensitivity makes him or her very susceptible to criticism. Should you have to reprimand a Capricorn, all you need do is point our the error calmly and quietly . . . once. There'll be no need to refer to it again. Capricorn will have heeded your words and taken them to heart.

It is not in the Capricorn nature to want to be a rebel or a trouble-maker. At school they're studious and compliant. You rarely hear of a Capricorn playing hooky. As teenagers, too, they know what's expected of them and will dutifully and willingly turn up at family gatherings, and pull their weight when it comes to pitching in with the preparations.

You can trust your Capricorn son or daughter. There's nothing flighty, silly, or impetuous in their nature. Since Capricorns are likely to be interested in the opposite sex (Capricorn, remember, is a very sexy sign), it will be reassuring to parents to learn that they are not risk takers. It's not that Capricorns won't want to go to a few wild parties, but at least you can rely on them to obey the rules and not spend their cab fare home.

Capricorn children often seem older than their years. And you're likely to find yourself thinking at times that they want to grow up *too* quickly. They'll be looking forward to the day when they can set up their own home and make their own way in life, but you need never worry that they won't be able to take care of themselves. Nor need you worry that your Capricorn will ever fail to think of you. They strongly believe in the ties that bind. And if you're bound to a little Capricorn now, that bond can never be broken. It can only get stronger . . . and stronger . . . as the years go by.

BORN UNDER CAPRICORN

Howard Hughes	Val Kilmer
Gypsy Rose Lee	Simone de Beauvoir
Paul Revere	Ted Danson
Mel Gibson	Henri Matisse
J. R. R. Tolkien	Aristotle Onassis
Joan of Arc	Rod Stewart
Isaac Asimov	Ibn Saud
Josef Stalin	Kate Moss
Joan Baez	David Bellamy
Henry Miller	Kevin Costner
Sophie Tucker	Jim Bakker
Gerard Depardieu	Sun Myung Moon
Muhammad Ali	Nicolas Cage
Joe Frazier	Yukio Mishima
Al Capone	Anwar Sadat
Louis Pasteur	Cary Grant
David Lloyd George	King Juan Carlos of Spain
Idi Amin	Diane Keaton
Dolly Parton	Carlos Castaneda
Michael Crawford	Jane Wyman
Maggie Smith	Paramahamsa Yogananda
Woodrow Wilson	Chuck Berry

AQUARIUS

January 21–February 19

Ruling planets

URANUS AND SATURN

I intend no modification of my oft-
expressed personal wish that all men
everywhere could be free.

Abraham Lincoln–born February 12

THE AQUARIUS NATURE

Everyone has said at some time, "I want to do my own thing." But if you've ever thought the words fall more frequently from the mouths of Aquarians, you're probably right. Being able to do their own thing is so crucial to the happiness of Aquarians that they've practically made it their personal credo.

There are plenty of other similar expressions that the "free agent" of the zodiac is fond of tossing around. If you've got an Aquarian friend and you phone to make a date, you're no doubt quite used to hearing "I'll pencil it in" or "Let's play it by ear" or We'll see how the day pans out." All of which are dead giveaways for their dread of getting tied up or tied down.

Even the most dutiful, family-oriented Aquarian enjoys escaping from the house regularly to take in a movie alone. Their family has come to expect them to sign up for an evening course in creative writing one year, and join an amateur drama group the next. They know how much Aquarius loves the conviviality of the big family get-together at Christmas, but they've given up trying to pin them down to a family vacation because they also know that Aquarius is likely to hedge their bets and will get no further than "penciling it in."

Already Aquarius is looking like a pretty contradictory and enigmatic sign. It's true that the Aquarian personality is so full of interesting paradoxes that it's hard to describe precisely what sort of people they are. And that suits Aquarians just fine. They themselves would strongly resist any attempt to be pigeonholed. Where's the individuality in that?

Much of the paradoxical nature of Aquarius can be explained by the fact that the sign is ruled by two planets, Saturn and Uranus, and two more different planets, you could not find. There are other signs that also have two planetary rulers, but none is ruled by two such disparate forces. It certainly makes for interesting people, even if they're not always easy to get a handle on.

Saturn explains the conservative side of the Aquarius personality. You've read about him in the Capricorn chapter. He's your earthy, feet-on-the-ground, pillar-of-society type, and he represents the side of Aquarius that wants the whole security package: house, family, regular income, and money in the bank for a rainy day. You'll meet plenty of modern Aquarians who strike you as predominantly conservative and old-fashioned. In short, thoroughly Saturnian.

Saturn has been a ruler of Aquarius since ancient times. Then, in 1871, Uranus appeared on the scene: a planet as strange and eccentric as the influence it wields. Even the discovery of Uranus was unusual. An amateur astronomer, Frederich Wilhelm Herschel (he was a musician by profession), was scanning the skies over England when he found what he initially thought was a comet. It turned out to be the first of the "modern" planets. Neptune and Pluto were still waiting to be discovered.

Astronomically speaking, Uranus seems to have a will all its own. It spins very rapidly, one revolution every ten hours and forty-nine minutes, compared with our twenty-four hours. And its north/south axis is only a few degrees above the plane of its orbit, which makes it look like it's spinning on its belly. There is virtually no spring or autumn on Uranus, only winter and summer. Uranus is a planet of extremes. There are no in betweens.

Astrologers soon observed that the astrological influence of Uranus matches his unusual astronomical profile. And so it was that Uranus became known as the planet of individuality, the offbeat, and the unorthodox. Today Uranus is recognized as the "new" ruler of Aquarius.

Uranus challenges the traditions and orderliness that Saturn values so highly. Saturn wants stability whereas Uranus embraces the new

and invokes change. Indeed, one very important and valuable function of Uranus is to sweep the old aside should it become a barrier
to progress. For Aquarians, the forces of Saturn and Uranus within
their personality can be a useful counterbalance to each other, and a
wonderful antidote to each other's extremes. Even if, in combination,
they produce those paradoxes that make Aquarians so interesting,
and occasionally so perplexing.

Just when you think that you've got an Aquarian worked out,
they'll do something or say something that forces you to rethink
your idea of who they are. It's hard to fathom that the friend who
turns up on your doorstep volunteering to help you paint the place
you've just moved into is the same person who, only a week ago,
ummed and aahed about whether they'd be there on moving day.
There are some Aquarians who feel so threatened by promises and
ironclad commitments that they will avoid being locked into any
more schedules than they absolutely have to.

Perhaps you know an Aquarian who adores nothing more than
getting together for a long Sunday lunch with half a dozen friends.
He or she always arrives beaming with smiles, armed with bottles
of wine and other treats. But if you're waiting for a reciprocal invitation, don't hold your breath. There are plenty of Aquarians who try
to avoid the kitchen as much as those ironclad commitments. Okay,
so you've dined chez Aquarius, and the food *was* fantastic. Are you
sure they cooked it all themselves? The take-out industry thrives on
the patronage of Aquarians.

The best get-togethers with Aquarians are those that are more or
less ad hoc. They just happen. And when they do, it may not be
going too far to say that there's just about no other person who
makes for such stimulating company. Aquarians are the friendliest
of people. In fact, Aquarius is the sign that rules friends, as well as
those people in our lives such as colleagues or members of any clubs
and groups that we belong to. Aquarians prefer their connections
with people to be friendly, free, and easy. The truth is, they are less
comfortable with close one-on-one relationships. It is not uncommon
to hear the spouses of Aquarians say that they often feel more like
a friend than a lover.

The Aquarius rulership over friendly relationships is why Aquarius is called the "humanitarian sign," and the sign of the "brotherhood of man." Ever since the sixties when people first heard about
the "dawning of the age of Aquarius," thanks to the song from the
musical *Hair*, the Aquarian "humanitarianism" has been rather
blown out of proportion. Yes, Aquarians are very concerned about
human rights and where the human race is heading. But as for harmony, peace, and understanding, well, they no more belong to

Aquarius than they do to Pisces, Libra, or Capricorn, or to any other sign for that matter.

Aquarius is an individualist, but most definitely not a loner. Socializing with friends is essential to their well-being, and they really light up when they're with people with whom they can share their ideas and their theories. They are invariably the first to have read the latest book on life on Mars, or why the pyramids were built, and they'll treat you to their review. If there's a controversial new film out, Aquarians will want to go see it—and spend hours discussing what all the fuss is about. A good controversy is always guaranteed to turn an Aquarian on.

The essence of the Uranian energy is to challenge the established order and to question the unquestioned—what we call the norm. People often describe Aquarians as eccentric, different, way out, bohemian, or just plain weird. But are these people who simply don't recognize that Aquarians are often brilliant, gifted, and blessed with the ability to see way ahead of others? Uranus flies in the face of the ordinary, the dull, and the pedestrian. On the one hand, it rules the genius, and on the other, the kook and the outsider.

Likewise, the mythological Uranus was no stranger to the unorthodox. He was the first god of the sky, born from Gaia, the primal earth mother. Before them, there existed only Chaos. Uranus was both son and lover of Gaia. From this incestuous union (or was it, since there was no one else around?) came some weird and wonderful offspring, including the titans and the one-eyed cyclops. But Uranus was a ruthless tyrant who treated his children harshly. And eventually Gaia put a stop to his rages by calling upon Saturn, the most dutiful and obedient of her children, to kill him. And so began the Saturnian golden age of order and prosperity.

The story is a message to all Aquarians whose minds would soar in the empyrean, that they must stay grounded. Saturn's earthy energies must be respected if Uranus is to bring forth his extraordinary originality. Uranus puts his mark on all human endeavors that are original. He is the innovative factor in the creative process. Every Aquarian has, at some time, had a fantastic idea for a new product, a new type of solar energy panel, a new TV series, or a new anything that will take off and make the world a better place. They've never got any shortage of good ideas. But unless they give due attention to the practicalities that Saturn is in charge of, their ideas risk remaining nothing more than ideas.

Uranus also rules truth. Pure, raw, unmitigated truth. The type of cold, incisive truth that is sometimes unpleasant and painful to look at, and is unsoftened by any gentle, more "feminine" influences. Uranus was the first male principle in mythology, and as such, he's a strong and confronting force. There can be a very willful, assertive, and uncompromising side to Aquarian men *and* women.

When Saturn avenged his father's violence by castrating him with his scythe, Uranus' blood fell to the earth, and from it sprang the Furies, whose work it was to seek their own revenge on human transgressors. Do something beyond the pale and you'll have the Furies to contend with, is what this subplot in the myth means. The genitals, however, were cast into the ocean, and his seed mixed with the primordial waters to create Venus, goddess of beauty and art.

Because the sign of Aquarius is symbolized by The Water Bearer, people often initially assume that it's a water sign. But when you delve into the Aquarius nature and discover their decidedly intellectual bent (not to mention their love of talking and stimulating company), there's really no mistaking them for anything but an air sign.

Air is the element of the mind. It is the realm of thought and ideas. Like the other air signs, Gemini and Libra, Aquarius is a sociable communicator. As the last of the air signs, Aquarius has refined the airy nature into a delight for abstraction and theory. All air signs are objective people who aim to keep a certain space between themselves and the murkier depths of complicated emotions.

The water that you see pouring from The Water Bearer's urn represents the humanitarian aspect of the sign. As humans, we cannot survive without water. But on a more esoteric level, the water can also be interpreted as electrical pulsations, the pure invisible life force of the cosmos. This is something beyond the physical, tangible realm, but it's as crucial to our survival as thinking, creative beings as the water we drink.

In the glyph, the shorthand symbol for Aquarius, the two wavy lines can, similarly, be interpreted as flowing water or waves of electricity. Uranus rules electricity. And it's not without reason that we use the language of electricity to describe the creative process, with words like *creative spark* and *flash of inspiration*.

Wolfgang Amadeus Mozart, said to be one of the most inspired creative minds of all time, was an Aquarian. It has even been suggested that his genius was so inspired that it was almost divine in origin. Whatever the source, his was a unique creativity. His music has a sublime quality that lifts the spirit. This was the pure genius of Mozart

Even your average Aquarian (as if there could be any such person as an "average" Aquarian) has an inimitable way of lifting your spirits. There's an extra charge to the atmosphere when they're around. They're guaranteed to liven up any company and can be very inspiring, sparking off all sorts of exciting new ideas.

In fact, there's nothing that Aquarians find quite as thrilling as something, anything, that's new. The "shock of the new" is no shock at all to an Aquarian. This is the least shockable sign of all. When Aquarian Édouard Manet first exhibited *Déjeuner sur l'Herbe (Luncheon on the Grass)*, it created an outrage in the Parisian art establishment. Today it's in every standard book on art history, and it doesn't even raise an eyebrow. It's the one with the two respectable gentlemen in suits picnicking with a naked woman. It wasn't as if Parisians hadn't seen pictures of naked women before. What was so shocking was the incongruity of seeing a naked woman lunching unabashedly with fully dressed men. Now, *that* was new.

You always find Aquarians in the advance troops of any movement—be it artistic, literary, political, or social. The Aquarian spirit *is* the spirit of the avant-garde. Though some avant-garde Aquarians seem to invite controversy over whether their work is truly innovative, or simply cashing in on shock tactics.

There are those who would say the Aquarius talent is frequently so far into the future that more earth-bound spirits can't grasp it, there are those who maintain that it's all a con, and there are many who can't decide.

Think of the painter Jackson Pollock and the writer Gertrude Stein. And, of course, there's the work of conceptual artist Yoko Ono. All of them Aquarians. Yoko once devised a group "artpiece" in which a hundred people in cities around the world synchronized their watches, and at the appointed hour, all simultaneously opened a window, breathed in, and turned around a few times. A Zen-style expression of group identity? A rare insight into the Aquarian concept of togetherness? Or just an Aquarian call for others to hail their originality? Aquarians love it when the spotlight shines on them.

Aquarians are progressive people whose vision is firmly set in the future. Uranus plays a leading role in the horoscopes of people whose discoveries herald dramatic changes that affect all of humanity—discoveries that have a universal application. A great many are born under the sign of The Water Bearer, including Thomas Edison, who invented the lightbulb, and André-Marie Ampère, who gave his name to the unit of electricity.

You'll find many Aquarians who are fond of their electrical whizbang gadgets. Computers are an Aquarian specialty, and it's an unusual Aquarian who isn't sold on the idea of unlimited information for everyone on the Net. Information technology comes under the domain of Aquarius. This is why as we enter the "Age of Aquarius" we're witnessing an explosion in computerization and information technology.

With their thirst for information, connecting with other minds on the Internet can sometimes be more appealing to Aquarians than personal interaction. For all its reputation as the "friendly" sign, most Aquarians are cool and somewhat detached. Interaction with others is terribly important to them, yet they like to maintain a certain emotional distance between themselves and other individuals.

Detachment versus closeness is actually a major Aquarian issue. Whatever the individual circumstances of their early years, you'll generally find that Aquarians have been raised in homes in which family members kept each other at arm's length, with less warmth and spontaneous physical affection than most people are used to. It's possibly why so many Aquarians back away from true intimacy and have an unconscious fear of drowning in what they see as a maelstrom of emotions.

Most Aquarians, at some stage in their lives, have felt a bit like the odd one out, which could be why they have such a need to define themselves by membership in a group, and why they are reluctant to get too close to any one individual. Aquarians are determined to be—and stay—their own person. The prospect that someone else could erode their personal freedom, or make too many emotional demands on them and prevent them from "doing their own thing," feels extremely threatening to them. In a group situation, the dynamics are nonthreatening. As part of a group, Aquarians can feel free to go their own way, yet still feel they belong, with all the security and support they need.

The most important group that an Aquarius wants to belong to is, of course, the family. They're not "family people" in the way that Cancerians or Taureans are, but they do nonetheless have a deep need to be part of a family, and have a great respect for the advantages of marriage and family life. Aquarians are not homebodies (not unless they have a Capricorn Moon or maybe a Cancer Ascendant, for example). Indeed, "home" may mean something entirely different to Aquarius than it does to other people. They need to know that home and family are there for them to return to, but they don't want the constant togetherness that many people associate with family life. Some family members have even been known to complain that their Aquarius treats home like a drop-in center.

No matter how much they subscribe to the family tribal structure— and conservative Saturn insists that they do—there's some part of Aquarius that always remains a little separate. Aquarians need their personal space. And they're prepared to give others their space too. You can't fence them in. They hate to feel possessed, and will avoid relationships that are too clinging and cloying. It's one of those Aquarian paradoxes that they need regular periods entirely to themselves, yet they also crave regular people input.

Individualistic Aquarians have a lot in common with natives of their opposite sign, Leo. Both are signs that espouse the "free to be me" philosophy. Both are also very dominant personalities within any group, team, or family structure. Yet the way each achieves pre-eminence within the group is quite different. There's no mistaking that Leos were born to rule. They naturally assume the leadership role, and others naturally and happily follow. But Aquarians are more subtle in the way they get people to revolve around them. They're less obviously autocratic, but they can be autocratic nonetheless.

Aquarians have their own kind of magnetic appeal. Along with their open and friendly manner, they have the most sensational smile. Think of actors Paul Newman, Alan Alda, Matt Dillon, and John Travolta—they all have that wonderful Aquarian smile that lights up their whole face. Indeed, that smile is often all it takes to completely disarm others and get them on their side. Just when you're feeling a warm glow of "harmony and understanding" and equality for all, you begin to become aware that Aquarius has taken the lead without your ever quite knowing how. Look around and you see that everyone seems to be doing what Aquarius wants. So don't be fooled by the light, easygoing approach. Aquarians have their ways. You may well come to the conclusions that the only person who's hanging loose and hanging free is Aquarius.

If you haven't got the message by now, the word *freedom* is practically synonymous with Aquarius. "Liberty, equality, and fraternity," proclaimed the French revolutionaries. When Herschel discovered Uranus, revolution was in the air and the "brotherhood of man" was the ideal of the times. A society in which everyone is free and equal is still an Aquarian ideal. Some would call it Utopia. In fact, it was an Aquarian, Sir Thomas More, King Henry VIII's right-hand man, who gave us the word *Utopia*. He wrote a story about an island called Utopia where people lived in a well-governed, harmonious state of fraternal bliss. *Utopia* is a pun. In Greek it means "somewhere," but it also means "nowhere." More's Aquarian Utopia was nothing more than a fantasy land. But a lot of people reading More's story, poring over the map he had drawn and examining the Utopian language he had invented, believed—or wished to believe—that Utopia really did exist.

Aquarius is the sign that rules our hopes and wishes for the future, both our individual and collective aspirations. In this sense, it's an optimistic sign. Aquarians never quite lose the belief that Utopia is a possibility. We know one colorful Aquarian interior designer who even called her shop Utopia Road with the intention of transporting people out of a dull and dreary existence into their very own Utopia.

With such strong convictions on the way the world ought to be, it's only natural that Aquarians should concern themselves with rights for all. These are the people who join labor unions and groups such as Amnesty International or the World Wildlife Society. Aquarians are big on causes. Uranus, you recall, is an instigator of radical change. If something has become outworn and is no longer relevant, Uranus comes along and turns things upside down. There is a rebellious, even a revolutionary, streak in Uranian individuals. Some Uranian-type Aquarians get so fired up that they become revolutionaries and rebels with—or without—a cause. James Dean (born February 8) cultivated the image of the archetypal Aquarian rebel. And Angela Davis was the real thing.

There's only one sign to rival Aquarius in optimism, idealism, and love of freedom. And that's Sagittarius. The two signs are quite similar in many of their attitudes and their interests. There's a connection between the two signs that lies in the story of The Water Bearer.

The water bearer of myth was a beautiful young man called Ganymede. Indeed, were it not for his astounding good looks, he would have remained one of the thousands of anonymous water bearers who trudged the streets of ancient Greece, scratching out a meager living. But one day Jupiter caught sight of Ganymede, was instantly mesmerized by his beauty, and whisked him off to Mount Olympus to spend the rest of his days pouring wine for the gods.

Jupiter was king of the Olympian gods. He is also the ruler of Sagittarius. It's an interesting coincidence (or is it?) that Ganymede is the name that has been given to one of the moons of Jupiter.

Two American presidents who are remembered as humanitarians were both born under the sign of The Water Bearer: Franklin D. Roosevelt and Abraham Lincoln. FDR is remembered for his New Deal, the program that gave people jobs in the depth of the Great Depression. He was the man who introduced Social Security to America, and the only American president to be elected a record four times.

Did FDR know how Aquarian he was when he said, "A radical is a man with both feet firmly planted in the air"? The patrician FDR saw no paradox in being both conservative and reformist. The Aquarian nature is one that is free to alternate between quite opposing positions. But Aquarians don't see this as contradictory or a potential source of conflict. If others do, then it's simply evidence of their mental limitations, figures Aquarius.

Then there's Abraham Lincoln who has gone down in history as the president who abolished slavery. His words "I intend no modification of my oft-expressed personal wish that all men everywhere could be free" are still inspiring. Notice how Lincoln said "everywhere." Aquarian ideals are universal. At their best, they are never confined to the narrow vision of "me and mine." They subscribe wholeheartedly to rights for everyone, everywhere. This is truly the finest side of the sign of humanity and brotherly love.

But for those who can grasp all the complexities of this complex sign, Lincoln's noble sentiments are also a subtle revelation of one of the less attractive sides of the Aquarian nature. The clue lies in the "I intend no modification . . ." bit. Think about it for a moment. Aquarius, as we know, is an air sign. They pride themselves on the clarity of their thinking and the rigor of their intellect. But Aquarius is also a fixed sign. The fixed quality provides them with tenacity and strength of purpose. Being both fixed and airy gives Aquarians fantastic powers of concentration. When they're absorbed in something or pursuing an interest, they can be as focused as a Scorpio, and every bit as determined as a Leo or a Taurus. But being both fixed and airy can also be the perfect recipe for obstinacy.

There are plenty of Aquarians who "intend no modification" of their wishes or their opinions. Because of their fixed mind-set, people are sometimes driven to accuse them of being intransigent and opinionated. You see, when an Aquarian's mind is made up, that's it. They get very attached to their beliefs and their opinions, and if they think that anyone is questioning one of those beliefs or opinions, they can be very condescending. It's irrelevant how well you present your case on the grounds of logic or evidence; they won't budge. Are some Aquarians contrary for the sake of being contrary? Do they get some sort of perverse satisfaction from it? There is a type of Aquarian who seems to suffer from a dreadful intellectual superiority complex and can infuriate others with their determination to always have the last word, and their inability to back down and admit they could be wrong.

When someone challenges one of their pet theories it strikes at the core of the Aquarian fixed mentality. Anyone who has ever tried to get an Aquarian to acknowledge another point of view or modify their stance feels like they're up against a stone wall—their very own Stonewall Jackson. He was the Confederate general who sat on his horse stony-faced, seemingly unmoved, while the battle raged and people were being slaughtered all around him.

It's not a bad thing to be detached at times. In fact, it can be very helpful to be able to access a certain detachedness in difficult circumstances. A cool head is essential in emergencies and in inflammatory situations. But some Aquarians—and Stonewall Jackson was obviously one of them—can appear so impervious to others' emotions, and so cut off from their own feelings, and so immovable that others see them as hard, cold, and even ruthless.

The problem with emotions is that they lie in the land of unreason.

And that's why Aquarians sense that the emotions are dangerous territory to venture into. There are times when the Aquarian detachment from the feeling capacity belies their humanitarianism. Some talk big about equality and love to philosophize on what's best for the world and mankind, but get them off the universal level and onto the personal plane, and you'll find their insensitive behavior is completely at odds with their fine words.

A friend of ours has an Aquarian photographer husband who berated her for years for not giving up smoking. Imagine, then, her shock when he came home one night and announced he had accepted a lucrative job shooting cigarette ads. She thought she was justified in calling him a hypocrite, but of course, he didn't see it that way. Aquarians have a way of rationalizing just about anything. *His* rationalization was, "Well, if I don't do it, someone else will." The job was worth big money—megabucks, in fact.

Aquarians would hate to think that money could ever determine the course of their lives. On the contrary, they'd much rather be seen as antimaterialistic. But practical, materialistic Saturn, never forget, is the ancient ruler of this sign. And he ensures that "modern" Aquarians always have one eye on their bank balance. Saturn helps Aquarians handle all their material needs very well. There are few Aquarians who go too many years without a home of their own, a car, and a nest egg. Financial security occupies a lot more of their thoughts than others would ever realize. Yet another one of those Aquarian paradoxes is their attitude towards money. Aquarians can be very generous at times and positively magnanimous with their own, yet they can be penny-pinching on the housekeeping and the everyday small pleasures such as the best cuts of meat, more expensive seats in the theater, or clothes that aren't purchased at the end-of-season sales.

The same Aquarian photographer often used to quote from graffiti on a wall in the seedier part of town that said "Isn't it funny—freedom costs money." Who better equipped to be aware of this practical Saturnian truth than the sign that so much desires a life of freedom?

Aquarian Jules Verne, the hero of latter-day science fiction writers, created an enigmatic character who personifies so many of the Aquarian paradoxes. He's Captain Nemo from *20,000 Leagues Under the Sea*. Nemo restlessly traveled the oceans of the world in his futuristic submarine, the *Nautilus*, a wonderland of high-tech innovations. He's the Aquarian eccentric with a brilliant inventive mind. But there's a dark side to Nemo that comes to the surface when he ruthlessly rams a foreign ship, killing all onboard. Why? The ship belongs to the nation that killed his wife and children. And Nemo has never let go of the hatred he bears for his "enemy." Were the men on board that ill-fated ship the same men who murdered his family? No. But that's not the point. They *belong* to the despised nation, and that is enough for Nemo.

Nemo's arrogance and his talent for justifying his actions paint a portrait of the very worst side of Aquarius. It led (as it often does) to the unleashing of the Furies. Remember the Furies—those nasty, uncompromising avengers that sprang from the blood of Uranus? Captain Nemo was fictional and was therefore allowed to be utterly possessed by fury. But you're bound to see the Furies occasionally erupting around real-life Aquarians. Aquarius is a highly strung sign. Physiologically speaking, Aquarius rules the nervous system, and when the pressure mounts, their reactions become unpredictable. Sudden bursts of anger and verbal lashings are often the way they unleash their frustrations.

Nemo had in his nature the capacity to destroy men against whom he had no personal vendetta. So much for the brotherhood of man. Anyone who has ever come up against an autocratic Aquarian may have good cause to question the Aquarian connection with brotherly love.

Every sign benefits from looking to the virtues of the opposite sign. And for Aquarius, that means Leo. Leos are people who need to express their individuality and be recognized as individuals in their own right. Hang on, thinks Aquarius, there's no one more individual than me—I'm all for individualism. That may well be true. But what is also true is that for all their love of humanity, Aquarians sometimes fail to see that humanity is made up of individuals. Certainly Captain Nemo couldn't—or didn't want—to see it.

Remember, Aquarians are people who tend to define themselves by the group they belong to. Look beneath the "Aquarius-speak" and you'll find they aspire to individuality in relation to the *group*, not the individuality of a person who stands alone. Nemo—that dark, angry Aquarian—was willing to tar every individual in the enemy group with the same brush. Leo, on the other hand, will always put the person before the race, the nation, or, for that matter, any other group the person belongs to.

Positive Aquarians are well tuned in to the fact that, as with everything in life, finding a balance is the answer. They admire nothing more than original, creative thinking, and are very conscious that everything progressive or innovative was originally conceived in the mind of an individual. These Aquarians can be like a breath of fresh air. Their goal is to seek a life without limitations. And their curiosity takes them to places—physically and mentally—that others wouldn't dream of journeying to.

Lewis Carroll, creator of *Alice's Adventures in Wonderland*, is perhaps the most Aquarian of Aquarians. And Alice is the most Aquarian of little girls. Curiouser and curiouser were the characters she encountered in Wonderland. But Alice was never daunted by any of the bizarre and unpredictable events that befell her. Such a self-contained little girl, Alice could conduct the most rational conversation about the most irrational things with the most extraordinary creatures, all without batting an eyelid. She's bright, mature, unflappable, and takes everything in her stride. But do you remember how Alice got into Wonderland in the first place?

"She saw a white rabbit scurrying across a field. When she heard it speak, it seemed perfectly natural to her. But . . . when the Rabbit actually took a watch out of its waistcoat-pocket, and looked at it, and then hurried on, Alice started to her feet, for it flashed across her mind that she had never before seen a rabbit with either a waistcoat-pocket, or a watch to take out of it, and burning with curiosity, she ran across the field after it, and was just in time to see it pop down a large rabbit hole under the hedge. In another moment down went Alice after it, never once considering how in the world she was to get out again."

Aquarians love the unusual and the unpredictable. And unlike the more stuffy signs who insist on knowing exactly where they stand today and tomorrow, it's in the Aquarius nature to explore whatever comes their way and takes their interest. After all, you never know where it may lead. It could take you to your very own Wonderland of new discoveries, new truths, and exciting new knowledge . . . that everyone can benefit from.

And as for "how in the world they are going to get out again," well, to know that would spoil all the fun. In any case, Aquarians are clever enough to figure that out along the way.

THE AQUARIUS CAREER AND DIRECTION

Whatever career an Aquarius chooses—whether they become a banker, a basketball player, or a brain surgeon—Aquarius needs to be able to put his or her own stamp on it.

Even better if that work has the freewheeling element that Aquarians like so much, and allows them to come and go as they please, get around to all sorts of places, and talk to all sorts of people. This is not a person who responds well to a strict nine-to-five routine. Aquarians can't abide jobs in which the work is much the same day after day, or they feel someone is breathing down their neck.

Even those who work in large organizations need the sense that they're running their own show. Some degree of independence is essential. That's why so many Aquarians are self-employed, or are drawn to fee-for-service jobs in which they are accountable to no one but themselves. This certainly doesn't mean that Aquarius is looking for an easy life. When Aquarians are engrossed in their work, they have been known to work all night if they have to.

The ideal Aquarian working environment is one where they can operate independently yet still feel a part of a team or a group of some sort. In spite of the Aquarian cry for independence, they want the congeniality of having friendly people around. The Aquarian freelance journalist, for example, will be much happier working in a shared office situation than alone at home. Aquarians are the people who set up "office communes" where everyone is responsible for their own work and their own clients, but where there's lots of interplay and mutual support.

There are some Aquarians though who are perfectly happy to work in a traditional office. But take a closer look, and you'll notice that Aquarius is not chained to a desk. All air signs have that magical ability to turn a humdrum day at work into a happening event. They're always a source of stimulation, and make the workplace a more exciting place to be for everyone. Aquarians are the first to rally the troops for a quick lunch at the local café, or drinks after work.

Aquarians alternate between loving the hype of a buzzing environment with phones ringing, people coming and going, and ideas and conversations whizzing around—and wanting to withdraw from it altogether. In fact, they are inclined to overload their nervous system, and only experience teaches them moderation.

Because their energy levels aren't consistent, a lot of Aquarians are erratic in their work production. It's either full on or not on at all. Their colleagues soon figure out that there are days when Aquarius puts their feet up on the desk and engages them in an hour-long animated debate on why the new computer program won't work and what should be done about it. In the afternoon, having got it all out of their system, the same Aquarius is eyes down, nose to the grindstone, with a "Do Not Disturb" sign dangling above his or her head.

Aquarians keep abreast of innovations, and many are hooked on information technology. If you're looking for a translation of the latest technobabble, speak to an Aquarius. Having said that, Aquarians also have a fascination with the very ancient. So it's not at all contradictory (is anything ever contradictory to an Aquarian?) that the proprietor of your favorite stall in the flea market should turn out to be an Aquarian antiquarian. They adore old and interesting artifacts, the older and odder, the better. There's nothing that turns an Aquarian on more than stumbling upon some bizarre African figurine decorated with arcane symbols, or an old oak refectory table on which they can install their new computer.

Aquarius is a scientific sign. Uranus, their ruler seeks the truth. He examines everything in an objective light, which is why Uranian people have such a gift for analytical thought. They have the ability to arrive at conclusions that are uncontaminated by personal bias. And because they think so quickly, they make connections that look like pure intuition but are really the result of rapid logical thinking.

The sudden flash of inspiration, the instant grasp of the truth, is a phenomenon ruled by Uranus. Don't be fooled by the classic image of the mad professor possessed by his machines and electrodes. He might be an eccentric Aquarius (there are plenty of those), but he's not as mad as he looks. He could even be a genius. Dr. Who comes to mind as the type of Aquarian whose idea of a good time is stepping into his Tardis (his space and time travel capsule disguised as a police box), pressing a few buttons, and being transported to somewhere strange, new, and exciting. Somewhere his fast and inventive Aquarian mind will be put to the test.

But science as a career is only for those Aquarians who have a strong methodical Saturnian side to their nature. For those who have, engineering is also a popular choice. The horoscopes of great inventors and scientists are always blessed with a strong Uranus *and* Saturn, and many have planets in Aquarius *and* Capricorn. Thomas Edison and Charles Darwin were both Aquarians and they both had Moon in Capricorn. And physicist Stephen Hawking is a Capricorn with a stack of planets in Aquarius.

All things electronic come under the rulership of Uranus, including television. Add to that the fact that Aquarius, like all the air signs, is a natural communicator and you can see why broadcasting is an Aquarian field. And why the linking of the world by satellite television is one of the most obvious signs that the Age of Aquarius is beginning.

Technology alone is exciting enough to Aquarians, but put them *in front* of a camera or a microphone and they're in their element. Quite literally. Aquarians are rarely shy of publicity or self-promotion. Actually the desire to be famous is a common Aquarian fantasy. The word itself, *fame*, has a special ring for Aquarians. They would love to be known as someone important in their field—whatever field that may be. These are the people who read the "Ten most . . ." lists in the weekend newspapers and dream of seeing their name among them.

Aquarians beam when they're praised for their work. To receive recognition at an annual award presentation gives them the chance to relish their own fifteen minutes of fame.

One of the most famous faces on television, Oprah Winfrey, is an

Aquarian. Aquarians can tackle the outrageous, the difficult, and the controversial. Nothing is taboo to Oprah. What other sign could feel so comfortable about hosting a public "let it all hang out" group experience?

Unions and professional associations of all kinds are also ruled by Aquarius. Socially aware Aquarians like to get involved in group politics, and it's an unusual Aquarian who doesn't have a firm opinion on the political issues of the day.

Aquarian Ronald Reagan began his political career as an actors' union representative in Hollywood. His ease with the camera was put to good use when he stepped onto the bigger stage as president of the United States. Reagan is a good example of one of those conservative Saturnian Aquarians. He is also a good example of how the horoscope of a leader always makes important connections with the horoscope of his or her country.

Countries have horoscopes, just like people. We know that the United States (born on the Fourth of July) is a Sun in Cancer country, but on that day the Moon was in the sign of Aquarius, and America's Aquarius Moon is very important to the "soul" of the country. It accounts for why the Aquarian concern with freedom of speech and human rights is such an integral part of the American national character, and why America plays the role of global watchdog on humanitarian issues. Any astrologer will tell you that the reason Reagan was able to touch a chord with the American people was that his Aquarian Sun makes a conjunction with America's Moon.

We've met many Aquarians who tell us how much they feel at home in America, especially California—the place where everything that is labeled New Age first takes off. In California, people are into anything and everything that is new, innovative, and offbeat, and occasionally bizarre and kooky. But who is to say what's bizarre and kooky? The Uranian energy is often just too ahead of its time for the average "limited" mind to grasp, as Aquarians would say. Though it must be said there are some Aquarians for whom nothing is too far out of this world. So it's only to be expected that many Aquarians are drawn to New Age vocations.

The new/ancient healing arts of acupuncture, color therapy, sound therapy, and any technique to do with electrical pulsations and energy vibrations are all Aquarian stuff. It's now even becoming commonplace to go to your local shopping mall and be able to consult a tarot reader or a numerologist or have someone lay crystals on your chakras and massage your aura, and emerge feeling far better for the experience.

The spiritual insight that comes as the flash of understanding, of just "knowing," is an Uranian phenomenon. This is part of the spiritual dimension of the sign of Aquarius, and it has produced some rare advanced souls. Thomas Merton and Sri Ramakrishna were Aquarians whose uncompromising search for spiritual truth still inspires many.

As the planet of truth and insight, Uranus rules the arcane arts, including astrology. Actually astrology is both a science and an art. Astrology requires an analytical mind but a mind that's also able to grasp the whole picture. Many Aquarians are interested in astrology and find that their interest quickly becomes a full-blown passion, and sometimes a full-time job. Although it must be said that Aquarians can often be the biggest skeptics of all. So don't be surprised if you meet one who proclaims, "Oh, I don't believe in *that*." You could point out that dismissing anything out of hand without objective investigation is hardly "scientific."

There is a lot that Aquarius shares with Gemini in their approach to work and their choice of career. It goes further than the simple fact of their both being air signs. Uranus is the "higher octave" of Mercury, the planetary ruler of Gemini, which means that Uranus incorporates the Mercurial qualities but expresses them on a more abstract and universal level. Like a Super-Mercury, so to speak.

Aquarians, like their Gemini cousins, are well suited to any job that requires a quick and efficient flow of ideas and information, and good verbal skills. Advertising, teaching, journalism, and the media are all good options for Aquarians—and Geminis.

Uranus lures Aquarians to the cutting edge of whatever field they're in. Creative work of some sort probably tops the wish list of Aquarian jobs. All creative people want to come up with something innovative that sets them apart from all the others, and Aquarians often achieve this.

Even if they're not working in fashion or interior design, or writing or running their own creative business, there are an awful lot who dream about how they could market their brilliant ideas. Many Aquarians dream, too, of penning a blockbuster.

Virginia Woolf was one of the kind of Aquarian writers who succeed in going beyond the decorative trimmings of social niceties in order to expose the truth. Despite her need for periods of solitude (*A Room of One's Own* is essential reading for every Aquarian), Woolf instinctively sought the security of membership of a group. *Her* group was called the Bloomsbury Set, the London literary avant-garde of its day, with Woolf as its leading light.

The theme of the work of a lot of Aquarian writers is social justice and the dynamics of getting on with each other. This is where the "humanitarian" sign has many important things to say and much to contribute to the progress of humanity.

The brotherhood of man could just as easily be the sisterhood of women. Aquarian Germaine Greer was among the first to get women—and men—talking and thinking about feminism with her book *The Female Eunuch*. The creative work of many Aquarians is considered radical in its time. They excel at throwing the cat among the pigeons. And there are plenty who do it in a savagely humorous way. Barry Humphries does it in the guise of his alter ego, Dame Edna Everage. Dame Edna is a parody of the hideously "normal," dubiously respectable middle-class housewife. When Dame Edna let a little fame go to her head, she turned into an outrageous international superstar who was then in the position *herself* to take a stab at the rich and famous.

Some of the wackiest and zaniest writers and performers around are Aquarians. They excel at the art of the spoof. Think of actor Leslie Nielson and his oddball send-ups of those who would take themselves too seriously. That's not to say that Aquarian humor is light or shallow. It often tackles some seriously twisted sides of human nature. There's something of the "if you can't join 'em, beat 'em" philosophy in the work of creative Aquarians.

If anyone can give the status quo a good shaking, it's an Aquarian. There's a revolutionary lurking somewhere inside even the most conservative of Aquarians. Okay, so there aren't too many jobs for revolutionaries advertised in the paper, but all Aquarians relish the chance—even if it's once in a lifetime—to buck the system, to think to hell with the consequences, and jump down the rabbit hole into the unknown. Just like Alice.

If Aquarius ignores the Uranian urge to make changes when change is clearly what Aquarius needs, then Uranus has a way of forcing their hand in his own sudden and unpredictable way. Should an Aquarian end up in a job or career that is clearly unsuitable or has outlived its interest, he or she would be well advised to exit as quickly—and as graciously—as possible.

You hear so many stories about Aquarians who received a terrible shock, and felt that their whole life was unjustly turned upside down when they lost their job or their work dried up. Dig a little deeper and you often find that they weren't happy in the job anyway. They'd simply chosen to ignore the warning signals of boredom, restlessness, and depression. If they don't jump ship, Uranus finds a way of making sure they're pushed. Turning up late for months on end, being difficult, offhand—even arrogant—doesn't win Aquarians any favors with their colleagues or the powers that be.

In all fairness to Aquarians, it can be very hard for them to make that decision to jump. It's a fixed sign, you recall, and what's more, the Saturnian part of their nature urges them to stay with what is safe, rather than go for change. Reconciling this with the Uranian part of their nature that *demands* change and freedom can be a nerve-racking business.

Aquarians—and indeed all who have Uranus strong in their horoscopes—often attribute any adverse twists in their working life to the cold hand of fate. Of course, we all experience setbacks that are not of our making. But a great deal of the time these dilemmas are actually manifestations of internal cries for a new direction. Aquarius is a sign that must learn to recognize when enough is enough, and move on.

It was an Aquarian, Robert Burns who gave us the line "the best laid schemes o' mice an' men . . ." After Aquarius has stopped bemoaning his or her fate, they come to realize that what seemed like a stroke of bad luck was actually a blessing in disguise. Years later, they look back and realize that they would never have gone on to bigger and better things had they not left that job.

Reversal of fortune goes both ways. Uranus is also the bringer of extraordinary opportunity that seems to come out of the blue. You'll hear stories from Aquarians about how a phone call changed everything overnight, about how they received an unexpected job offer and had to make a decision on the spot.

It's Uranus who brings Aquarians a lucky break just when they think things have never looked so bleak. When your ruling planet is the planet of unexpected occurrences, you need to roll with the punches. And you must never say no to the marvelous opportunities that will come your way when you least expect them. And they will. Uranus will see to that.

LOVE AND FRIENDSHIP

No one is easier to make friends with than someone born under the sign that rules friends. Spending time with their friends means a lot to Aquarians, and with their open and welcoming nature, they're the friends others want to spend time with, too.

One of the loveliest things about Aquarians is that they enjoy mixing with all types of people on a basis of true equality. You'll be no less important a friend if you're a struggling student than if you're president of your own empire. They won't judge you by your clothes, and won't think any less of you if you happen to have a skeleton or two in your closet. Any little quirks or idiosyncrasies will only raise your interest value.

Wealth for its own sake doesn't necessarily impress them. But fame, or a little brush with it, excites Aquarians. They'll be there to share the triumph of the friend who's been an unknown Sunday painter for years, and is now being discovered and having his first big exhibition. Especially if the TV cameras have turned up.

As a friend of an Aquarian, you'll be in a circle that's part of another ever-widening circle. An Aquarian's network of friends extends in all directions. Even if a friend goes abroad for ten years, Aquarius will keep in touch. They can be the most enthusiastic of correspondents.

Aquarius, remember, is an air sign. So a meeting of like minds is a necessary prerequisite to any relationship. The communication channels must be open. The typical Aquarian is quick to strike up friendships with co-workers. If you work together, you've clearly got things in common.

There is just about nothing you cannot discuss with your Aquarian friends, and there are few things that they're not interested in hearing about. The conversation will flow from speculations on the time space continuum to why there's the risk of a fascist resurgence and then just as easily turn to who's having an unlikely affair with whom and why it nevertheless suits them perfectly. With Aquarius the discussion will never fizzle into pleasantries such as whether it's going to rain. At least, boredom is not a state that you'll ever drift into in any sort of relationship with an Aquarius.

There's a definite taste for the bohemian life in most Aquarians, though they may live in the suburbs and catch the bus to the city five days a week with people they privately think of as the lemmings of the world, smug in the knowledge that they're not really "one of them."

They're the best at having a good time on a tight budget. We know one Aquarian woman who's so *au fait* with the café scene in her city that she's finally given in to her friends' suggestions that she should write a guide on where to go for the best deal in coffee and cake. The same woman has conducted all her friends to a popular Cambodian diner where you can eat as much bean curd and chili noodles as you can manage for under five bucks. So what if you eat out of plastic rice bowls on orange laminate tables? The food's great—and it's cheap. Aquarians can make do without a tablecloth and matching plates. They're not stingy, but they can be thrifty, and any fun times are a lot more fun for Aquarians when they're getting good value for money.

Suitably fortified with noodles, Aquarius will be ready to take in something cerebral. The more avant-garde, the better. This is a person who (even if you scarcely know them) you can safely take to an exhibition of kinetic sculpture or a performance by a nude ballet.

And if there's a party on, then Aquarius will want to be there.

Aquarius is one of the great partygoers of the zodiac. They're up there with Gemini, Leo, and Sagittarius. So if you're tagging along, be prepared to stay up all night or make your own way home. The Aquarius body clock has a timing all its own.

If your intentions are set on something more serious than just "hanging out" together, then you're going to discover that the Aquarian attitude towards love and romance is like no other. How can you compare Aquarians, renowned for their love of freedom and independence, to anyone else? You can't. And in any case, why would you want to? You've had enough of boring, predictable people who live a boring, predictable life. With Aquarius you've met someone who will keep you interested, and keep you guessing.

Their air of nonchalance is part of what makes ever-enigmatic Aquarians so attractive. Aquarian-style courtship can be a nail-biting experience for the other party, but the "take it or leave it" method hardly ever fails to add to their allure. The heady cocktail of mixed messages can get to even the most resistant of admirers. Just when you think things are really heating up and you reckon the time is ripe to suggest a rendezvous for a quiet Sunday lunch *chez vous* (hinting that you've put aside the whole afternoon and evening for dessert), Aquarius will oh so casually drop the news that he or she has already made plans. Of course, Aquarius won't feel they need to mention what those plans are, which makes *you* feel that you shouldn't ask. It's not surprising that feelings of paranoia begin to creep up on you and you start to wonder, "Is there someone else? Have I got the signals wrong?" Maybe you have. All air signs like to play mind games. Our advice is to give as good as you get. The moment you find terminal flirting no longer any fun, perhaps you should go in search of another Sun sign.

The trouble is, once you're hooked on an Aquarian, it can be hard to leave. Often that's because they're simply so utterly gorgeous. There's a definite Aquarian "look" that's very à la mode and highly desirable. It's lean and laid-back, with suitably crumpled faded jeans and a well-worn T-shirt, with a few pieces of rare ethnic jewelry as an optional extra. Even when they break all the rules of fashion coordination (which they often do), it somehow all comes together and works.

Aquarians have their own kind of natural uncontrived sexiness. Maybe it's got something to do with their hair, which has that wild, just-got-out-of-bed look. Or maybe it's their sparkling eyes, or clear, almost translucent skin. A lot of Aquarians go for the androgynous look. They were the first to teach us not to get hung up on gender stereotypes. Aquarians have an almost intuitive understanding that we are human beings first, and male and female second, though there are some Aquarian women who effect a superfeminine posthippie, Pre-Raphaelite style, and some men who look like they've just stepped out of the pages of a volume of nineteenth-century romantic verse.

One of the most famous descriptions of an Aquarian lover was given by one of his long-suffering mistresses. The poet Lord Byron was "mad, bad, and dangerous to know," according to Lady Caroline Lamb. Byron was infuriating, he was a heartbreaker, and he was lame. But that didn't stop women from falling at his feet. Byron was an irresistible challenge. Many Aquarians are.

There's a pattern Aquarians fall into in relationships, of being drawn to a person and then suddenly pulling back when things look like they're getting too "heavy." It unnerves them to discover that someone has made too much of an inroad into their mind space. Aquarians don't want to be possessed, organized, or controlled by anyone. If someone gets too intense, they interpret it as a serious threat to their personal freedom. Big outpourings of emotion or overwhelming passion can send them running. The best-known exit line ever—"Frankly, my dear, I don't give a damn"—was uttered by that most Aquarian of lovers, Rhett Butler. Lovers of Aquarians may need to keep a lid on the Scarlett O'Hara within if they don't want to see their own Rhett Butler close the door on the relationship. Clarke Gable was an Aquarius, too. And it has been suggested by more than one astrologer that Scarlett O'Hara could only have been an Aries.

The best way—in fact, the only way—to hold on to an Aquarius is not to "hold on" to them at all. Give Aquarius the stimulating companionship they want and the space they need, and you will be the most desirable thing on the planet.

Brain meets Brain is the preferred Aquarian foreplay. So if Aquarius spends the night with you talking about all manner of things, you can consider the relationship to be virtually consummated.

When Aquarians decide that a relationship is for keeps, they'll be just as keen as any other sign to settle down and get married. Aquarius is a fixed sign, and once they make up their mind, it's usually made up forever. The Aquarian need to be their own person and have their personal space has somehow led to the fallacious myth of Aquarius as the reluctant bride or groom. Think of the Aquarians you know. Most of them are married, and leading thoroughly respectable, normal family lives.

The wedding, however, might have been a little unorthodox. Most Aquarian weddings are interesting; some are positively extraordinary. The nuptials of one Aquarian woman we know spring to mind. Off she flew with her husband-to-be to Barbados, where they tied the knot barefoot under a breadfruit tree. It was so romantic, so free.

And all so Aquarian. The bride wore a billowing off-the-shoulder white muslin dress, and put frangipanis in her windswept hair.

Once the frangipanis have lost their intoxicating perfume and you settle down to the realities of everyday life with an Aquarian, things may not turn out to be quite as easygoing and harmonious as you imagined they would be. "Easygoing" for an Aquarius can mean "too hard to live with" for other people. Partners may find themselves struggling with the Aquarian version of "house beautiful," and wondering whether they've become overly neurotic about housework. Living with an Aquarian inevitably means turning a blind eye to the boxes and piles of papers that are breeding silently in corners all over the house. At the root of their abhorrence of housework lies the Aquarian fear that domestic chores could take over their life.

The positive side of the picture is that Aquarians will be tolerant of the husband who wants to pull apart a motor on the kitchen table, or the wife who soaks the plants in the bathtub overnight, or wants to start stripping the wallpaper at 11:00 P.M.

Unless you've married one of those rarer types of Aquarians who are superneat and orderly (they're sure to have a Virgo or Pisces Moon, or Libra or Capricorn on the Ascendant), you're about to discover that there are plenty of Aquarians who can't remember where the vacuum cleaner is kept, let alone how to assemble it. You could save your sanity (and your relationship) by marking out some space for yourself and forbidding your Aquarius to cross the line.

Don't expect Aquarius to keep a mental memo of all the little things that keep a home humming. The fridge won't be bursting with an array of precooked dishes (unless you like to cook yourself). Indeed, there are some Aquarians who regard spending any more than minimum time in the kitchen as a violation of human rights. Partners of Aquarians who don't want to be making the midnight dash to the all-night store to pick up a carton of milk or a can of cat food may find it easier to just assume charge of the housekeeping themselves.

Aquarians seem to have their own interpretation of what you previously thought were universally defined concepts. "Dinner," for example, can take on a whole new meaning for Aquarians, who seem able to eat at any hour of the day or night. There are some single Aquarians who regularly "breakfast" at 1:00 P.M. and could well be enjoying Saturday night dinner when everyone else is tucking into Sunday brunch. Flexible mealtimes don't seem to upset an Aquarian's metabolism at all. But partners who dine alone with the TV too often have been known to cite it as grounds for divorce.

Other things that you may need to redefine are: "coming home soon" (Aquarian translation: "I'm not sure when, but three hours is soon enough") and "Let's take a vacation" (translation: "You arrange it and I'll see how I feel nearer the time"). And when it's your birthday and your Aquarius says, "It's your birthday—leave it all to me," they could be thinking something along the lines of "I'll grab a bunch of flowers on the way home." And the romantic candlelit dinner for two could be a case of which take-out joint has a vacant parking spot. BYO candles, of course. If you can manage not to take any of these things personally and are happy to go along with a fairly unstructured approach to living together, then Aquarius could be your perfect partner.

But there are some partners of Aquarians who end up yearning for a more traditional relationship, the kind that you read about in the romance novels. You know the sort of thing—boy meets girl, they fall in love, boy proposes, wedding bells ring, and Sunday mornings are spent with breakfast and the newspapers in bed. You plan your holiday together, and dinner is on the table every evening (well, almost every evening) at 7:00 P.M.—and it's comforting that way, not a bore . . . or a chore.

The most common complaint directed at "friendly" Aquarians is their lack of spontaneous affection. Their partners sometimes wish for a bit more old-fashioned togetherness of the holding-hands-in-the-movies and smooching-on-the-sofa variety. The sign that likes to keep people at arm's length can sometimes be a bit of a cold fish. Aquarius is not a sign renowned for scaling the heights of passion or plunging into the depths of eroticism. How can it be when it is in Aquarians' very nature to stay a little disinterested and detached? There are many Aquarians who have a little trouble with the concept that a relationship with a lover is in an entirely separate category from a relationship with a friend, or anyone else for that matter.

Which makes it all the more bewildering when Aquarians come across in an effusive manner to people they hardly know. It's not at all unusual for Aquarius to greet a stranger in such a familiar way that you can see people taking a visible step backwards. It seems so out of character because you'd never think of Aquarius as the gushing type. To be fair, they themselves don't realize that their behavior could be a little over the top, and socially inappropriate. It's just their way of being friendly.

It is in the intimacy of a one-on-one relationship—which is, after all, what marriage is all about—that Aquarius can run into serious problems. Aquarius may be a clear-thinking communicator, but when the topic is feelings or, heaven forbid, heavy emotional issues, there could be a total communication shutdown. When partners of Aquarius try to get down to the deep and meaningful, they see Aquarius getting visibly twitchy and restless, so they never quite get around to talking about what's on their mind. And they give up. Gemini and Libra individuals may not have too much of a problem with the Aquarian detachment, but water and earth sign types can find it very distressing.

The wheel of the zodiac is a symbolic cycle of the development of the individual in which each sign anticipates the qualities of the sign to come. If we can acquire even a little of those qualities, it's a big step towards personal growth. Pisces follows Aquarius. Sensitivity to other people's feelings and the ability to tune in to the vibes and create a gentle, soothing ambiance come naturally to Pisceans but demand more conscious effort from Aquarians. The Aquarian who genuinely tries to accommodate other peoples' needs and can bring themselves to admit that their opinions may not always be the only valid ones, will find his or her personal relationships run more smoothly.

Ex-partners of Aquarians often report that one of the most infuriating things about Aquarians is their fondness for two little words: "I know." Two seemingly innocent words that stick in your mind as evidence of Aquarians at their most opinionated. Aquarians have a propensity for dismissing other people's dreams and aspirations. And should they decide they're not in favor of something their partner wants to do, The Water Bearer is perfectly capable of picking up their pitcher and throwing cold water all over their desires. Especially if realizing that desire might require Aquarius to take on more responsibility and give away some of their precious independence. When they're at their most intransigent and most adamant, otherwise encouraging and enthusiastic Aquarians can be terribly discouraging.

Should a relationship go sour, Aquarius will not rush to make the break. Fixed signs don't, they hang in there. But if there is a parting of ways, Aquarius will be able to cut so completely, it's as if the ex has become someone from a past life.

We must be honest. If your idea of marriage is something out of a romance novel, there are other Sun signs that are more suitable— a Leo, a Cancer, or a Pisces, for example. Aquarius is one sign, if not *the* sign, least likely to fit the description of the girl who will give up everything for true love, or the knight in shining armor who will adore you and protect you forever.

But if you're grown-up enough to know that such things only happen in fairy tales, and you're looking for someone who can give you a relationship based on equality and mutual respect, then you can do no better than to settle down with an Aquarian.

When you're married to an Aquarius, you'll know that you belong, but you won't feel that you're owned. Aquarius will understand your need for space and freedom because they need it so much themselves. It's good to know that when you fall in love with an Aquarian, you will always be able to be your own person.

One thing is for sure; life with an Aquarian will never be dull. As the words to that classic Aquarian song go:

When the Moon is in the Seventh House
And Jupiter aligns with Mars,
Then peace will be around us
And love is in the stars . . .

Any Aquarian who knows a little about astrology (and there are plenty who do) knows that the "seventh house" is the house of marriage. And many people happily married to an Aquarian believe that their love was written in the stars.

THE AQUARIAN PARENT

Thank heavens Aquarians are such fast and fantastic organizers. Because there are plenty of Aquarians who are still as involved as ever in their work and all their other interests right up to the day when baby arrives.

These are not the types to waste time fantasizing over the big event before it happens, and they probably won't have the nursery all decked out with mobiles and a tribe of teddy bears waiting in a corner. The efficient, no-nonsense side of Aquarius knows that bottles and baby clothes can be obtained in no time at all.

Adoring parents, Aquarians will be when baby arrives, but there's a limit to their fascination with hand-knitted booties and frilly cribs. The chores of diaper changing and the piles of extra laundry will also quickly lose their charm. Baby or no baby, Aquarius is not a sign that cares to be locked into domestic routine. So before baby arrives is the time for Aquarians to do a bit of honest reflection on their own nature and work out just how much of their own pursuits and their own freedom they'll be willing to sacrifice.

It's a rare Aquarian woman who dreams of renouncing her career and independence to become the ultimate earth mother. Yoko Ono may have been speaking from somewhere near the extreme edge of the Aquarian woman's concept of motherhood when she informed John Lennon, "I am carrying the baby for nine months and that is enough, so you can take care of it afterward. If a mother carries the child and a father raises it, the responsibility is shared." But even the most devoted and loving of Aquarian mothers is a little daunted by the idea of twenty-four-hour, hands-on baby care.

Remember, Aquarian men and women pride themselves on approaching all relationships in a cool and rational manner. They would like to think that any problem can be discussed and resolved with the aid of logic and reason. Unfortunately, that theory doesn't hold with babies and infants, who are not logical and reasonable beings. They cry, they demand, and their emotions are pretty primitive. And that's exactly what Aquarians find difficult to deal with. They soon learn that you can't always appeal to children on an intellectual basis. It just doesn't work.

If it all gets too much, partners of Aquarians may find themselves left literally holding the baby as Aquarius finds some excuse to grab his or her coat and utter those magic Aquarian words, "I'm outta here . . ."

The sensible solution for many Aquarian mothers is to look for support. If the grandmas aren't competing with each other for babysitting rights, it might even be a good idea for Aquarius to consider hiring a professional nanny. This is exactly what one Aquarian mother we know did when she feared she was on the brink of cracking up because it was impossible to have a stimulating conversation with her two-year old. Most Aquarian parents have a psychological need to make regular excursions back into the freedom of a single person's existence. They need to sometimes step off an airplane unencumbered by bags bursting with bottles and diapers.

If a nanny is out of the question, it could be the ideal time in an Aquarian's life to stay home and take up a course of study or do something she never had the time to do when she was working. With computer and fax machine installed, there are many jobs that smart Aquarians can do from home.

Fortunately, Sun signs are inherited. Even if Aquarius hasn't produced a little Aquarius, it's probable that the child will have some planets in Aquarius, and will share the parent's need for his or her own space. Aquarian parents are keen on encouraging their children to become independent. Their children are definitely not going to grow up with the hang-ups caused by a smothering, overprotective parent.

Instead, they will have fond memories of all the exciting things their Aquarius parent introduced them to. Aquarians are keen to share their knowledge and are great believers in children never being too young to start their education. They'll enjoy making model pterodactyls and taking trips into the country to look for river stones possibly even more than the children will. There'll be plenty of fun times for the children when mother or father is an Aquarian.

And is there a parent with a bigger smile anywhere in the auditorium when their son or daughter appears in the school play, or sings a solo with the first grade choir? And when their child takes first prize in the state essay competition, Aquarius will photocopy the winning piece, mail it off to all the relatives, and read it aloud to everyone who comes to visit.

Their children will grow up knowing they can broach any topic with their broad-minded, liberal parent. Mother or father won't fob them off when the conversation turns to politics, sex, or religion. Nor will Aquarius flip out or freeze up if their children bring home friends with an unusual dress sense weighed down by half a dozen earrings and nose rings.

But sometimes Aquarians don't grasp the difference between giving children their own space—and not being there for them. Some children of Aquarians pick up intuitively that their parent would rather not be bothered by certain things, particularly anything that is too emotionally heavy.

There are times when Aquarius may miss the subtle clues that all is not well. They're the first to say that their children are fine and don't have any problems, but is it because they sometimes can't see what they don't want to find? Aquarians are not very big on hugs, cuddles, and heart-to-heart talks. Perhaps the most important breakthrough an Aquarian parent can make is a little modification of their desire to remain detached.

For all their liberal approach to childraising, and for all their respect for the child as an individual, there is a Saturnian streak in all Aquarians that can get stuck in a certain mode of thinking about their offspring's future. If Aquarius has been harboring the expectation that Junior, who is top of the class in math, will go on to a career in science, or become a teacher like father, then he or she may struggle to accept that a future in something entirely different is okay. Some children of Aquarius may have to assert their *own* will to escape the blueprint that their parent has drawn up for them.

When the children are grown, they'll remember the mother or father who taught by example that your life is your own to live. Whoever remembers whether Sunday lunch was always served right on time?

THE AQUARIUS CHILD

Is it your imagination or does your Aquarius baby really stand out from the others? Are all babies so bright and alert? Already they seem to want to know what's going on around them. As the months go by you discover that yes, they are more bright and alert. And by the time they're crawling, you know you've got a real live wire on your hands.

Even as children, Aquarians are never predictable. Don't count on their being the same today as they were yesterday, and be prepared for them to be different again tomorrow. The Aquarian child is often thought of as the one who is different, the wild card in the family.

One thing is certain; Aquarius is not a child who wants to fade into the background. They're quite emphatic about what they like and don't like, what they want to do and what they're not prepared to do, and it will be hard to convince them otherwise. The willfulness of Aquarius shows itself early.

You'll be amazed by some of the ideas they come up with. Even very young Aquarians can be entertaining, and they know how to get good mileage out of their bright personality and their quick-thinking minds. But they're going to give you a run for your money. When little Aquarians have decided they want to go to the park to play with their friends, the fact that it's cold and raining and their friends won't be there won't detract them one little bit. Moments like these are designed to teach you two essential lessons on raising an Aquarian child. First, for a rational and logical thinking sign, Aquarius can be very hard to reason with. Appeals on the grounds of common sense will be countered by apparently commonsensical retorts along the lines of "I'll put on my raincoat and boots." It's hard to argue with that. Secondly, it's difficult to keep them behind closed doors for long. Yes, they do love the sense of being one of the family circle, but the Aquarian need to get out and about starts young, too.

On top of that, they can be remarkably short-sighted about the immediate consequences of their actions. Perhaps it's because their sights are so focused on the excitement that's waiting around the next corner that they don't see the lamppost right in front of them. Aquarius can be a bit accident- and incident-prone at times. The ankles and the lower legs are ruled by Aquarius, so you can expect to be patching up a few bumps and bruises, and bandaging a sprained ankle or two. You can expect, too, some fantastic tales to accompany some of the bruises and mishaps. "I was hit by an orange on the way home" or "I'm late because the bus was early." You know the bus runs every ten minutes. And you know oranges don't just fly through the air unless somebody throws them. Aquarians have a way of making the implausible sound plausible. That inventive little Aquarian mind can be put to good use creating all sorts of perfectly good excuses.

Does this remind you of someone on TV? A boy who would test the patience and the intellect of any parent. He's got an answer for everything and is famous for his back-talk. Bart Simpson, the know-it-all Aquarian child of bumbling, sentimental Homer and long-suffering Marge. Some would call Bart street-smart. Others call him a smart aleck. But Bart is the modern American cool kid. He's out for himself, but when the chips are down, he looks after his own. So what is it about Bart that grates? Has he got an attitude problem? Bart doesn't think so. He seems blissfully unaware that he makes plenty of adults wish for a return to the days when children were seen and not heard. In fact, it was a ten-year-old Aquarian who informed us that Bart is an anagram for Brat and made us realize that Bart, too, could only have been born under the sign of The Water Bearer. It all makes sense. A little research revealed that Bart's creator, Matt Groenig, is also an Aquarian, so he ought to understand perfectly what makes an Aquarian child tick.

Who better than an Aquarian to create a cartoon program about the group dynamics of your average dysfunctional family? And who better than a person with a sentimental, appealing Moon in Cancer—like Matt Groening—to make "The Simpsons" such a likable lot? (Students of astrology will already have picked Homer as a Cancer.) Bart Simpson is an omnipresent reminder to the parents of Aquarius children that they may occasionally need to nip the "Bart factor" in the bud.

Aquarians are confident sociable people. So it's going to be very important to them to fit in with "the gang" or "the club." They'll feel terribly hurt if they're ever excluded. As they grow up, an issue emerges that will stay with them for the rest of their lives—their need to identify with the group while at the same time fearing being just like everyone else. As adults, Aquarians will value their individuality, and others will admire it. But all children, including Aquarians, are essentially conformists. Peer-group pressure dictates that to be one of the group, you can't be *too* different. It can be a young Aquarian's first lesson in conformity versus individuality.

Aquarian children also have a tendency to get hyped up. It's only through experience that Aquarians learn just how much their nervous system can take. The "live wire" can easily short-circuit. Overload is always a potential danger to Aquarians of all ages, and you'll know an Aquarius child is approaching that point when the electrical voltage in the air is palpable and your own nerves are getting zapped.

For all his or her desire to be with people, your young Aquarius needs periods of quiet time to get grounded and restore inner calm. The inquiring Aquarian mind benefits enormously from time alone to follow up on ideas and to ponder discoveries. These are the children who treasure their collections of rocks or shells. The natural world fascinates them. Many Aquarians are budding scientists who will want to study the life cycle of ants and silkworms, or press wildflowers.

Try to choose a school that is neither too liberal nor too disciplinarian. A place that will keep a check on their willfulness yet won't squash their individuality. Most Aquarian children can't wait to go to school. Simply tell them about all the new things they're going to learn and new friends they're going to make, and they'll be dragging *you* to the school gates and running in without once looking back (unless, of course, your Aquarius child has the Moon in one of the more reticent signs such as Cancer or Pisces).

By the same token, you'll find that Moon in Aquarius children— no matter what their Sun sign—will be eager to start school. In childhood our Moon sign lies closer to the surface of our personality. If your child has an Aquarian Moon, you can expect him or her also to be individualistic, independent, and enthusiastic about learning.

Both Sun and Moon in Aquarius children are attracted to the way out and the wacky. Nothing is deemed too weird for some Aquarian children. And if they can manage to rattle their parents' nerves a little, so much the better. Mobiles made from dead spiders and lizards are at least visible and avoidable. But best not to investigate the boxes under the bed. It could be a good idea to designate your Aquarian's bedroom a "no go zone" and send in a robot vacuum cleaner once a week.

The rebellious streak is bound to surface in Aquarius children sometime, somehow. Prepare yourself now for the day when you come home to be greeted by a teenage daughter with green stripes in her hair. And it would be a rare Aquarian child who didn't once, in an otherwise untarnished school career, play hooky with friends.

One Aquarian mother we know told us she was mortified by what she saw as the first signs of the perverse rebel in her fourteen-year-old Aquarian son. She lamented how her previously nature-loving, artistically gifted boy had taken to manufacturing fiendish but ingenious weaponry from junk he found in the garage and the bamboo patch at the end of the street. He had decided to become a mercenary when he left school. "Where did I go wrong?" she said. "He listened to Mozart in utero and I fed him on brown rice and pawpaw—now he wants to kill people."

He doesn't, of course. He's just winding her up, exploring his native inventiveness, and putting out the first message that he won't necessarily be fitting in with her plans for his future. Parents of Aquarian children would at times be better off turning one blind eye to the antics of their offspring and some of the ideas they come up with (but keeping the other eye wide open). This is not a sign that tolerates too much regimentation or close supervision. Give them an inch, and most of the time you can trust that they won't take a mile. A lot of Aquarius's rebelliousness is just hot air. Perhaps the most important lesson you can give young Aquarians is to learn to think before they act. But just like Bart, Aquarians have got the brains to get themselves out of most sticky situations.

You may suspect that over the years you've been summoned to the school for more than your fair share of chats with the teacher, and you might reckon that you've spent more than most parents on Band-Aids and antiseptic. But how proud you're going to be when your Aquarius grows up and does something the other kids never even dreamed of.

You always knew that face beaming at you from the first-grade class photo was never destined to end up on the conveyor belt of life . . .

BORN UNDER AQUARIUS

Betty Friedan	Charles Darwin
William Burroughs	Neil Diamond
Farrah Fawcett	Susan B. Anthony
Charles Dickens	John McEnroe
Alice Cooper	Burt Reynolds
Yasser Arafat	Anton Chekhov
Evangeline Adams	Carole King
Princess Caroline of Monaco	Oliver Reed
Princess Stephanie of Monaco	Benny Hill
Vanessa Redgrave	Jack Nicklaus
Bob Marley	Greg Norman
Charlotte Rampling	Nastassia Kinski
Christopher Marlowe	Phil Collins
Eva Braun	Lisa Marie Presley
Boris Pasternak	Boris Yeltsin
Zsa Zsa Gabor	Babe Ruth
Jack Lemmon	Laura Dern
Michael Jordan	Axl Rose
Mary Quant	Tom Selleck
Mia Farrow	

PISCES

February 20–March 20

♓

Ruling planets

NEPTUNE AND JUPITER

He who would know the world, seek
first within his being's depths; he
would truly know himself, develop interest in the world.

Rudolf Steiner—born February 27

THE PISCES NATURE

Why is it so difficult to identify a Pisces? What is it about the last sign of the zodiac that defies classification? With their love of a good time and good company, they behave just like a Leo. At least some of the time. At other times they display such dry, sardonic wit and talk so knowledgeably about the stock market that you'd swear you were talking to a Capricorn. Then sometimes they sparkle like a Gemini and are every bit as chatty. That's, of course, when they haven't retreated into a private world of their own. Just like a Scorpio.

The last sign of the zodiac is the hardest to pick because it's actually a composite of all the personality traits that have developed along the way in the previous eleven signs. The Pisces man or woman is like a myriad of people in the one person. And each and every one is a Pisces.

Like chameleons, Pisceans are able to draw on whatever facet of their personality they want to, changing colors to match their surroundings. One day they're the best of hosts, the next they're the hermit, home alone, savoring their own company.

It may be hard to put a finger on their nature, but there are certain traits that come to mind when you think of Pisces. They're sensitive, even hypersensitive at times. They're gentle and prefer to avoid any kind of confrontation. They're highly imaginative (which can work both for and against them). And they're intuitive. There are many Pisceans who are so intuitive they're psychic, though they may never give their gift a name.

There's something else that distinguishes Pisceans from the rest of the crowd. Pisces is the sign that rules man's longing to transcend the self and connect with something greater. Call it the Divine. The Numinous. The ineffable. The One. Call it God. Whatever you call it, all Pisces individuals—whether they realize it or not—need to seek a spiritual meaning to their lives.

It may sound like pretty esoteric stuff, but it's impossible to fully understand Pisces without coming to grips with the spiritual journey of this, the final sign.

In the first sign, Aries, the soul makes its symbolic entrance as the infant of the zodiac. The ego is born. It runs the gamut of human experience and arrives at Aquarius, who aspires to be an independent individual within the whole of humanity. What could possibly be bigger than humanity? The concept of the Divine.

No other person is more in touch with the ephemeral realms. In fact, Pisces is called the "sign of the mystic." There is something a little otherworldly about Pisceans, as if part of them inhabits a dimension that most others only ever get a glimpse of. Mind you, the Piscean familiarity with that "other dimension" also makes Pisces very *unworldly* at times. There is definitely one type of Piscean whose friends think they are "lost in space" a great deal of the time. Even the average well-adjusted Pisces seems to get a little confused and overwhelmed by the practical matters of the everyday material world. Pisces can slip into a kind of inertia and apathy over quite ordinary things such as paying the bills on time or fixing the fence. Some would call it laziness, and they could be right. But from Pisces' point of view, there are some things that are just not worth investing too much time and energy in.

So how is it that some of the greatest doers and achievers of this or any other age have been Pisceans? People like George Washington, Michelangelo, Alexander Graham Bell, and Yuri Gagarin—the first man in space.

The answer lies in the symbol for Pisces—two fish joined by a cord swimming in opposite directions. One fish swims towards the spiritual realm, the other towards the material. Often the fish are depicted without the cord. But the meaning of the symbol is lost if the cord is missing because the cord is what keeps the fish connected and in balance. One fish can never pull too far away from the other. As different as they are, the two fish must learn to coexist. The astrologer's glyph for Pisces is a stylized shorthand version of The Fish and their cord.

The balance between the spiritual and the material is one that we all need to find in life. But achieving that balance is a core issue for Pisceans. The Pisces individual needs to make a conscious effort to respect both of the fish that dwell within his or her nature.

Pisces is a dual sign, meaning it's two creatures in one image. There's a multiplicity about the Pisces personality that's very similar to the other dual signs, Gemini and Sagittarius. They're multidimensional, multiskilled, multicolored, and often, it appears to others, multieverything. Their malleable nature is what makes them such marvelous actors, both onstage and in real life. A Pisces can be whatever you want him or her to be. If Pisces is in a room full of bankers, he or she can credibly play the part of Mr. or Ms. Corporate Flyer. If found in the company of artists, Pisces will talk postmodernism and abstract expressionism like a professional.

All the dual signs have what astrologers call a mutable quality, which means adaptability is one of their best assets. There is probably no one as adept as Pisceans at swimming with the current. And no one with such an understanding of how futile it is to swim against the tide. "Go with the flow" is an expression that was probably first said by a Pisces.

Pisces is also the last of the water signs. And along with Cancer and Scorpio, Pisces people function primarily on the intuitive emotional plane. How they *feel* about something or someone governs their reactions and a lot of the decisions they make in life. All water-sign people are sensitive to the "vibes" they pick up from people and their environment. But Pisceans have what psychics call an "open aura." They can sense things that others miss altogether, absorbing messages and signals almost subliminally.

All the water signs are sympathetic souls. The nurturing quality is well developed. Rarely is a Pisces judgmental. They genuinely feel for the unfortunates of the world. When they see others who are suffering or down on their luck, they are likely to think, "There but for the grace of God go I." Compassion is perhaps the noblest of the Piscean qualities.

There are many charitable acts, big and small, performed by Pisceans that restore your faith in human nature. One Piscean gentleman (literally a gentle man) gave us food for thought about the compassionate Piscean nature. He was standing in a line waiting to pay his telephone bill and listening to a woman at the counter asking for an extension on her account and pleading not to have her phone disconnected. She had three children in tow and was obviously strapped for cash. Unobtrusively our Pisces friend went up to the counter and paid her bill.

Every Pisces needs to be needed. When they perform acts of kindness without any thought of return, they seem to know that they're actually doing something very fulfilling for themselves as well.

Because they are aware of the oneness of all life, there is no anguish, no suffering, that a Pisces cannot relate to. Like the opposite sign, Virgo, Pisces derives a deep soul-satisfaction from caring for people and animals. Both signs share a special reverence for nature. There are many Pisceans among those who leave seed in the park for the birds and food on the back doorstep for the stray cats.

Springing from the Pisces watery sensitivity comes their great power of imagination. The world of the arts is full of Pisceans. But the Pisces imagination is not limited to poetry, painting, and music. Abstract thought requires imagination, too. And you're just as likely to find creative and imaginative Pisceans interested in philosophy, mathematics, and science. Young Pisceans may be unenchanted with arithmetic, but develop a love for mathematics when they're introduced to the abstraction of algebra and the beauty of geometry.

"Imagination is more important than knowledge," said Pisces Albert Einstein (born March 14). There must be something to it because it's become a slogan emblazoned on T-shirts everywhere. And Einstein himself has become something of a pop icon.

Think of Einstein and you think of genius. You visualize a slightly disheveled, absentminded old gentleman in slippers and a cardigan. Here was a man who helped rewrite the laws of physics, yet couldn't find a pair of matching socks to put on in the morning. How can you be expected to worry about your wardrobe when your mind is on greater things? Besides, nonmatching socks can always be turned into a fashion statement. There's one fashion-conscious advertising executive we know who has made the Einstein nonmatching socks his trademark. He's a Pisces, too, of course.

All creative minds need time out to be alone with their thoughts. And Pisceans are no exception. No matter how fond they are of family and friends, they have an almost biological need for regular periods of solitude. Solitude and serenity restore the Pisces body and soul. Pisces is not a tough sign with energy to burn, and they're not very resistant to the hurly-burly of a competitive world. They do, however, possess endurance and a self-containment that carry them through stressful situations better than many. As Pisceans become increasingly aware of their nature and realize that their energies are easily drained, they learn to cultivate a self-protective detachment and learn to stay clear of certain environments and certain people.

But there are plenty of young Pisceans who ignore the warning signals of fatigue and overload and who work too hard at having a good time. Einstein also said, "I live in that solitude which is painful in youth but delicious in maturity." Words that every older Piscean will relate to. And a very young Piscean might like to reflect on.

The possession of a vivid imagination naturally sets you up for a rich fantasy life. And that can be the Piscean double-edged sword. There's a Walter Mitty type of Fish who, to others, would seem to squander much productive time on pipe dreams. But as every creative person will tell you, it is in dreaming that the creative process begins.

Imagination, sleep, and dreams come under the auspices of Neptune, the ruling planet of Pisces. King Neptune of myth reigned over the oceans of the world, riding across the waves in his chariot pulled by winged white horses. Neptune has a benign side to his character, but a darker, destructive side, too. He has the power to give sailors a safe passage across calm waters or to call up mountainous waves and violent storms that seem to come from nowhere. The open sea can be a terrifying place. Neptune can cause people in his thrall to become becalmed in situations in which it's impossible to make any headway, and listlessness takes over. Neptune has much to do with the infamous Piscean procrastination.

Water is the symbol of fertility—of body and mind. The primordial oceans that Neptune rules represent the receptive womb where the creative spark can implant and grow. Anyone who has achieved success in the arts or work that demands a fertile imagination is bound to have planets in Pisces or a strong and powerful Neptune in his or her horoscope.

It's one of those wonderful examples of astrological synchronicity that the planet Neptune has two moons that are named after the king and queen of fairies—Oberon and Titania, whom we know from Shakespeare's *A Midsummer Night's Dream*. Indeed, Neptune's influence is often as hard to pin down as a dream. He rules the intangible, the nebulous, and the indefinable. But such is the nature of imagination, the very stuff that dreams are made of.

It is Neptune who causes situations to shift and turn, to dissolve and reappear in another form. Astrologers counsel clients who are experiencing a Neptunian influence that all may not be entirely the way it appears. It's hard to get a clear view when Neptune is in the air. Nothing is certain. Nothing is for sure. Only after the Neptunian mists of confusion have lifted can you see again with clarity. If you have the feeling that, deep down, all is not quite right, you can be sure that Neptune is lurking in the background. Neptune is the planet of deception . . . and self-deception. He's also incredibly seductive and beguiling.

All those beautiful mythological beings such as the Sirens and the Lorelei who lured sailors to a watery grave were mysterious Neptunian creatures. Like them, Neptune leads you into the land of illusion where it's very easy to fall into delusion.

Who can say precisely where the borderline lies between imagination and delusion? Pisces least of all. All Pisceans have a tendency to see only what they want to see. They always keep a pair of rose-colored glasses tucked in their pocket to put on when the occasion calls for it. They can't see—or more to the point, they don't *want* to see—that the man or woman they've fallen in love with is totally unsuitable. Or that the colleague at work who has befriended them is actually exploiting them. Things that are crystal-clear to others are not to those Pisceans who set themselves up for a grand delusion.

When Pisceans become prey to other people's schemes and scams, it's as if their famous intuition deserts them. But just as it's easy for Pisceans to be deluded, so, too, is it easy for them to delude others. If Pisceans can fall for dubious deals and people, they themselves can be quite shameless about misleading other people in all sorts of ways. Often for the sake of expediency, it must be said. But it's still deception. Pisceans have a bit of a bad reputation for taking the easy way out and slipping into a kind of moral laziness when it suits them.

You see, most Pisceans don't want life to be any more difficult than it need be. And if that means telling a little white lie occasionally to make life easier for them and for everyone else, then is it such a terrible thing? It's far less upsetting, for example, for a Pisces to simply stop phoning a lover rather than put him or herself on the line and deal with the uncomfortable job of saying the relationship is over. The Pisces who really wants a job is quite capable of dismissing any moral qualms about telling a prospective employer that they've got heaps of experience when actually they've got very little—or none at all. Pisces is the master of bluff.

Most Pisceans are prepared to bend reality and the truth to avoid the messy explanations and confrontations they hate so much. Occasionally Pisceans trip themselves up, though usually they manage to swim away just in time. How do they get away with it? The answer to that may lie as much with Jupiter as it does with Neptune.

Before Neptune was discovered in 1846, Jupiter was the sole ruler of Pisces. And it would be a mistake to forget that Jupiter, the king of the gods, still rules Pisces as he accounts for a lot of the Piscean characteristics, such as the good luck that often turns up at the eleventh hour when things are looking hopeless. In spite of their regular retreats into wistful melancholia, most Pisceans, rather like Sagittarians, have an underlying optimism that things will somehow work out.

Pisces, in fact, shares Jupiter with Sagittarius, which explains some of the similarities between the two signs. Both Pisceans and Sagittarians are philosophical by disposition and are very interested in spiritual and metaphysical matters. Their minds have scope, but attention to detail bores them. Both love to travel, and there are many Pisceans—and Sagittarians—who take up residence in a foreign country, even if only for a year or two.

Pisces is just as clever as Sagittarius at sniffing out a good opportunity. And they're equally devoted to good living. There are some Pisceans for whom no amount of the good life is enough. These are the ones who frequent nightclubs, turn up at every party, and never go to bed before 2:00 A.M.

Pisces takes first prize for escapism. There is more than one way to avoid facing reality, responsibility . . . and yourself. The commonest one—the endless pursuit of a good time—might not even be thought of as escapism, but it is.

There's a character in a well-loved story written by a Piscean who encapsulates the Pisces desire to escape into a more glamorous and exciting life. In *The Wind in the Willows,* by Kenneth Grahame, Toad, the Pisces, is eventually saved from himself by his loyal and eminently sensible friends, Mole, Rat, and Badger (all of whom are, without doubt, practical earth-sign types). If you're not familiar with this wonderful story, it's worth reading because it's full of insights into the Pisces personality—from the first page to the last.

The young Toad belongs to the landed gentry. He lives in the grandest house in the district. While Mole, Rat, and Badger are content with their modest, respectable lives by the riverbank, Toad craves excitement. His first encounter with a motorcar sends him into a spin. Instantly he is infatuated with the romance of the open road, and all he can do is sit by the road imitating the "poop poop" of the horn. Enthralled, Toad immediately procures one for himself and becomes the terror of the countryside. As Rat says, *"He is now possessed. He has got a new craze, and it always takes him that way, in its first stage. He'll continue like that for days now, like an animal walking in a happy dream, quite useless for all practical purposes . . ."* For Toad, the Piscean self-destructive spiral has just begun.

Following his first serious mishap with his motorcar, his friends set out on a mission of mercy to teach him to be a "sensible Toad." After some initial resistance and throwing of tantrums, Toad subsides into sobs of contrition and seems ready to repent. Badger takes Toad aside and gives him a good fatherly talking to before bringing Toad to confess to the general company that he's sorry for what he's done. There's a long pause. At last Toad shouts, "No!" The Badger is scandalized. "You backsliding animal, didn't you tell me just now, in *there*—" "O, yes, yes, in *there*," said Toad impatiently. "I'd have said anything in there . . . I'm not a bit sorry or repentant really, so it's no earthly good saying I am; now, is it?"

So, Mole, Rat, and Badger decide to confine Toad to the house for his own good. But Toad feigns illness, and while Rat goes in search of a doctor, he escapes. He steals a car, lands in jail, escapes dressed as a washer-woman, tricks a barge woman and a train driver into a free ride, and finally, in a state of utter distress, he is once again rescued by his long-suffering friends, only to discover that he can't return to his ancestral home because it's been invaded by evil stoats and weasels.

For Toad, a stroke of Jupiterian luck always manages to forestall total disaster. As if often the case with the real-life Pisceans who push their luck, Toad quickly moves back and forth between depression and desperation, and outrageous optimism. The tale has a happy ending. The stoats and weasels are sent packing, and Toad finally becomes a truly reformed Toad. Being the good-hearted and generous fellow that he fundamentally is (why else would his friends tolerate his antics?), he throws a banquet to celebrate his homecoming.

Toad renounces his futile, foolish, and costly ways of trying to "transcend" responsibilities and real life. His adventures—and the desires that motivated them—hardly seem so terribly wicked, but as the story reveals, they always lead to trouble.

Among Pisceans there is no shortage of "Toads" who are intent on living a sybaritic life of self-indulgence and who cover up their fears or misgivings with bravado and self-inflation.

And if it's not self-inflation, it's the opposite—self-deprecation. The "I'm not good enough" or "I can't do it" Piscean response is, curiously, another cover-up and another excuse for not realizing their potential. There are some Pisces who offer their disinterest in worldly affairs as a valid excuse for not trying to do their best. They conveniently push responsibilities aside and always have a bag of ready-made excuses for why they've decided not to write the book they've been talking about for ten years, or why it's no use completing their degree, or why they can't revise their résumé so they don't miss the deadline for that job application. Some of the classic Pisces excuses run along the lines of: "I've still got some research to do . . ." "My head's not in the right place . . ." "The place I'm living in is not right . . ." "I'm waiting for a good Jupiter transit . . ." What a waste of talent, think the friends of Pisces.

They can be the greatest of time wasters, with every rationalization in the book, but ultimately they can't fool themselves. Inwardly Pisceans *do* sense the futility and they *do* have a fear of failure. Sometimes Pisces can't bring themselves to put an idea into some tangible form because they worry too much about whether it would ever be as good in reality as it is in their imagination. Pisces can sabotage their ideas before they ever get going. But if they don't tackle the job, the poem, the film, or even painting the house, it can drag them down into a serious depression, and into that famous Pisces self-undoing. It's a vicious circle. The more Pisces procrastinates and indulges in self-destructive thinking and behavior, the more nothing gets done.

Yet Pisceans, like Toad, are often blessed with the support of indispensable key people in their lives. They're usually trusted friends who can see the goodness and potential in Pisces and give encouragement, all the while being careful not to crush Pisces' spirit.

It is often, though, a fine line between helping someone and allowing him or her to become dependent on you. Pisceans have a passive, even lazy streak in their nature that can become parasitical. There are some who deliberately set out to avoid the full responsibility of running an independent life. Paradoxically, independence and having only yourself to answer to is a Pisces dream. It's a common Pisces aspiration to be able to live solely unto yourself and have the tedious tasks taken care of by someone else.

It is, remember, the purpose of this sign to seek a connection with something beyond the self, to reach out for a spiritual meaning to life. The Pisceans who have a compulsion to buy themselves something new every week, who must own a flashy car, who regularly blow out their credit cards, and who are always the last to leave the party are looking for meaning in all the wrong places.

These hedonistic Pisceans who crave external stimuli as a means of transcendence are trying to take themselves out of themselves by wanting to maintain a constant "high." Pisces is a sign easily seduced by the transcendental qualities of drugs and alcohol. At their worst, they can be terribly weak-willed and easily succumb to temptation. If it's not substance abuse, it can be people abuse. Pisceans can fall in love overnight and lose themselves in their "beloved" who becomes the instantaneous solution to all their problems. Again, they're seeking a blissful union with something that, because it's external, cannot last.

There are many creative, gifted Pisceans who have enormous potential but for whom escape—in the form of drinking too much too often, spending too much too often, or partying too hard too often—is an attempt to anesthetize their personal pains and soften the blow of what they see as a gross, unfeeling, and hard world. Part of Pisces' function as the last sign of the zodiac is to be the sign of "self-undoing." Some Pisceans can be their own worst enemy.

In many ways it's not an easy destiny to be born under the sign that must deal with the spiritual dimension of life. But those who push aside this fundamental Piscean issue invariably experience an emptiness because they sense something integral to their nature is missing.

Pisces is a sign with a deep religious and spiritual urge. For personal fulfillment, they must face this fact. Those who don't may appear to have taken the easy way out, but in the long run it's harder on Pisces to deny their true nature. The Pisceans who *do* pursue their interests in spiritual and esoteric matters find they have a natural counterpoint to living in the material world.

Rudolf Steiner was a spiritual teacher who devoted his life to this core Piscean issue. As he said, "Those who disregard the mystery of the human being, either because of their condition in life or a lack of interest, very easily fall prey to a kind of soul hunger and to what happens as a result of this—a sort of atrophy in the life of the soul, an uncertainty and powerlessness, an inability to find one's way in the world."

Steiner was a Pisces, born at the time when scientific materialism was the accepted philosophy and it was fashionable to believe that man had no need of divine aid. In intellectual circles, anything religious or esoteric was synonymous with superstition. Steiner was an advocate of the human need for a spiritual life, but he was a well-educated man, and he certainly wasn't advising anyone to drop everything and join a monastery.

A Pisces, or anyone for that matter, who is spiritually inclined is wise to keep an open, objective, and inquiring mind. And you can only do that by keeping one foot (or one fish) in the real world. The two "worlds" are inextricably linked, just like The Fish of Pisces. If you "would know the world," as Steiner said, you must look within. Likewise, if you want to look within and tend to your spiritual well-being, you must not turn away from the practical demands of the outside world.

Astrology teaches that in our opposite sign we find the qualities that bring out the best in our own Sun sign. For Pisces, the lessons from earthy Virgo are self-discipline, a strong work ethic, and plain common sense. Virgos don't cut corners or look for the easy way out. As opposite ends of the same pole, there is also much that Pisceans and Virgoans share. They are both nature lovers who see the interconnectedness of all things.

Steiner's approach to spirituality—and to life—was holistic. Most people know his name through the Steiner (or Waldorf) schools. But few know that he was the pioneer of biodynamic farming, that he developed a form of spiritual dance called eurythmy, and that he practiced color therapy. You could say he was a man well ahead of his time, a harbinger of a renewed search for meaning beyond the material. Funny how times change. There are still plenty of materialists around, but it's no longer fashionable to decry the spiritual, or even to be antireligious.

There's so much talk about the coming "Age of Aquarius." Talk that fills us with expectation and hope for a better future. But what is largely ignored is the fact that the "Age of Pisces" is now drawing to a close. A Great Age in astrology lasts a little over two thousand years. And the beginning of the Age of Pisces roughly coincided with the birth of Christ. The Christian mysteries are part of the myth of Pisces. Indeed, the first symbol that Christians adopted was the Fish, and the idea of sacrifice to a higher force belongs to this sign. The current resurgence of interest in spirituality and metaphysics has as much to do with the end of the Piscean age as it does with the beginning of the Age of Aquarius.

Just as some Sun sign descriptions play down the Piscean connection with spiritual issues (understandably, perhaps, since these matters are hard to put into words), so, too, are they quick to portray Pisces as a weak-willed and "wishy-washy" sign.

It's true that Pisceans often don't take definitive action when perhaps they sometimes ought to. They are rarely combative by nature (unless they have a fiery Ascendant), and there are some who will do anything to avoid anger or hostility even to the point of sacrificing their own needs in order to make life with a more dominant personality bearable.

But maybe Pisces knows something that more aggressive types don't. Maybe they understand that there's usually no point in wasting energy on angry scenes. Pisces knows when it is better not to take the bait or rail against the bullies and the bad guys. When The Fish flicks its tail and swims off downstream, is it weak? Or is it wise?

Ambitious is not a word you see at the top of the list of typical Pisces characteristics. Ambition, after all, requires a certain combative and competitive temperament. But it would be a big mistake to write off all Pisceans as unambitious and unworldly.

Jupiter lends his entrepreneurial skills to Pisceans. And, like Sagittarians, Pisceans are prepared to take risks. Big risks. The Jupiterian gambling instinct frequently works in their favor. Even when they do have to cut their losses, they'll philosophically pick themselves up in the knowledge that there's always another day . . . and another deal.

Global media baron Rupert Murdoch is a Pisces. Surprised? He certainly doesn't come across as your brutal business tycoon. He speaks softly and courteously, and doesn't like formal meetings. Yet this is the man who owns the TV satellite service that can reach two thirds of the people in the world and has been called a "pirate" and a "predator."

Murdoch is one of those entrepreneurial Pisceans who takes enormous risks, moves quickly, and acts on intuition. Many of his methods, in fact, are very Piscean.

It's hard to say exactly where Murdoch stands politically or idealistically. He changes his colors, and has even changed his nationality. Take the story of his entrance into the lucrative China market. Murdoch's "Star" network used to beam the BBC world service into China, but when he discovered that the BBC was a stumbling block to expansion into that huge market, he simply took the BBC off Star and replaced it with Chinese movies. If objective, unbiased news upset Beijing, then it had to go. As Murdoch said, "The BBC was driving them nuts. It's not worth it." The chairman of *The Financial Times* explained it another way, "When matters of principle and expediency clash with Rupert, expediency wins every time." Mutable Pisces can sometimes justifiably be accused of having mutable morals.

There are many "successful" Pisceans who are happy to do whatever they have to do in order to win. As far as they are concerned, expediency demands that the division between what's right and what's wrong remains blurred. Does Murdoch push expediency further than it should be pushed, or is he one of the world's smartest businessmen, with all the best Piscean attributes of adaptability, flexibility, tolerance, and creative intuition? As Pisces would say, you be the judge.

As the last sign, Pisces is, in one sense, postegoic. It can rise above the self. But because the zodiac is a wheel, with Pisces preceding Aries (the sign of the emergence of the ego), it is also *preegoic*. In this sense it has the potential to be anything it wants to be. All those wonderful, highly imaginative ideas are gestating, just waiting to emerge. The Pisces time of year (February and March) is the time when nature is busy underground, preparing to burst forth into the energy of spring . . . and a profusion of life and color.

Pisces must never for a moment think that their dreams are unachievable. If the talents of this sign are not to remain latent or be stillborn, Pisces need only look to the powerful symbol of the two Fish. Their challenge is to keep the fish of the material world and the fish of the spiritual world in healthy stasis. Then neither one can turn into a piranha. When Pisceans have achieved this happy balance, they know instinctively when it's time to let their imagination run wild, and when it's time to "get real." When they need to push forward, and when they need to pull back. When to put on their work boots and when to put on their slippers.

One of the best-loved holy men of modern times, Meher Baba (born February 25), was a Pisces. His name means Compassionate Father. Meher Baba founded no religion, sect, or cult, and said his message was for all nations and creeds, rich and poor. Meher Baba is famous for taking a vow of silence and not speaking for forty-four years. But he is even more famous for instructing us, "Don't worry— be happy."

These words do not imply that Meher Baba was a Piscean who gave everyone permission to do whatever they pleased. What is frequently omitted are his preceding words. Words that are key to his message, and key to the meaning of the sign of Pisces. What Baba actually said was:

"Do your best. Then don't worry—be happy."

Every wise Pisces knows that when you do your best, you have no reason in the world to worry. And every reason in the world to be truly happy

THE PISCES CAREER AND DIRECTION

Ovid, the great Roman poet, once said, "Let your hook be always cast; in the pool where you least expect it, there will be a fish." As a Pisces, he understood that the secret to Pisces' success is remaining open to all possibilities. Indeed, staying receptive is just about the most important thing a career-minded Piscean can do.

Should Pisces' intuition tell them that something's worth pursuing, or that they've got what it takes to become a writer, a teacher, a trader, or even prime minister, they shouldn't allow anyone to put them off. Nor should they try to talk themselves out of it either (which they can be pretty good at).

After all, if a Pisces can make a hugely successful movie about a pig who thinks he's a sheepdog, then is there anything that Pisceans cannot turn themselves to? Is there anything that is too way out or too out of reach? George Miller, doctor-turned-film-director (so many Pisceans end up in work they never started out in), is sure to have known that he was on to something that would capture the public imagination when he discovered *Babe.*

There's certainly no doubt that Babe is a Pisces, because he has proved that pigs—or Pisceans—can do things that people think pigs—or Pisceans—can't do. Babe's owner, Farmer Hoggett, must be a Pisces too. He was broad-minded and imaginative enough to see Babe's potential and give him a go, much to the disbelief of his wife and the other farmers who thought he'd lost his marbles. They were all forced to eat humble pie when Babe won the sheepdog trials, and the hearts of animal lovers and filmgoers everywhere.

Neptune rules film and photography. And the magical, Neptunian, real-but-not-real world of film attracts many Pisceans. The movie theater is still the place where we lose ourselves for a couple of hours.

Often imagination is the very best asset Pisces have, no matter what field they work in. It's said that success is 5 percent inspiration and 95 percent perspiration. True enough. Whoever said it first was obviously born under an earth sign and was keen to extol the hard-work factor. But without that elusive but essential 5 percent, no amount of blood, sweat, and tears will produce anything special. Pisces have little or no trouble with the 5 percent. It's that other 95 that they can have difficulty coming to grips with.

Every possible kind of artistic career is open to Pisces. It's a sign that knows no boundaries. The entertainment industry is teeming with Fishes of all varieties. Their particular affinity is with music and dance. Two of the greatest dancers ever, Nijinsky and Nureyev, were both Pisceans.

You'll find Pisceans who excel in every type of musical expression. People who don't know anything about classical music have heard the music of Antonio Vivaldi. They've probably got a copy of *The Four Seasons* in the car, which they listen to when they need to transcend the long traffic jam home. Interesting, is it not, that the greatest of the Venetian composers was a Pisces, and that Venice is a city that astrologers have long believed comes under the sign of Pisces. How could such a soulful and otherworldly place belong to any other sign?

Frédéric Chopin, who was also a Pisces, wrote music you can pour your soul out to. It's uncanny how artists unconsciously reveal their Sun sign in their choice of names and titles. Piscean Glenn Miller's most enduring title is "In the Mood." At the other end of the musical spectrum is Nirvana, the band led by ill-fated Piscean Kurt Cobain. Unfortunately, Cobain (like a few too many Piscean musicians) pushed the pursuit of an altered state of consciousness too far.

Few artistic Pisceans are destined to end up in the same league as Vivaldi or Ovid, or as Michelangelo, Rossini, or Handel (all born under the sign of The Fish), but the commercial world is bursting with opportunities for imaginative and creative Pisceans.

Fashion is a Neptunian business because fashion is all about trends, and Neptune is the planet that rules trends. Whether they design, sell, buy, promote, photograph, or write about it, a career in fashion is perfect for Pisceans with flair, as well as for anyone born under any sign who has Neptune strong in his or her horoscope.

The Neptune effect is subliminal and elusive. It's subtle, but powerful enough to dictate what the next wave will be. Neptune plays a big role in the tastes and the desires of the masses, which is why Neptune has much to do with the *zeitgeist* and why Neptunian people are often one step ahead of the rest. Indeed, there are some Neptunian types who are so far ahead of their time that some of their brilliant ideas are initially rejected.

This was the case for one Piscean fashion designer we know whose ideas were cast aside in the "too way out" basket so often that she started to doubt her own abilities and ended up in a crisis of confidence. But she hung in long enough to see somebody else come up with concepts that were virtually the same as hers . . . a couple of years later. Experience taught her that her ideas were rarely wrong. It was just that her timing was often premature. Now she files away all those way out designs and pulls them out when everyone else is catching up.

The intuition of Neptunian people gives them this ability to "see" a whole new look or "hear" a whole new sound before it reaches the airwaves. It comes close to being mediumistic, and indeed there are some Pisceans who make a living from this gift. Psychic consultants of all sorts employ the powers of Neptune.

Because Neptune dictates what will speak to the mass mind, he always has a role to play (subtle as it may be) in politics. There have been many Piscean politicians and statesmen who have successfully accessed this Neptunian grasp of collective desires. Pisces is not a sign that is usually intent on wielding power for its sake. Often the opposite is true. But every sign has its own way of making its mark in politics, and has its own style of leadership. The Pisces who arrives in a leadership position is amenable, tolerant, flexible, and open to other people's opinions.

Mikhail Gorbachev was a politician with an unmistakably Piscean style. He put *Glasnost* into the global vocabulary when he "opened up" the Soviet Union, and proclaimed openness as the way for Russia to go.

The first president of the United States was also a Pisces. It was George Washington who chose the pyramid with the mysterious eye for the American one-dollar bill. Washington and many of the founding fathers were students of arcane lore. Power, as Pisces has always known, is not something man alone can create or control. It ultimately comes from something higher. Only Scorpio rivals Pisces in its understanding of the unseen forces that are at work in the world.

Advertising is an industry that relies on people who've got a handle on fads, fashions, and trends. When you consider that advertising is all about coming up with ideas that the masses will relate to, you can see why Pisces are so good at it. Pisceans and Neptunian types are well represented in advertising agencies and all the businesses that support them. The horoscopes of commercial illustrators, makeup artists, jingle writers, directors, producers, and photographers all need the Neptunian input. What's more, ads are generally short-term projects, and that appeals to Pisces. On the whole, they're not suited to the long-haul jobs and will instinctively avoid them because they know they can have a problem maintaining focus.

Knowing what people will buy is a Pisces talent. And when it comes to consumerism, Pisceans can be the most dedicated of consumers themselves. Pisces loves stumbling upon old curios in thrift shops, but this is not your bargain-basement shopper. When they are in the mood to indulge, Pisceans go in for divine decadence. Then nothing is too sumptuous, too gorgeous, or too lavish. Beautiful Venus comes to the aid of the Pisceans who make a career from their special ability to create ambiance and their talent for interior decor. In astrology, Neptune is said to be the higher octave of Venus, which means Pisceans are not just interested in beautiful objects per se, but more in the effect they have on the senses, and how they elevate the spirits.

Moreover, Venus is exalted in the sign of Pisces, where she blossoms as the goddess of beauty. Aesthetics can become almost be a "calling" for some Pisceans. How wonderful to make money by providing beautiful things that will help people escape from the ugly "real" world, and spend your working day surrounded by things that are absolutely fabulous.

If you've watched the British comedy series "*Absolutely Fabulous*," you can see why Edina could only be a Pisces. We suspect she's got a Sagittarius Ascendant (she knows she was made for the big time) and a Taurus Moon (she receives alimony from not one but *two* ex-husbands). But there are plenty of giveaway signs that she's a Pisces. She heads up a PR company, and public relations is a perfect occupation for many Pisceans because it's all about creating an image that will appeal to the public. Edina also pushes the Piscean divine decadence to the point of absurdity. When she announces that she's opening her own shop that will sell "lovely things," she's in pure Pisces territory.

Like many Pisceans, Edina is a bit of an easy touch. She keeps her alcoholic friend Patsy in champagne and lunches, and the pair of them, Pisces and Scorpio (water signs understand each other so well), are hooked on their shopping sprees in Harvey Nichols. Edina is perpetually chastised and corrected by Saffy—her long-suffering, sensible Virgo daughter. Another clue that Edina is a Pisces is her love affair with metaphysical aids; the float tank, the crystals, the mantras, and the chanting that she claims delivered her gorgeous house. Edina may have her little delusions and eccentricities, but she recognizes a good opportunity when it comes her way and is never slow to grab it.

Jupiter, the bringer of opportunities, can lead real-life Pisceans into careers in exciting high-flying, high-risk areas where their willingness to gamble is part of the job.

People are often surprised when they first learn that Pisceans are numerous in the ranks of stockbrokers and traders. Their famous intuition is often what gives them the extra edge, and many successful Piscean brokers are prepared to confess that they rely on their sixth sense and their gut instinct as much as *The Wall Street Journal*. Pisces knows that equally indispensable to success in this hard-nosed field is their ability to maintain a "win some, lose some" philosophical attitude.

Even though Pisces seems less driven than other signs, they can be just as ambitious. It's just that they often find less traditional ways of earning a living and getting all those "lovely things" that they enjoy so much. So don't be fooled by their casual, low-key "I can take it or leave it" manner, or by their less than dynamic persona. And never make the mistake of underestimating a Pisces.

When the job demands it, Pisceans can cleverly present themselves as the sort of person their client or their boss is looking for. The natural actor in every Pisces thinks a role and becomes it. For Pisces, it's as simple as that.

Acting is, in fact, a classic Neptunian profession. Pisces actors usually manage to avoid being typecast. Glenn Close is one who displays the Piscean versatility for assuming any sort of character. Male Pisceans always come across as strong yet sensitive. Think of John Mills, David Niven, Rex Harrison, and William Hurt.

Pisceans love the glamour and fantasy of show biz, and no matter how shy or retiring they are in private life, the stage is one place they can display their feelings and emotions, because onstage you're not who you really are, are you? And Pisces loves that.

Their acting ability serves Pisceans well in all sorts of situations. Presentations run smoothly when a Pisces is in charge. Any little hiccups are cleverly covered up or glossed over without anyone suspecting that anything has gone awry. Pisces is a good performer who makes contact with the audience. In interviews they can tap-dance their way through the trickiest questions. They may be shaking in their shoes, but you'd never know it. In fact, it may only take a few minutes for a skillful Pisces who wants the job to convince the boss that they've found their man . . . or woman. We've heard more than one true-life Piscean story about how a few harmless white lies or a little bit of embroidering on the truth about their qualifications and lean experience clinched them the job. Having cleverly talked their way in, Pisceans will just as cleverly—and quickly—learn on the job if they have to. They will feel no guilt about accepting a job "under false pretenses" if they know they can do it, and their cover won't be blown.

Sometimes, though, their willingness to bend the truth and their disregard for the unspoken rules can lead Piscean opportunists into some rather dubious acts. Such as the one related to us by the Cancerian ex-girlfriend of one Pisces man. They were both working as advertising art directors at competing agencies, and when Ms. Cancer was made responsible for a new-business pitch for a huge account, she knew that this was her big opportunity. Mr. Pisces was the perfect Pisces boyfriend. He listened attentively while she ran her ideas past him, reassuring her that she was heading in the right direction. What he failed to tell her was that he was pitching for the same account. So you can imagine her shock when she read in the trade magazines a few weeks later that her boyfriend and his agency were in the running for the same business. She was understanding (as most Cancerians would be) and believed him when he said he'd kept it quiet so she wouldn't be put off her job. But she wasn't so understanding when he won the account and she saw his ad on television. It was all her own work—exactly as she'd described it to him.

How could this sweet, understanding, kind Piscean man she was so much in love with do such a dastardly deed? Warning. When something big is in it for them, and there's an easy way to get it, Pisceans can be shifty and conniving—even downright dishonest. When it suits Pisces to keep a secret, only a Scorpio could be as covert.

Pisceans can do some pretty audacious things. Not in a brash, aggressive, in-your-face way, but in ways that often leave people thinking, "What an operator." Superficially, this sort of behavior appears to fly in the face of the image of Pisces as someone who's not terribly competitive or pushy, someone who's even inclined to suffer from a lack of confidence. But does it really? In many cases, it's simply evidence of their insecurity.

Other clues lie in the cynical remarks that Pisceans make about "the system" and those blatantly ambitious types who want to make it in the system. Many Pisces have misgivings about the system and working yourself into the ground (and you have to admit they've got a point). But their cynicism is often a smoke screen to hide their anxiety about not making it. Perhaps they know better than anyone that they are inclined to fall into apathy and laziness. Maybe they secretly fear that they could become one of those people who wake up on their fiftieth birthday and wonder what they've done with their life.

It's a pity, because so many Piscean wanna-bes are genuine could-bes. And indeed, many of those would remain could-bes if it were not for that Jupiterian good luck that so often turns things around at the eleventh hour. Often that luck arrives in the form of a person, a facilitator who has confidence in their potential and who gives them a gentle but firm push in the right direction.

Pisceans take longer than most to gain a firm sense of identity and the confidence that comes with it. Until they do, many opt for safe and easy jobs that won't challenge them and are well below their capabilities.

Because the zodiac is a symbolic cycle of development, each Sun sign can benefit by looking ahead to the sign that follows. After Pisces, the last sign, we return to the first sign, Aries. When it comes to confidence, self-image, and motivation, no one shapes up like an Aries. Motivation and confidence are things that Pisceans might need to work on. As soon as they make the effort to consciously cultivate some of those fiery Aries qualities, they can surprise themselves—and others.

One meaning attributed to the sign of Pisces is "life removed from the world." In this sense, Pisceans are very attracted—and well suited—to working from home. But wherever Pisceans work, the environment itself is of utmost importance. They are particularly susceptible to sick-building syndrome and are likely to suffer more than others from faulty air conditioning, bad lighting, screen fatigue, and high noise levels. To be at their most productive and enjoy their work, they need calm, nonthreatening, physically attractive surroundings.

In another sense, a working life away from the nine-to-five world takes many Pisceans into academia. Science or any field that involves abstract or speculative thought is perfect for the broad scope of the Pisces mind. A lot of Pisceans are scholarly types.

There are many Pisceans who make excellent teachers. They are unlikely to bore students because they're creative and the natural actor in them can command the attention of their audience. Pisces are very good at pulling a rabbit out of a hat when they can see that attention is waning.

The learned professions, law, and medicine are also appealing. And provided they can put enough distance between themselves and the suffering of others (and there are some particularly sensitive Pisceans who cannot), they can make wonderful doctors and nurses.

Institutions come under this sign, and many Pisceans work in prisons or hospitals, and places where people need special care. Pisceans have the understanding that is needed to work with the elderly, the handicapped, and the underprivileged. Because of their empathy for others, Pisceans make skillful counselors. The bereaved, the deeply troubled, and the addicted all benefit from the Piscean understanding and compassion. Likewise, social and welfare work or working for charitable organizations gives Pisceans a sense of making a real contribution to the happiness of others.

A religious vocation is a very special calling, but one, it is said, that calls many Pisceans. Not many of these will go so far as to devote themselves completely to the contemplative life. Though it has been suggested that if you did a head count in a monastery or a convent, you'd find a high percentage of Pisceans. The clergy attracts Pisceans, and outside of the traditional religions, you'll also find plenty of Pisceans teaching meditation and courses on everything from spiritual awareness to Taoism and Vedanta. Who better to run weekend retreats for the harassed workaholic than a Pisces?

Pisceans, by and large, have little taste for the tough corporate culture. Many intuitively shy away from the top jobs, knowing that rising to the position of CEO is not the meaning of life. If you stay somewhere in the middle, you're more likely to get your weekends to yourself and be able to pursue your other interests, figures Pisces.

There are though, of course, plenty of Piscean bosses in the workplace. And if you work for one, you'll appreciate his or her understanding, flexibility, and willingness to cut through the red tape. Pisceans are more interested in a job well done than *how* it is done. They themselves tend to work in fits and starts and hate being closely supervised. So they'll understand if you take it easy one day so long as you're madly productive the next. If your boss is a Pisces, you won't have to put up with someone constantly looking over your shoulder.

Okay, so they may not keep the neatest filing system in the building, and they are prone to overlook those important practical details in their enthusiasm for the bigger, more exciting picture. If you work with a Pisces, you might have to accept a few little idiosyncrasies and the occasional late arrival or early disappearing act. But Pisces know what's expected of them, and when it comes to producing quality work, they will do everything not to let the team down. Most Pisceans are anxious to please and will work well beyond the call of duty, without fanfare. You see, the Pisces person, like their opposite sign Virgo, gets a deep satisfaction from knowing that his or her work really matters.

So when those tedious humdrum tasks pile up into a mountain of overtime, and when Pisceans can't bring themselves to tackle the long, hard slog, they might do well to remember the motto of Piscean Lord Baden Powell, the founder of the Boy Scouts.

"Be prepared."

The Pisces who is prepared to back up their inspiration with some perspiration can achieve extraordinary things. The Pisces who is prepared knows no limits, feels no restrictions, and will allow no one to distract him or her from their goal.

There are primordial fish swimming deep down in the depths of the ocean that never see the light of the sun. And there are fish that can fly. When a Pisces makes up his or her mind that they're going to fly, then look out, world . . . be prepared.

LOVE AND FRIENDSHIP

No one falls in love like a Pisces. Hook, line, and sinker, they literally fall.

And if you've just met an irresistible Piscean, you'll probably find yourself falling too. The Pisces man or woman has something that's totally alluring. When Pisces looks at you, those beautiful deep eyes speak volumes. There's no need for words so you may be left wondering whether the signals you're picking up are real, or if your imagination is working overtime.

Like all the sensitive water signs, Pisceans are often reluctant to make the first move and put their feelings and their ego on the line. Consequently they become expert in seduction by telepathy.

With seemingly no effort on their part, Pisces will bewitch you, and before you know it, you're man—or woman—overboard. It's no use reaching for a life raft. After you've sat up all night talking from the heart about things that you've never even told to your best friend, you may well believe that you've found your soul mate.

One of the loveliest things about Pisceans is that they're not hung up on looks. In other words, if you don't look like Sharon Stone or Kurt Russell (both gorgeous Pisceans), there's no need to fret. That beauty is only skin-deep is something that most people only pay lip service to, but not Pisces. They can be attracted to as many different sorts of fish as there are in the sea. From big blue-eye cods and yellowfin tunas to ornamental goldfish and Atlantic salmon. Unfortunately, a few sharks and slippery eels can also find their way into Pisces' pool.

Friends of Pisces, too, come in all varieties. It's natural for Pisces to befriend the rich, the poor, the worldly and powerful, and the local greengrocer. Those in need will always have a special place in a Pisces heart. There are a lot of Pisceans whose spare bed is permanently occupied by a temporarily homeless friend.

Friends of Pisces love them dearly for the kindness and generosity they give in so many different ways. As Piscean songwriter James Taylor sang, "You've got a friend." Friendship, as Pisces understands, is knowing that someone will always be there for you.

People are not the only strays that Pisces rescues. All manner of suburban wildlife seem to know to make a beeline for dinner at Pisces' back door. To nurture is in the Pisces nature. The Pisces home has a lived-in and welcoming feel. Though it must be admitted, there is one type of Piscean who is allergic to housework. But the vision of old beer cans under the couch and dish towels that are adding to the biodiversity in the kitchen of the single Piscean male is a bit of a myth. There are many Pisceans who are almost as persnickety as Virgos and get quite anxious should they feel they're descending into domestic chaos.

Even the most retiring and homey of them enjoy a dose of glamour every now and again, which is worth knowing if you're wondering where to take them on a date. As a rule, they prefer to avoid noisy, crowded places. A brightly lit, canteen-style eatery with lots of clatter and action may be the new wave, but it's unlikely to whet a Piscean's appetite. Better stick to the classic dinner by candlelight. You can't be too romantic with a Pisces. They love being by the water, so a thoughtfully packed picnic on the beach—having checked the weather reports to find out what time the moon rises above the ocean—is sure to put Pisces in a relaxed and receptive mode.

Pisces is definitely someone to take to the ballet or theater, and flowers and chocolates are practically de rigueur. But it's the gesture that Pisces will appreciate. They'll be just as impressed—if not more—by a hand-picked posy from your garden as an extravagant bunch of red roses.

As a devotee of home comforts, Pisces will be keen to check out where—and how—you live. Minimalism is not their style, as you'll no doubt discover when you're invited over to *their* place.

Home is Pisces' sacred space where they can find the seclusion and peace of mind they need. Pisces knows all about ambiance. Some Piscean homes are a testament to their taste for the exotic, and most display a fondness for chairs you sink into, velvet drapes, and old lamps they've picked up at flea markets, with bibelots and dusty books on every surface.

Pisceans hate the cold and love to putter around the house in warm, woolly, baggy clothes (they can't bear tight clothing) and comfy shoes. There are some Pisceans whose friends laugh at the old, worn-out shoes that Pisces can't bear to throw away. The feet are, in fact, the part of the body ruled by Pisces, and some Pisceans are almost fanatical about footwear. Pisceans come in two varieties as far as feet are concerned: those who have good feet and those who are forever complaining about their bunions and fallen arches.

There are also two types of Pisceans when it comes to overall body shape. The tall, slender Piscean is in the minority, but he or she does exist. Think no further than Fabio, the model for the illustrations on the covers of popular romance novels. Fabio, in true Neptunian style, is hired just to be fab, to be the ultimate fantasy lover. On the whole, though, most Pisceans are shorter than average and on the fleshy side. Even when they're slim, their bones are well-covered. Many have soft faces with rounded features and beautiful full lips. Some have "chipmunk cheeks."

But the first thing most people notice about a Pisces' appearance is the eyes. They are large, round, and soulful, and dominate their face. The area around the eyes is usually noticeably larger than in other signs. Think of Pisceans Spike Lee, Liza Minnelli, Andy Gibb, and the unforgettable eyes (and eyelashes) of Tammy Faye Bakker.

Romance will never die while there are Pisceans. That's not to say that all Piscean romances run smoothly. Pisceans tend to have a history of ill-fated romances or marriages, when they're young and haven't yet figured out why they keep falling for unsuitable prospects.

Their desire to find true love seems to cloud their intuition, not to mention their judgment. If true love is not on the menu, Pisces will cook it up anyway. They can be blind to a person's obvious unsuitability, maximizing the good points and ignoring the shortcomings. In matters of romance, Pisces can live in the most fantasy storybook land of all. True love transcends all, believes Pisces. True love overcomes all differences of age, class, and background. The beautiful thing is that with Pisces, it can. But only when true love doesn't rule out reality.

The love between poet Elizabeth Barrett Browning and her rescuer and fellow poet, Robert Browning, is one of the great Piscean true-life love stories. Following a fall from a horse when she was fifteen, Elizabeth became a semi-invalid, virtually confined to her room by her overprotective father. Her only companion was her little dog, Flush. But Robert Browning was determined to meet her. He successfully circumvented her father, and when Robert and Elizabeth finally met, they fell deeply in love. The story of her secret flight from the house, their elopement, and their life of love and devotion together in Italy is more poignant than any romantic novel. Under Robert's love and care, Elizabeth's health improved and they had a child. Even though their time together was brief—Elizabeth died a few years later in his arms—she found happiness, and left some of the most beautiful love poems ever written.

So how does the image of Pisces the romantic sit with the not entirely undeserved reputation many Pisceans have acquired for having a quick turnover? Pisceans are notorious for jumping into a relationship with total abandon. "This is IT," Pisces tell themselves. Until they wipe the fairy dust off their shoes and realize that the man or woman of their dreams is only human, after all, and not nearly as attractive as he or she first seemed. But hey, the new hero/heroine has just walked in, and wouldn't you know it, "*This* is it" all over again.

What Pisces loves about being in love is the sense of anticipation, the thrill of looking forward to the day and the hour of the next meeting with their beloved. There's something of the divine discontent in their nature that keeps them searching for a kind of elusive high. Love is the drug of preference for many Pisceans, male and female.

The day after the night before, these Neptunian lovers can't keep from giving in to their imagination and allowing themselves to be carried away on a tidal wave of fantasy about what their new life will be like with their new love. What sort of wedding will we have? Where will we live? How many children will we have? What will we call them? Pisces is already in danger of drowning and in serious need of rescue, because the inevitable tumble back into reality is going to hurt. Neptune can be a wonderful support to lovers. He can make love truly the most otherworldly of experiences. Or he can fill you with delusion. The most extreme expression of the Piscean fixation with the object of their desire is unrequited love. There are plenty of Pisceans who, at some stage in their life, have fallen victim to unrequited love and held out for much longer than they should have in a hopeless situation.

Unrequited love goes both ways. Pisceans themselves are not above keeping someone hanging on when they have no serious intention of getting into a relationship. And if you *are* in a relationship with a Pisces and it looks like you're getting more serious than he or she would like, then Pisces could very well swim off downstream without any explanation. They hate confrontation and will do anything to avoid a scene or recriminations. Yet both male and female Fish find it hard to completely let go of their old flames, and after a while the "We're still good friends" line might wear a bit thin with some partners of Pisces.

The sign that so much wants to lose itself in love can reach the kind of abandonment that makes sex a transcendental experience. With the right atmosphere and the right person, Pisces is an uninhibited lover, capable of making all your erotic fantasies come true.

If you're both hooked on each other, then it won't be long before wedding bells are ringing. The sentimental Pisces bride is one who is still sold on the ideal of the white satin dress with the long train. Unless, of course, she opts for the romantic Elizabeth Barrett Browning–style elopement

If the good life is to be had, Pisces will relish it. It's a rare Pisces who will buy a two-dollar can of tuna when for an extra three dollars they can buy smoked salmon, and enjoy it a hundred times more. Even if he or she can't, strictly speaking, afford the good life, Pisces knows that there are times when it's better to have a little gratification of the senses . . . and worry about the money tomorrow. Something will always come along, thinks Pisces.

We know one Neptunian lady who told us how she once spent her monthly paycheck in two weeks and, struggling with a mixture of guilt and depression, decided to blow her last twenty dollars on a huge bunch of flowers and a bottle of gin. Who's to say that it was a waste of money? To this day, she still figures it was money well spent. Besides she knew her friends wouldn't see her starve. Pisces is a friend indeed, and others are usually there to return the favor when Pisces is a friend in need. Should circumstances absolutely demand it, however, Pisceans can be surprisingly thrifty. They can tighten the domestic belt in such a clever way that they never seem to be doing it.

On the whole, Pisceans are some of the easiest people to live with. They're understanding, accommodating, and tolerant. Does this sound all to good to be true? Yes—if being understanding, accommodating, and tolerant means that Pisceans have slipped into their habit of repressing their dissatisfactions and playing the martyr. It goes back to childhood (as these things usually do) when mother loomed large and was someone to whom Pisces felt very beholden. Because they developed a feeling of deep obligation to the person who cared for them, there are many Pisceans who act out the same scenario in marriage. They tend to put so much into caring for their partner that they can fall into the role of the sacrificial lamb, forever putting their own needs second. Is it any wonder that in time they begin to feel miserable and resentful?

Pisceans are people who don't like to get angry. But they do feel anger. And if they take the path of least resistance in a relationship and always let the opportunities to express their needs pass by, their anger turns inward where it gets stored up and manifests as depression. And when Pisceans get depressed, they become depressing to be around. If their partner moves away emotionally, it makes Pisceans more depressed and it all becomes a downward spiral.

It's very important for Pisceans not to push their own needs or opinions into the background. They need to practice thinking and *saying*, "I need . . ." or "I want . . ." It's usually a lesson that time, maturity, and experience teach Pisces well.

Pisceans have their mutable nature on their side. Although they don't like too many disruptions to their daily routine, they are able to change when change is needed, which is why you should never take a Pisces for granted. That's an error that many have fallen into and regretted later as they watched their Pisces swim away into the arms of another. So if you want to keep your love alive, don't just tell Pisces that you love them. Show them that you love them. Surprise them with a bunch of flowers on the anniversary of the day you met. Bring home their favorite chocolates regularly. Always phone if you're going to be late. And know when to lend a sympathetic ear, and when to give Pisces a day to him or herself. When Pisces knows that your love is real, no sign is more devoted.

There's a lovely myth about how Neptune and Jupiter, the ruling gods of Pisces, came to the aid of a pair of star-crossed lovers. Idas and Marpessa wanted to marry, but her father was against it. It looked like a hopeless situation until Neptune lent them his chariot and winged horses so they could escape. As they were speeding away, Apollo the Sun god appeared and declared his intention of taking Marpessa for his own. Suddenly all seemed lost again. But this time Jupiter came to the rescue. So touched was he by their tender devotion to each other that he overruled Apollo and declared that Marpessa had the right to choose.

For Marpessa, there really was no choice. She knew that Apollo, as an immortal, would remain young and beautiful forever, while she was destined to grow old and die. How could she expect his love to last? She chose Idas, knowing that as they grew old together, their love would grow stronger.

Pisces believes that true love is strong enough to triumph over all. And that when love is true, it's there in everything you say and do. As Elizabeth Barrett Browning wrote: "How do I love thee? Let me count the ways, I love thee to the depth and breadth and height my soul can reach . . ."

Those who have won the Piscean heart will also count the ways they love their Pisces. And they will never forget the day they fell in love . . . the day their dreams came true.

THE PISCES PARENT

Quietly bursting with joy will be the Pisces mother or father when they're presented with their first child. A sentimentalist at heart, Pisces will lovingly store away all the precious mementoes: the congratulation's cards, baby's first pair of shoes and first lock of hair.

Every one of their children will be special to Pisceans, and they would hate the idea of having a favorite, but if there is one who steals their heart, it will be the one who is less demanding than the others, the one who is less confident, or not so tough. Pisceans have a soft spot for the child who, for whatever reason, is vulnerable. Grazed knees and bumps and bruises will probably hurt Pisces more than the child. And when it comes to soothing away hurts and sorrows, Pisces has a special touch.

The Pisces mother is not usually one who wants to be a superwoman. Not for her the dream (or nightmare) of juggling career and family, and running to a tight schedule with no room for spontaneity. No, thank you. She looks forward to taking time out in those important early years and is usually content to stay home with baby. Likewise, Pisces fathers may not be averse to the idea of being a househusband for a year or two. They won't see it as a sacrifice to put their career on hold, knowing that this time with their child will never come again.

Pisces is a fertile sign, and there are plenty of Pisceans who end up having a bigger family than they planned, and some who never planned on becoming parents at all, but do. Indeed, some Pisces find themselves "mothering" other people's children too. They find it hard to say no when friends ask them to baby-sit, and need to learn to take in the welcome mat from time to time to protect their privacy.

No matter what their age, all Pisceans are at home in the childhood wonderland of fantasy and make-believe. They're great storytellers who've always known that tales of witches, goblins, and secret passages to the castle in the attic never lose their appeal. It's debatable who will enjoy pulling out the fancy-dress box or setting up a teepee in the garden more, parent or child.

Never short on ideas, Pisces parents know how to make learning fun. They understand why laptops and video games for eight-year-olds will never be a replacement for the smell and the touch of pop-up books of dragons and monsters, Chutes and Ladders, and dollhouses with miniature brooms and lampshades. Pisces effortlessly sows the seeds of creativity in young, receptive minds.

Dr. Seuss, the creator of *The Cat in the Hat* and *Green Eggs and Ham*, was a Piscean. At first glance the Dr. Seuss' books might look rather silly, but they're actually very clever. He taps into the old-fashioned but eternally valid ideas that rhythm and rhyme help children acquire language, and his books remain perennial favorites. They touch a chord with children, and they work.

No one can create a calm and tranquil home quite like a Pisces can. And since Sun signs run in families, it's likely that Pisces' child will also have planets in Pisces and will thrive in the atmosphere of a peaceful, orderly home. If, however, Pisces has produced a more extroverted child (such as an Aries, Sagittarius, Leo, or Aquarius), then Pisces will accept that this child is not a chip off the old block and won't try to dampen the energy of someone whose nature is different from his or her own.

Pisces understand the importance of privacy and personal space, and they're not the overly possessive types who want to run their children's lives or live their lives through their children. They're warm and loving, but they're not smotherers. In fact, Pisces will encourage a child to take his or her first steps towards independence. That's partly because achieving independence from their own parents is probably something that Pisceans have had to struggle with themselves.

There are some Pisceans, however, who haven't yet reckoned with their own childhood conditioning and who may be guilty of slipping into the old, familiar pattern of cocooning their children and trying to keep them in a mutually dependent relationship. They may be only too willing to overindulge their children in the mistaken belief that the children will love them more for it. Unfortunately, the end result is that Pisces may foster the same guilt complex in their children that they carry around themselves.

The Pisces parent may be a softie, but he or she is not a laissez-faire, "anything goes" parent in matters of discipline. Busy, noisy households are not their cup of tea. There's only so much assault on the senses that Pisces can take. They rarely shout or even raise their voice, but Pisces can be the gentle disciplinarians of the zodiac, and are undoubtedly among the most understanding when it comes to helping their children over those early stumbling blocks. Pisces will kindly and diplomatically turn a blind eye to their many mistakes, knowing that it's best not to trample on bruised feelings and an already contrite heart. They know when to make their point, and when to leave well enough alone.

When children of Pisces are no longer children and they go to visit their parents, they will have the deep satisfaction that they're really "going home"—home to a place that's as warm and comforting as it's always been . . . and where they are reminded that they are truly lucky to be the son or daughter of a Pisces.

THE PISCES CHILD

For those who believe, it's said that Pisces is an old soul. Certainly there is something very "knowing" about the Pisces child. If intuition is something you're born with, Pisceans are simply born with more. Even as babies, they're extraordinarily perceptive; they don't miss a thing.

Any change in the atmosphere of the home, and all the joys and worries of those who live there, will be felt by little Pisces. They never forget who kissed their sore finger better and tucked them in at night. Parents who've been blessed with a sensitive, gentle Pisces child have a great responsibility to be sensitive and gentle themselves. This child is easily upset by reprimands, and every cross word or angry look will go straight to the heart.

Pisces is the closest thing to the ideal of the calm, contented child. Rarely do they set out to create a disturbance or throw tantrums. Most often the opposite is true. It's in the Piscean nature to want to please. Making allowance for an Aries Ascendant, Mars Rising, or maybe a strong Jupiter aspect (and there are some Piscean children who have all of these and are a handful), the Pisces child is quiet, cooperative, and easy to train. Show your Pisces how to pick up precious objects and put them back carefully, and you can relax secure in the knowledge that this is a child you can safely leave alone with your Persian carpets and heirloom crystal. Pisceans love beautiful things. They don't have it in them to destroy your objets d'art.

You certainly won't have to do battle at bath time. They love water. The tub is a playground for the Pisces child, and the more rubber ducks and boats, the better. Rain is no reason, in Pisces' mind, not to be allowed out to play. But Pisces are particularly susceptible to colds and flus, and have a tendency to weak lungs. So make sure you keep them warm against the cold and the damp.

Likewise, Pisceans of all ages who are born with Moon in Pisces are prone to chest complaints. If you have a Pisces Moon child, no matter what the Sun sign, you'll also need to make allowances for his or her hypersensitive nature. Neither Sun nor Moon in Pisces children are robust. And parents need to be vigilant and not brush aside any complaint as inconsequential or imaginary.

Most Piscean children are reserved, sometimes timid, and it can take a long time for their confidence to build. Never forget to praise them when praise is due and you'll help develop their self-esteem. It's a delicate balance, though, between encouraging Pisces children to occasionally take center stage, and not forcing them into the limelight against their wishes.

An ideal way to help boost their confidence is through things they have a natural talent for, such as music, dancing, and drama. Pisces are usually drawn to the performing arts anyway, and while not every Pisces child is a budding Chopin, or Nureyev, most are keen to learn.

Excursions to museums and art galleries are wonderful for every child, but they are a must for Pisceans. The more inspiring, the more grand and exotic the venue, the more Pisces will love it. Don't plan vacations full of scheduled, organized fun. Pisceans will enjoy themselves much more exploring a beach, playing in the rockpools, and bringing back a collection of tiny shells.

If at all possible, give your Pisces child a pet. The special rapport they have with animals will last all their life. The delights of the garden will keep the young Pisces amused for hours. Pixies and goblins will be residing in every tree and behind every rock. Let them build their own castle out of your old tablecloth and a couple of boxes, and they'll enjoy the pleasure of just being unto themselves in their own fantasy world.

Science and chemistry kits are also popular with Piscean children. They like quizzes and puzzles, and they can be quite bookish.

Sports are not usually high on their agenda. They love swimming and physical activities in which they can pitch themselves against themselves, but they're generally not too keen on competitive team sports. Their combative instinct is not strong enough. Pisces hate too much rough and tumble. So think carefully before sending them off to a noisy, rowdy day-care center packed with dozens of excitable children.

It's not that Pisces is antisocial. Far from it. Pisceans of all ages are friendly and easygoing and like to mingle with all sorts of people, but they can't bear to be stuck in crowds. Even after the most exciting day out, Pisces always loves to come home.

A little extra emotional protection may be called for if you have a Pisces child—protection from pictures on the TV news, for example, that aren't intended for young eyes. On the other hand, the Pisces child will one day become the Pisces adult, and you won't be doing him or her any favors if you are *over*protective, or take on the responsibility for every little thing in their life.

Beware of setting up a situation in which Pisces can become a dependent personality. It's precisely because they are reluctant to assert themselves, and are quite happy to let other people take charge, that they can fall into a pattern of dependency. Better that the Pisces child is taught valuable living skills when young. On top of that, Pisces know exactly how to exploit their sensitivities. All water-sign children can become well versed in the art of parental manipulation. But Pisces children are perhaps the subtlest of them all at using the full range of emotional ploys to get their own way.

The Piscean gift for a little bit of creative lying starts young. Piscean children learn quickly how to camouflage their little sins and how to wriggle out of blame. Their overactive imagination can stand them in good stead at moments when they need to come up with their own plausible version of what *really* happened. Somehow, Pisces are never the ringleaders, it was never their idea, it was all an accident. For all their gentle, self-effacing ways, don't make the mistake of assuming that Pisces children are immune to perpetrating their share of nasty deeds. It's just that they're better than most at judging the likelihood of being caught.

The key to raising a happy, well-adjusted Pisces is to be kind but not unquestioning. Don't neglect the old-fashioned values of a sound moral and religious education, even if you're not observant yourself. Pisces is a spiritual sign. And though they may choose later on to reject the religious background they were raised in, it's important for them to have some kind of starting point for their spiritual journey.

At school Pisces will show the range of his or her talents and won't quickly be identified as a budding artist or a future scientist. Pisces is a sign that rarely reveals its full potential in childhood. Einstein's teacher was convinced he would never amount to anything, and this should be enough to remind parents that the Piscean talents need cultivation. As students, Pisceans tend to do well in the classes of the teachers they like best, irrespective of the subject. They don't have a burning ambition to lead and are unlikely to want to put themselves forward for the role of class president.

During their teenage years, early romances will probably lead to at least one broken heart. The combination of lack of confidence and wanting to believe the best of their beloved can set them up for disappointment. Parents who are there but don't judge can do a lot to help Pisces weather the early emotional storms.

Pisces does not forget any kindness. You will appreciate the blessings of having a Pisces son or daughter from the start, but as the years go by and you discover that he or she is the first to repay your love and support, you'll count your blessings even more.

BORN UNDER PISCES

Hubert de Givenchy	Sidney Poitier
W. H. Auden	H. W. Longfellow
Drew Barrymore	Jack Kerouac
Ted Kennedy	Karen Carpenter
Peter Fonda	Jean Harlow
George Harrison	Emilio Estefan
Yitzhak Rabin	Kiri Te Kanawa
Zeppo Marx	Gabriel García Márquez
Prince Andrew	Denis Waterman
Prince Edward	Tom Arnold
Johnny Cash	Ron L. Hubbard
Fats Domino	Lord Snowdon
Michael Bolton	Bruce Willis
Sally Jessy Raphael	Anne Lee
Victor Hugo	Bobby Fischer
Ron Howard	Billy Crystal
Edgar Cayce	Michael Caine
Harry Belafonte	Quincy Jones
Roger Daltrey	Isabelle Huppert
Lou Reed	Jerry Lewis
Patty Hearst	Nat King Cole

SUN SIGN COMPATIBILITY GUIDE

True compatibility between two people is a complex thing. "Which sign is the best one for me?" is a question people still ask astrologers, and they're invariably disappointed to discover there's no definitive, clear-cut answer. Obviously the astrological chemistry and harmony must be there to create the attraction in the first place. But without a certain amount of tension, there would be no spark and probably not enough interest value to keep a relationship alive. Too much tension, though, and trouble is bound to loom.

Your astrologer will tell you Mercury, Venus, Mars, Jupiter, and all the other planets form part of the picture of how a relationship operates. They will also tell you that in intimate relationships the Moon sign of each partner is of paramount importance.

Our Moon sign reveals much about our emotional makeup, what kind of home life we want, and what we need from a lover. It is a very important factor in how we function domestically with another person on an everyday basis. So if you're serious about someone, you'll get a valuable insight into what love and living together will be like by doing a little extra research and finding out their moon sign. To do this, you'll need to consult an astrologer or give your partner's birth data to one of the many astrological computing services listed in the popular astrology magazines.

Compatibility depends on many factors. What Sun sign comparisons will tell you is how similar—or dissimilar—your whole approach to life is. Is one of you essentially more ambitious than the other? Do you share the same goals? Is one of you a homebody by nature and the other a restless spirit always on the move? These are the fundamental sorts of things that Sun sign compatibility can reveal.

ARIES

Aries and Aries

Fire meets Fire. This will be hot. It could be dynamite. In any case, it won't be long before they find out since neither is prepared to waste unnecessary time in getting down to it. A terrific combination if they've both got their sights set on the same goals. They will believe there is nothing they cannot achieve together. On the other hand, if these two particular Rams don't turn out to be same-sign soul mates, the relationship could fizzle out as quickly as it flared up. One of the main problems is that their egos are so large they may not be able to get through the door at the same time—one is going to have to walk behind some of the time. The female Aries is no lamb and won't be content to take permanent second place. This relationship will last only if both Rams are willing to take turns deferring to each other and do their fair share of those perfunctory chores such as washing the kitchen floor that Arians are only too happy to leave to someone else.

Aries and Taurus

Sex is unlikely to be a problem. They're both lusty types. Even though Aries is a little more experimental than Taurus, The Bull's love of the pleasures of life—and the flesh—will turn Aries on. Beyond the bedroom, Aries senses that Taurus can show them what patience can achieve, and help keep Aries grounded. But there's a big difference between feeling grounded and feeling fenced in, which is how Aries may end up viewing life with Taurus. In the long run, the Taurus lifestyle may be too routine for Aries' liking. If they can find a happy compromise, this couple can be very productive and make a formidable team, with Aries providing the courage and drive, backed up by the Taurean practicality and staying power. Warning. Money may be an issue. Taurus likes to save and Aries likes to spend. Best sort out the finances before you tie the knot. If disagreements ever get out of hand, the scene could be devastating, even irreparable. Aries is quick to anger, and is unafraid to hit below the belt. But not even The Ram can be as emotionally annihilating as a raging Bull.

Aries and Gemini

Sparks will fly when these two meet. This can be an electric combination, with each bouncing energy and ideas off the other. They are unlikely to get bored with each other and will probably spend their first evening together talking till dawn, and still have plenty more to say. Aries is turned on by a challenge, and Gemini knows how to tease and titillate, so there may be some game playing to start with, but neither is the patient type who believes in postponing pleasure for too long. And two hours could be too long. Socially they're well matched—they're extroverts who love to get out and about and meet people. But if a permanent relationship is on the agenda, the issues of commitment and responsibility will need to be ironed out. Both can be a little too quick to pull out and move on the minute things get difficult.

Aries and Cancer

Both are ambitious and have a clear idea of what they want to get out of life. If they establish from the start that their goals are the same, and that neither partner will move the goalposts later on, then these two could make a terrific team, accomplish a great deal, and enjoy some pretty steamy sex. An Aries man and Cancer woman will probably fare better than vice versa since neither is likely to entirely relinquish the notion of traditional male/female roles. Male or female, Aries may assume that Cancer will be willing to always do things Aries' way. Big mistake. And Cancer may figure that Aries is going to be happy playing house. Bigger mistake. Alarm bells will start ringing when it becomes clear—possibly painfully clear—that emotionally they're from different planets. The Ram takes the direct, head-on approach to everything. Crabs scuttle sideways around problems. It won't be long before Aries says something too pointed for Cancer's supersensitive feelings, or before the Cancerian changing moods and frequent tears become all too much for Aries.

Aries and Leo

The King and I? Who rules . . . regal Leo or Aries the firstborn? Both believe it is their birthright, and that could be the main source of drama in what is otherwise a fantastic combination. These two fiery types will fan each other's flames, and sex is unlikely to ever burn down to embers. This is a striking pair who will turn heads. Both take pride in their appearance and expect their partner to do them proud. Both are also big spenders, but on the whole, Leo—who loves the glamour and the good life maybe even more than Aries—is a better money manager. One thing is certain; life will never be boring. Energy and enthusiasm flow back and forth between the two of them.

The main pitfall is that the relationship could turn into a bonfire of the vanities. When you've got two healthy egos, a battle of wills is bound to be waged sometime. Leo, as the fixed partner in this duo, has more staying power and is better equipped to hang in there if the going gets tough.

Aries and Virgo

When this interesting combination works, it's because each finds the missing components of themselves in the other. In just about every way, these two are coming from different places, but if they can appreciate what the other has to offer, they need not end up going to different places. If Aries respects the value of Virgo's help in home, finances, and general organization, and if Virgo is inspired by the Aries boldness and enthusiasm, then it can work well. But Aries can be far too brash and assertive for Virgo to tolerate long term. And Virgo can be too nitpicky and pedantic so far as Aries is concerned. When the criticism is directed at Virgo (and it will be, because Aries can't keep their complaints to themselves), Virgo will take it hard and withdraw emotionally and sexually. Aries lacks the patience and the sensitivity to understand what makes Virgo tick. So Virgo could feel terribly unappreciated and begin to ask who's doing the giving and who's doing the taking. The initial physical attraction is usually strong. But apart from that, there isn't a lot that these two have in common.

Aries and Libra

Opposites attract. And with this pair the attraction is instantaneous. Aries is quick to pounce, and Libra won't put up too much resistance if he or she reckons Aries is the one. Both want the good life and have an excellent head for money and business. This is a combination that works best when there is no conflict caused by differences in background and culture. Both like to feel they are a sought-after couple in their milieu and are often the beautiful people of the social scene. They look like the perfect couple, but unless they sort out the me/we factor, it could be a case of opposites repel. Independence and being "free to be me" is everything to an Aries. Libra, however, can push togetherness too far, wanting to do everything as a couple. If they can't meet each other halfway, then Aries will feel suffocated and will look elsewhere for a better prospect. Libra will feel unloved and abandoned . . . until a better prospect (with a bigger bank account) comes along.

Aries and Scorpio

Both are ruled by Mars, the god of war and sex. You get the picture. Let's start with the sex . . . as it usually does with these two. It's all very primordial. First-man-and-first-woman-on-earth kind of stuff. In—and out of—the bedroom it's hard to say which one is more dynamic, active, and demanding. Aries can be fascinated and turned on by the depths of Scorpio's emotions. And Scorpio responds to the direct, stimulating, and uninhibited Aries approach to life and love. But too much of Scorpio's emotional dramas and deep, dark brooding could douse the Aries flames. And too many of Aries' insensitive remarks may hurt Scorpio, who's then likely to shock The Ram with the strength of the venom at the tip of their tail. This relationship could turn into a battleground if war breaks out over who's calling the shots and who's got the power. Then the thin line between love and hate will become even thinner.

Aries and Sagittarius

Physically, this could be the perfect match. Life and sex are there to be experienced and enjoyed to the full. "Seize the day and seize the night" is this pair's motto. This is the couple who think they can conquer anything . . . and everything. No mountain is too high, no plan too ambitious. They're both big personalities, and if they can manage to temper their boundless optimism with reason, there is little they cannot accomplish. Both will be able to keep pace with the other's desire for action, excitement, and travel. Skeptical Aries may have a little difficulty going along on Sagittarius' mental and metaphysical adventures. But independent Sagittarius won't have a problem going his or her own way at times. Since both are pretty up front with their opinions, there shouldn't be too many stored-up resentments. So long as they don't continually pit themselves against each other physically and burn the candle at both ends, this is one couple who could find the lifestyle and the happiness they want together right from the start.

Aries and Capricorn

Although their general approach to life is radically different, the chemistry between these two can be strong. Capricorn is one of the very few signs that can match the Aries libido and test their stamina in the boudoir. Happy indeed are The Ram and The Goat who can make their differences work for them. Both are highly ambitious. If Aries can see the benefits in Capricorn's more cautious approach and if Capricorn can see that the Aries bold "can do" attitude has its virtues, then this couple can go far indeed. If not, money is bound to be a source of disagreement. Moreover, a serious clash could arise if Capricorn is too fearful and too intent on doing every little thing by the book, or if Aries is too flamboyant and rash. Aries can make Capricorn feel insecure, and Capricorn's occasional black mood and emotional shutdowns can irritate The Ram. Keeping this relationship in balance may take a bit of effort, but if they put in that effort, it can be a recipe for big achievements.

Aries and Aquarius
This is a brilliant combination for two strong individualists who want a stimulating relationship but still want the freedom to do their own thing. The rapport is good, communication is clear, and they're basically on the same wavelength. Sexually speaking, Aries is always keen to get physical, whereas Aquarius is more interested in the mind connection. There is, though, something energizing and youthful about this duo, and they're unlikely to ever become old fuddy-duddies. But not even the most compatible of couples are going to see eye to eye on everything, and when these two disagree, their differences become all too obvious. Aquarius digs in his or her heels and wrongly assumes that Aries will eventually give up and comply. Aries, if provoked, will turn into a battering ram and try to force the issue. It could turn into a Mexican stand-off, with neither one the winner. But on the whole they have a lot going for them and should be able to find ways around their differences.

Aries and Pisces
The odd couple are not as odd as they at first seem. Being so different is not such a bad thing. If they are both aware enough to realize that they have much to offer each other, they can settle into a harmonious complementary relationship. Then Pisces can draw on the Aries drive, confidence, and enthusiasm, and receive the extra push they sometimes need. And Aries' life will be all the richer for taking a lesson out of the Pisces book and learning to relax and go with the flow. In the bedroom they make an imaginative, playful, and uninhibited pair. The most likely problem is that Aries will mistake the Pisces accommodating nature and desire to please as a sign of weakness and end up taking Pisces for granted. If the relationship is to last, Aries will need to examine their urge to dominate. Aries is turned on by challenge, so Pisces, in turn, will need to cultivate some independence, learn to stand their ground, and clearly state their needs.

TAURUS

Taurus and Aries
See Aries and Taurus (page 386)

Taurus and Taurus

Two happier peas in a pod, you couldn't hope to meet. This is more than a case of same-sign compatibility. Taurus wants a relationship with someone of like mind, so this couple has a good chance of contentment. Together in the king-size bed in the king-size palace, they could well live happily ever after. Both have expectations of satisfaction guaranteed in the bedroom and the dining room—gourmet sex is a Taurean *spécialité de la maison*, and it's likely to be on the menu with regularity. Taurus enjoys a sense of routine in everything, including sex, so their mate will love the certainty that Sunday night is reserved for romance. They are not, however, immune to the danger that exists in all same-sign combinations—namely, that of magnifying their worst side. Obstinacy. When two Bulls do battle, it's the stuff that family dramas are made of. Neither finds it easy to say sorry, and both prefer to just wait for any trouble to blow over. Since Taurus is loath to divorce, some conflicts could remain unresolved forever.

Taurus and Gemini

Since these two generally have a very different outlook on life and different priorities, there has to be a lot more going for them, astrologically, than their Sun signs. Stability and security-conscious Taurus will, nevertheless, be intrigued by Gemini's more casual, easygoing approach, and will enjoy the Geminian wit and sparkle. And if Gemini is honest, they'll admit they respect the way practical Taurus manages life so well. But too much of the Taurean predictability will quickly bore Gemini, and too much of the Geminian unpredictability will push Taurus' patience too far. Since neither sign is good at compromise, conflicts, big and small, are bound to arise over how money—and time—are spent, and what goals are worth striving for. When this combination works, it's a strange fascination, and it could be because their compatibility in the bedroom overcomes the differences in their personalities.

Taurus and Cancer

A very popular combination. Why? Because Taurus and Cancer have so much in common. Both seek their security in domestic contentment and both want to acquire things for the home, which will quickly fill up with every creature comfort and modern appliance (including several priceless antiques). Money makes the world go around, and money keeps this relationship bubbling away nicely. Whoever brings home the larger slice of bacon is likely to rule the roost, but because their goals are essentially the same, and they both believe "what's yours is ours," this usually isn't a problem. By pooling their resources, this couple can live a very rich and comfortable life. Sex is mutually satisfying for these two sensualists. And since both love their food and both love to cook, the kitchen could well become the heart of the home . . . The only danger is, they could end up looking like a pair of matching bookends. All in all, a relationship with an excellent potential for lasting happiness.

Taurus and Leo

This is a relationship that was surely clinched over a bottle of Veuve Clicquot '64 and an excellent dinner. Both, in their own way, are dedicated to the pursuit of the good life (although Leo's spending sprees could make Taurus break out in a cold sweat). Sex between a red-blooded Bull and a passionate fiery Lion could be very hot indeed, and there'll be few inhibitions in the bedroom. Both Leo and Taurus are warm, loyal people who take commitment seriously. Which is terrific when they're traveling in the same direction. But since both have very clear ideas as to what they want in life, and both are stubborn, problems will arise if they're *not* traveling in the same direction. The Lion and The Bull are strong personalities, and in disagreements neither yields, which means there could be dramas of Vesuvian proportions. Tenacity is a double-edged sword. They won't walk away at the first sign of difficulty. On the other hand, if the relationship is clearly not working out, they may hang in there far too long.

Taurus and Virgo

These two earth signs are naturally in tune with each other. Both are reliable types who seek commitment and place high value on a calm and harmonious home life. Both want comfort, but neither is into displays of extravagance. They'll love communing with nature, and if possible, they should find a home where they can create a garden of their own. But it won't be without a few thorns and thistles. Taureans are very set in their ways, and Virgos simply can't let things be if they think things could be better. There might be times when Taurus wishes Virgo would stop fussing and fretting—and times when Virgo wishes Taurus would bother a bit more about the washing up and the laundry. Taurus is likely to be the more dominant, but it would be a mistake if Taurus were to take Virgo's willingness to please for granted. Virgo is not one to create a scene. Should the time come when enough is enough, they'll simply up and leave. If they can keep the channels of communication open, this couple has a good chance of happiness because they both seek financial security and a stable family life.

Taurus and Libra
Although these two are essentially quite different, they both seek a traditional kind of marriage, with traditional kind of roles. Venus, the goddess of love and beauty, rules them both. So there'll be no shortage of flowers, beautiful pictures, and divine home furnishings. In short, these two together will create the sort of home the Joneses want to keep up with. Taurus will provide Libra with loyalty and a sense of security. And sophisticated Libra will give Taurus every reason to beam with pride. But there will be problems if Taurus feels that Libra is a little too cool, distant, and fastidious. Or if Libra feels that Taurus is too demanding and a bit boorish. The Bull is a very stolid, earthy animal who may at times upset the delicate balance of Libra's scales. Neither is the independent type. And neither will contemplate living the single life, so they'll make every effort to smooth over any differences and keep the marriage alive and well. Marriage? Yes, these two won't be reluctant to say "I do."

Taurus and Scorpio
A compelling and powerful attraction if ever there was one. There's no doubt that when these two get together they can make the earth move. This has the potential to be a very sexy, passionate union. It also has the potential to blow apart if there are too many disagreements caused by who's in control. Both are possessive, stubborn, and willing to hold out until they get their own way. And since these are the two money signs of the zodiac, issues over money (who earns it and how it's spent) are sure to be the cause of some strife. Taurus and Scorpio have a respect for each other's strengths and tenacity, but Scorpio can't help thinking that habit-bound Taurus is in danger of collecting cobwebs, and Taurus can't tolerate too many of Scorpio's emotional dramas and taste for the mysterious. Compromise is always the key to a successful relationship between opposites. If these two can appreciate each other's qualities, it can be a truly loving relationship based on loyalty and their mutual belief in the importance of family life.

Taurus and Sagittarius
Initially this could be an exciting and sexy pairing. The ebullient, uninhibited side of Sagittarius will definitely appeal to Taurus, and the sensuous Bull will appear very attractive to the animal half of The Centaur. Once the dust has settled, they may discover that their attitudes towards life are fundamentally very different. Sagittarius is a restless, impulsive sign that likes to be on the move, whereas Taurus doesn't like to move anywhere—in a hurry (or without due consideration). Independence is everything to Sagittarius, and Taurus—who craves constancy and stability—can be far too possessive for a

Sagittarian's liking. Too many interruptions to the peace of their home is a red flag to a Bull. And since both signs, in their own way, attempt to dominate a household, there are bound to be a few angry words. Since these two are basically traveling down different paths, lasting happiness will probably depend on Moon sign compatibility and harmonious aspects between their other planets.

Taurus and Capricorn

This is the stuff that dynasties are made of. They can go far, and achieve great success as a team. Each feels reassured by the other's fundamentally conservative nature. Neither is into anything untoward, wild, or unreliable. But it won't be all counting the coffers. The Bull and The Goat are both horny animals. And since they are both earth signs, the gratification of the senses includes the pleasures of the flesh. When Taurus gets a bit complacent and habit-bound, Capricorn can encourage them to extend themselves. And when Capricorn gets too preoccupied with future goals, he or she can learn much from Taurus about slowing down and enjoying today. These two have much to give each other, including warmth, steadfastness, and the knowledge that each is solidly behind the other. It's a good combination that will be even better if they meet after thirty, since Capricorn is a late bloomer who gains in confidence with the years.

Taurus and Aquarius

Put one of the most possessive signs of the zodiac together with one of the least possessive and you've got an interesting—and not always easy—combination. Frankly, their Moon signs and other planets will determine the success of this partnership. They are essentially poles apart. Aquarius, the free spirit, may feel Taurus is too staid, too stuck in their ways, and too predictable. And Taurus may feel disturbed by the Aquarian disregard for timetables and routine. Moreover, some of the Aquarian's ideas are far too wacky and way out for The Bull. Sexually, it's a hit-and-miss affair. Taurus craves physical affection, and Aquarius is happy to live without constant coochycooing, and would rather connect on the mental plane. Yet, for all their differences, both very much want the security of belonging to a family unit, and because they're both tenacious, they could make it work— that is, if they can conquer the failing they share, namely refusing to acknowledge that they're not always right. If these two can cultivate the art of compromise, they can achieve a lot together.

Taurus and Pisces

Taurus and Pisces can fit together like two pieces in a jigsaw. And what a pretty picture it makes. A peaceful home with beautiful things, a lovely garden, and good home cooking. Both appreciate the simple comforts of life, and neither is averse to a little self-indulgence. Sensitive Pisces will lift Taurus into a more ephemeral realm, and practical Taurus will help Pisces feel grounded. But if The Fish spends too long out of their imaginative spiritual waters, they could find themselves unable to breathe. Pisceans want to please, and that will please Taurus no end. So long as Taurus doesn't take Pisces for granted, and so long as Pisces can be self-assertive when need be, this should be a good match, because although they're quite dissimilar, this can be a very complementary duo. Making the relationship work will not be an uphill battle; there's a natural spirit of cooperation between individuals born under these two signs. This combination works best, by tradition, when the man is the Taurus and the woman is the Pisces.

GEMINI

Gemini and Aries
See Aries and Gemini (Page 387)

Gemini and Taurus
See Taurus and Gemini (Page 391)

Gemini and Gemini
When like meets like, you'd think it would have a great chance of success. Geminis are gregarious, restless extroverts who want to keep their options open and hate to feel fenced in. And that could be precisely the problem. They could be like two ships—or rather two speed boats—that pass in the night. The initial attraction will be instantaneous and volcanic, with no time wasted between small talk and pillow talk. But unless these two take the time that's necessary to really connect and get to know each other well, then all that volcanic passion could die down and lie dormant for another five hundred years. Both like the sound of their own voice, and provided one voice doesn't always drown out the other, there'll be lots of interesting exchange. This relationship could make for a stimulating, exciting match if they can get the right balance between quality time together and the independence and separate interests they both need.

Gemini and Cancer
Their natures and their needs are fundamentally different. So Moon sign compatibility or harmonious vibrations between their other planets is probably what brought this pair together in the first place.

Understanding where each other is coming from and where they're going to is essential to the success of this relationship. So is respect for each other's differences. Cancers live through their feelings. Gemini approaches life in a cool, easy-come-easy-go manner, and could find Cancer's supersensitivity and moods all too much. Conversely Cancer could find Gemini insensitive and unemotional. For Cancer, home is definitely where the heart is, and they suspect that for Gemini, home is wherever they lay their hat. When the wheels of their domestic and working life are rolling along smoothly and predictably, Cancer is at his or her happiest. But that's going to make Gemini feel claustrophobic and restless. Striking a happy medium is the key to this couple finding lasting happiness.

Gemini and Leo

From the start, these two will hit it off. They're both bright, friendly, sociable individuals who enjoy a good time and will play off each other's best side very well. Leo's boldness and savoir faire will spark off Gemini's wit and wickedness, and in no time at all, they'll be leaving the party . . . together. The Lion loves to have their mane and their ego stroked. And Gemini will happily oblige, partly because Gemini loves the fun and glamour that Leo brings to his or her life. If Leo can refrain from bossing Gemini around, Gemini will appreciate how well Leo organizes their home and their life. Both have great admiration for each other. Leo seeks a partner who is clever, attractive, and presents well. And Gemini is all that. These two complement each other, and so long as they don't end up competing with each other, there's an excellent chance of a happy life together. Though they might like to put a padlock on their purse: Both enjoy spending money—lots of money.

Gemini and Virgo

How did they ever meet in the first place? Gemini is forever late, and Virgo has a fetish for being on time. Once they've made the connection and adjusted their watches, there'll be no stopping them. Here are two mercurial people, fueled by good ideas and stimulating conversation, so the talkfest may never end. Of all the earth signs, Virgo suits Gemini best, giving Gemini a sense of security without turning into a clinging vine. Gemini's less serious approach to life will keep Virgo's spirits up. "What's the use in worrying?" is something that Gemini can teach Virgo. But Virgo *will* worry and become resentful if they're left with all the boring chores because fast-moving Gemini always manages to wriggle out of them. When Gemini does a vanishing act, it could be to escape Virgo's fussing over undone tasks. Both can be sharp-tongued, and because they're both highly strung, those channels of communication could become clogged with frayed nerves and crossed wires. Thank heavens they're such adaptable individuals. That's the secret to their success as a couple.

Gemini and Libra
"What a perfect couple!" people will exclaim when they walk in together. The darlings of the social set are always beautifully turned out and never fail to delight and entertain others with their company and clever conversations. This can be a very successful pairing because their tastes and their attitudes dovetail so well. Good manners and looking good are all part of the lifestyle that these two create together. Sexually, too, they'll be in tune with each other. Neither likes to swim too deep in muddy emotional waters, and they both know that a little charm goes a long way . . . in all relationships. Libra's desire for harmony may be occasionally shattered by Gemini's ability to make important decisions in five minutes. Libra takes at least five days to decide what to wear to a cousin's wedding. The biggest hurdle they'll have to cross is Libra's need for constant togetherness, and Gemini's need for a certain degree of personal freedom. Once they sort this out, it could be "I do" and living happily ever after.

Gemini and Scorpio
In many respects, this is one of the odd couples of the zodiac. But curiously, it can be a very sexy combination precisely because their natures *are* at odds with each other. The sexual tension will be palpable. Both are cool—at least on the surface—and both have a taste, and a talent, for the wicked. But it will take more than good sex to keep them together. It will take extra sensitivity on Gemini's part, and extra effort from Scorpio to lighten up and not take everything so personally. If Gemini begins to feel like a character in Scorpio's epic miniseries, they'll run, accusing Scorpio of being "all too dramatic and difficult." If Scorpio walks, Gemini will be told that they're "superficial and an emotional bonsai." It's all or nothing with this pair. Like magnets, they'll either stick together or instantly repel. When they do stick together it's usually because Gemini has enough sensitive water in his or her horoscope, and Scorpio is blessed with planets in rational air.

Gemini and Sagittarius
If it's true that opposites attract, then this is the combination that proves it. A meeting of minds—very quickly to be followed by a meeting of bodies—is the way these two operate. There'll never be a dull moment as this pair jet around everywhere. Both place high

value on their independence and will immediately see the attraction of someone who's not going to clip their wings and expect them to stay home and watch TV every night. Sexually it's a good match. They're both young at heart with few inhibitions, although Gemini is not into sexual marathons and may reach burnout sooner than fiery Sagittarius. Unless one or the other has a bucketful of earth in his or her horoscope, they could spur each other on to take big risks where money, security, and careers are concerned (even though they're both highly adept at extracting themselves out of sticky situations). This is definitely the carefree couple of the zodiac, and so long as they don't become care*less,* it's a union with great potential for success and happiness.

Gemini and Capricorn

Appearances can be deceptive. Their natures are so dissimilar you might wonder what these two see in each other. Well, a mutual taste for the old hubba-hubba is what. This can be one of those wild, deliciously wicked combinations. With Gemini, Capricorn feels a sense of liberation and learns the value of having fun for fun's sake. And Gemini will be quick to appreciate that life has more to offer when Capricorn is around to help them get organized and plan their life more than a week ahead. But there is a limit to the amount of organizing that Gemini can take, and a limit to the Geminian "easy come easy go" unstructured existence that Capricorn can tolerate. If Capricorn starts to look too hung up on stability and security, and Gemini starts to rattle Capricorn's nerves—and budget—the excitement could evaporate. Ultimately the success of this relationship hangs on honest up-front communication and being able to bridge the gap between their fundamentally different natures.

Gemini and Aquarius

"At last—someone who understands me, someone who doesn't think I'm off the wall . . ." think both Aquarius and Gemini five minutes after they meet. Each is turned on by the other's brilliant brain. Indeed, nothing, it seems, is too way out or fantastic for this pair to contemplate. And since they both want to be free to come and go and do as they please, this could easily turn into the mutual admiration society of the zodiac. Sexually, both place a high priority on technical prowess and tend to steer clear of the troublesome emotional stuff that wastes your energy and complicates your life. Well suited as they are, there could be a few dingdongs over money. Aquarius is more hung up on money than they like to admit, and may have a seizure when Gemini blows the monthly budget on another "I had to have it" item. Separate bank accounts and financial

independence is the simple solution and the way to keep this relationship blissful. They find in each other not only a lover, but a true
companion and best friend.

Gemini and Pisces

When these two click they can be anything and everything to each
other. Two highly adaptable, multifaceted individuals with a wide
range of interests is a fantastic recipe for keeping a relationship sparkling. The Piscean imagination combined with the Gemini dexterity
ensures that sex will never descend into the boring monotony of
once a week on Sunday. Both like their own time and space, but
Pisceans are more sensitive and emotional, and Gemini is bound to
irritate Pisces at times and invade the peace and serenity Pisces values so much. The problem is that when Pisces *is* left alone, they start
to long for Gemini's return and anxiously await the sound of the key
in the door. Independent, freedom-loving Gemini may find Pisces a
bit unfathomable, and quickly back off if it all gets too clingy and
cloying. If they can't talk about their feelings, they could end up
drifting apart. Long-term happiness depends on a lot of straight
talking.

CANCER

Cancer and Aries
See Aries and Cancer (Page 387)

Cancer and Taurus
See Taurus and Cancer (Page 391)

Cancer and Gemini
See Gemini and Cancer (Page 395)

Cancer and Cancer

With two such sensitive souls who understand each other perfectly,
you'd think this couple was made for each other. And indeed, they
often are. As a same-sign combination, each provides much of what
the other is looking for, including lots of tenderness, physical affection, and security. Two Cancerians can lead a very cozy life together, arms wrapped protectively around each other. Nothing, you
can be certain, will be allowed to come in the way of their home
and family, and here lies a source of potential problems. They can
become so embroiled in family politics and the lives of their children
that their own relationship is pushed down on the list of priorities.

Two such sensitive souls can easily become *over*sensitive, and double sensitivity is going to mean double floods of tears and hurt feelings. To work best, both need the objectivity of air in their horoscopes so they can stand back and still give each other all the warmth, love, and security they crave so much.

Cancer and Leo

They could have stepped out from the cover of a romance novel. Of all the fire signs, Leo is undoubtedly the best for Cancer. The Crab will bask in the warmth of The Lion's love and loyalty, and vice versa. Cancer senses that Leo is someone who can broaden his or her horizons, and Leo can benefit from Cancer's more cautious approach to money and career. Both are in pursuit of the good life and gain enormous pleasure from having children, so family gatherings will be times to remember. Who rules the roost, though, may become an issue, and it could come down to whether Leo's bossiness overrides Cancer's desire to have the last word on everything domestic. Emotionally, Leo is a straightforward, uncomplicated type who may find Cancer's complicated, emotional mood swings irksome and annoying. What Cancer will find annoying is the sheer overwhelming force of The Lion's big personality. But because this couple believe that love can overcome all differences, they have an excellent chance of finding lasting happiness

Cancer and Virgo

What a team. They have complementary attitudes towards money, job, and security, so there won't be any differences about where their future is heading. Virgo's earthy sensuality is beautifully in tune with the warmth and tenderness of Cancer, and they can get along very well—despite some basic differences in their nature. Virgos are into self-improvement, whereas Cancerians have no real desire to change their ways. When the nitpicking perfectionist Virgo meets the carping Cancerian who just can't let something drop, it could become an exercise in conjugating the verb *to nag* . . . I nag, you nag, we nag. Moreover, Cancer is a highly emotional person who needs constant reassurance, and Virgo, who is more controlled and self-contained, pulls back from too many tears and dramas, which in turn makes Virgo look cold and uncaring to Cancer. More tears, more withdrawal. You get the picture. If they can manage not to get drawn into this cycle and hung up on each other's foibles, the relationship can work very well.

Cancer and Libra

Neither Cancer nor Libra aspires to living the single life. On the contrary, they both want to settle down into a life of domestic bliss.

So when these two meet, they'll like each other's attitude towards relationships, and it will turn serious fast. Socially they're well matched, and the wedding could be the talk of the town. They make a brilliant business couple, and since they're both acquisitive, their beautiful home will soon be overflowing with every "must have" item and every labor-saving device. One stumbling block could be that Cancer wants to buy into emotional scenes, and Libra wants to buy out. Supersensitive Cancer finds release by letting their emotions flow. But this doesn't suit cool, objective Libra at all, who will do anything to avoid a scene. On top of that, Cancer thinks in terms of the family unit, and Libra sees him or herself, first and foremost, as one of a couple. If however, their Moon signs are compatible, they can find fulfillment.

Cancer and Scorpio
There's an unmistakable affinity between these two. They find it easy to open up to each other and will develop an emotional bond and an intuitive understanding of each other that time will never break. Intense, passionate sex will add to the magic that a Cancer can spin with a Scorpio. Both seek stability in their lives, and loyalty from a partner. Scorpio, though, is prepared to take more risks than Cancer, which can help bring Cancer out of their protective shell and lead them into a more exciting and interesting world. By the same token, if Scorpio can heed Cancer's play-it-safe advice, they can achieve so much more. Scorpio may be surprised to discover that the sweet-natured Crab is not as easy to control as Scorpio initially thought. Crabs are expert at getting their own way. Two crusty invertebrates with sharp pincers can actually hurt each other a lot. Because they're both highly emotional people, getting an objective view on any problems that pop up between them can be hard. But it's all they need to live happily ever after.

Cancer and Sagittarius
Both like a good laugh, a good dinner, and a good time—and that's probably what attracted them to each other in the first place. But essentially these are two very different types of people. Cancer puts security number one on their list. Sagittarius puts it number . . . well, way down somewhere after freedom, flexibility, and room to roam. At times Sagittarius is going to be far too insensitive for Cancer to bear. Sagittarius, in turn, will find Cancer's moods all too heavy, and will hate the way Cancer throws cold water over their ideas. If The Centaur gallops out the door (which is likely), it will upset Cancer dreadfully. Their attitudes towards home, money, and job are so out

of sync that when the initial laughter dies down, they may wonder what they have in common. In truth, that could be very little. At some stage, Sagittarius is sure to accuse Cancer of being too tame and always the same. And Cancer will tell Sagittarius they're fool-hardy and have got their priorities wrong. Much mutual adjustment and genuine appreciation of each other's qualities are needed if this is to work.

Cancer and Capricorn

Two opposite signs with much in common. Both place great store on traditional values, on having a secure job and a nice home with the mortgage paid off. With heaps of initiative and a healthy respect for money, they make a terrific business team. Home is a haven for them both, and Sunday lunch will be a family institution. They can be very compatible since Capricorn is a closet sentimentalist and Cancer is more career-minded than he or she would ever admit. Both demand loyalty and they'll give each other the emotional security they both need. Capricorn, though, hates schmaltz; Cancer loves it, and occasionally will do something that Capricorn finds undignified or embarrassing. And Capricorn is bound to strike Cancer as cold and insensitive from time to time. Cancer's reluctance to forgo present-day pleasures for a bigger and better future might frustrate Capricorn's long-term financial vision, and Capricorn can be far too frugal with the daily treats that Cancer loves so much. All things considered, though this can be a good match.

Cancer and Aquarius

These two come from different planets. Indeed, their destinies are so radically different, it's unlikely they'll ever get together in the first place. If they do, it's because Cancer is intrigued by the Aquarian free, wild, and way-out approach to life, and Aquarius sees a warm, comforting partner who's so clever at taking care of all those little daily tasks that make life so cozy and comfortable. So they may well bumble along for a while in semidomestic bliss. But because their emotional needs conflict, it won't be long before they find themselves at odds with each other. Cancer is far too possessive, jealous, and clinging for Aquarian's liking. The Crab needs lots of intimate tête-à-têtes, cuddles, and emotional reassurance, and may be forced to conclude that Aquarius would rather be tapping away at the computer. It's possible that each could become the living example of the other's worst relationship nightmare. If it's to work, it will depend on many harmonious links between their other planets.

Cancer and Pisces

With so much natural affinity between them, this can be a richly satisfying relationship. Sexually, they're both sensual and responsive and they're both sentimentalists. Two sensitive water signs together will care for each other, and because they both feel things deeply, they'll try never to upset each other. On the contrary, they'll want to build a love nest together away from the cruel, hard, unfeeling world, and will spend many a happy time cooking up delicious meals and enjoying long chats. One danger is that Cancer could end up dominating on the domestic front, and because Pisces is too willing to yield in order to keep the peace, it might be hard to redress the imbalance. Cancerians justify their desire to take charge on the grounds that they are more organized and have more get up and go. Provided they don't get locked into a closed, claustrophobic world revolving around recipes and what's on TV, and avoid developing a symbiotic relationship, it makes for a loving and enduring combination.

LEO

Leo and Aries
See Aries and Leo (Page 387)

Leo and Taurus
See Taurus and Leo (Page 392)

Leo and Gemini
See Gemini and Leo (Page 396)

Leo and Cancer
See Cancer and Leo (Page 400)

Leo and Leo

Such warmth, such passion, such excitement—this same-sign combination looks like a sure fire thing. With their devotion to the good life, it seems there can never be enough lavish entertaining, grand dinners, and dressing up. If the dollars permit (and even if they don't), they'll want a home bursting with sumptuous furniture and wonderful things. This pair could make other couples look positively plain and dreary. Put two passionate people together and you've got twice the passion. So sex is going to be hot and mutually satisfying. But since both Lions are born to rule, there could be a few impasses and battles royal if someone doesn't occasionally back down. On top of that, both are achievement- and goal-oriented individuals with healthy egos, and they might end up competing against each other for the spotlight. That would be a great pity because when each supports the other's ambitions, they can get exactly what they want from a relationship—a loyal, loving, and strong partner.

Leo and Virgo

Although their natures are very different, this can be a successful combination because each offers the other something that the other is rather short on. Leo benefits from Virgo's reservoir of common sense and restraint. And Virgo, likewise, can thrive with an injection of Leo's pizzazz and glamour. The Lion can induce Virgo to be a little more bold and adventurous, and together they can pull off some well-calculated moves for material success. They're both hard workers who want to get ahead. Physically it can be warm, richly fulfilling, and enduring. The fact that Leo is born to rule and Virgo enjoys caring for others makes them seem highly compatible, but if Leo takes advantage of Virgo's giving nature and becomes too demanding, or if Virgo is irked by Leo's vanity, Virgo could quietly disappear and leave Leo alone on their throne. The proud Lion won't tolerate too much of Virgo's carping and nitpicking. But with some mutual adjustment, these two will discover they have much to give each other.

Leo and Libra

What a good match, says everyone when this couple walks into the room. They look so fine together, so confident and happy with each other. This charming pair has a well-developed taste for the good life—even the high life. No restaurant, no opera house, no store, is too grand for them. In fact, their credit cards will be in constant competition with each other. With their need to look good at all times, separate bathrooms are essential and separate bank accounts are advisable. So long as life is good, the relationship will be good. But should real life cease to resemble the celluloid ideal, there could be a few arguments over who's to blame. Libra's procrastination and dilly-dallying could drive fast-acting Leo crazy. By the same token, Libra may find Leo a little too loud, pushy, and brash on occasion. Yet with the ready spirit of cooperation that exists between these two signs, this relationship has a good chance of lasting success.

Leo and Scorpio

Passion is what draws these two together, and passion is undoubtedly what will keep them together. Leo is big on romance and not averse to a touch of fantasy, and since Scorpio seeks ecstasy of body and spirit, it won't be long before they're enthralled with each other.

Both are powerful personalities in their own right who have a natural tendency to dominate any domestic scene (though Scorpios are more subtle in their methods). On top of that, both can be extremely stubborn and unwilling to compromise when their sights are set on something they want. Other problems could arise from the fact that Scorpio is the more complex of the two and needs an ongoing deep emotional exchange, which Leo could find all too heavy and intense. If that's the case, Scorpio will figure Leo is far too superficial and be turned off by their loud "I'm so wonderful" attitude. But when each learns to occasionally yield to the other and accept the other's differences, this is a loyal, steadfast, and mutually supportive match.

Leo and Sagittarius

Two people who are full of lust for life—and lust for one another. They're energetic and energizing, and they fuel each other. Is there anything they cannot do or achieve? Nothing is too adventurous, no project too ambitious, no vacation destination too glamorous or exotic. The trouble is, it all costs money. And if you've heard that two can live as cheaply as one, it was never said with this pair in mind. So long as they don't push their enthusiasms and their lifestyle to the point of burnout, they could find their true soul mate in each other. Sagittarius is, on the whole, more easygoing and flexible, whereas the loyal and royal Lion likes the certainty that their consort will always be home at the palace on time. Leos may also have their mane—and ego—ruffled by the Sagittarian talent for brutal honesty. Where are all the compliments that Leo likes so much? But these two have so much in common that such minor irritations are sure to fade away in the warmth and the magic they weave together.

Leo and Capricorn

Only the best will do for Leo and Capricorn individuals—which means that these two status seekers could figure they've found the best in each other—and only each other will do. They've got a lot more to give each other than first meets the eye. Socially they're well matched; both seek approval, respect, and the evidence of material success. Sexually, too, it can be an exciting and passionate pairing. Leo gives Capricorn carte blance to release their lusty desires and become more spontaneous in all areas of life, while Capricorn provides Leo with astute advice and a great sense of safety and security. But since Capricorn is basically an introvert and Leo is an extrovert, there are bound to be times when Capricorn looks all too controlled and stitched up for Leo, and Leo looks embarrassingly showy and superficial to Capricorn. If each appreciates how much the other has to offer, then there is little that these two cannot achieve together and little to get in the way of their love and admiration for each other.

Leo and Aquarius

When one big personality connects with another big personality, there's fantastic potential for love and friendship. With no shortage of creative sparks flying between them, they'll soon feel like kindred spirits. Both Leo and Aquarius are eminently sociable, and together they make a colorful couple who like to be seen everywhere—and with everyone. Their own social events will be grand happenings with a cast of thousands. But they are opposite signs and their differences will become all too clear. Leo's fiery passions blow hot and hot, and detached Aquarius tends to blow hot and cold. Leos always like to know where they stand, and Aquarians hate to be pinned down on anything, hence the dilemma of personal freedom versus togetherness. And since both are obstinate and will hold out to get their own way, they could build up blocks between them that become insurmountable. Ultimately, long-term compatibility for this pair depends on tolerance of each other's different needs. Harmonious Moon signs will help.

Leo and Pisces

They may look like the odd couple, but they're both great romantics with a taste for luxury and an appreciation of the arts, so curiously, this can be a very happy and fulfilling relationship. Both, in their own way, are creative thinkers who hate the idea of living an ordinary life. There's nothing dull about their sex life either. Leo and Pisces are both into the pleasure principle and will bring out the sensual, uninhibited best in each other. Pisces, who is only too happy to please, will never threaten Leo's top-cat position. And Leo, who is more dynamic and generally better organized, will give Pisces a prod when needed, a boost to their confidence and faith in themselves and the future. So long as Leo doesn't become overly bossy and organize Pisces to death (there's a limit to how much organization a Pisces can take), and so long as Pisces doesn't come across as too meek and mild without a firm sense of purpose, this can actually be a stimulating, rewarding relationship.

VIRGO

Virgo and Aries
See Aries and Virgo (Page 388)

Virgo and Taurus
See Taurus and Virgo (Page 392)

Virgo and Gemini
See Gemini and Virgo (Page 396)

Virgo and Cancer
See Cancer and Virgo (Page 400)

Virgo and Leo
See Leo and Virgo (Page 404)

Virgo and Virgo
What more could a Virgo want? Someone of like mind who is just as conscientious and has the same desire for a secure, harmonious life. It could be a dream come true. Certainly these two mercurial types will never be short of interesting things to talk about. Though at times two Virgos together can get all too analytical and theoretical. They might do well to practice just enjoying life for its own sake. With any same-sign combination, there's the risk they will feed off each other's negativities, so in the worst case scenario their life could end up revolving around the minutiae of everyday life such as the price of grapefruit, the best value in multivitamins, the bills, and the vacation bookings. It could all get very tedious indeed. But if one of them has fire signs strong in his or her horoscope, it will inject the sparkle and desire for excitement that will enable these two to relish the security, comfort, and reassurance they give each other, and provide a lot more besides. Then it will be a mutually satisfying relationship with great potential for growth.

Virgo and Libra
At first glance, these two polite, gentle individuals appear so right for each other. Both have well-honed social skills and are careful to say and do the right thing and not give offense. But it won't be long before Libra discovers that Virgo (who has a more serious attitude to life) is not as keen on the party circuit. And Virgo will soon be enlightened on Libra's desire to acquire all the best that money (be it their own or their partner's) can buy. Such a modest, thrifty person could begin to get a little nervous. In fact, lifestyle and spending habits are likely to become bones of contention. The combination of Virgo's worrying and Libra's dependency could lead to a semitortured state of limbo. Though if Libra appreciates the values of Virgo's common sense and practicality, and if Virgo enjoys breathing the fresh air of Libra's lighter, more sociable ways, it can work well. To

love or not to love, to leave or not to leave—that is the question. The answer depends on other compatibilities in their horoscopes, because in spite of appearances, these two have very different philosophies of life.

Virgo and Scorpio

These two instantly see each other as a serious person of substance, and they like what they see. When the analyst and the investigator of the zodiac get together, they'll find plenty to analyze and investigate in each other. Although they come at things in different ways, each admires the other's thinking. Virgo marvels at what Scorpio can perceive with gut instinct, and Scorpio will be impressed by the sharp Virgoan rational brain. They can do great things together . . . and not just in business, either. The more earthy type of Virgo will bloom under the erotic care of sexy Scorpio. They can cultivate a cooperative, complementary relationship provided Virgo doesn't get too hung up on what Scorpio regards as the trivia of life, and provided Scorpio (who can be too intense and controlling for Virgo) knows when to lower the force field. Both place great importance on loyalty, so there's a good possibility of an enduring love, especially since both are able to figure out what adjustments need to be made to make it work.

Virgo and Sagittarius

A Virgo and a Sagittarius are bound to have connected on a "clean up the beaches" campaign or in a discussion on reduction of greenhouse gases or what direction education ought to be taking. It is undoubtedly a meeting of minds. Both are restless, bookish types who like to be *au fait* with what's going on. Sagittarius can encourage a greater sense of fun and adventure in the more retiring Virgo and bring Virgo out of his or her worrying . . . that is, of course, if Sagittarius doesn't give Virgo cause for more worrying. Virgo hates any displays of excess and the kind of impulsive behavior that Sagittarius is sure to exhibit at some time. And when Virgo points out the foolishness of some of Sagittarius' ways (which Virgo won't be able to resist doing), they'll be seen as a wet blanket by The Centaur, who may disappear into the distance. And what a pity that would be because Virgo has all the earthy assets to help Sagittarius realize their wonderful ideas. It can be touch and go—literally and metaphorically speaking—with this pair.

Virgo and Capricorn

Two realists with so much in common—is it any wonder they are so attracted to each other? Both are earthy, practical traditionalists who believe you get from life what you're prepared to put in, and for these two, that is often a great deal. With similar attitudes towards work and money, they make a brilliant business partnership, though Capricorn's sights are set on the bigger, more distant picture. Duty can hang heavily at times since both tend to feel guilty about taking time out to relax. Doing-nothing days rarely happen for these two—there's always something that needs to be done. So they may need to schedule a night of passion in their diaries. Jokes aside, their compatibility definitely extends to the bedroom, where they make a lusty, sensual couple. One reason the long-term prognosis is so good is that they would have been astute enough to discuss their likes, their dislikes, and their goals before they make a commitment to each other—so there won't be any nasty surprises. Like a fine old port, these two just get better and better with the years.

Virgo and Aquarius

Because they're coming from such different places—and are going to such different places—it's likely to be a brief encounter of two sharp minds if they happen to connect on the way. Initially this talkative duo are sure to be fascinated by what each other has to say. But beyond the brain and into the body, they probably don't have enough in common to keep them interested. If Aquarius should misread Virgo's modest, restrained manner as a sign that Virgo shares Aquarius' own cool, faintly disinterested approach to sex and personal relationships, it would be a big mistake. Earthy Virgo wants the delights of a rich and satisfying sex life and will not tolerate the Aquarian detachment for too long. Moreover, there could be serious fallout over Virgo's timetable addiction versus Aquarius' timetable allergy. Fussy Virgo will have good grounds for fussing about Aquarius' rather freewheeling domestic habits, which in turn will send Aquarius crazy over Virgo's obsession with order and hygiene. Permanent happiness will depend on brilliant connections with their Moons and other planets.

Virgo and Pisces

This pair possibly receives top rating among the opposites of the zodiac. They could settle down to enjoy the gentle pleasures of life together in a well-run home with a well-run kitchen, the herb garden, the library, the animals, the birds, and everything else they both love. The sensitivity and the natural flexibility of spirit they share give them the ability to appreciate their similarities and tolerate their differences. But opposites are opposites, even if they do get on well. And at some stage Virgo, the total realist, will be frustrated by Pisces, the impractical dreamer, and the critic in Virgo is bound to emerge if Pisces becomes lazy and aimless. Virgo would be better off giving Pisces an encouraging nudge rather than resorting to nagging because Pisces can often show Virgo possibilities that Virgo never dreamed of. Let the Piscean imagination take care of the big picture, and let Virgo take care of the practicalities, and you could have a wonderful harmonious, happy, and productive partnership.

LIBRA

Libra and Aries
See Aries and Libra (Page 388)

Libra and Taurus
See Taurus and Libra (Page 393)

Libra and Gemini
See Gemini and Libra (Page 397)

Libra and Cancer
See Cancer and Libra (Page 400)

Libra and Leo
See Leo and Libra (Page 404)

Libra and Virgo
See Virgo and Libra (Page 407)

Libra and Libra
When two peace-loving Librans get together, the stage looks set for domestic bliss. One thing's for sure; neither intends to stay single, so the relationship is likely to turn very serious very quickly. All same-sign combinations understand each other. But for Librans, who want so much to please their "better half," it's like looking in a mirror and seeing someone as keen as they are to live a comfortable and uncomplicated existence with as many material pleasures as they can afford. And seeing as they're both aware that dollars are what pay for their indulgences, they'll work brilliantly as a team to obtain those dollars. Though there will be plenty of occasions when their joint indecisiveness makes decision making a nightmare. Should we opt for green or blue in the bathroom? Stainless steel or marble in the kitchen? Paris or New York for the vacation? Whichever they choose, they'll never be totally convinced they made the right deci-

sion. The one thing they will be convinced of is that life really started the day they met each other.

Libra and Scorpio

Their natures may be fundamentally different, but should gracious, gorgeous Libra be picked up by Scorpio's radar for anything scintillating and sexy that enters their zone, then it could be an instant physical attraction. After the initial fascination has faded, however, they could find they have little to talk about and wonder what on earth they have in common. Answer: not a lot. Libra's light, uncomplicated approach to life doesn't always sit well with Scorpio's need to question, probe, and dig below the surface. Libra recoils naturally from the intense emotional scenes that Libra figures Scorpio stirs up for the sake of it. And Scorpio is sure to get frustrated by Libra's refusal to engage in anything deeper than what Scorpio regards as superficial niceties. Unless their horoscopes contain compatibilities between the other planets, there's usually not enough to keep these two sufficiently interested in each other to form a fulfilling long-term relationship.

Libra and Sagittarius

This can be a perfect recipe for happiness since neither wants a stay-at-home, claustrophobic relationship. Both are hugely sociable people, so their calendar will be full. Indeed, they could get very twitchy if there's no one interesting to talk to and nowhere exciting to go. It won't be without a few hiccups, though. Sagittarius is far too blunt at times for Libra, who may quietly take umbrage at such undiplomatic honesty. And Sagittarius will find it hard to hide his or her annoyance at Libra's preciousness. Moreover, they tend to live their lives at a different pace. Fiery Sagittarius believes in spontaneity and likes to take off at a moment's notice. Libra considers the pros and cons of everything. But because Libra's nature is to defer to their partner, Libra will accept much of Sagittarian's fiery, impulsive, and seemingly irrational behavior. This couple has an excellent chance of making allowances for each other's differences, and when they do, they can form a stimulating, satisfying relationship.

Libra and Capricorn

Because they present themselves so well together and because they've basically got the same goals in life, this can be a successful combination. It's certainly a match that friends and family will applaud. And since each wants the respectability of a traditional marriage and the admiration of other people, it won't be long before wedding bells are ringing. This doesn't mean that these two don't have their differences. Capricorn values integrity above all and will sometimes be irked by Libra's preoccupation with the social scene. Capricorn will see it as a case of sham versus sincerity. But Libra may interpret it as a case of gloom versus glamour. Capricorn can get all too heavy and depressing for Libra at times. And Capricorn, who has a high libido, may sometimes be too sexually demanding for Libra. Even so, this is a couple whose mutual drive to get on in life will ensure that those differences will be downplayed. The fact that they come across as a dignified, successful pair with a good image will give them both great satisfaction and contentment.

Libra and Aquarius

They'll talk all night. Okay, so that might be all they do, but they'll love it and they'll be back for more. Two socially oriented people, each with a wide and interesting circle of friends, are soon going to find themselves in an even wider circle. Even though these two could have found a compatible partner in each other, they're not two peas in a pod. Libra is a very polished and sophisticated creature for whom the social graces rate high. Aquarians, with their bohemian, occasionally madcap ways, are not well noted for their decorum or well-ironed shirts. Libra cares about image, and Aquarius is certain to embarrass Libra at some time with "inappropriate behavior." Both like to keep their distance from heavy emotional scenes, but Libra needs someone who is there for them in body, not just in spirit, and because Aquarius wants to keep their options—and timetable—open, Aquarius may begin to resent Libra's desire for constant togetherness. Yet because they're both air signs and on the same mental wavelength, their shared interests should keep their love alive.

Libra and Pisces

Who said romance is dead? Certainly never a Libra or a Pisces. When these two fall for each other, it's Romance with a capital *R*, maybe even romance bordering on fantasy. They both want a lovely home with lovely things and a lovely life where they can cushion themselves and each other from that horrible hard place called the real world. Creating an aesthetic existence is very important to this couple, who could become the darlings of the art scene. In their search for harmony and bliss, each will be careful to try to please the other, but Pisces is an emotional water sign, and if there's any uncomfortable emotional issue that needs to be broached, Libra tends to go into reverse. That will make Pisces depressed and they could both end up consoling themselves with a bit of retail therapy—or in the loving arms of another. And that would be a shame, because this partnership has the potential to stay as magical as the moment they met.

SCORPIO

Scorpio and Aries
See Aries and Scorpio (Page 388)

Scorpio and Taurus
See Taurus and Scorpio (Page 393)

Scorpio and Gemini
See Gemini and Scorpio (Page 397)

Scorpio and Cancer
See Cancer and Scorpio (Page 401)

Scorpio and Leo
See Leo and Scorpio (Page 404)

Scorpio and Virgo
See Virgo and Scorpio (Page 408)

Scorpio and Libra
See Libra and Scorpio (Page 411)

Scorpio and Scorpio
Because Scorpio is the sign of extremes, the tendency that same-sign combinations have to bring out the best and worst in each other is magnified tenfold with this pair. Is it possible that Scorpio could ever be totally unnerved by someone else? Yes, if that someone is another Scorpio. Despite an initial wariness between them, the sexual attraction is usually so strong they can't resist moving in closer. Add to that the feeling that this is a soul connection, and these two will already be swimming around in those deep Scorpionic waters of emotion, hooked on each other. But since both are into power games and neither knows the meaning of compromise, if things go awry, it may be so hard for them to say "I'm sorry" that they never do. Indeed, the hurt they can inflict upon each other might take more than one lifetime to heal. When it works, they make a rock-solid, deeply committed, loving couple. It's a powerful relationship that can bring enormous personal happiness as well as worldly success.

Scorpio and Sagittarius

When the fire of Sagittarius meets the water of Scorpio, it could be so hot and steamy it feels like a sauna. Both are strong, forceful personalities who have firm ideas about what they want out of life, which means they'll soon discover that what each one wants is different. The way they operate is very different, too. Scorpio may be altogether too possessive and stubborn for Sagittarius, who aspires to a life of freedom and spontaneity, and hates the thought of being controlled by anyone. The extroverted nature of Sagittarius can be way too open and indiscreet for Scorpio, who values privacy. The Archer's flexibility and lighter touch may also irritate Scorpio, yet a little of that Sagittarian hang-loose philosophy is exactly what Scorpio sometimes needs to dilute that Scorpionic intensity. Scorpio craves intimacy, and Sagittarius wants space—and that could become an issue. At least they're both honest and forthright enough to confront any problems head-on, and on that basis they could work things out.

Scorpio and Capricorn

A formidable duo indeed. Two ambitious, focused people fueled by a sense of purpose and the desire to move onward and upward. Is this what they admired in each other to start with? Their combined business brains are not the whole picture. It's by no means all work and no play for this couple. Because Scorpio and Capricorn both have a very high sex drive, it should be satisfaction guaranteed in the bedroom. Maintaining a feeling of control is essential for each, so the question of who's calling the shots could become a stumbling block, and they could both become very cold and uptight. If it goes seriously wrong, each can be so unforgiving and uncompromising that reconciliation is impossible. Thankfully, though, these two signs find it easy to cooperate with each other and have a better than average chance of sorting out any differences of opinion. They both rank fidelity and commitment high, and both work hard to create a comforting and rich home life. A combination with an excellent chance for enduring happiness.

Scorpio and Aquarius

Put together two of the most obstinate signs, with their completely different approaches to life and love, and you obviously have to look to other factors in their horoscopes for relationship compatibility. Even then they'll need truckloads of mutual understanding if this relationship is to work. Scorpio is a highly emotional being who thinks with his or her feelings. Aquarius (who is very suspicious of feelings) needs lots of personal space and will respond to Scorpio's intensity and desire for deep intimacy by backing right off. This will make Scorpio distraught, cold, and more intense, which in turn will see Aquarius heading towards the horizon. The distance between them could become so great that they end up viewing each other from the North and South Poles—unless Aquarius can overcome their distaste for emotional matters, and unless Scorpio can learn to modify their propensity for drama. If they ever reach the point of total standoff, there's no going back, because both have very definite ideas about what they want in a relationship and who their ideal partner is—and ninety-nine times out of one hundred, it's not each other.

Scorpio and Pisces

A natural attraction exists between these two, based on an understanding of each other's sensitivities. Each intuitively knows what the other is feeling and cares enough to do what he or she can to be supportive, and neither will dismiss the other's feelings as inconsequential. Since both are into a little fantasy and otherworldliness, they could live out their fantasies with each other. Sex between them could include rewriting the *Kama Sutra*. But not even these two individuals are without their differences. Scorpio may be irritated by the Piscean talent for swimming away when answers and action are what's called for. But then, Scorpio can come on too strong for Pisces' taste, and some Pisceans find themselves becoming too compliant in the face of the Scorpionic force of personality. It takes a strong Piscean and a very aware Scorpio to make the best of this potentially fulfilling partnership. But all things considered, they have a lot to give each other, and it's a union that's likely to survive the test of time.

SAGITTARIUS

Sagittarius and Aries
See Aries and Sagittarius (Page 389)

Sagittarius and Taurus
See Taurus and Sagittarius (Page 393)

Sagittarius and Gemini
See Gemini and Sagittarius (Page 397)

Sagittarius and Cancer
See Cancer and Sagittarius (Page 401)

Sagittarius and Leo
See Leo and Sagittarius (Page 405)

Sagittarius and Virgo
See Virgo and Sagittarius (Page 408)

Sagittarius and Libra
See Libra and Sagittarius (Page 411)

Sagittarius and Scorpio
See Scorpio and Sagittarius (Page 414)

Sagittarius and Sagittarius
If there was ever a vital couple, this is it. With all those hooves galloping around the house and out the door into the big wide world, these two seem to live a life of perpetual motion. Being a same-sign combination means they can see eye to eye on just about everything. It certainly won't be a mismatch in the bedroom since they both like it hot, physical, uncomplicated—and lots of it. But the lover of a Sagittarius must also be a good companion, and provided these two are the best of buddies with shared interests and the same philosophical outlook, it could be a brilliant combination. Without lots in common, it will probably be a flash in the pan. But two Sagittarians are bound to appreciate the space and freedom that each happily gives the other. This couple will talk each other into the ground and love it. It has an excellent chance of lasting, and when they're old and gray they'll look back on all those adventures they had together that they could never have had with anyone else.

Sagittarius and Capricorn
With Sagittarian's instant-response mechanism and Capricorn's not-so-obvious but possibly stronger sex drive, there is bound to be fascination and fireworks—at least to start with. But when one partner invests in hope, faith, and optimism, and the other invests in insurance policies, you get a pretty good idea of the essential difference in the natures of these two. If it works, it's because it's a complementary arrangement that successfully balances the Sagittarian exuberance and high spirits with the Capricornian caution and common sense. If they can't find that balance, it could resemble a case of optimist meets pessimist, or "act first think later" meets "think first act later." Basically these two have a completely different approach to how they run their lives, as well as very different priorities, so unless their compatibility is reinforced by other planetary factors, there's not a great deal that will keep them together in the long term.

Sagittarius and Aquarius

This combination is quite common. And it's not surprising, because when one freedom lover meets another, each is thrilled to have found someone who wants to be in a relationship but also wants to do their own thing. Neither wants to be owned or confined to domesticity. Indeed, life will be so full of travel and stimulating conversations with stimulating people that the nitty-gritty of the housework could become a source of disharmony. The solution is simple—hire a cleaner, and turn mind and body to more exciting things. Speaking of body, fiery Sagittarius may complain about Aquarius' cooler approach to sex. And Aquarius will cleverly avoid what she regards as Sagittarius' excessive demands on their person. Any arguments could be material for a miniseries since Sagittarius gets very loud and heated, and Aquarius will stand his or her ground and refuse to budge. If it ever reaches the point of "take it or leave it," they'll probably both decide to take it, because fundamentally their lives and their lifestyle dovetail nicely.

Sagittarius and Pisces

They seem so well matched. Jupiter casts his optimistic, indulgent rays over both signs, so these two could be the last of the good-time boys and girls who really know how to have fun. Undoubtedly Sagittarius is the best fire sign for Pisces, and Pisces is the best of the water signs for Sagittarius. Both are flexible, accommodating types, but on the whole, sensitive Pisces needs a quieter, more gentle existence than Sagittarius. Problems will surface if Sagittarius' tendency to dominate is given too much of a free rein by the Piscean inclination to defer. Pisces will go along with Sagittarius' desires and demands—but only up to a point. The Fish can take only so much of the Sagittarian full-on approach before swimming off. And The Centaur can endure only so much of the Piscean dampening of their spirits. As both can be evasive, neither may have a clear picture of where they stand with each other, and it could be a case of easy come, easy go, with the emphasis on the *go*. If both have planets in earth, it will stabilize the relationship and give it a much better chance of success.

CAPRICORN

Capricorn and Aries
See Aries and Capricorn (Page 389)

Capricorn and Taurus
See Taurus and Capricorn (Page 394)

Capricorn and Gemini
See Gemini and Capricorn (Page 398)

Capricorn and Cancer
See Cancer and Capricorn (Page 402)

Capricorn and Leo
See Leo and Capricorn (Page 405)

Capricorn and Virgo
See Virgo and Capricorn (Page 408)

Capricorn and Libra
See Libra and Capricorn (Page 411)

Capricorn and Scorpio
See Scorpio and Capricorn (Page 414)

Capricorn and Sagittarius
See Sagittarius and Capricorn (Page 416)

Capricorn and Capricorn
From the start, he knows what he wants, she knows what she wants, and naturally, they both want the same thing. How wonderful that these two ambitious, thoroughly realistic—and very sexy—individuals should have found each other. The thing Capricorn places top of the list in a relationship is respect, and since this is a same-sign combination, there'll be plenty of mutual respect and consideration—as well as practical support—to keep them both happy. Their goals in life are in perfect accord. Both want to acquire security as soon as possible, so they will work very hard to put money in the bank and move into a home of their own. There is a risk that work could consume their lives. Capricorns who don't factor in the fun times could end up far too serious and dour for their own good. But with so much common ground, this couple stands a very good chance of finding long-term happiness. Certainly these two realists will never delude themselves over what they can reasonably expect from life—and love. It's a relationship that will only get better with time.

Capricorn and Aquarius
There are two types of Aquarians: the wild, freedom-loving, and unorthodox Uranian-type Aquarius, and the security-conscious Saturnian-type who likes to play it safe. Should Capricorn encounter the latter, sensible, grounding Saturn will be a wonderful anchor and keep the

relationship together. If, however, the Aquarian is of the unconventional Uranian type, then it's highly unlikely they'll get very far past first base. How can they when Capricorn aims to be a solid citizen and values order, reliability, and steadfastness, and Aquarius questions social convention and wants personal freedom and open-ended, unstructured existence? In either case, their sexual needs are likely to be different. Capricorn is the sexy dark horse of the zodiac, and Aquarius dislikes too many expectations in any aspect of a relationship. This is definitely a couple for whom compatibility between their Moons and other planets is worth researching.

Capricorn and Pisces
A Capricorn and a Piscean have wonderful gifts to bring to each other. With the vast Pisces imagination and the supreme Capricorn organizational ability, it can be a very satisfying and complementary match on many levels. They could take the prize as one of the most devoted, caring couples of the zodiac. They feel safe with each other, and sexually, it can be warm, sensual, and erotic. Capricorn is a grounding influence and can provide the kick start Pisces needs to fulfill his or her potential. And Pisces can show Capricorn the advantages of a little R and R, which is just what the hardworking Goat needs. They both place great store on the peace and quiet of a secure home life. The main problem is Capricorn's natural tendency to assume control. The Piscean inability to get their act together at times will drive Capricorn crazy. But Capricorn will come to realize that gentle Pisces is not as undisciplined and untogether as they assumed. A partnership between the ultimate realist and the ultimate dreamer can actually make dreams come true.

AQUARIUS

Aquarius and Aries
See Aries and Aquarius (Page 390)

Aquarius and Taurus
See Taurus and Aquarius (Page 394)

Aquarius and Gemini
See Gemini and Aquarius (Page 398)

Aquarius and Cancer
See Cancer and Aquarius (Page 402)

Aquarius and Leo
See Leo and Aquarius (Page 406)

Aquarius and Virgo
See Virgo and Aquarius (Page 409)

Aquarius and Libra
See Libra and Aquarius (Page 412)

Aquarius and Scorpio
See Scorpio and Aquarius (Page 414)

Aquarius and Sagittarius
See Sagittarius and Aquarius (Page 417)

Aquarius and Capricorn
See Capricorn and Aquarius (Page 418)

Aquarius and Aquarius
Provided their quirks, eccentricities, and firm opinions are the same quirks, eccentricities, and firm opinions, two Aquarians could be just right for each other. Neither wants to get bogged down in too much sentimental, emotional stuff—exclusive togetherness is not their cup of tea. Both like their own space and will appreciate a partner who doesn't give them the third degree over their whereabouts at all times. It's possible that these two can give each other the soul-mate understanding that same-sign combinations are so good at. Aquarians are usually far more savvy with money than appearances would suggest, so if they disagree on expenditures, there could be much digging in of the Aquarian heels. And with two people who are so immune to domestic chaos, it's likely that radical action will have to be taken every so often, so who dusts off the vacuum cleaner may become another source of disagreement. With their "free to be me" attitude, this could be a case of how to have a relationship when you're not really having a relationship.

Aquarius and Pisces
On the mind level, they can turn each other on. Both are original thinkers with ideas that reach the outer edge. They also share a certain self-containedness, but problems are bound to arise if Aquarius misreads the Piscean need for personal space and time to be unto themselves as the Aquarian-style desire for a less intimate relationship. This would be a big mistake as the opposite is, in fact, true. Pisces is a sensitive water sign, and needs regular emotional feed-

back—as well as the occasional thoughtful sentimental gesture. On the physical level, it could be hit and miss—but mostly miss. Pisces is a "nester" and needs a calm, harmonious home life—and could accuse Aquarius of treating home like a hotel. But Aquarius could think Pisces is far too precious and hung up on unimportant things like whether there's milk in the fridge and tea bags in the cupboard. If they've got planets in each other's signs, it could save the day and save the relationship.

PISCES

Pisces and Aries
See Aries and Pisces (Page 390)

Pisces and Taurus
See Taurus and Pisces (Page 394)

Pisces and Gemini
See Gemini and Pisces (Page 399)

Pisces and Cancer
See Cancer and Pisces (Page 403)

Pisces and Leo
See Leo and Pisces (Page 406)

Pisces and Virgo
See Virgo and Pisces (Page 409)

Pisces and Libra
See Libra and Pisces (Page 412)

Pisces and Scorpio
See Scorpio and Pisces (Page 415)

Pisces and Sagittarius
See Sagittarius and Pisces (Page 417)

Pisces and Capricorn
See Capricorn and Pisces (Page 419)

Pisces and Aquarius
See Aquarius and Pisces (Page 420)

Pisces and Pisces

Two Fish could happily swim around together in their nice little glass bowl forever. What is so wonderful for a Pisces about loving another Pisces is having someone who really understands why they're often misunderstood. So much of their life together will be centered on making a beautiful home with all the comfort and coziness they love so much. There'll be lots of mutual pouring out of hearts, and spooning out of TLC and chicken soup. With so much kindness and tenderness to give to each other, what little storms could ruffle their idyllic waters? Well, a little too much swimming around in circles might see this couple getting nowhere. They can be a pretty aimless pair at times. Without identifiable goals, they can easily fall into a kind of restless dissatisfaction and apathy, which they try to compensate for by overspending, overpartying, or overindulgence in anything else they fancy. Planets in earth are desirable for both to keep them from getting lost at sea.